Rationale for the Design of the Ada® Programming Language

The Ada Companion Series

There are currently no better candidates for a co-ordinated, low risk, and synergetic approach to software development than the Ada programming language. Integrated into a support environment, Ada promises to give a solid standards-orientated foundation for higher professionalism in software engineering.

This definitive series aims to be the guide to the Ada software industry for managers, implementors, software producers and users. It will deal with all aspects of the emerging industry: adopting an Ada strategy, conversion issues, style and portability issues, and management. To assist the organised development of an Ada-oriented software components industry, equal emphasis will be placed on all phases of life cycle support.

Some current titles:

Proceedings of the 1985 Ada International Conference
Edited by J.G.P. Barnes and G.A. Fisher

Ada for specification: possibilities and limitations
Edited by S.J. Goldsack

Concurrent programming in Ada
A. Burns

Selecting an Ada environment
Edited by T.G.L. Lyons and J.C.D. Nissen

Ada components: Libraries and tools
Proceedings of the 1987 Ada-Europe International Conference
Edited by S. Tafvelin

Ada: the design choice
Proceedings of the 1989 Ada-Europe International Conference
Edited by A. Alvarez

Distibuted Ada: developments and experiences
Proceedings of the Distributed Ada '89 Symposium, Southampton
Edited by J.M. Bishop

Ada: experiences and prospects
Proceedings of the 1990 Ada-Europe International Conference
Edited by Barry Lynch

Rationale for the Design of the Ada Programming Language

J. Ichbiah
J. Barnes
R. Firth
and M. Woodger

*HONEYWELL, Systems and Research Center, Minneapolis, USA
and ALSYS, La Celle Saint Cloud, France*

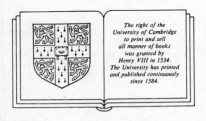

The right of the
University of Cambridge
to print and sell
all manner of books
was granted by
Henry VIII in 1534.
The University has printed
and published continuously
since 1584.

CAMBRIDGE UNIVERSITY PRESS

Cambridge
New York   Port Chester   Melbourne   Sydney

Published by the Press Syndicate of the University of Cambridge
The Pitt Building, Trumpington Street, Cambridge CB2 1RP
40 West 20th Street, New York, NY 10011, USA
10 Stamford Road, Oakleigh, Melbourne 3166, Australia

Original edition published by the Ada Joint Program Office 1986

This corrected edition first published by Cambridge University Press 1991

Printed in Great Britain at the University Press, Cambridge

Library of Congress Cataloguing in Publication data available

British Library Cataloguing in Publication data available

ISBN 0 521 39267 5

Table of Contents

1. Introduction and Preface

1.1 GOALS

This document, the Rationale for the design of the Ada programming language (ANSI/MIL-STD-1815A), has evolved over a number of years.

A first version appeared in 1978 as the Rationale for the Green programming language, and this was revised in 1979 at the time that Green was finally selected as Ada. The purpose of these documents was to explain the motivation for the language design, and to justify and defend its position against the other competitive languages and the Ironman (later Steelman) requirements. No corresponding document was written in 1980 when Ada was proposed as a standard, nor in January 1983 when Ada finally became both an ANSI and Military Standard. The present version completes and revises a draft issued in January 1984 and which was the subject of public review.

The goal of these documents has also evolved. The original goal was both motivational and defensive; a major concern was implementability (in potentially controversial areas such as overload resolution) especially since there were no compilers then in existence. This last concern is now substantially reduced since implementability is well demonstrated by a number of production quality compilers.

Equally the goal is not to document and justify every language design decision: it would be difficult to replace the archive containing the hundreds of study notes and thousands of comments produced between 1977 and 1983.

The present goal is thus now more inspirational: to give the reader a feel for the spirit of the language, the motives behind the key features and to create the basis for understanding how they fit together both globally as viewed from the outside and in detail as viewed from the inside; above all to impart an appreciation of the main architectural lines of the language and its overall philosophy. It is only by knowing this philosophy that a real understanding for the detail will be obtained.

It is now 1986, and it may well be asked why this ultimate Rationale has taken so long to emerge. We must admit that the main reason is simply that we have been deeply involved over the past years in a number of activities aimed at creating an infrastructure that would ensure the success of the Ada language, – in particular, the development of training material and compilers. The success of Ada has now relieved that pressure and allowed us to complete the work started in 1978, and to make available what we hope will be an important addition to the Ada literature.

1.2 STRUCTURE

This document is divided into chapters covering different aspects of the language. Most chapters correspond to chapters of the Reference Manual. Expressions and statements are here regrouped in a single chapter, since the subject is fairly classical. Conversely, in view of the importance of the subjects, special chapters are devoted to numeric types, access types, and derived types, in addition to the chapter on types. The chapters of the Rationale are fairly independent (at the cost of some repetition) and can be read in any order.

Most chapters of the Rationale have a common structure. They start with an introduction to the topic discussed. An informal description of the language features follows. This description is made in terms of examples chosen to reflect the major classes of uses of the features considered.

We believe that the reader will get the spirit of the language reading these examples. They should help the development of an intuition for programming style in the Ada language.

A discussion of the technical issues follows, or in some cases is interspersed with the informal description. Such discussions cover the major design decisions, their justification, and the interactions with other aspects of the language.

1.3 ACKNOWLEDGEMENTS

We would like to take this opportunity to acknowledge the contributions of several others to the Ada Rationale: Jean-Raymond Abrial, Bernd Krieg-Brueckner, Jean-Claude Heliard, Henry Ledgard, Ian Pyle, Olivier Roubine, Steve Schuman, Stan Vestal, and Brian Wichmann contributed to the 1978 and 1979 initial versions. Brian Wichmann also contributed to the 1984 draft.

Other significant contributions were derived from the Language Study Notes by Jean-Loup Gailly and Paul Hilfinger and by comments from the Distinguished Reviewers.

We are also indebted to the comments on the 1984 draft from the Ada Europe Review Group organized by Kit Lester, the comments by Henry Dancy and Vincent Amiot, and the dedicated technical support of Marion Myers.

The Ada Rationale was developed by Alsys and Honeywell under a contract from the United States Government (Ada Joint Program Office).

Jean D. Ichbiah
John G.P. Barnes
Robert J. Firth
Mike Woodger

2. Lexical and Textual Structure

A program is a text that specifies actions to be performed by a computer.

Programs are written by human programmers, and read by their authors or by other programmers for checking and maintenance purposes; they are also processed by compilers and other automatic tools. The need to accommodate these various forms of communication permeates every level of consideration of a programming language, including the most immediate levels where we are only concerned with the physical appearance of a program text.

The lexical and textual structures of a programming language are of course important for ease of program compilation, and for compilation – time detection of errors. The importance of lexical and textual structures is even greater for ease of reading and understanding programs – in particular, for detection of logical errors – and for ease of teaching the language. We believe that our understanding of programs can be greatly simplified if our intuition is able to rely on textual forms that convey the logical structure of the program. This is the justification for giving major consideration to readability and teachability in the design of lexical and textual structures in Ada; moreover, special attention has been devoted to structural analogies.

2.1 LEXICAL STRUCTURE

A program is written in characters forming lines on a printed page. The arrangement on the page is primarily to assist the human reader, and consequently is mainly in free format. The allowed characters belong to the ISO (ASCII) character set, and the text of a program may contain both upper case and lower case letters. For portability reasons, it is possible to write any program in a 56 character subset of the ISO character set.

On a higher level than that of characters, a program is considered to consist of lexical elements. Both the mechanical compiler and the human interpreter of programs will tend to work in lexical elements, so it is important that these elements should be clearly specified. Lexical elements are clearly delimited and may not straddle line boundaries – a restriction that assists human reading and helps compilers to recover after having detected an error.

The lexical elements are:

- Identifiers, including those for reserved words and attribute designators

- Single-character delimiters and two-character compound delimiters

- Numeric literals: integer literals and real literals

- Character literals and string literals

Each literal is a lexical element that stands for a value, namely the value *literally* represented: for example, 10 and 1E1 are two integer literals which both stand for the integer value ten. In addition, a program text can include elements that have no influence on the meaning of the program but are included as information and guidance for the human reader or for the compiler. These are:

- Comments

- Pragmas

Identifiers start with a letter which may be followed by a sequence of letters and digits. In addition, an underline character may appear between two other characters of an identifier. This underline is significant and plays the role of the space in ordinary prose (but without breaking the integrity of the identifier). The need for such an underline is seen from good choices of names such as BYTES_PER_WORD rather than BYTESPERWORD. Furthermore the significance of the underline makes SPACE_PER_SON a different identifier from SPACEPERSON or SPACE_PERSON and A_NYLON_GRIP different from ANY_LONG_RIP.

Reserved words are special identifiers that are reserved for special significance in the language. There are 63 such words. Many of them play an important role in the definition of the overall syntax of the major program units of the language, for example:

procedure   is   begin   end

Other reserved words play a syntactic role at a more detailed level, for example:

constant   in   out   range

Finally, seven of them are used as operators. These are the reserved words

and   or   xor   not   abs   rem   mod

Reserved words other than operators cannot be redeclared, and operators can only be redeclared as operators and with the same precedence. Hence programmers cannot write obscure programs by redefining the meaning of words that play an important syntactic role in the definition of the structure of Ada texts. Similarly, declarations written by programmers cannot affect overall properties of the syntax, for example, the fact that if two adjacent lexical elements are identifiers, one of them (at least) must be a reserved word.

Special printing of reserved words is recommended for highlighting programs on an appropriate output device. The method chosen in this book is boldface (and lower case). Since the language does not distinguish between character fonts, one can envisage methods of highlighting the reserved words by the use of a different font, such as lower case, italics, underlining, color, and so on. Clearly, this does not contradict the use of the ISO character set for program input. On the other hand, for program printouts, it is currently possible to get excellent renditions via graphical printers, color screens, or photocomposers; and it is important to exploit this ability in order to enhance the readability of programs.

The identifiers for attribute designators are not treated as reserved words; they are always preceded by an apostrophe (pronounced *prime* or *tick*) and can thus be distinguished from declared identifiers and reserved words purely on the basis of lexical information. The identifiers for predefined attribute designators are in fact different from the reserved words, excepting only DIGITS, DELTA, and RANGE.

Ada uses attributes as environment enquiries and to refer to predefined properties. Other languages have used functional notation or dot notation for this purpose. These alternative forms both have the disadvantage of restricting the user's free choice of names. For example, if the address of an object were denoted by a function, this function would have to be overloaded on all data types. Furthermore any user definition of ADDRESS would hide the predefined one and thus make it unavailable. Similarly, dot notation would prevent declaration of record components with the same identifier as an attribute designator. Neither of these consequences is acceptable in light of the fact that the number of attribute designators can be large, and that some of them may be specific to an implementation. Both problems are avoided by the Ada notation for attributes.

The choice of identifiers for reserved words and attributes depends primarily on convention. Preference is given to full English words rather than abbreviations since we believe full words to be simpler to read. For instance **procedure** is used rather than **proc** (in Algol 68) and **constant** rather than **const** (in Pascal). Shorter words are also given preference: for example **access** is used in preference to **reference**, and **task** is used in preference to **process**.

The following special characters can be used as single-character delimiters between lexical elements:

    & ' ( ) * + , - . / : ; < = > |

Two-character compound delimiters are constructed by juxtaposition of two such characters, as follows:

    => .. ** := /= >= <= << >> <>

Naturally, in listings of Ada programs, the compound delimiters can be represented following conventional notations where the corresponding characters exist:

    /= as $\neq$ >= as $\geq$ <= as $\leq$

Numeric literals are all introduced by an initial digit. A requirement that has long been recognized when printing numeric tables is for a character to break up long sequences of digits: in Ada, the underline character serves this purpose. In contrast to identifiers, underlines in numeric literals do not alter the meaning, so that 12_000 naturally has the same value as 12000.

A simple sequence of digits is an integer literal written in decimal notation. For other bases from 2 up to 16, the base is given first and is followed by a sequence of digits enclosed by sharp characters (#) or by colons (:), the colon being used as replacement character for the sharp, but only when the sharp is not available. The enclosed digits may include the letters A to F for bases greater than ten. Thus, the conventional ways of expressing bit patterns in binary, octal, or hexadecimal are provided.

Real literals must contain a period, which represents the radix point. They may be expressed in decimal notation or with other bases. Finally, both integer and real literals may include the letter E followed by an exponent.

Examples of numeric literals are given below:

```
10                        -- an integer literal
10.0                      -- a real literal
1E3                       -- an integer literal of value 1000
1.5E2                     -- a real literal of value 150.0
2#1111_1111#              -- an integer literal of value 255
2#1#E8                    -- an integer literal of value 256
2#1.1111_1111_111#E11     -- a real literal of value 4095.0
```

Other forms of lexical element are character literals and string literals. A character literal is formed by enclosing a single character between two apostrophes (') – its value belongs to a character type. A string literal is formed by enclosing zero or more characters between double quotes (") – the value of a string literal is a sequence of character values.

String literals (like all lexical elements) are limited to a single line: otherwise for sequences straddling line boundaries the number of spaces in the string would not be clear since the end of line is not visibly delimited. Furthermore, the limitation to one line reduces the consequences of compilation errors arising from the (unintentional) omission of a closing quote character.

To represent a long sequence of characters, the sequence is split into several string literals, each on a single line, and connected by the catenation operator (&). Apart from long sequences, there may be a need to split sequences that contain characters that are not in the 56 basic character subset of ASCII. Examples of catenations of string literals are as follows:

```
"A long line of printed output which" &
"is continued on the next line of the program."

"END OF LINE " & ASCII.CR & ASCII.LF & "START OF NEXT LINE"
```

Comments may appear alone on a line or at the end of a line. As an end of line remark, the comment should appear as an explanation of the preceding text -- hence the use of a double hyphen (doing duty for a dash) is natural and appropriate, as illustrated by this sentence. For simplicity, a space is not allowed between the two hyphens. No form of embedded comments (within a line of text) is provided, as their utility is insufficient to justify the extra complexity. Single comments that are larger than one line are not provided. Such comments would require a closing comment delimiter and this would again raise the dangers associated with the (unintentional) omission of the closing delimiter: entire sections of a program could be ignored by the compiler without the programmer realizing it, so that the program would not mean what he thinks. Long comments can be written as a succession of single line comments, thus combining elegance with safety.

A *pragma* (from the Greek word meaning *action*) is used to direct the actions of the compiler in particular ways, but has no effect on the semantics of a program (in general). Pragmas are used to control listing, to define an object configuration (for example, the size of memory), to control features of the code generated (for example, the degree of optimization or the level of diagnostics), and so on. Such directives are not likely to be related to the rest of the language in an obvious way. Hence the form taken should not intrude upon the language, but it should be uniform. Thus, the general form of pragmas is defined by the language. They start with the reserved word **pragma** followed by a pragma identifier, optionally followed by a list of arguments enclosed by parentheses, and terminated by a semicolon. The overall syntax of the pragma identifier and arguments is similar to that of a procedure call. Pragmas are allowed at places where a declaration or a statement is allowed; also at places where other constructs that play the role of declarations (for example clauses) are allowed. Examples of pragmas are as follows:

```
pragma LIST(ON);          -- listing wanted
pragma INLINE(SET_MASK); -- in line inclusion of call
pragma OPTIMIZE(SPACE);
pragma SUPPRESS(RANGE_CHECK, ON => TABLE);
```

Some pragmas are defined by the language (see Annex B of the reference manual). It is expected that other pragmas will be defined by various implementations, in particular for the programming support environments developed around the Ada language.

2.2 TEXTUAL STRUCTURE

Above the lexical level, the text of a program is structured as an arrangement of lexical elements. This structure is described by the Ada syntax in the conventional manner. However, a number of issues require separate discussion to clarify the decisions taken.

Declarations and statements are always terminated by semicolons – this differs from the Pascal practice, in which a semicolon is used as a separator. The Ada convention simplifies the insertion of another declaration or statement: normal layout places the semicolon at the end of a line and thus, where semicolons are separators, insertion of a line often entails changing the previous line as well. This is an argument against separators between items that are likely to be on separate lines. We want each line to be a complete unit – therefore including a terminator – so that adding a line does not require changing a previous line. (Fortran achieves this by having the end of line be a terminator.)

The use of semicolons as terminators aids recovery by the compiler after finding a syntax error; recovery from omission of the semicolon itself is usually quite simple for the parser. Finally, comparative analyses of programmer errors have shown the use of semicolon as a terminator to be less error-prone than its use as a separator [GH 75].

Having dealt with the lines of text themselves, we next consider the two-dimensional arrangement of lexical elements to form a page. Reading a page of a program normally proceeds on a line by line basis, at least consciously. But reading and vision are indeed more complex than is suggested by this purely linear process. While the eye consciously concentrates on a given point (a given line), peripheral vision is actively at work in a parallel fashion. This *unconscious* reading activity provides us with information on the overall structure of the text – the textual structure – and gradually develops our intuition of what is coming in subsequent lines, and also our perception of the spatial relationships of different parts of the text.

A readable textual structure is one that facilitates this parallel decoding activity: readability is thus improved by suitable paragraphing (layout) of the program text. This facet of readability has influenced the design of Ada textual structure in several ways. For each of the major program structures, we have defined a textual structure that reflects the underlying logical structure (this point will be substantiated later by examples). This textual structure is given by the recommended paragraphing specified in the Ada reference manual through the layout of the syntax rules. Finally, the syntax was designed in such a way that this recommended paragraphing can be produced by very simple mechanical tools, on the basis of the reserved words alone.

We should therefore expect Ada programs to be paragraphed in a systematic and automatic manner. This consistency and uniformity of presentation is a significant advantage for readers, in particular when reading programs written by others. The resulting textual structure is what will be perceived when looking at a program from a distance, when the individual details (the individual lexical elements) can no longer be seen distinctly. Even at this first level of perception, a good program will provide us with some intuition of its organization into major parts.

Some program structures have simple brackets, for example the **loop** and **end loop** of the loop statement, and similarly the **record** and **end record** of the record type definition. This simplifies the insertion of additional statements or declarations. Thus, adding a statement to the Ada if statement

```
if COUNT < AVERAGE then
   INCREASE(COUNT);
end if;
```

requires a single line insertion:

```
if COUNT < AVERAGE then
   PRINT(COUNT);    -- added
   INCREASE(COUNT);
end if;
```

Note that the similar transformation of the Pascal if statement

```
if COUNT < AVERAGE then
   INCREASE(COUNT);
```

would be more cumbersome since it would require more modifications:

```
if COUNT < AVERAGE then
begin                  {added}
   PRINT(COUNT);       {added}
   INCREASE(COUNT)     {; deleted}
end;                   {added}
```

and forgetting the **begin ... end** makes the increase of count unconditional!

Several other program constructs exhibit a *comb*-like structure, which is best illustrated with the if statement as in the following example:

```
if ... then
   ...
elsif ... then
   ...
elsif ... then
   ...
end if;
```

This structure is built around four markers: an initial opening marker (**if ... then**), two intermediate markers (**elsif ... then**), and a closing marker (**end if**). Each of the three major parts bracketed by two consecutive markers is a sequence of statements that forms one of the alternatives of the if statement. Thus each major part of the comb structure correspond to a logical alternative of the if statement. A similar comb structure is exhibited by the case statement:

```
        case LIGHT is
          when GREEN =>
            ...
          when AMBER =>
            ...
          when RED =>
            ...
        end case;
```

Here again the layout defines three major parts of the text, which correspond to the three logical alternatives of the case statement. Further examples of the comb structure are

```
        procedure P is
          ...
        begin
          ...
        exception
          ...
        end P;
```

```
        select
          ...
        or when ... =>
          ...
        or when ... =>
          ...
        else
          ...
        end select;
```

Note that each large-scale comb structure has the terminating reserved word **end**. For declarations and statements, this is followed by a reserved word echoing the corresponding opening marker:

case	**end case**
if	**end if**
loop	**end loop**
record	**end record**
select	**end select**

For named constructs such as subprograms, packages, and task units the name of the construct may be written after the final end to assist in the recognition of the structure, something which is quite useful in the case of long program units:

```
package KEY_MANAGER is
   ...
end KEY_MANAGER;
```

When program constructs are nested, this pairing of opening and closing markers will assist in reading the program. Special tools used for printing (or displaying) programs may also print additional vertical lines that further enhance the major structures as in the example below:

```
task body CONTROLLER is
...
begin
  loop
    select
      accept READ ... do
        ...
      end READ;
    or
      accept WRITE ... do
        ...
      end WRITE;
    end select;
  end loop;
end CONTROLLER;
```

Naturally, these structural vertical lines are not part of the input text submitted to an Ada compiler, any more than are font indications such as the use of boldface for reserved words. Such enhancing techniques are not superfluous: they have an important role in facilitating the reading of programs, an important activity in our profession.

In general, language constructs which do not express similar ideas should not look similar. Thus, unlike Pascal which used a colon in both cases, Ada uses different notations for statement labels (used by goto statements) and for choices (in case statements). Statement labels have angle brackets << >> placed around the label identifier; they emphasize that this is a special point in the program. Conversely, choices express preconditions for executing the statements that follow. Their form is therefore as follows:

when ... =>

The same form is also used in select statements and exception handlers, since it corresponds to the same idea of a precondition.

Whenever possible, a uniform notation is used for similar constructs. The clearest example of this principle is the case structure, which is used for variant parts in records as well as for case statements. In Ada, both constructs have the same morphology, so as to reflect the common idea of discrimination among several alternatives: seen from a distance the two structures are indistinguishable. This should simplify teaching of the language and avoid programming errors.

Pascal variant parts and case statements, although similar, do not follow our principle. The contrast is illustrated by an example:

A graphics data structure in Pascal:

```
type SHAPE = (CIRCLE, TRIANGLE, POINT);

type FIGURE =
  record
    X, Y : REAL;
    case KIND : SHAPE of
      CIRCLE:
        (RADIUS : REAL);
      TRIANGLE:
        (INCLINATION, ANGLE   : REAL;
        LEFT_SIDE, RIGHT_SIDE : REAL);
      POINT:()
  end
```

A case statement in Pascal:

```
case A.KIND of
  CIRCLE:
    PRINT(A.RADIUS);
  TRIANGLE:
    begin
      PRINT(A.INCLINATION); PRINT(A.ANGLE);
      PRINT(A.LEFT_SIDE);   PRINT(A.RIGHT_SIDE)
    end;
  POINT:
end
```

The equivalent data structure in Ada:

```
type SHAPE is (CIRCLE, TRIANGLE, POINT);

type FIGURE(KIND : SHAPE) is
  record
    X, Y : REAL;
      case KIND is
        when CIRCLE =>
          RADIUS : REAL;
        when TRIANGLE =>
          INCLINATION, ANGLE    : REAL;
          LEFT_SIDE, RIGHT_SIDE : REAL;
        when POINT =>
          null;
      end case;
  end record;
```

The equivalent case statement in Ada:

```
case A.KIND is
  when CIRCLE =>
    PRINT(A.RADIUS);
  when TRIANGLE =>
    PRINT(A.INCLINATION); PRINT(A.ANGLE);
    PRINT(A.LEFT_SIDE);   PRINT(A.RIGHT_SIDE);
  when POINT =>
    null;
end case;
```

In Ada, the structural analogy between the declarative case structure (the variant part) and the case statement should assist the human reader and help in learning the language. The approach will also simplify pretty-printing of programs by mechanical tools which need not be able to distinguish the two (semantically different) versions of the case structure, namely variant parts and case statements.

A similar structural analogy exists between the case statement, the select statement, and exception handlers. Other structural analogies, which are adequately reflected by the syntax, are shown by the textual structure of functions, procedures, package bodies, task bodies, and blocks. In each case the syntax defines three major logical parts (a declarative part, a sequence of statements, and exception handlers) that are reflected by the textual structure

function F ... is	procedure P ... is	declare
begin	begin	begin
exception	exception	exception
end F;	end P;	end;

package body P is	task body T is
begin	begin
exception	exception
end P;	end T;

and similarly for package and task specifications

package P is	task T is
end P;	end T;

These structural analogies have been used quite systematically. They should develop a feeling of familiarity for the reader and simplify the teaching of the Ada language.

3. Classical Programming

Programs achieve actions by executing statements. These may contain expressions that are formulas defining the computation of values. The major entities involved in a program are declared by declarations, and the creation of the declared entities is achieved during program execution by a process that is called the elaboration of declarations.

Declarations, expressions, and statements are fairly *classical* aspects of most programming languages. Hence we will limit the discussion to the most prominent points.

3.1 SIMPLE DECLARATIONS: VARIABLES AND CONSTANTS

Variables and constants are declared by the simplest kind of declaration, called an object declaration; the general form is similar to that used in Pascal but there are some differences.

A delicate balance is necessary in the handling of variables and constants. Reliability and security demand that the two concepts be clearly separated. On the other hand it is convenient if a variable declaration can be changed into a constant declaration by a very simple alteration of the program text. Ada meets these two goals by having two distinct but related forms of declaration for the two concepts. Thus the following object declaration:

```
C : constant REAL := 300_000.0;
```

declares a constant, whereas the following object declaration declares a variable with an initial value:

```
SPEED : REAL := C/1500.0;
```

The adjective **constant** which appears in the declaration of a constant states that the value of this object must not be altered after its initialization. By writing this adjective, the programmer expresses his intent in an explicit manner and requests the assistance of the compiler in forbidding attempts to alter the value – whether by accident, by mistake, or deliberately.

Following Algol 68 however, the adjective **constant** does not mean that the initial value must be known at compilation time (that is, in Ada terminology, the initial value expression need not be *static*).

For example, a function to determine whether a given integer number is prime may declare an upper bound on divisors:

```
function PRIME(X : INTEGER) return BOOLEAN is
   UPPER_BOUND : constant INTEGER := INTEGER(SQRT(X));
begin
   ...
end PRIME;
```

and clearly the value of this upperbound, although constant for a given call of the function, will be computed in terms of the actual parameter of the function, and hence dynamically.

Good programming style in Ada will systematically emphasize constants, even for short texts where the danger of accidental alterations would be very slight. For example, an Ada formulation of the classical procedure to exchange the values of two variables will emphasize the fact that the *temporary variable* – OLD_LEFT – is indeed a constant:

```
procedure EXCHANGE(LEFT, RIGHT : in out INTEGER) is
   OLD_LEFT : constant INTEGER := LEFT;
begin
   LEFT  := RIGHT;
   RIGHT := OLD_LEFT;
end;
```

An initialization is required in the case of a constant. For variables it is allowed but not required. Allowing initialization of a variable in its declaration enables one to ensure that the initial state of variables is well-defined. Furthermore, this avoids long sequences of initialization assignment statements, which are divorced from the declarations and hence hard to locate.

3.2 DECLARATIVE PARTS – LINEAR READING

Object declarations and declarations of other forms are grouped in declarative parts together with other declarative items such as bodies (of subprograms and packages) and representation clauses.

The spatial arrangement of declarative items in a declarative part is (almost) free. This means that constant and variable object declarations, and type and subtype declarations can be mixed in groupings that best reflect the logical needs of a program.

An Ada program can be read *linearly*, line by line in a sequential manner, very much in the same way as we read good English prose. This means that our understanding of a text progresses line by line (declaration by declaration) and that we can reuse in later lines the knowledge acquired in earlier lines, as is shown in the following example where each declaration is made in terms of the one on the previous line:

```
declare
   LENGTH : constant INTEGER := 100;
   SQUARE : constant INTEGER := LENGTH*LENGTH;
   subtype AREA is INTEGER range 0 .. SQUARE;
   SURFACE, EXTENT : AREA;
begin
   ...
end;
```

Several rules of the language were designed to serve this purpose of linear reading. For example, the scope rules allow declarations to appear in the order used above. But they would not allow the initialization of SQUARE to refer to LENGTH if the declaration of LENGTH were given after that of SQUARE: the Ada rules forbid forward references: we can refer only to what we have already read. Other specific rules that support this linear reading will be seen later, when we discuss subprograms and access types (Chapters 8 and 6).

Reading is linear and so also is *elaboration* of declarations. During program execution, declarations are elaborated (that is, they achieve their effect), one by one, in the linear order in which they appear.

For example, the constant LENGTH and the variable SURFACE do not exist before the execution of the above block statement. This execution will start by the elaboration of the four declarations that form the declarative part: one after the other. Thus after elaboration of the declaration of LENGTH, this constant will exist; but the variable SURFACE will exist only after the elaboration of its declaration − the last one. Finally, after executing the statements enclosed by begin and end, all the entities created by the elaboration of the declarative part will disappear (or at least become unreachable).

The above illustrates the logical model of execution of an Ada program. In this model, elaboration is a process that takes place dynamically, at run time. This does not, however, prevent a compiler from using a more static approach − for example, for storage allocation − as long as it can guarantee that this implementation technique will yield an effect equivalent to that of the logical model.

The only limitation imposed by the language on the order of declarative items is that bodies must appear after simpler declarative items such as object declarations. This rule was devised to avoid the poor degree of readability that would result from mixing *large* and *small* textual items. In Algol-like languages that allowed this mixing, the occurrence of an isolated variable between the bodies of two large subprograms was a well-known source of error. Although good programming practice would avoid such isolated variable declarations, they could still be generated by faulty uses of a text-editor and cause subtle errors when hiding outer declarations:

```
declare
   X : INTEGER := 0;
begin
   ...
   declare
      ...                    -- several procedures

      procedure P is     -- very long
         ...
      end P;
      X : INTEGER;       -- a mistake: not legal Ada
      procedure Q is     -- also long
         ...
      end Q;
      ...                    -- more procedures
   begin
      ...
      X := 2;            -- should modify X ...
   end;
   if X = 0 then        -- but apparently did not!
      PUT("SOMETHING STRANGE is HAPPENING");
   end if;
   ...
end;
```

With the Ada rules, the declaration of a variable between two procedure bodies is not allowed and therefore this error will be detected and signaled by the compiler. Note that these rules do not forbid a local declaration of X hiding the outer one – there may be good reasons for such a declaration – but the hiding declaration will have to occur before the bodies and therefore in a portion of text that is easier to inspect than the potentially much longer text of the sequence of bodies.

3.3 MULTIPLE DECLARATIONS

An object declaration may declare more than one object, in which case it is called a multiple object declaration. For example

```
DIVISOR, STEP : POSITIVE := 5;
```

is a multiple declaration that declares two variables of subtype POSITIVE which are initialized with the value of the literal 5. A large number of multiple declarations are of the above form: the initial value is given by a literal or by a *pure* expression that delivers the same value each time it is evaluated. But consider now the multiple declaration:

```
YESTERDAY, TODAY, TOMORROW : DAY := GET_NEXT_DAY;
```

where the function GET_NEXT_DAY returns a different day each time it is called. Then there are two possible interpretations. One of them would be equivalent to:

```
some_day   : constant DAY := GET_NEXT_DAY;

YESTERDAY : DAY := some_day;
TODAY     : DAY := some_day;
TOMORROW  : DAY := some_day;
```

in which case all three variables would have the same value, obtained by the single evaluation of the function. However, the semantics selected for Ada is different. In fact the multiple declaration is equivalent to the following sequence of single declarations:

```
YESTERDAY : DAY := GET_NEXT_DAY;
TODAY     : DAY := GET_NEXT_DAY;
TOMORROW  : DAY := GET_NEXT_DAY;
```

in this order. This means that the function will be called three times and the variables will therefore be given three successive day values, as one expects in the present example.

Clearly, the two semantics do not differ when the initialization always yields the same value (the most frequent case). However we have found that when multiple evaluations yield different values, the most natural semantics is almost always the one involving multiple evaluations – hence the choice for Ada. Other examples are:

```
JOHN, PAUL : PERSON_NAME := new PERSON;
```

where we certainly want to allocate two new persons, and similarly:

```
FIRST, SECOND : constant STRING := GET_NEW_TEXT;
```

In this last example these two constants may have different values, and they need not even have the same length. Thus FIRST and SECOND need not even be of the same subtype of the type STRING. The same situation would also arise with

```
A, B : STRING(1 .. F) := (others => "*");
```

if F were a function and the two implied calls of F delivered different values.

In later chapters, when we discuss default expressions for record components and for parameters, we will see that the Ada semantics requires dynamic evaluation of these default expressions – as the need arises; this is quite consistent with the semantics of multiple evaluation selected for multiple declarations.

3.4 NAMES

A single object declaration associates an identifier with a declared object. The identifier, like every lexical element, is only a sequence of characters. But by virtue of the declaration, it becomes possible to use the identifier to refer to the declared object. We say that the identifier is a *name* for the object: a name that *denotes* the object. As we shall see, there are several forms of name. The simplest form is just an identifier, which is therefore also called a *simple name*.

To illustrate other forms of name, consider the following declarations (given in skeletal, but hopefully self-explanatory form):

```
type PERSON(SEX : GENDER) is
  record
    BIRTH : DATE;
    ...
    SPOUSE : ... ;
  end record;

subtype KING is PERSON(SEX => M);

JOHN  : KING;
LOUIS : array (1 .. 18) of KING;
```

The above declarations have defined several simple names: for example JOHN is the simple name of an object of subtype KING, and LOUIS is the simple name of an array of kings. Now, starting with simple names, we can form more complex names: a *selected component* such as

```
JOHN.SPOUSE
```

which denotes a component of the record object that is itself denoted by JOHN; and similarly an *indexed component* such as

```
LOUIS (9)
```

which denotes a particular component of our array of kings. We can also combine selected components and indexed components to form yet more complex names such as

```
LOUIS(15).SPOUSE
```

but not as in PL/1

```
LOUIS.SPOUSE(15)
```

Following Simula (and unlike Pascal), Ada allows function calls to be part of names. For example we can define a function HEIR as follows:

```
function HEIR(N : POSITIVE) return KING is
begin
  if N < 18 then
     return LOUIS(N + 1);
  else
     raise LINEAGE_ERROR;
  end if;
end;
```

Now we can form names such as

```
HEIR(14).SPOUSE
```

which include function calls. Note that the function call HEIR(14) delivers a value (not a variable), so that the above name allows the SPOUSE component to be read, but not updated.

The ability to use function calls in names is especially useful when dealing with data structures constructed with access types. Thus an algorithm in a tree traversal may include names such as

```
NEXT(N).PART
```

where NEXT(N) delivers an access value, and where PART is a component of the object designated by the access value. In this case, reading and updating of the component PART are both possible.

This ability goes some way toward the principle of *uniform referents* advocated by Ross and others [Ro 70, GM 75]. Following this principle, Ada uses round brackets rather than square brackets for denoting array components, thereby unifying the syntax of indexed components and function calls. In the same spirit, the syntax of selected components is used for component selection of records, whether the records are statically or dynamically allocated (see 6.3.4).

3.5 AGGREGATES

For an array or record type, Ada provides a basic operation that combines component values into a composite value of the type. This basic operation is expressed by an *aggregate* and there are two possible syntaxes for this construct.

The first is the traditional *positional* notation, in which the composite value is defined by an ordered sequence of component values: each value is implicitly associated with the component that has the same position in the array or record.

The second – and often preferable – notation provided in Ada is the so-called *named* notation, in which the component-value pairings are given explicitly by component associations of the form

```
component => value
```

using the names of the components (in the simplest case).

The examples given below show that named notation is often much more readable than positional notation, since it allows more explicit formulation of the intent. It is also more reliable, being insensitive to order and permutation. Consider for example the following type:

```
type DATE is
  record
    MONTH : INTEGER range 1 .. 12;
    DAY   : INTEGER range 1 .. 31;
    YEAR  : INTEGER range 1 .. 3000;
  end record;
```

Then we can define dates by positional aggregates such as

```
(12, 4, 1983)
```

but we can express our intent in a more explicit way if we use named notation as in the three equivalent aggregates given below:

```
(MONTH => 12,   DAY   => 4,  YEAR => 1983)  -- the American way
(DAY   => 4,    MONTH => 12, YEAR => 1983)  -- the European way
(YEAR  => 1983, MONTH => 12, DAY  => 4)     -- the ISO way
```

A reformulation of the type DATE is possible in which an enumeration type is used for months. In that case a permutation error such as

```
(4, DECEMBER, 1983)
```

would be detected by a compiler. In the above all-integer formulation, however, the named notation is more reliable since the meaning does not rely on order.

Similar possibilities exist for an array type such as

```
type TABLE is array (1 .. 10) of INTEGER;
```

Given the object declaration

```
T : TABLE;
```

we can assign to T a positional array aggregate such as

```
T := (0, 0, 0, 0, 0, 0, 0, 0, 0, 0);
```

But the intent can be made more explicit by writing the aggregate in any of the equivalent named forms given below

```
(1 .. 10 => 0)
(TABLE'FIRST .. TABLE'LAST => 0)
(T'FIRST .. T'LAST => 0)
(TABLE'RANGE => 0)
(T'RANGE => 0)
(others => 0)
```

Other forms of named notation allow the explicit mention of component indexes, as in the following example

```
(1|3|5|7|9 => 0, 2|4|6|8|10 => 1)
```

Other examples of aggregates will be presented in Chapter 4 when we discuss overloading resolution for aggregates.

3.6 EXPRESSIONS

An expression is a formula that defines the computation of a value by the application of operators. Six classes of operators exist in Ada. They are listed below in increasing order of precedence:

```
logical            and   or    xor
relational         =     /=    <     >     <=    >=
binary adding      +     -     &
unary adding       +     -
multiplying        *     /     mod   rem
highest precedence **    abs   not
```

When defining levels of precedence it is very important to follow common usage, and we found six levels to be the minimum number compatible with accepted practice.

Different levels are clearly required for relational, binary adding, unary adding, multiplying, and exponentiation operators. These levels have a very deep intuitive foundation, going back to algebra learned at school.

Logical operators must be on a different (and lower) level if expressions such as

```
TODAY = MON or TODAY = SAT
LOWER_BOUND <= X and X <= UPPER_BOUND
```

are to be written without parentheses. In the case of a succession of operators with the same precedence, Ada adopts the traditional rule of binding from left to right. However, the syntax recognizes that intuition of logical operators is not as deeply rooted as in the case of arithmetic operators. For example, consider the following expression (not allowed in Ada) written in two different ways:

```
COLD and SUNNY   or   HUMID
COLD    and    SUNNY or HUMID
```

Many programmers are likely to rely on the spacing for their interpretation of such expressions, whereas nobody would be fooled by misleading spacing in the case of arithmetic operators

```
X*Y + Z           -- yes
X * Y+Z           -- no
```

For this reason, the syntax requires explicit parentheses in the case of a succession of different logical operators. For example:

```
A or (B xor C)   -- parentheses required
(A or B) xor C   -- parentheses required
                 -- (not always equal to previous expression)
A or (B and C)   -- parentheses required
A or B or C      -- no need for parentheses
A and B and C    -- no need for parentheses
```

Finally, the precedence of **abs** is chosen higher than that of multiplying operators so that

```
abs A   * B           -- and
abs (A) * B
```

both mean (abs A) * B. For similar reasons, the precedence of **not** is higher than that of logical and relational operators so that

```
not SUNNY or WARM
```

is equivalent to

```
(not SUNNY) or WARM
```

In practice most expressions are simple. The inconvenience of parentheses should not be exaggerated, as programmers tend to introduce additional parentheses anyway for readability purposes (to reassure themselves when in doubt) whether they are required or not.

3.7 STATEMENTS

The classical forms for sequential processing are included in Ada: assignment statements, procedure call statements, if and case statements, loop statements, and (control) transfer statements. Less classical control structures, such as the raise statement and the statements used for tasking, are discussed in later chapters.

It is customary to distinguish simple and compound statements: a simple statement contains no other statement; compound statements may include other sequences of statements.

The Ada syntax is such that wherever a single statement may appear, a sequence of several statements may also appear. This simplifies program modification since insertion of a statement can be done without the need to insert extra begin and end markers (as was the case in Algol and Pascal).

A sequence of statements contains at least one statement: an empty sequence is not allowed. For readability reasons, Ada provides an explicit null statement for situations where other languages would use (implicit) *empty* statements. For example, if nothing needs to be done for a given alternative of a case statement, it is preferable to state this explicitly by a null statement:

```
case TODAY is
   when TUE | THU | SAT => null;
   when MON | WED |
        FRI | SUN        => ACTION;
end case;
```

rather than convey the same impression by an empty statement which could be taken as an unintentional omission, as in the Pascal formulation given below:

```
case TODAY of
   TUE, THU, SAT : ;
   MON, WED,
   FRI, SUN: ACTION
end;
```

3.8 ASSIGNMENT STATEMENTS – THE ADA MODEL OF TIME

The assignment statement is usually regarded as the simplest of all statements, and we will use this statement to discuss the Ada model of time flow.

One issue that must be addressed in any language design is the definition of the sequencing of elementary operations. One extreme corresponds to *operational* definitions in which this sequencing is defined exhaustively, for all features of the language, and for all possible elementary operations.

The view adopted in Ada, following the Algol 68 concept of *collateral* evaluation, uses a somewhat simpler mental model of sequencing. We consider that time differences only matter at certain specific points of the program – mainly at the semicolons that terminate statements and declarations. This means that the sequencing of certain actions that occur between two consecutive semicolons is not necessarily defined by the language. Consider for example, the following assignment statements:

```
OUT_ROW(FLOOR(X)) := IN_ROW(CEIL(Y));
X := SIN(Y)*COS(Y) - TAN(Z);
```

where we assume OUT_ROW and IN_ROW to be arrays, FLOOR, CEIL to be functions, and X, Y, Z to be variables. For assignments statements, the Ada reference manual specifies that the evaluation of the left and right hand sides is done *in some order that is not defined by the language*. This means that the language does not define which of FLOOR and CEIL is called first. Similarly, whereas the precedence rules require the right hand side of the second assignment to mean

```
(SIN(Y)*COS(Y)) - TAN(Z)
```

the rules of expression evaluation leave the order of evaluation of the function calls undefined. Thus it would be possible for the functions to be called in any of the following orders:

```
(1) TAN   (2) SIN   (3) COS
(1) TAN   (2) COS   (3) SIN
(1) SIN   (2) COS   (3) TAN
(1) COS   (2) SIN   (3) TAN
```

The only (and partial) order imposed comes from the ordering of statements and from the logic of operations. Thus the ordering of the two statements requires that a function call (such as FLOOR) of the first assignment statement occur before a function call (such as SIN) of the second. Similarly, the logic of operations requires that the multiplication be performed after the evaluation of its two operands (SIN(Y) and COS(Y)).

The Ada reference manual further specifies (RM 1.6) that if different parts of a given construct are to be executed *in some order that is not defined by the language*, then the construct is incorrect if execution of these parts in a different order would have a different effect: this kind of error is called an *incorrect order dependence*.

In terms of programming methodology, this means that we must consider the flow of time to be given by the sequencing of statements, each simple statement being considered as an indivisible action. In the above example, the first assignment would be incorrect if its effect depended on the order of evaluation of FLOOR and CEIL. Should this order actually matter, then the proper way to write the program would be to give a sequence of assignments that defines the intended order explicitly. For example:

```
U := FLOOR(X);     -- guarantees that FLOOR
V := CEIL(Y);      -- is called before CEIL
OUT_ROW(U) := IN_ROW(V);
```

Similar considerations apply to expression evaluation. All constituents of an expression (aside from short-circuit control forms) must be evaluated, although the evaluation order is not defined for all terms. Hence if an exception is raised by the evaluation of some term, then this exception cannot be avoided. In this sense an expression such as

```
A = 0 or X/A > 10
```

although syntactically correct, is not proper since the validity of the right operand of or depends on the value of the left operand. Whenever there is such a dependence, it should be made explicit by means of conditional statements, or by short-circuit control forms (see 3.10), in order to emphasize the possibility of incomplete evaluation. For example:

```
A = 0 or else X/A > 10
```

Note finally that whenever order is not defined, the reference manual uses the phrase *in some order that is not defined*, rather than the phrase *in any order*. The intent of the chosen wording is to leave the order undefined but nevertheless require that it be done in some order, and thus exclude parallel evaluation.

To illustrate this point, consider again the calls of FLOOR and CEIL, and assume that the values obtained do not depend on whether FLOOR or CEIL is called first. It is nevertheless possible that parallel evaluation of FLOOR and CEIL will yield a different effect. Thus FLOOR and CEIL could be *memo-functions*, which remember past intermediate results (for efficiency). Should some of these intermediate results be used by both FLOOR and CEIL, then it would be possible for interleaved executions of these functions to deliver different – and probably incoherent – results.

3.9 IF STATEMENTS

An if statement is used to select a sequence of statements for execution on the basis of a condition. The syntax

> **if** *condition* **then**
>   *sequence_of_statements*
> **else**
>   *sequence_of_statements*
> **end if;**

is fairly classical. For nested if statements, the **if** and **end if** bracket structure avoids the *dangling else* ambiguity that results from not using **end if**. An if statement containing **elsif** alternatives can be used to select among several sequences of statements, depending on different conditions:

```
if RAIN then
   -- sequence of statements describing
   -- what to do when it rains
elsif SUN_SHINE then
   -- sequence of statements describing
   -- what to do when the sun shines
else
   -- sequence of statements describing
   -- what to do for other weather conditions
end if;
```

Strictly speaking, **elsif** alternatives are redundant: the corresponding statements can always be rewritten in the form of nested if statements. However this nesting is generally awkward and does not convey the correct impression, namely that the alternatives are on the same logical level, and this is quite apart from the fact that the conditions should be evaluated in the order in which they appear.

3.10 SHORT–CIRCUIT CONTROL FORMS

The operands of a boolean expression such as A **and** B can be evaluated in any order. Depending on the complexity of the term B, it may be more efficient (on some but not all machines) to evaluate B only when the term A has the value TRUE. This however is an optimization decision taken by the compiler and it would be incorrect to assume that this optimization is always done. In other situations we may want to express a conjunction of conditions where each condition should be evaluated (has meaning) only if the previous condition is satisfied.

Both of these things may be done with short-circuit control forms such as:

```
if NUMBER /= 0 and then TOTAL/NUMBER > MEDIAN then
   ...
end if;
```

Clearly it would not be proper to express this condition as a boolean expression using the **and** operator, since an exception would be raised if NUMBER were zero and the second operand were evaluated. Similarly, short-circuit disjunctions can be expressed with **or else** clauses as in the following example:

```
exit when NEXT = null or else NEXT.AGE = 0;
```

In this case the condition following **or else** will only be evaluated if the previous condition is not satisfied.

In Algol 60 one can achieve the effect of short-circuit evaluation only by use of conditional expressions, since complete evaluation is performed otherwise. This often leads to constructs that are tedious to follow:

```
if(if NUMBER = 0 then TRUE else TOTAL/NUMBER > MEDIAN) then ...
```

Several languages do not define how boolean conditions are to be evaluated. As a consequence programs based on short-circuit evaluation will not be portable. This clearly illustrates the need to separate boolean operators from short-circuit control forms.

3.11 CASE STATEMENTS

A case statement selects for execution one of a number of alternative sequences of statements: the alternative selected is defined by the value of an expression. Each sequence of statements is preceded by a list of *choices* defining the values for which that alternative must be selected. The main criteria in the design of the case statement are reliability and generality.

For reliability, the compiler must be given the opportunity to check for the accidental omission of some alternatives. For that reason, Ada requires that all possible values of the type of the discriminating expression be provided for in the choices. This rule is weakened if the discriminating expression is a name whose subtype is static: the choices that must be provided are then all the values of this subtype. Finally, a qualified expression can be used to restrict the possible choices, and a final choice **others** may be used to represent all values not previously specified.

As an example consider the declarations

```
type DAY is (MON, TUE, WED, THU, FRI, SAT, SUN);
subtype WORKDAY is DAY range MON .. FRI;
subtype RESTDAY is DAY range SAT .. SUN;

TODAY : DAY;
START : WORKDAY;
```

With the above declarations all values of the type DAY (the type of TODAY) must appear in one selection, as in

```
case TODAY is
    when MON | TUE | WED | THU | FRI => WORK;
    when SAT | SUN => REST;
end case;
```

This could have been written in the equivalent form

```
case TODAY is
    when MON | TUE | WED | THU | FRI => WORK;
    when others => REST;
end case;
```

If in a given context it is known that the case discriminant belongs to a given subtype, a case statement with a qualified expression may be used. Only the values of the corresponding subtype can appear in the selections.

```
case WORKDAY'(TODAY) is
    when MON | WED | FRI => LATE;
    when TUE | THU => EARLY;
end case;
```

Should the value of TODAY not belong to the subtype WORKDAY (for example if TODAY = SAT), then the exception CONSTRAINT_ERROR would be raised by the evaluation of the qualified expression. This cannot arise in the following example, which uses the fact that the subtype of START is static:

```
case START is
    when MON | WED | FRI => LATE;
    when TUE | THU => EARLY;
end case;
```

The other main criterion in the design of case statements is generality: the syntax of selections should accommodate all situations that are likely to arise, given that the case discriminant has a discrete type. Hence it should permit ranges as well as lists of values.

Thus the first example above is more likely to be written using ranges:

```
case TODAY is
   when MON .. FRI => WORK;
   when SAT .. SUN => REST;
end case;
```

or (better) using the subtype names:

```
case TODAY is
   when WORKDAY => WORK;
   when RESTDAY => REST;
end case;
```

Such ranges and subtype names are very useful for case choices. They avoid long lists that can be tedious to read and therefore error-prone.

In many ways a case statement is similar to an *array of statements* and this is somewhat reflected in the syntax. For example we may compute the opposite of a given direction by means of a case statement:

```
type DIRECTION is (NORTH, WEST, SOUTH, EAST);
COURSE : DIRECTION;
BACK    : DIRECTION;
...       -- a value is given to COURSE
case COURSE is
   when NORTH => BACK := SOUTH;
   when WEST  => BACK := EAST;
   when SOUTH => BACK := NORTH;
   when EAST  => BACK := WEST;
end case;
-- now BACK is the direction opposite to COURSE
```

Another formulation of this computation uses an array of directions declared as

```
INVERSE : constant array(DIRECTION) of DIRECTION :=
                        (NORTH => SOUTH,
                         WEST  => EAST,
                         SOUTH => NORTH,
                         EAST  => WEST);
```

and the assignment statement

```
BACK := INVERSE(COURSE);
```

As can be seen from the above example, the conceptual similarity is actually reflected in the similarity of the syntaxes for case statements and for array aggregates.

A very important diagnostic facility that the compiler should provide is the listing of all values of the discriminating type that do not appear in the listed choices. For an incomplete (and therefore incorrect) case statement, the compiler has the information and should provide it to the programmer. In the absence of this kind of diagnostic, it might be quite difficult for the programmer to discover missing values for an enumeration type with a large number of values.

Case statements are conventionally implemented with an implicit transfer table. This table will generally contain one place for each possible value of the discriminating type. Quite often however, if some of the alternatives include null statements, the compiler may optimize the code generated, by using a shorter table and an explicit range check. As an example

```
case TODAY is
   when SAT    => SHOP;
   when SUN    => SLEEP;
   when others => null;
end case;
```

may be compiled to produce code equivalent to

```
if TODAY in RESTDAY then
   case RESTDAY'(TODAY) is          -- no check needed
   when SAT => SHOP;
   when SUN => SLEEP;
   end case;
end if;
```

thus leading to a two-place transfer table. Finally, case statements with very sparse selections or with ranges as selections can be compiled as equivalent if statements. Thus for our first example we may have:

```
if TODAY in WORKDAY then
   WORK;
else
   REST;
end if;
```

3.12 LOOP STATEMENTS

The main form of loop statement allows conditional or unconditional exit statements to appear anywhere within the sequence of statements enclosed by the brackets **loop** and **end loop:**

```
loop
    READ_CHARACTER(NEXT);
    exit when NEXT = '*';
    PRINT_CHARACTER(NEXT);
end loop;
```

Although this form of loop is quite general, a special form also exists to single out the cases in which a continuation condition appears at the start of the loop:

```
while MORE_TO_DO loop
    ...
end loop;
```

Similarly two forms of for loop are provided to iterate over ranges either in *normal* (increasing) or in *reverse* (decreasing) order:

```
for COUNTER in 1 .. 10 loop          -- 1 2 3 ... 9 10
    ...
end loop;

for COUNTER in reverse 1 .. 10 loop  -- 10 9 8 ... 2 1
    ...
end loop;
```

In both cases (unlike Pascal), the loop parameter is local to the loop (which solves the problem of its value after the loop). It is declared by the loop parameter specification of the for iteration scheme. The following two forms of loop parameter specification are equivalent:

```
COUNTER in 1 .. 10
COUNTER in INTEGER range 1 .. 10
```

A null range – that is, a range whose upper bound is less than its lower bound – specifies zero iterations. Within the sequence of statements of the loop, the loop parameter is constant and therefore protected against accidental attempts at modification.

More complicated forms of loop constructs such as the so-called Zahn's construct [Za 74] and the related construct provided in Modula were considered in this design but in the end rejected. As shown in the example below, situations for which such constructs would be used can be dealt with quite easily with the existing forms.

```
declare
   type CAUSE is (TOO_LOW, NORMAL, TOO_HIGH);
   STATE : CAUSE := NORMAL;
begin
   for ... loop
      ...
      STATE := TOO_LOW;   exit;
      ...
      STATE := TOO_HIGH;  exit;
      ...
      STATE := TOO_LOW;   exit;
      ...
   end loop;

   case STATE is
      when TOO_LOW  => ...
      when TOO_HIGH => ...
      when NORMAL   => ...
   end case;
end;
```

The major emphasis in the design of the loop statement has been on simplicity: loops should have an intuitive meaning and users should not have to consult a reference manual to understand their meaning. Several studies on the use of programming languages have shown that the vast majority of loops are very simple. Hence generalities such as the *step* expression of Algol 60 should be avoided. The redundancy provided for conditional exits is itself motivated by readability considerations: loop termination conditions should be marked very conspicuously. Thus, in the recommended paragraphing,

```
exit when CONDITION;
```

is certainly more conspicuous than the equivalent form in which the exit statement is nested within an if statement:

```
if CONDITION then
   exit;
end if;
```

Guarded commands were also considered for this design and not retained. They have advantages for the development of program proofs. However, they are not compatible with other looping constructs with explicit exits. Hence if they had been retained it would have been to the exclusion of other forms of loop statement, a decision which seemed too drastic.

4. Types

4.1 INTRODUCTION

The notion of type has gradually emerged from the past twenty years of the history of programming languages as the way by which we impose structure on data. A now widely accepted view of types is that a type characterizes the set of values that objects of the type may assume, and the set of operations that may be performed on them. This common view is also taken in the Ada language.

There are several important reasons why it is found desirable to associate a type with constants and variables:

- *Factorization of Properties, Maintainability*

  Knowledge about common properties of objects should be described and collected in one place and a name should be associated with that description. A type declaration serves that purpose. Subsequently, the type name may be used to refer to the common properties in object declarations. This factorization improves program maintainability: if later a given property is to be changed, then the type declaration will be the only part of the program text to be affected by the change.

- *Reliability*

  Objects with distinct properties should be clearly distinguished in a program, and the distinction should be enforced by the compiler. Requiring that all objects be typed thus contributes to program reliability. Experience has shown that a well-written program in Pascal can be recognized easily by the use made of the typing facility to increase the reliability, readability, and security of the program.

- *Abstraction, Hiding of Implementation Details*

  Abstract or external properties of objects and operations should be separated from underlying and internal implementation-dependent properties, such as the physical representation on a specific machine. The abstract properties of an object are the only ones that need to be known for its use. Implementation details should therefore be hidden from the user. The need for such a separation is particularly strong in the case of disjoint sections of a program text, produced and maintained by different programmers, and presumably separately compiled.

Several classical problems are associated with the formulation of a type facility in a programming language. Some are the subject of ongoing debate among language designers and users, in particular:

(a) *Static versus Dynamic Properties*

Should both the *static* properties – those which are determinable from an analysis of the program text at compilation time – and the *dynamic* properties – those which may depend on the dynamic execution of a program, such as reading from an input device – be covered by a single notion of type?

(b) *Type Equivalence*

Should the language provide some form of *equivalence* or *compatibility* among types with logically related properties?

(c) *Parameterization*

Should the language provide some form of parameterization for types and their associated properties? Should the evaluation of type parameters be performed at translation time or should it be deferred until execution time?

The Ada solutions to the above problems are now summarized. A detailed discussion of these design decisions is given in later sections of this chapter.

(a) *Static versus Dynamic Properties*

Two notions are distinguished: the notion of type and the notion of subtype. A type characterizes a distinct set of values and its static properties, such as the applicable operations.

Constraints may be imposed on named types: for example a range constraint for a scalar type, or an index constraint for an array type. In general, constraints define certain requirements whose satisfaction is to be checked dynamically. A subtype name serves as an abbreviation for a type name together with a constraint associated with the type. Several difficulties in the types of Pascal that have been noted by Habermann and others [Hab 73, WSH 77] are overcome in Ada by the notion of subtype.

(b) *Type Equivalence*

Each type declaration defines a distinct type. In consequence, each type name denotes a distinct type. Values of a given type can be assigned only to objects that have this type. Values of different types cannot be intermixed.

In contrast, objects that have different subtypes of the same type are compatible: the value of an object may be assigned to a variable that has the same type, whether or not the object and the variable have the same subtype. Constraints are normally checked at execution time, although in many cases these checks can be done at compilation time, in anticipation.

Certain explicit conversions are allowed between closely related types. Such explicit conversions are defined among numeric types, among sufficiently similar array types, and among derived types of the same family. Being explicit, these conversions are safe. On the other hand, no *implicit* conversion is possible among user-defined types.

(c) *Parameterization*

Parameterization at execution time is closely associated with the notion of constraint. In particular this applies to array and record types:

- An unconstrained array type declaration has unspecified index bounds. These are subsequently specified by an index constraint for a given array object so that different array objects of the same type may have different numbers of components. If such an array is a formal parameter of a subprogram, its bounds are obtained from the actual parameter for each call.

- A record type may have special components which are called discriminants and whose values are used at execution time to discriminate among alternative variants of the record type. For example, the value of a discriminant may be used to determine a bound of a record component that is itself an array. It is possible to constrain a record by a discriminant constraint, which imposes (and establishes) certain values for the discriminants. As in the case of arrays, it is possible to write subprograms of general utility which operate on records with arbitrary discriminant values.

Parameterization at compilation time is achieved by the very powerful mechanism of generic units. Whereas parameterization at execution time by index bounds and discriminants is limited to scalar values, the parameters of generic units can even be subprograms and types. For example, we could model the length of a stack by a discriminant; but, to allow for different types of elements, we would need to define stacks within a generic package and have the element type be a generic parameter. We could then create several instances of the generic package, for example one for stacks of integers, one for stacks of characters, and so on.

These solutions are detailed in the following sections of this chapter (and, in the case of generic units, in a later chapter). We first introduce the concept of type by means of the simplest form – enumeration types – and further use these types for the discussion of type equivalence and the concepts of constraints and subtypes. We then proceed to a discussion of array types, record types, and discriminants; and the general problems of type composition.

4.2 THE CONCEPT OF TYPE

Ada provides a capability to define new types. The language construct used to declare a new type is called a type declaration. Examples of type declarations appear below:

```
type INT    is range -2**24 .. 2**24;           -- integer type
type SCALE  is (LOW, MEDIUM, HIGH);             -- enumeration type
type MASS   is digits 8 range 0.0 .. 1.0E9;     -- floating point
type VOLT   is delta 0.01 range 0.0 .. 1_000.0; -- fixed point type

type LINE   is array (1 .. 128) of CHARACTER;   -- array type
type PAIR   is record X, Y : INTEGER; end record; -- record type
type MY_INT is new INTEGER;                      -- derived
type TEXT   is access STRING;                    -- access type
type FILE   is limited private;                  -- private type
```

As stated in the introduction, a type is characterized by a set of values and a set of operations. To illustrate this we can use enumeration types: in many ways they are the simplest form of type, yet they are sufficient to discuss the most important aspects. Consider for example:

```
type DAY is (MON, TUE, WED, THU, FRI, SAT, SUN);
```

Each of the identifiers thus enumerated is called an enumeration literal and can be viewed as a (parameterless) function that always delivers the same value. Hence we have a distinct value for each enumeration literal, and so we have seven values for the type DAY.

Consider now the set of operations that is – implictly – defined by this type declaration. This set includes

- Equality and inequality:　　　`=  /=`

- Ordering relations:　　　`<  <=  >  >=`

- The assignment basic operation: `:=`

- Other basic operations called attributes. These all start with the type name followed by an apostrophe (`'`). They include attributes such as

```
DAY'FIRST   -- yields MON
DAY'LAST    -- yields SUN
```

and other attributes that are functions with a single parameter; the latter include

```
DAY'SUCC    -- for example, DAY'SUCC(MON) = TUE
DAY'PRED    -- for example, DAY'PRED(TUE) = MON
DAY'POS     -- for example, DAY'POS(MON)  = 0
DAY'VAL     -- for example, DAY'VAL(0)    = MON
```

• Finally, the basic operations involved in membership tests (**in** and **not in**), and qualification by the type DAY itself.

Thus the declaration of the type DAY has implicitly defined the above set of values and operations, and thereby what we are allowed to do with objects and values of type DAY. To appreciate the contribution of this concept to program reliability consider the interactions of three important rules in typed languages such as Pascal and Ada:

(a) All objects (variables and constants) must be declared.

(b) The declaration of an object must specify its type.

(c) Any operation on an object must preserve its type.

It results from the above rules that the type of an object is invariant during program execution: it is the type given in the object declaration. All properties characterized by the type are therefore static and must be checked at compilation time by Ada compilers. To illustrate this point consider the additional declarations:

```
type DIRECTION is (NORTH, EAST, SOUTH, WEST);
GOAL  : DIRECTION;
TODAY : DAY;
START : DAY;
```

With these declarations, an Ada compiler will accept assignment statements such as

```
TODAY := MON;
GOAL  := WEST;
START := TODAY;
```

Consider for example the first one: TODAY is a variable declared to be of type DAY; there is an assignment operation (:=) defined for this type; assignment to a variable is allowed, but it requires a value of the same type: and there is actually a literal MON that yields a value of type DAY. Using similar simple rules, an Ada compiler must reject each of the following illegal assignment statements:

```
TODAY := WEST;          -- Illegal: WEST is not a DAY value
TODAY := 5;             -- Illegal: 5 is not a DAY value
TODAY := TODAY + START; -- Illegal: "+" is not defined for DAYS
```

In the last case, TODAY and START are both of type DAY but the operation "+" is not defined for this type and this knowledge allows rejection of the statement.

This example demonstrates that the contribution of enumeration types to the quality of programs goes far beyond increased readability. We could actually achieve a comparable degree of readability in languages such as Algol 68, which do not provide enumeration types (or even in Fortran, using *data* or *parameter* statements). The set of Algol 68 declarations could be as follows

```
¢ days of the week: ¢
int MON=1, TUE=2, WED=3, THU=4, FRI=5, SAT=6, SUN=7;
¢ directions: ¢
int NORTH=1, EAST=2, SOUTH=3, WEST=4;
int GOAL, TODAY, START;
```

thereby allowing the same degree of readability as Ada for statements such as

```
TODAY := MON;
GOAL  := WEST;
START := TODAY;
```

The real difference is one of reliability. The following statements would all be accepted by an Algol 68 compiler, whereas they would all be rejected by an Ada compiler in the Ada formulation:

```
TODAY := WEST;
TODAY := 8;
TODAY := TODAY + START;
START := 2*GOAL - NORTH + SUN*WEST;
```

By declaring DAY as an enumeration type we expressed the intent that there be seven distinct values with well-defined operations. This intent was expressed in a form that permits a compiler to verify that further uses of days are consistent. Furthermore, in declaring DIRECTION to be a different type (instead of having a single enumeration type with eleven values), we have conveyed our intent that days and directions should not be mixed; and again, we have done so in a form that allows verification at compilation time by an Ada compiler.

In all cases to be examined in later sections, we will find that types allow the explicit formulation of certain logical requirements of programs. Explicit formulation allows these logical requirements to be verified by a mechanical tool – the Ada compiler – thereby contributing to program reliability.

4.3 TYPE EQUIVALENCE

As stated before, one of the objectives of a type system is to disallow incorrect (in particular unintentional) mixing of objects of different types. Hence a key issue in the design of a type system is the formulation of the conditions that must be satisfied by two objects in order that they have the same type.

Alternative resolutions of this issue of type equivalence have been put forward in a paper by Welsh, Sneeringer, and Hoare [WSH 77]. These are classified into two families, called *name* equivalence and *structural* equivalence.

Name equivalence is used in Ada. It is based on the principle that each type declaration declares a distinct type: hence two type declarations always declare two distinct types, even if the included type definitions are textually identical. Consequently, for two objects to have the same type, their declarations must refer to the same type name (whether directly, or indirectly by a subtype, as we shall see later). Consider for example the declarations:

```
type COLOR  is (WHITE, RED, YELLOW, GREEN, BLUE, BROWN, BLACK);
type COLOUR is (WHITE, RED, YELLOW, GREEN, BLUE, BROWN, BLACK);


TINT       : COLOR  := BROWN;
SHADE      : COLOR  := RED;
HUE, SPOT  : COLOUR := GREEN;
```

Then, according to the above stated principle, COLOR and COLOUR are two distinct types; TINT and SHADE are of the same type (COLOR); HUE and SPOT are of the same type (COLOUR). Thus the following assignments are legal:

```
TINT := SHADE;
SPOT := HUE;
```

On the other hand, SPOT and TINT are of different types, so that the following assignment is not allowed:

```
SPOT := TINT;        -- Illegal!
```

Structural equivalence refers to formulations in which some form of equivalence rule is defined between types on the basis of their structural properties. For example, in the case of enumeration literals several degrees of structural equivalence would be conceivable: the same number of literals (unlikely); the same literals, although not necessarily in the same order; textually identical, including spaces and line breaks and so on. For example COLOR and COLOUR would be considered as structurally equivalent for all but the last of these formulations.

We have rejected structural equivalence in order to avoid pattern-matching problems for the compiler and for the human reader: in the case of enumeration types, this could involve comparisons of very long lists of identifiers.

We also believe that structural equivalence tends to defeat the purpose of typing. Thus, objects could be considered as being of the same type because their structures happen to be identical – by accident – or because they have become identical as a result of textual modifications performed during program maintenance: in the case of enumeration types, after deleting or inserting a literal. Such objects could then be mixed unintentionally, without causing compiler diagnostics, and the error would go undetected.

Name equivalence is therefore both simpler and safer. If we want several objects to have the same type, then we must declare the type, thereby giving it a name, and we must subsequently refer to this name in the declarations of these objects.

Further arguments supporting name equivalence are presented in the sections concerning arrays (see 4.5.3) and records (see 4.6.1).

4.4 CONSTRAINTS AND SUBTYPES

So far we have seen that a type characterizes a set of values that may be assumed by objects of the type, and a set of operations that may be applied to these values and objects. The fact that an object has a certain type is a static property of the program: it follows directly from the declaration of the object.

We shall now see how to restrict the values that may be assumed by an object to a subset of the values of the type. Such a restriction is called a *constraint*, and it does not affect the set of applicable operations. A subtype is a type together with an associated constraint. An object can be declared to have a certain subtype, and this is then a static property of the object. But in general it will not always be possible to determine statically (at compilation time) whether or not a value satisfies a constraint and thereby belongs to a corresponding subtype. Thus constraints and subtypes are concepts that are, in general, related to the dynamic behavior of programs.

4.4.1 Constraints

A constraint can be used to restrict the set of values that may be assumed by an object of a given type, as in the following example:

```
START : DAY range MON .. WED;
```

Had we declared the variable START as

```
START : DAY;      -- only on MON, TUE, and WED
```

then all values of this type would be assignable to START – the comment notwithstanding. Given the constraint, however, the only assignable values are those in the range MON .. WED, that is, the values MON, TUE, and WED.

Constraints may be used effectively by compilers for optimization purposes. Their major purpose, however, is for greater program reliability: a constraint expresses a logical requirement on our program in an explicit manner, and it therefore opens up the possibility of reporting violations of this logical requirement, should they ever occur.

In principle these violations will be reported at execution time by raising the exception **CONSTRAINT_ERROR**. This means that, in general, compilers will generate code that dynamically checks constraint satisfaction. In practice however, compilers will be able to report certain potential constraint violations at compilation time. In other situations they will be in a position to omit a given check, since success has been guaranteed by a prior check.

Examples of assignments are given in the block statement below. The comment *static check* refers to situations where the check can be done at compilation time (in anticipation). The comment *dynamic check* refers to situations where a check at run time is actually required.

```
declare
    TODAY : DAY;
    START : DAY range MON .. WED;
    STOP  : DAY range MON .. FRI;
    MID   : DAY range WED .. THU;
begin
    START := TUE;   -- static check : since TUE is a literal
    STOP  := FRI;   -- static check : since FRI is a literal
    ...
    TODAY := START; -- static check : any value is allowed for TODAY
    STOP  := START; -- static check : the range of STOP
                    --                 includes that of START
    ...
    START := STOP;  -- dynamic check : STOP <= WED
    MID   := TODAY; -- dynamic check : TODAY in WED .. THU
    ...
    STOP  := MID;   -- static check : the range of MID is
                    --                 included in that of STOP
end;
```

4.4.2 Subtypes

It is good programming practice to factor out the knowledge of common properties, and this applies to constraints as well. Assume for example that at several places in a program we find objects declared with a type and constraint such as

```
DAY range MON .. FRI
```

Then it would be better to associate a name with this group and use this name for the corresponding object declarations. This can be achieved by a subtype declaration (a type name followed by a constraint is actually called a *subtype indication*):

```
subtype WORKDAY is DAY range MON .. FRI;
```

where the name chosen for the subtype is carefully chosen to convey the intent.

The name of a subtype is an abbreviation for the associated type name and constraint. Thus a subtype declaration does not define a new type, and objects of different subtypes of a given type are compatible for assignment. In an expression, such objects can be used at any place where a value of the given type is expected; the constraint on an object need be checked only upon assignment to the object, as shown in the previous examples.

The advantages of using subtypes are the usual maintainability advantages of any factoring mechanism. For example, if we want to change the range of workdays, then a single textual change is needed, namely in the subtype declaration. Without named subtypes, it would be necessary to inspect all occurrences of the range MON .. FRI in the program, in order to detect those occurrences where the intent was to use this range for workdays.

We can also define hierarchies of subtypes by constraining other subtypes. Consider for example the type CHARACTER. In Ada this is a predefined enumeration type whose enumeration literals are character literals (such enumeration types are called character types). Now we can define a subtype such as

```
subtype LETTER is CHARACTER range 'A' .. 'Z';
```

for upper-case letters. Subsequently we can define a subtype such as

```
subtype LAST_11 is LETTER range 'O' .. 'Z';
```

For this to be correct, the range 'O' .. 'Z' must be compatible with that of LETTER, that is, it must be a subinterval of 'A' .. 'Z'. This is checked, and so an error such as writing the character '0' (the digit zero) instead of the upper-case letter 'O' would be detected – the character '0' (zero) does not belong to the range 'A' .. 'Z'.

4.4.3 Evaluation of Constraints

All the examples presented so far included constraints that can be evaluated statically. Certain constraints that determine critical space requirements must be known at compilation time, since space optimization would not be possible in the case of dynamically computed values. For example, the range of an integer type had better be known statically, in order to allow the compiler to select the appropriate single-length or double-length machine instructions.

However, requiring static evaluation in every case would be much too restrictive. The assertions expressed by range constraints would be too coarse, ranges could not be used as general loop iteration ranges, and arrays could only be of static size. A balance must be struck in this respect, and the rules of Ada represent a deliberate choice of when evaluation must be static.

An issue to be considered is the time when the expressions appearing in constraints should be evaluated. Consider the subtype declaration:

subtype PAST **is** DAY **range** MON .. TODAY;

where TODAY is a variable. The rule adopted in Ada is that the bounds of a range constraint are evaluated when the subtype declaration is elaborated. This means that the subtype declaration is equivalent to the following sequence:

today_now : **constant** DAY := TODAY;
subtype PAST **is** DAY **range** MON .. *today_now*;

where *today_now* represents an identifier not used elsewhere. The bounds of the subtype PAST are denoted by the subtype attributes PAST'FIRST (same as MON) and PAST'LAST (same as *today_now*).

Note that if the bounds of the range are not known at compilation time, the compiler will often need to generate (implicitly) a descriptor containing the value of the bounds. Hence, to minimize descriptor overhead, it is important to localize the knowledge about equivalent constraints in a single subtype declaration and then to use the name of this subtype, instead of repeating the constraint in several variable declarations.

Note also that, for reliability and maintainability, using a subtype is far better than repeating the corresponding constraint at various points of the text, since the value of an expression defining a bound may differ at these points. Thus it is preferable to write:

```
declare
   subtype INDEX is INTEGER range K*M .. K*N;
   TABLE : array (INDEX) of FLOAT;
   ...
   procedure UPDATE(X : INDEX) is
   ...
   end UPDATE;
begin
   for J in INDEX loop
      if TABLE(J) < TABLE(INDEX'LAST) then
      ...
      end if;
   end loop;
end;
```

rather than to repeat the range K*M .. K*N at various points of the text or to use K*N directly (for INDEX'LAST).

In the case of the subprogram UPDATE the language does not even leave us this choice, since it requires a type or subtype name for subtype indications of formal parameters.

4.5 ARRAY TYPES

An array type declaration specifies the subtype of array components, and the subtype of index values for each index position. On the other hand, the index bounds are not specified. This means that the set of array values defined by an array type contains arrays with different numbers of components. Consider for example the formulation of the predefined array type STRING:

> **type** STRING **is array** (POSITIVE **range** <>) **of** CHARACTER;

This declaration specifies that values of type STRING are one-dimensional arrays whose components have the type CHARACTER. It further specifies that the index values must be positive integers, the subtype POSITIVE being declared as

> **subtype** POSITIVE **is** INTEGER **range** 1 .. INTEGER'LAST;

On the other hand, it does not specify which values should be assumed by the index bounds. This is stressed by the box (<>) in the index subtype definition

> POSITIVE **range** <>

The box symbol (here as elsewhere in the language) stands for something that is to be filled in later; something that is left unspecified, but only temporarily.

Later on, it will be possible to partition the set of array values into subsets corresponding to some specific index bounds. Each such subset defines a subtype of the array type. The form of constraint used to specify the range of index values (and hence the bounds) for a given index position is called an index constraint. For example:

> BUFFER : STRING(1 .. 1000);

This declares the variable BUFFER of type STRING: an index constraint is required in such a declaration and, in the case considered, it specifies that the lower and upper bounds are the positive numbers 1 and 1000.

We can also declare a subtype, and thus give a name to the subtype indication formed by the name of the array type followed by an index constraint. Subsequently, we can use the subtype name in object declarations:

> **subtype** LINE **is** STRING(1 .. 80);

> LEAD   : **constant** LINE := (LINE'RANGE => ' ');
> HEADER : LINE := LEAD;

We have used the array attribute LINE'RANGE in the initialization of LEAD: it provides the index range of the subtype LINE in a symbolic manner, and is therefore easier to maintain than stating the range literally, as 1 .. 80.

Other examples of array attributes are given below:

```
BUFFER'FIRST          -- 1
BUFFER'LAST           -- 1000
BUFFER'LENGTH         -- 1000
LINE'LAST             -- 80
LEAD'LAST             -- 80 (same as LINE'LAST)
```

In some cases we want all declared objects of a given array type to have the same index bounds. This can be achieved by providing an index constraint directly in the array type declaration. For example

type SCHEDULE **is array** (DAY) **of** BOOLEAN;

This form is actually a contraction of the declaration of an *anonymous* array type followed by the declaration of a subtype:

type *schedule* **is array** (DAY **range** <>) **of** BOOLEAN;
                              -- arbitrary range of days
subtype SCHEDULE **is** *schedule* (DAY'FIRST .. DAY'LAST);
                              -- always 7 days

This means that SCHEDULE is actually a (constrained) array subtype and all objects that have this subtype therefore have the same bounds (MON and SUN).

There are two cases in which the subtype of an array object (and hence the bounds) can be inferred, and therefore is not required to be explicit in the declaration of the object. The first case is for constants. In a way, constancy is the ultimate form of restriction: whereas an index constraint freezes the index bounds but not the values of the array components, everything is invariable in the case of a constant: the component values and hence also the bounds. Thus a constant declaration such as

MESSAGE : **constant** STRING := "how many characters?";

is allowed. The implied lower bound is 1 – that is, POSITIVE'FIRST – and the implied upper bound is given by the number of characters of the string (which we can subsequently obtain from the attribute MESSAGE'LENGTH).

The second case is for formal parameters. We want to provide a subprogram of general utility that is applicable to any array of a given type, whatever the index bounds. This is achieved by declaring the formal parameter to have this array type. Then, for each call of the subprogram, the formal parameter will be constrained by the bounds obtained from the associated actual parameter. For example a function MIRROR, returning the mirror image of a string of arbitrary bounds, is defined as follows:

```
function MIRROR(A : STRING) return STRING is
  RESULT : STRING(A'RANGE);
begin
  for N in A'RANGE loop
    RESULT(N) := A(A'LAST - (N - A'FIRST));
  end loop;
  return RESULT;
end MIRROR;
```

For each call, the formal parameter A is constrained by the bounds of the associated actual parameter. This means that the bounds A'FIRST and A'LAST (and hence the range A'RANGE) have well-defined values during a given call. Consider for example:

```
EGASSEM : constant STRING := MIRROR(MESSAGE);
-- the string "?sretcarahc ynam woh"
```

then during the call MIRROR(MESSAGE), the value of A'FIRST is MESSAGE'FIRST; that of A'LAST is MESSAGE'LAST; and the range A'RANGE is defined by MESSAGE'RANGE. These values are invariable for the call considered, but they need not be the same for different calls.

To complete our discussion of array types we need to mention the set of operations defined by an array type. Some of, them such as indexing, are fairly classical: indexing the array BUFFER by the index value N is achieved by BUFFER(N) and refers to the Nth component of that array (since the lower bound is 1). The discussion given in the following subsections will concentrate upon features that are less classical: slices and aggregates.

4.5.1 Slices and Sliding

Slices are quite useful for programs that deal with strings and more generally for one-dimensional arrays. Consider, for example, setting the headline of a given page of a dictionary. Assuming the headline declared as

```
HEADLINE : STRING(1 .. 60) := (others => ' ');
```

it could later be filled by slice assignments such as

```
HEADLINE(1 .. 10)  := "battle cry";
HEADLINE(29 .. 32) := " 125";
HEADLINE(46 .. 60) := "Bayeux tapestry";
```

More realistically, our application would have functions defining the left, middle, and right sides for a given page number:

```
function LEFT  (N : POSITIVE) return STRING (1 .. 20);
function MID   (N : POSITIVE) return STRING (1 .. 4);
function RIGHT (N : POSITIVE) return STRING (1 .. 20);
```

so that the composition for the page 125 could appear as follows:

```
HEADLINE(1 .. 20)  := LEFT(125);
HEADLINE(29 .. 32) := MID(125);
HEADLINE(41 .. 60) := RIGHT(125);
```

Another way of programming this headline composition is to declare an eight character blank filler and then use string catenation. So for the current page P:

```
FILLER : constant STRING(1 .. 8) := (others => ' ');
  ...
HEADLINE := LEFT(P) & FILLER & MID(P) & FILLER & RIGHT(P);
```

In another part of the program, in which we analyze the header, we may define another string

```
PLACE : STRING(1 .. 60);
```

and write the slice assignment

```
PLACE(1 .. 20) := HEADLINE(41 .. 60);
```

Finally, we may want to compare a slice to a string literal or to nother slice:

```
if PLACE(1 .. 20) = "    BAYEUX TAPESTRY" or
   PLACE(1 .. 20) = HEADLINE (41 .. 60) then
```

Having reviewed these typical uses of slices, we now consider what they are and what is involved in slice assignments and comparisons. Consider first the type of a slice such as

```
PLACE(41 .. 60)
```

This type is the same as that of PLACE, that is, the type STRING. Remember that an array type defines the subtype of the index bounds but not the bounds themselves. Thus STRING was defined as

```
type STRING is array (POSITIVE range <>) of CHARACTER;
```

Consequently PLACE and PLACE(41 .. 60) are both of this type, although they have different subtypes. The subtype of PLACE is

    STRING(1 .. 60)

whereas the subtype of

    PLACE(41 .. 60)

is

    STRING(41 .. 60)

Note that we can have slices even in the case where the array type is anonymous. For example, given the type SCHEDULE declared in the previous section we can declare

    A, B : SCHEDULE;

and then perform slice assignments such as

    A(MON .. FRI) := (MON .. FRI => TRUE);
    A(SAT .. SUN) := (SAT .. SUN => FALSE);

Similarly we can catenate slices as in

    B := A(WED .. SUN) & A(MON .. TUE);

    -- B = (TRUE, TRUE, TRUE, FALSE, FALSE, TRUE, TRUE)

In the above cases, slices such as A(MON .. FRI) and A(SAT .. SUN) have the anonymous type *schedule* (and this is quite legitimate, as is amply demonstrated by these examples).

Consider next what is involved in an assignment statement such as

    PLACE(1 .. 20) := HEADLINE(41 .. 60);

The two objects do have the same type (STRING) but their subtypes are STRING(1 .. 20) and STRING(41 .. 60) respectively, and are thus different. The assignment is nevertheless correct: the language rules specify that before assigning HEADLINE(41 .. 60), this array value undergoes a *subtype conversion* to the subtype of the left-hand side, that is, to STRING(1 .. 20). This subtype conversion – sometimes called *sliding* – is possible only if the two arrays have the same length (which is true for our example). If the lengths differ, the subtype conversion fails and the exception CONSTRAINT_ERROR is raised.

Sliding is also involved in comparisons such as

```
PLACE(1 .. 20) = HEADLINE(41 .. 60)
```

so that equality does not require the same subtype (and bounds): it only requires that the lengths be the same and that matching components be equal – *matching* components are those that have the same *relative* position. If the lengths differ, the two slices are unequal (no exception is raised).

So far we have given examples of sliding in the case of slices, but subtype conversions are also involved for array objects that do not have the same bounds. For example, having declared

```
BANNER : STRING(101 .. 160);
```

the following assignment is correct and involves a similar subtype conversion:

```
BANNER := PLACE;
```

To conclude, sliding corresponds to a view of arrays for which *the bounds are not part of array values but rather of array objects*. The logical consistency of the model moreover requires that array bounds be transmitted to formal parameters. The sliding semantics selected for equality can actually be described in Ada itself:

```
function "=" (LEFT, RIGHT : STRING) return BOOLEAN is
begin
   if LEFT'LENGTH /= RIGHT'LENGTH then
      return FALSE;
   end if;
   for N in LEFT'RANGE loop
      if LEFT(N) /= RIGHT(N + (RIGHT'FIRST - LEFT'FIRST)) then
         return FALSE;
      end if;
   end loop;
   return TRUE;
end;
```

Sliding actually corresponds to the term (RIGHT'FIRST - LEFT'FIRST) in the indexing of the right array.

Without slices the necessity for a sliding semantics of assignments would not be as obvious: after all it would be possible to restrict assignments to cases where the bounds were the same. Another alternative would have been to consider that sliding is part of the slicing itself. This would mean, for example, that the lower bound of any string slice is POSITIVE'FIRST. However this semantics does not appear very intuitive. Consider for example the following function:

```
function LOCATE(C : CHARACTER; S : STRING) return INTEGER is
begin
   for N in S'RANGE loop
     if C = S(N) then
        return N;
     end if;
   end loop;
   return 0;    -- not found
end;
```

With the Ada semantics of slices we can call this function in the following manner:

```
LOCATE('X', BUFFER)
LOCATE('*', BUFFER(30 .. 90))
LOCATE('?', BUFFER(100 .. 200))
```

and so on, and we expect the result, if not zero, to be usable as an index indicating a position where the character was located in the buffer. Now this relies essentially on the fact that both the lower and upper bounds of the actual array are passed to the formal array. This would not be the case if slicing already implied sliding, since all STRING slices would have a lower bound equal to 1.

4.5.2 Array Aggregates

The syntax of array aggregates allows for *named* aggregates, aggregates with the choice **others**, and *positional* aggregates. These forms are justified by readability and by convenience, and also, in the case of positional aggregates, by tradition. Their design had to take into account certain limitations, inspired either by efficiency or by consistency with other rules, such as sliding.

The different forms of aggregate are reviewed in what follows. For each form we discuss what is allowed, and consider the determination of the subtype of the corresponding aggregates – that is, how to determine the lower and upper bounds. Most examples will presuppose the following declarations:

```
subtype INDEX is INTEGER range -1 .. +200;
type    TABLE is array (INDEX range <>) of INTEGER;

subtype QUINTET  is TABLE(0 .. 4);
subtype TRIPLE   is TABLE(1 .. 3);

TRIO    : TRIPLE;
QUINT   : QUINTET;
ROW     : TABLE(1 .. 50);

procedure DISPLAY  (T : TABLE);
procedure TRIANGLE (T : TRIPLE);
```

Named Aggregates

Named associations are provided for reasons of readability: they make the association between index values and component values fully explicit. For example:

```
(1 .. 10 => 0, 11 .. 50 => 25);
```

The choices being explicit, the lower and upper bounds are fully defined by the smallest and largest choice values, respectively, so that the subtype of the above aggregate is TABLE(1 .. 50), in the present context. Thus for the call

```
DISPLAY((1 .. 10 => 0, 11 .. 50 => 25));
```

the attributes of the formal parameter T have the corresponding values: T'FIRST = 1 and T'LAST = 50.

For assignment statements, sliding applies as usual, and the following assignment is therefore well-defined:

```
QUINT := (1 .. 5 => 33);
```

The limitations imposed on named aggregates are justified by efficiency considerations: the choices must be static (computable at compilation time), unless the aggregate includes a single component association, and this component association has a single choice. Thus an aggregate with a single choice such as

```
(1 .. N => 25)
```

where N is computed at run time, is allowed. But an aggregate such as

```
(M .. N => 25, K .. L => 12)
```

where M, N, K and L are not static is not allowed, since this would require a rather complex check at run time that the ranges were adjacent and did not overlap.

The Choice Others

In many cases most components of an array will have the same value and it will be convenient to obtain the array value by an aggregate of the form:

(... , others => COMMON_VALUE)

The particular case where all components have the same common value is also frequent; in this case the form of the aggregate reduces to

(others => COMMON_VALUE)

In contrast to the situation encountered with previous named aggregates, the presence of an **others** choice implies that no information about the bounds can be derived from the aggregate itself and this information will therefore have to be obtained from the context. An aggregate with the choice **others** will be illegal in a context that does not define the bounds. For this reason, a call such as:

DISPLAY((others => 25));   -- illegal

is illegal since no information on the bounds can be obtained from the context; indeed it is the other way round: since the formal parameter is unconstrained, it expects the bounds to be supplied by the actual parameter. For similar reasons the comparison

if TRIO = (others => 10) then ...

is not allowed, since the predefined operator "=", which is implicitly declared by the declaration of the type TABLE, has the following profile:

function "=" (LEFT, RIGHT : TABLE) **return** BOOLEAN;

so that the right parameter is of the (unconstrained) array type TABLE, which does not provide information on the bounds.

For the above reasons an aggregate containing the choice **others** is only allowed in contexts where we know the array subtype, whether by declaration or by qualification, as in the following examples:

```
TRIANGLE((others => 15));                   -- subtype TRIPLE
DISPLAY(TRIPLE'(others => 21));             -- qualified: a TRIPLE
DISPLAY(QUINTET'(0 .. 1 => 5, others => 15));-- qualified: a QUINTET
```

For assignment statements, the choice **others** is also allowed, since the subtype of the variable on the left-hand side is always known. So we can write:

```
TRIO  := (others => 0);
QUINT := (others => 1);
```

Note that an **others** choice need not be static, as is shown in the following example:

```
for N in 1 .. 4 loop
  ROW(10*N .. 12*N) := (others => 3);
end loop;
```

Whereas the above aggregate is allowed, an aggregate combining the choice **others** with other named associations is not allowed as the right-hand-side expression of an assignment statement (unless the aggregate is qualified). To understand this restriction, remember that an array assignment involves sliding of the bounds of the value of the array expression. In combination with the choice **others** this could have led to surprises. Consider for example the variable:

```
FIVE : TABLE(2 .. 6);
```

and the (illegal) assignment statement

```
FIVE := (3 => 8, others => 1);   -- illegal
```

One might expect the resulting value of FIVE to be $(1,1,8,1,1)$, because of the explicit choice, or perhaps $(1,8,1,1,1)$, because of the lower bound of FIVE. However, before sliding the subtype of the aggregate would be TABLE(-1 .. 3), with INDEX'FIRST = -1 as lower bound, therefore placing the value 8 in fifth position and with the resulting value $(1,1,1,1,8)$. The combination of these two degrees of freedom – sliding on the one hand, and **others** with other associations on the other hand – would thus have unintuitive and therefore unreliable consequences; it is not allowed in Ada.

Note that, as usual, an explicit qualification resolves all doubt, so that the following assignment is allowed:

```
FIVE := QUINTET'(3 => 8, others => 1);   -- (1,1,1,8,1)
```

Positional Aggregates

For positional aggregates we again have to consider whether or not the subtype is defined by the context. Thus for:

```
TRIANGLE((4, 6, 8));          -- subtype TRIPLE
TRIO := (4, 6, 8);            -- subtype TRIPLE
DISPLAY(TRIPLE'(4, 6, 8));    -- qualified: TRIPLE
```

the subtype is known and therefore defines the bounds. Consider on the other hand a call such as

```
DISPLAY((4, 6, 8));
```

where the declaration of the formal parameter is unconstrained: in such a case the lower bound of the aggregate is (implicitly) taken to be INDEX'FIRST, the lower bound of the index subtype (here -1).

4.5.3 Equivalence and Explicit Conversions

Name equivalence, as explained in section 4.3, is used systematically for all types in Ada, and in particular for array types. As for other types, the main arguments in favor of name equivalence are simplicity and the desire to avoid unintentional equivalence: It would not be desirable to treat two arrays as having the same type just because the component type is the same:

```
type OPTION_SET is array (OPTION) of BOOLEAN;
type COLOR_SET  is array (COLOR)  of BOOLEAN;
```

and (in this case) just because the number of options happens to equal the number of colors. From a conceptual point of view, these two array types have nothing to do with each other, apart from their common component type.

On the other hand, the design of Ada recognizes that this safety argument does not apply to *explicit* type conversions: being explicit, they are unequivocally intentional and cannot be just accidental.

Explicit type conversions are clearly desirable among array types that satisfy certain conditions. To illustrate their need, consider first a package defining sorting operations. It could appear as:

```
with MATHS; use MATHS;    -- defines REAL
package SORTING is
   type VECTOR is array (INTEGER range <>) of REAL;
   procedure SORT(X : in out VECTOR);
   ...
end SORTING;
```

For the definition of the type VECTOR the number of decisions to be made was rather limited: first there was the component type, for which it appeared convenient to use the type REAL defined in the library package MATHS (along with useful mathematical functions); then there was the selection of INTEGER as index subtype. Given this limited number of decisions, it is not unlikely that the same decisions could be made in another package defined totally independently, say by a different software producer. For example a package performing table listings could be specified as:

```
with MATHS; use MATHS;
package LISTING is
   type TABLE is array (INTEGER range <>) of REAL;
   procedure LIST(X : in TABLE);
   ...
end LISTING;
```

These two packages are of general use and hence they would probably be made available as library packages, so that a user performing both sort and listing operations would naturally write a procedure such as the one given below:

```
with MATHS, SORTING, LISTING;
use  MATHS, SORTING, LISTING;
procedure APPLICATION is
   ...
   V : VECTOR(1 .. 200);
   ...
   T : TABLE(0 .. 3000);
begin
   ...
   SORT(V);
   ...
   LIST(T);
   ...
end APPLICATION;
```

The SORT operation is applicable to vectors and thus to V; similarly the LIST operation is applicable to tables and thus to T. However, a dilemma would arise for an array that must be sorted before being listed: should it be declared as a VECTOR or as a TABLE? – neither of the two would work. Similarly, an array might have been declared as

```
A : array (1 .. 1000) of REAL;
```

without knowing in advance whether it would ever be sorted (or listed), and it would be cumbersome to have to change the declaration of A just because it needed to be sorted in one part of the program.

For these reasons, explicit conversions are allowed between two array types if both types have the same component type and the same dimensionality, and if for each dimension the index types are the same (or convertible to each other: see RM 4.6). Syntactically, an explicit conversion appears as a call of a function whose name is that of the target type. For example:

```
SORT(VECTOR(T));
   ...
LIST(TABLE(V));
   ...
SORT(VECTOR(A));
```

Note that conversions are still possible when the constraints on the component type are different. Consider for example the array types

```
type CHAR_LINE is array (1 .. 120) of CHARACTER;
type TEXT_LINE is array (1 .. 120) of CHARACTER range 'A' .. 'Z';

CL : CHAR_LINE;
TL : TEXT_LINE;
```

Explicit conversions such as

```
TL := TEXT_LINE(CL);
CL := CHAR_LINE(TL);
```

are allowed. The fact that they are explicit warns the user that they may (but need not) be costly. For example, the conversion of CL to the type TEXT_LINE requires an implicit loop to check that each component of CL is in the allowed range of characters; on the other hand, no check is involved for the conversion of TL to the type CHAR_LINE. Similarly, for an in out parameter that is implemented by reference, an actual parameter that has the form of a type conversion may require the creation of a copy on the calling side if the compiler has chosen different representations for the two types.

Array types are the only types for which Ada provides anonymous type definitions. However, all array objects declared in this manner are of different types, even in the case of multiple declarations such as

```
U, V : array (1 .. 12) of INTEGER;
```

since this multiple declaration has the same meaning as the following succession of single declarations:

```
U : array (1 .. 12) of INTEGER;
V : array (1 .. 12) of INTEGER;
```

Two type definitions imply two distinct types, and thus we cannot assign U to V, although we could assign a component of U to a component of V since they are both of type INTEGER. Should we want U and V to be of the same type (and the ability to assign U to V), the only solution is to name the type and use this type name in the declaration of U and V:

```
type DOZEN is array (1 .. 12) of INTEGER;
U : DOZEN;
V : DOZEN;
   ...
U := V;
```

4.6 RECORD TYPES

The basic form of record type is similar to that provided in Pascal: the component declarations are enclosed by the reserved words **record** and **end record**, as in the following example:

```
type DATE is
  record
     MONTH : MONTH_NAME;              -- a suitable enumeration type
     DAY   : INTEGER range 1 .. 31;
     YEAR  : INTEGER range 1 .. 3000;
  end record;
```

Here the set of values consists of all ordered triples containing a month, a day, and a year in this order and having the specified component names MONTH, DAY, YEAR. The set of operations includes assignment, test for equality, component selection, and aggregate formation. For example, having declared

```
TODAY : DATE;
```

we can select the corresponding year by a selected component

```
TODAY.YEAR
```

as in the following assignment

```
TODAY.YEAR := TODAY.YEAR + 1;
```

Selection of the component YEAR can actually be viewed as achieved by a basic operation ".YEAR" which can be applied in postfix manner to the name of any object of type DATE. These basic operations are implicitly declared by the record type declaration itself, although Ada does not allow the explicit declaration of postfix operations such as ".YEAR".

Aggregates have already been discussed in section 3.5: in particular we have seen that Ada provides both positional aggregates and aggregates in named notation:

```
(DEC, 12, 1983)                          -- positional
(DAY => 12, MONTH => DEC, YEAR => 1983)  -- named
```

4.6.1 Equivalence

Name equivalence is used for record types, as for other types. To emphasize the arguments against structural equivalence, consider the following record type declarations:

```
type PAIR is
  record
    LEFT  : INTEGER;
    RIGHT : INTEGER;
  end record;

type RATIONAL is
  record
    NUMERATOR   : INTEGER;
    DENOMINATOR : INTEGER range 1 .. INTEGER'LAST;
  end record;
```

Several alternative forms of structural equivalence rules can be considered, involving increasing amounts of checking, especially if the record types have a large number of components:

(a) Two record types are equivalent if the texts of their type definitions (what appears after is) are identical (disregarding textual layout such as spaces, new lines, and so on).

(b) Two record types are equivalent if they have the same number of components, and at each component position, corresponding components have the same name and are declared with the same type name.

(c) Same as (b) but the names of corresponding components need not agree, only the type names. This is a more mathematical point of view, where one considers a record as a cartesian product.

(d) Same as (b) but the order of components is not significant.

(e) Same as (c) but the constraints on corresponding components may differ.

(f) Same as (e) but the subtypes must be the same.

(g) Same as (e) but the component types must be equivalent, while their names need not be identical.

(h) Same as (g) but a type name is also equivalent to the text of the corresponding type definition (which could even be anonymous).

The types PAIR and RATIONAL given above would be equivalent under all the rules if their component names were accidentally the same and if the constraint on DENOMINATOR were not expressed in the type declaration. More specifically, under rule (b), PAIR would be equivalent to

```
type ANOTHER_PAIR is
  record
    LEFT, RIGHT : INTEGER;
  end record;
```

Rule (c) makes sense for a language for which all aggregates are in positional notation. It complicates the checking by the compiler, since all permutations must be considered. Conversely, the rule (d) is sensible for a totally non-positional language where components must always be named in record aggregates. Rule (e) complicates the implementation of constraints and subtypes for components, since they must be checked for each component on record or array assignments. Rule (f) cannot be checked statically. Rule (g) requires a recursive matching algorithm. In addition, rule (h) requires type expansion, and even an algorithm of cycle reduction in the case of mutually recursive access types.

All these complexities for the implementation – and above all, for the reader – are avoided in Ada by adopting the simple rule that every declaration declares a distinct type.

4.6.2 Default Initialization of Record Components

Default initialization can be specified for some or for all components of a record. Consider for example:

```
type FRACTION is
  record
    DIVIDEND : INTEGER  := 0;
    DIVISOR  : POSITIVE := 1;
  end record;
```

The indicated initializations will be performed by the elaboration of the declaration of an object of type FRACTION, in the absence of explicit initialization. Thus after the elaboration of

```
F : FRACTION;
G : FRACTION := (2, 3);
```

the value of F is well-defined and is equal to (0, 1), whereas the value of G is equal to (2, 3) as specified by the explicit initialization.

Note that initial values need not be static, as is illustrated here:

```
type BUFFER(LENGTH : POSITIVE) is
  record
    POS   : NATURAL := 0;
    VALUE : STRING(1 .. LENGTH) := (1 .. LENGTH => ' ');
  end record;

type TRIPLE is
  record
    A, B, C : PERSON_NAME := new PERSON;
  end record;
```

The following example shows that default initializations (in combination with access types) can even be used to construct quite elaborate dynamic structures:

```
type NODE(LEVEL : POSITIVE := 1);
type LINK is access NODE;
function BRANCH(N : POSITIVE) return LINK;

type NODE(LEVEL : POSITIVE := 1) is
  record
    VALUE : ITEM := NULL_ITEM;
    LEFT, RIGHT : LINK := BRANCH(LEVEL);
  end record;

function BRANCH(N : POSITIVE) return LINK is
begin
  if N = 1 then
    return null;
  else
    return new NODE(N - 1);
  end if;
end;
```

Thus whereas the declaration

```
TERMINAL : NODE(1);
```

will create a single node, a declaration such as

```
TREE : NODE(5);
```

will lead to the dynamic creation of a complete binary tree with 5 levels (thus including 1 node of level 5, 2 nodes of level 4, 4 nodes of level 3, 8 nodes of level 2, and 16 nodes of level 1).

The previous example is mainly intended to show the power that can be achieved by default initializations. Clearly more power also creates more danger and an incorrect program could certainly enter an infinite recursion during the elaboration of declarations.

The main motivation for allowing default initialization is however one of program reliability. In many applications, it is found desirable to have a consistent initial state for all objects: the services offered by the program may critically depend on objects being well initialized. To achieve this, we could of course define an initial value to be used for all declarations, or provide the users with an initialization procedure to be applied before any other use is made of objects. The weakness of these approaches lies in the fact that our program would remain vulnerable to users that do not follow this initialization discipline (whether unintentionally or not). The only safe solution is therefore to have a default initialization that is invoked without any reliance on the user.

4.7 DISCRIMINANTS

The form of record type presented so far corresponds to a pure Cartesian product (as described by C.A.R. Hoare in Notes on Data Structuring [DDH 72]), aside from the requirement that components be named. A typical example of such record types is the type `PAIR` with two components of type `INTEGER`: there is no dependence between these components – any pair of integers will be of type `PAIR`, so that the set of values of this type is actually the Cartesian product `INTEGER x INTEGER`.

There are however composite objects in which there is dependence between components. For example, in a record describing an attendance list, the length of one component – the table of attendants – may be given by another component of the record. More generally, the overall structure of a record, in particular the presence or absence of certain components, may depend on the value of a specific component.

Because of these dependences, such composite objects cannot be modelled as simple Cartesian products. Their description will require the use of special components called discriminants.

4.7.1 Record Types with Variants

A record type with a variant part specifies several alternative variants of the type. The variant part depends on a special component called a *discriminant*, and each variant defines the components that exist for a given value of the discriminant. Consider for example a formulation of the type `PERSON`:

```
type GENDER is (M, F);

type PERSON(SEX : GENDER := F) is
  record
    AGE : INTEGER range 0 .. 123;
    case SEX is
      when M => BEARDED  : BOOLEAN;
      when F => CHILDREN : INTEGER range 0 .. 20;
    end case;
  end record;
```

Here the discriminant is the component SEX declared in the discriminant part, immediately after the name of the type. This special syntax brings out the fact that discriminants are not ordinary components: it will be possible for other components to depend on discriminants. Furthermore, as we shall see when presenting packages, this syntax will allow us to declare private types for which the discriminants are known, while keeping the rest of the type hidden.

In the record type definition we next encounter the declaration of the component AGE (all persons have an age), and then the variant part, expressing a dependence on the discriminant SEX:

```
case SEX is
  ...
end case;
```

Within the variant part, we next find the two variants – one for each possible value of the discriminant. For example we find the variant

```
when M => BEARDED : BOOLEAN;
```

that declares the boolean component BEARDED to exist for persons of sex M (only men are bearded); and similarly, another variant that declares the component CHILDREN to exist for persons of sex F (only women bear children):

```
when F => CHILDREN : INTEGER range 0 .. 20;
```

It follows from this description that the set of values of the type PERSON is the union of disjoint subsets, which correspond to the two possible variants. Thus we have a subset of values of the form

```
(SEX => F, AGE => integer_value, CHILDREN => integer_value)
```

and another subset of values of the form

```
(SEX => M, AGE => integer_value, BEARDED => boolean_value)
```

4.7.2 Discriminant Constraints – Record Subtypes

We have seen that different subsets of values are associated with different variants. Seen in this light, a subtype of the record type is associated with each of its variants. When declaring an object, we can actually specify that it may only assume values of a given subtype: this is achieved by a *discriminant constraint* that imposes a specific value on the discriminant. Thus whereas

```
ANYONE : PERSON;
```

declares a person of either sex, each of the two following declarations includes a discriminant constraint and declares an object constrained to one of the two possible subtypes:

```
HE  : PERSON(M);          -- positional notation
SHE : PERSON(SEX => F);   -- named notation
```

We can also name the two possible subtypes by means of subtype declarations:

```
subtype MALE   is PERSON(SEX => M);
subtype FEMALE is PERSON(SEX => F);
```

The compiler may take advantage of the information provided by constraints, when setting the amount of space to be used for a given record variable. However, as with other forms of constraint, the main purpose of discriminant constraints is reliability: the requirements specified by constraints can be checked at execution time, unless it can already be shown at compilation time that the checks are not needed (either because they would always succeed or because they would always fail). The possible situations are illustrated below:

```
declare
   ANYONE : PERSON;

   HE    : MALE;        -- equivalent methods of
   PETER : PERSON(M);   -- declaring males

   JOAN  : FEMALE;
   SHE   : FEMALE;
begin
   ...
   ANYONE := HE;        -- No run-time check needed since
                        -- MALE is a subtype of PERSON

   ANYONE := JOAN;      -- Similarly no run-time check needed

   HE := PETER;         -- No run-time check needed: both are males
```

```
    HE := JOAN;          -- Error! Can be reported at compilation time
                         -- since MALE and FEMALE are disjoint subtypes

    SHE := ANYONE;       -- check at run time that ANYONE.SEX = F and
                         -- raise CONSTRAINT_ERROR if check fails
end;
```

4.7.3 Denoting Components of Variants

Variants define certain components that exist only for specific values of the discriminant. Checking the validity of names that denote such dependent components is part of the security that must be provided by Ada compilers. This implies that a reference to the component

```
    ...  ANYONE.BEARDED  ...
```

is logically equivalent to the following text

```
if ANYONE.SEX /= M then
    raise CONSTRAINT_ERROR;
end if;
...  ANYONE.BEARDED  ...
```

We will show in section 4.7.4 that this check can always be done because the language rules guarantee that discriminants are always initialized. Furthermore direct assignment to a discriminant

```
ANYONE.SEX := F;     -- illegal!
```

is forbidden and will be rejected by the compiler. The only allowed way to change the value of a discriminant is by assignment to the record as a whole. Thus

```
ANYONE := (SEX => F, AGE => 13, CHILDREN => 0);
```

is a whole-record assignment which (legally) sets ANYONE.SEX equal to F. Similarly, whole-record assignments such as

```
ANYONE := PETER;
ANYONE := JOAN;
```

are legal and each has the effect of establishing a new value for ANYONE.SEX.

Denoting components of constrained records – such as the component JOAN.CHILDREN of the record JOAN, or the component PETER.BEARDED of the record PETER – is always secure and never requires any discriminant check at run time since the discriminant value is specified by the constraint and is static. Furthermore the discriminant value is invariable: this is guaranteed by the constraint checks that are performed before any assignment to these constrained variables – whether these checks are actually performed at run time or are anticipated at compilation time.

When denoting dependent components of an unconstrained variable (such as ANY-ONE), discriminant checks will usually have to be done at run time – unless they become unnecessary because of prior explicit or implicit checks. Such explicit discrimination may take several forms. It can be achieved by an if statement:

```
if ANYONE.SEX = M then
   -- No check needed when denoting ANYONE.BEARDED
   ...
end if;
```

or similarly by a case statement:

```
case ANYONE.SEX is
   when M =>
      -- No check needed when denoting ANYONE.BEARDED
      ...
   when F =>
      -- No check needed when denoting ANYONE.CHILDREN
      ...
end case;
```

Of course, the check can only be omitted as long as the discriminant is not changed as a result of a whole record assignment. Consider for example:

```
case ANYONE.SEX is
   when M =>
      ...   ANYONE.BEARDED   ...      -- occurrence 1
      ...   ANYONE.BEARDED   ...      -- occurrence 2
      UPDATE(ANYONE);
      ...   ANYONE.BEARDED   ...      -- occurrence 3
      PRINT(ANYONE);
      ...   ANYONE.BEARDED   ...      -- occurrence 4
   when F => ...
end case;
```

No checks are needed for the first two occurrences. A check is needed for the third (assuming the mode of the parameter of UPDATE to be in out), but no check is needed for the fourth occurrence (assuming the mode of the parameter of PRINT to be in).

Note that additional problems exist if a record is shared by two tasks. One task could perform a whole record assignment (thereby changing the discriminant) while another was reading a component. We consider this problem to be a danger inherent in the use of shared variables rather than a problem concerning the formulation of record types. The tasking facilities of the language are powerful enough to make unsynchronized access to shared variables virtually useless. If they are nevertheless used, the appropriate precautions should be taken by the programmer. On the other hand, we did not believe it right to distort the semantics of the language just to deal with such possible misuse.

It might be felt that the checking code is a high price to pay. It is, however, essential for security with variant records. Previous experience with languages such as Simula and Algol 68, which force a similar discrimination of variants, show that these checks are not as frequent as one might suppose. The parts of the programs that operate on a given variant tend to be textually discriminated as well as dynamically discriminated. Hence the checks can be achieved at a rather low cost (see also [We 78]).

One should not underestimate the importance of secure access to components of a variant part. This is well demonstrated by actual experience on large programs with Pascal compilers that perform such checks [Ha 77]. Further confirmation has been obtained from experience with large Ada programs – Ada compilers in particular.

4.7.4 Initialization of Discriminants

Discriminants are components of special importance: We have seen that the structure of a record may depend on the value of a discriminant, and that this value is also critical for determining whether or not it is possible to denote a component defined by a corresponding variant.

For safety reasons therefore, it is essential that discriminants always be initialized; and this is actually guaranteed by the language rules. Before discussing these rules, let us review two possible ways of initializing a discriminant. One way of ensuring discriminant initialization is by a constraint. For example, the elaboration of the constrained declaration

```
JOAN : PERSON(SEX => F);
```

initializes the discriminant JOAN.SEX to the value F specified by the constraint (and the discriminant value is thereafter invariable, because of the constraint). However, as we have seen earlier, some objects are unconstrained; for example,

```
ANYONE : PERSON;
```

For this unconstrained object, the initialization of the discriminant is obtained by another device, namely, by means of the default expression specified in the discriminant part of the type PERSON:

```
type PERSON(SEX : GENDER := F) is ...
```

So the elaboration of the declaration of ANYONE evaluates the default expression and uses the resulting value (F) to initialize the discriminant: ANYONE.SEX is initially equal to F, but this value may be changed later, by whole record assignments, since ANYONE is unconstrained.

Safety of variant records is achieved in Ada by requiring that discriminants be always initialized in one of the two ways described above.

For a type declared with a discriminant part, the language rules require:

(a) If default expressions are provided for discriminants, then declarations of constrained and unconstrained objects of the type are both allowed.

(b) In the absence of default expressions, all object declarations must be constrained.

Thus unconstrained declarations are not allowed in the latter case: In the absence of a default expression, the discriminant value of such objects would be unspecified.

To illustrate these rules, we first introduce a few additional type declarations

```
type HUMAN(SEX : GENDER) is
  record
    AGE : INTEGER range 0 .. 123;
    case SEX is
      when M => BEARDED  : BOOLEAN;
      when F => CHILDREN : INTEGER range 0 .. 20;
    end case;
  end record;

subtype LENGTH is INTEGER range 0 .. 200;

type TEXT(SIZE : LENGTH) is
  record
    POS  : LENGTH := 0;
    DATA : STRING(1 .. SIZE);
  end record;

type LINE(SIZE : LENGTH := 100) is
  record
    DATA : STRING(1 .. SIZE);
  end record;
```

We may now declare constrained objects, very much in the same way as for the type PERSON:

```
JOAN    : PERSON(SEX => F);   -- must be of sex F

MARIA   : HUMAN(SEX =>  F);   -- must be of sex F
JOHN    : HUMAN(SEX =>  M);   -- must be of sex M
PAUL    : HUMAN(M);           -- must be of sex M

LARGE   : TEXT(SIZE => 130);  -- must have 130 characters

SMALL   : LINE(SIZE => 20);   -- must have 20 characters
MEDIUM  : LINE(80);           -- must have 80 characters
```

In the case of types PERSON and LINE, we may also declare unconstrained objects such as

```
ANYONE  : PERSON;    -- Initially: ANYONE.SEX = F
MESSAGE : LINE;      -- Initially: MESSAGE.SIZE = 100
                     -- but later could vary up to 200 characters
```

On the other hand, unconstrained object declarations are not allowed for types such as HUMAN and TEXT, for which there are no default discriminant values:

```
ILLEGAL : HUMAN;     -- Illegal! What would the sex be?
ERROR   : TEXT;      -- Illegal! What would the size be?
```

4.7.5 Discriminants and Type Composition

Ada provides a very general ability to compose types from more elementary types: we can have arrays of records that contain other arrays and records, and so on to an arbitrary depth. This type composition ability can be parameterized by means of discriminants. Thus the language allows two forms of parameterization of the subtype definitions of record components:

(a) The value of a discriminant may be used to specify a bound in an index constraint for a record component – the component being an array.

(b) The value of a discriminant may be used in a discriminant constraint for a record component – the component being again a record.

The first form of parameterization is what we have in the type TEXT:

```
type TEXT(SIZE : LENGTH) is
  record
    POS  : LENGTH := 0;
    DATA : STRING(1 .. SIZE);
  end record;
```

Thus the declaration of the component DATA specifies SIZE as the upper bound in the index constraint for this component. The implication is that when we declare

```
LARGE : TEXT(SIZE => 130); -- or, equivalently:
LARGE : TEXT(130);         -- in positional form
```

then the discriminant value (130) is used to dimension the corresponding string, so that LARGE.DATA is a string of 130 characters.

The second form of parameterization is illustrated by the following type:

```
type DUPLEX(DIMENSION : LENGTH) is
  record
    FIRST  : TEXT(SIZE => DIMENSION);
    SECOND : TEXT(SIZE => DIMENSION);
  end record;
```

in which the discriminant of the type DUPLEX is itself used to specify the discriminant values for the first and second components. So when we declare

```
DISTICH : DUPLEX(40);
```

the dimension of the type DUPLEX is used to specify the size of the first and second texts, so that we have two strings of 40 characters.

We have given different names to the discriminants to emphasize the two levels, of type composition. But this is not necessary, and we could have written

```
type DUPLEX(SIZE : LENGTH) is
  record
    FIRST  : TEXT(SIZE => SIZE); -- size of text => size of duplex
    SECOND : TEXT(SIZE => SIZE);
  end record;
```

or even simply

```
type DUPLEX(SIZE : LENGTH) is
  record
    FIRST  : TEXT(SIZE);
    SECOND : TEXT(SIZE);
  end record;
```

Nothing prevents the composition of types to further levels, and we may for example define a type such as

```
type QUAD(SIZE : LENGTH) is
  record
    LEFT, RIGHT : DUPLEX(SIZE);
  end record;
```

and so on.

Note that the first form of parameterization (that is, that of an index bound) would not suffice alone. For example, it would not be satisfactory (in general) to define DUPLEX in the following manner

```
type OTHER_DUPLEX(SIZE : LENGTH) is
  record
    POS_1, POS_2 : LENGTH := 0;
    FIRST  : STRING(1 .. SIZE);
    SECOND : STRING(1 .. SIZE);
  end record;
```

since operations defined for the type TEXT such as

```
procedure APPEND(TAIL : in TEXT; TO : in out TEXT) is
begin
  TO.DATA(TO.POS+1 .. TO.POS+TAIL.POS) := TAIL.DATA(1 .. TAIL.POS);
  TO.POS := TO.POS + TAIL.POS;
end;
```

would not be applicable to components of records of the type OTHER_DUPLEX.

To conclude this presentation of discriminants, it will be interesting to compare this form of parameterization with the form offered by generic units. It is certainly possible to define a generic formulation of the type TEXT, in which the size is a generic parameter. But, as we shall see, the functionality offered would be quite different. Consider for example:

```
generic
  SIZE : POSITIVE;
package TEXT_HANDLING is
  type TEXT is
    record
      POS  : NATURAL := 0;
      DATA : STRING(1 .. SIZE);
    end record;
  ...
  procedure APPEND(TAIL : in TEXT; TO : in out TEXT);
  ...
end TEXT_HANDLING;
```

We could later create instances of this generic package such as

```
package TEXT_20 is new TEXT_HANDLING(SIZE => 20);
package TEXT_50 is new TEXT_HANDLING(SIZE => 50);
```

The main drawback of this formulation is that the types TEXT_20.TEXT and TEXT_50.TEXT are now two distinct and completely unrelated types, with the consequence that we cannot intermix their objects in operations such as APPEND.

What this example shows is that if objects differ only in size, it is better to consider that they are still objects of the same type, but belonging to different subtypes: this form of parameterization is therefore better dealt with by discriminant constraints.

Parameterization by generic units is more appropriate if we want to parameterize by types, or if we are prepared to accept the consequences of the fact that several instances of the generic unit will create several types. For example, the two forms of parameterization are used in conjunction in this further formulation of text handling:

```
generic
  MAXIMUM : POSITIVE;
package TEXT_HANDLING is
  subtype LENGTH is INTEGER range 0 .. MAXIMUM;

  type TEXT(SIZE : LENGTH) is
    record
      POS  : LENGTH := 0;
      DATA : STRING(1 .. SIZE);
    end record;
  ...
end TEXT_HANDLING;
```

Different instantiations will result in different text types (and in fact the compiler is likely to use different representations for texts having a maximum of 256 characters and for larger maximum lengths). For a given maximum length however, we can use discriminant constraints to represent texts of different lengths, which are nevertheless objects of the same type.

4.8 MUTABILITY

The term *mutability* refers to the ability to change the value of a discriminant of a given record (by a whole record assignment). The problems addressed in this discussion of mutability are those of efficiency of representation and efficiency of implementation of the parameter passing rules.

As regards efficiency of representation, consider again our canonical examples of types with discriminants. Then for unconstrained objects such as

```
ANYONE  : PERSON;
ANYLINE : LINE;
```

we expect the compiler to reserve enough storage to accommodate the largest possible value for the type considered. For example, in the case of ANYLINE, 200 characters must be reserved for the string component ANYLINE.DATA. On the other hand, for constrained objects such as:

```
PAUL  : PERSON(SEX => M);
JOAN  : PERSON(SEX => F);
TITLE : LINE(SIZE => 30);
```

we expect the compiler to reserve no more space than is dictated by the corresponding constraint. Thus in the case of TITLE, just 30 characters are needed for the corresponding string.

Parameter passing rules for objects of record types do not specify whether the effect is to be achieved by *copy* or by *reference*. For example, for an **in out** parameter the semantics specifies that both reading and updating of the associated actual parameter are allowed. But the implementation has freedom to implement parameter passing by copy (for example, for small objects) or by reference (for example, for large objects): this should not matter for correct programs, that is, for programs that are not erroneous. The motivation for these rules is discussed elsewhere (see 8.2), but consider now their interactions with representation and mutability.

Consider for example a procedure to invert a given line (arrange the letters in reverse order) using the function MIRROR previously defined for strings (see 4.5):

```
procedure INVERT(L : in out LINE) is
begin
   L.DATA := MIRROR(L.DATA);
end;
```

The formal parameter must have the mode **in out**, since we update the formal parameter. This procedure can be used indifferently for constrained or unconstrained objects:

```
INVERT(TITLE);      -- constrained
INVERT(ANYLINE);    -- unconstrained
```

In either case, it does not matter whether the compiler implements parameter passing using the by-copy or by-reference mechanism, since the procedure does not change the size of the line. This would remain true if, in INVERT, we had used a whole record assignment such as

```
L := (SIZE => L.SIZE, DATA => MIRROR(L.DATA));
```

But consider now a procedure, such as CHANGE, that performs mutations:

```
procedure CHANGE(L : in out LINE) is
   SAFE : constant LINE := L;
begin
   ...
   L := (SIZE => 45, DATA => ... );         -- (1)
   ...
   L := (SIZE => 117, DATA => ... );         -- (2)
   ...
   L := (SIZE => SAFE.SIZE, DATA => MIRROR(SAFE.DATA));
end;
```

Calls with an unconstrained object such as

```
CHANGE(ANYLINE);
```

clearly raise no problem. But consider the treatment of a call with a constrained object, such as

```
CHANGE(TITLE);
```

If the parameter passing semantics were purely by copy, such a call would be acceptable:

before the call the unconstrained formal parameter would be initialized with the value of the actual parameter TITLE; upon return, the value of the formal parameter would be copied back into TITLE, and this would work since the discriminant value would be the same upon return as before the call. However, the important optimization of passing large records by reference would not be possible. (Alternatively assignments such as (1) and (2) would require a local copy.)

The above call will fail with the Ada semantics: *the formal parameter is constrained in exactly the same way as the associated actual parameter.* For the formal parameter L, the language actually provides the attribute

```
L'CONSTRAINED
```

which is TRUE if the associated actual parameter is constrained (such as TITLE), FALSE if unconstrained (such as ANYLINE). In the case of the procedure CHANGE called with TITLE as actual parameter, these rules mean that the assignment (1) is incorrect, and will raise the exception CONSTRAINT_ERROR.

4.8.1 The Case Against Static Mutability

The Ada solution for mutability, as presented above, is dynamic solution, which involves dynamic transmission of the *constrained* attribute across subprogram calls. During the course of the Ada design several solutions that allow compilation-time verification of mutability were examined. We next review two of these static solutions and the reasons for their rejection.

One approach to static mutability would be to associate this quality with the type itself: allow types with objects that are always constrained (never mutable), allow types with objects that are never constrained (always mutable), but not types with both constrained objects and unconstrained objects.

With this approach the type PERSON would not be allowed, but we could declare the following types:

```
type HUMAN(SEX : GENDER) is        -- immutable: must be constrained
   record
     AGE : INTEGER range 0 .. 123;
     case SEX is
        ...                        -- as in PERSON
     end case;
   end record;

-- What follows is not in Ada:

type MUTANT(SEX : GENDER := F) is  -- cannot be constrained
   mutable record
     SELF : HUMAN(SEX);
   end record;
```

A constraint is required for each object of type HUMAN. This allows the compiler to allocate the exact (minimum) space needed for each such object. Furthermore we know that this space cannot vary, because of the constraint, so that parameter passing by reference can safely be used for all objects of this type.

Conversely, no constraint would ever be allowed for objects of type MUTANT, so that the maximum space would be allocated for each such object. Parameter passing by reference would therefore again be safe.

Whereas this solution allows efficient parameter passing by reference, its drawbacks become apparent precisely in those situations where we need to have both mutable and immutable objects. The first drawback is verbosity. Instead of writing the Ada declarations and statements:

```
PAUL : PERSON(SEX => M);     -- constrained
JOAN : PERSON(SEX => F);     -- constrained
ANY  : PERSON;               -- mutable
...
ANY  := PAUL;
...    ANY.AGE ...
```

we would have to write:

```
PAUL : PERSON(SEX => M);     -- constrained
JOAN : PERSON(SEX => F);     -- constrained
ANY  : MUTANT;               -- mutable
...
ANY  := (M, PAUL);
...    ANY.SELF.AGE ...
```

in which the use of mutable objects is complicated by the extra component.

The second – and more important – drawback is in terms of space efficiency. Consider the formation of any structure that involves objects of a given type with different discriminant values: for example a genealogy, using another formulation of the type PERSON with an access type:

```
   ...
type PERSON_NAME is access PERSON;

type PERSON(SEX : GENDER := F) is
  record
     ...
     FATHER  : PERSON_NAME(SEX => M);
     MOTHER  : PERSON_NAME(SEX => F);
     SPOUSE  : PERSON_NAME;
     SIBLING : PERSON_NAME;
     ...
  end record;

MARY : PERSON_NAME(F) := new PERSON'(SEX => F, ... );
JACK : PERSON_NAME(M) := new PERSON'(SEX => M, ... );
```

The above Ada formulation will take advantage of the fact that objects dynamically created by allocators (see chapter 6) are constrained upon allocation. For example, although the component SPOUSE is not constrained (and can thus designate an object of either gender), a given gender must be selected upon allocation, and the allocated object is thereafter constrained by this value and is immutable:

```
MARY.SPOUSE := new PERSON'(SEX => M, ... );
JACK.SPOUSE := new PERSON'(SEX => F, ... );
```

In terms of space efficiency this is optimal: the minimum space is reserved for the object designated by the SPOUSE component. With the static alternative presently being analyzed, however, this would not be the case. The component SPOUSE would have to be declared as follows (assuming the appropriate access type declaration):

```
SPOUSE : MUTANT_NAME;
```

so that the allocation for the above example would become:

```
MARY.SPOUSE := new MUTANT'( ... );
JACK.SPOUSE := new MUTANT'( ... );
```

and in both cases we would have to allocate the maximum space.

The Ada formulation therefore allows an important kind of space optimization. It is very well suited to a quite common situation in the construction of interrelated data structures: although the discriminant of the object designated by a given variable is not known statically (as in the case of SPOUSE and SIBLING) it will be very unlikely to change after allocation. Conversely, the Ada concepts also allow the declaration of a type such as MUTANT in terms of the type PERSON (the inconvenience is inverted):

```
type MUTANT is          -- cannot be constrained
   record
      SELF : PERSON;     -- unconstrained
   end record;
```

Another approach to static mutability would be to associate the mutable quality with formal parameters, rather than with types. For example, consider again the type LINE:

```
type LINE(SIZE : LENGTH := 100) is
   record
      DATA : STRING(1 .. SIZE);
   end record;

SPACE : constant CHARACTER := ' ';
```

Then we could define a procedure as follows

```
-- The following is not in Ada:

procedure BLANK(L : in out LINE(<>)) is     -- not mutable
begin
   for N in 1 .. L.SIZE loop
      L.DATA(N) := SPACE;
   end loop;
end;
```

In this hypothetical formulation the subtype indication

```
LINE(<>)            -- not in Ada
```

would mean that the formal parameter is indeed constrained (and hence immutable) although the discriminant values are borrowed from the associated actual parameter. Parameter passing by reference would be quite safe because of the immutability. Conversely, in this formulation mutability could be indicated by the type mark LINE alone as in

```
procedure CHANGE(L : in out LINE) is
begin
   L := (SIZE => 80, DATA => (1 .. 80 => SPACE));
end;
```

and would be applicable only to objects that are unconstrained such as

```
ANYLINE : LINE;
```

thereby ensuring the safety of by-reference parameter passing in this case as well.

The major drawback of this approach to static mutability (aside from the additional rules and notations) is that it would make it impossible to define an operation that performs mutations in the case of unconstrained objects but not in the case of constrained objects – note that this is actually what happens for the basic operation (:=) of assignment. Thus:

```
PAUL : PERSON(SEX => M);      -- constrained
JOAN : PERSON(SEX => F);      -- constrained
ANY  : PERSON;                -- unconstrained: initially SEX = F
...
ANY  := PAUL;                 -- ":=" mutates
ANY  := JOAN;                 -- ":=" mutates again
JOAN := ANY;                  -- ":=" does not mutate
```

If this property exists for assignment, we are likely to need it also for user-defined operations, which would not be possible with this static approach to mutability. For example, it would not be possible to write a procedure COPY that copies the whole line in the case of unconstrained lines but only the common part in the case of constrained lines. Such a procedure can be written as follows in Ada:

```
procedure COPY(SOURCE : in LINE; TARGET : out LINE) is
begin
   if TARGET'CONSTRAINED then
      declare
         SIZE : LENGTH := TARGET.SIZE;
      begin
         if SIZE > SOURCE.SIZE then
            SIZE := SOURCE.SIZE;
         end;
         TARGET.DATA(1 .. SIZE) := SOURCE.DATA(1 .. SIZE);
      end;
   else
      TARGET := SOURCE;
   end if;
end COPY;
```

4.8.2 Implementation Considerations

The CONSTRAINED attribute may be implemented in a variety of ways. First there are several cases where we know the objects to be always immutable, so that no run-time representation of the attribute is ever required (CONSTRAINED is always true). These are:

- Any object whose type is a type with discriminants defined without default expressions.

- Any object designated by an access value: such objects are constrained by the discriminant value specified for the allocator that creates the object.

When run-time mutability information is needed for a formal parameter, the CONSTRAINED attribute must be passed (as a descriptor) along with the actual parameter.

Note that the CONSTRAINED attribute cannot be considered as part of the value itself (that is, as a component). To see this point, consider the following example:

```
subtype TITLE is LINE(SIZE => 45);
ANYLINE : LINE;
  ...
procedure SET(A_LINE : in out LINE) is
begin
  ...
end;


  ...
procedure PREPARE(A_TITLE : in out TITLE) is
begin
  ...
  SET(A_TITLE);
  ...
end;


  ...
ANYLINE := TITLE'(SIZE => 45, DATA => (others => ' '));
PREPARE(ANYLINE);
```

Then if the CONSTRAINED attribute were considered as a boolean component of the value of ANYLINE, it would have to be FALSE (and not updated by the assignment of the value of A_TITLE). However, consider the call SET(A_TITLE) issued from the body of PREPARE when called with the actual parameter ANYLINE. We must have successively:

```
ANYLINE'CONSTRAINED = FALSE    -- since ANYLINE is declared as LINE
A_TITLE'CONSTRAINED = TRUE     -- since A_TITLE is declared as TITLE
A_LINE'CONSTRAINED  = FALSE    -- since A_LINE is declared as LINE
```

But this would not be the case in our example: For a by-reference implementation, A_TITLE and A_LINE would both refer to ANYLINE; for a by-copy implementation the value of ANYLINE would be copied to A_TITLE and further to A_LINE; and for either implementation the attribute would be incorrect within the body of PREPARE, and if corrected there, within the body of SET.

5. Numeric Types

5.1 INTRODUCTION

The importance of numerical calculations in the use of computers dates from their earliest days. The floating point hardware of the second generation of machines resulted from the need to perform fast calculations with approximate representations of numerical data that varied over a wide range of values. However, in spite of this long history of numerical computation, the handling of both fixed point and floating point data types is unsatisfactory in most programming languages.

Fortran is widely used for scientific computation and compilers are available on almost all machines. Several large packages of numerical routines of a high professional standard, such as the library of subroutines of the Numerical Algorithms Group (NAG), have been implemented in Fortran and made available on a wide range of computers. Nevertheless, numerous defects can easily trap the unwary. For example, when a floating point value is assigned to an integer variable the value is truncated; this obvious trap is compounded by the lack of any definition of this effect – the standard does not say whether -3.8 truncates to -3 or to -4, that is, whether the sign is considered after truncation or with it. Moreover Fortran provides no facilities for fixed point arithmetic, for which there is a particular need on computers without floating point hardware.

5.1.1 Floating Point: The Problems

The most difficult area is the control of floating point precision, for which no entirely adequate solution is available. Fortran does not define the accuracy of *single precision* values. Consequently, the number of bits in the mantissa of a single precision value can be 48 on one system and 24 on another; to achieve a given precision, say 30 bits, one would have to specify single precision on the first system but double precision on the second.

To change the precision for a Fortran 66 program is extremely awkward, and requires a careful review of the program text: the exponents of floating point literals must be changed, all intrinsic functions must be altered, and so on; some functions such as FLOAT have no double length counterpart. The Numerical Algorithms Group overcame this by an elaborate text processing package [HF 76]. By adopting suitable programming conventions, most of the changes can be made with a simple text edit, but there is no simple complete solution. For instance, use of double length throughout is not effective because of its excessive cost, changing the type by IMPLICIT is not standard Fortran, and in any case IMPLICIT cannot be used for literals.

Changing precision is much easier for a Fortran 77 program, because many of the problems identified above have been eliminated. Some problems remain, however: thus it is still not possible to specify the precision of a type explicitly – say in decimal digits. Moreover the change from single to double precision is sometimes difficult: for instance single length COMPLEX is a defined data type but DOUBLE COMPLEX is not. It should be noted that the proposed standard Fortran 8X attempts to overcome all of these problems, and others, and in consequence has features similar to those of Ada.

Several languages in the Algol 60 tradition, such as Pascal, Coral 66 and RTL/2, admit only one floating point data type. In some cases this simple solution meets the users' requirements better than Fortran does. The two Algol 60 compilers for the IBM 360 provide a directive to specify 32 or 64 bit precision – substantially easier to change than the corresponding precision in Fortran. In essence, unless the declarations can determine different precisions, it is best to use the same precision for all floating point quantities, and therefore to have only one floating-point data type in the language.

Control of precision in Algol 68 is by declaration of types *real, long real,* or even *long long real.* Although the precision of *real* is implementation-dependent, so that declarative changes to a program may still be needed in order to maintain the required accuracy when moving it from one implementation to another, these changes are rather easy.

Any language that has user-defined types, and some method of controlling precision, has the essential mechanism for an effective solution of this problem. It is, of course, imperative that the programmer use the typing facility in such a way that the floating point declarations can easily be remapped when a change of precision is needed.

5.1.2 Fixed Point: The Problems

There is also considerable difficulty in formulating a satisfactory fixed point facility. The Steelman requirements [DoD 78] specify exact fixed point computation:

> ... *fixed point numbers shall be treated as exact numeric values. ... The scale or step size (i.e., the minimal representable difference between values) of each fixed point variable must be ... determinable during translation. Scales shall not be restricted to powers of two.*

Thus the possible values of a fixed point variable must be integral multiples of a fixed quantity called the scale. Exact addition and subtraction do not cause problems, but multiplication and division do.

To illustrate these problems, let us consider the case of calculations on electrical insulation, using Ohm's Law: current multiplied by resistance equals voltage. Suppose that we measure the leakage current to an accuracy of one milliampere, and adopt this as the step size or scale of a variable LEAKAGE. This means that only whole numbers of milliamperes can be represented: the value of LEAKAGE will always be an integer L times the scale of 0.001 amperes. In like fashion we may measure the resistance of the insulation to an accuracy of 1000 ohms, and use a variable RESISTANCE whose value will always be an integer R times the scale of 1000 ohms, that is, R kilo-ohms.

Now the potential supported by the insulation is the value of LEAKAGE*RESISTANCE, and because the scale factors happen to cancel it will be LR volts. This is again an integer, but we cannot simply assign it to a third fixed point variable POTENTIAL having scale factor one volt, and treat this variable in the same way as the others, because only a *subset* of the possible values of POTENTIAL can arise in this way. Thus a given value of POTENTIAL, say P volts (an integer) cannot be divided by a given value of RESISTANCE, say R kilo-ohms, to get L milliamperes exactly (which must be an integer) because P/R will usually not be an integer. In addition there are size problems because single length factors give a double length product. The Ironman requirements [DoD 77] recognized this, and required built-in operations for integer and fixed point division with remainder. This would allow a double length representation of P to be divided by R to yield an integer quotient L1 and integer remainder L2, each single length:

    P = R*L1 + L2

and it would be in the hands of the programmer to ignore or use L2 as he wished. The operation would be exact, and L1 could be assigned to LEAKAGE for further use, as a quantity whose inaccuracy was known.

Cobol apparently meets the Ironman requirements, but only by using decimal scales, which are not adequate for two reasons. First, this is not necessarily the scaling required by the application, and secondly, 10 is too coarse for the standard 16-bit minicomputer. A glance at a Cobol manual will also indicate that explaining the implicit decimal point to the programmer is not easy.

In view of the difficulty of providing exact fixed point computation to meet the Steelman requirements, we considered what was really needed by the users. An analysis of actual applications in many real-time situations revealed that there was a need for cheap approximate computation. Small but frequently executed computations are performed upon digital input signals. Simple machines do not have floating point hardware, and emulation of floating point operations by software or firmware is not fast enough, hence some other means is required to perform approximate computations rapidly on such machines. To say that in the future floating point hardware will always be available may not be the answer: source data input is inevitably captured in fixed point representation, and floating point representation requires more space. Hence approximate fixed point is better matched than floating point to the needs of common applications.

It must be admitted that, as we shall see, programming with fixed point is much more difficult than with floating point. On the other hand, fixed point is potentially more reliable because effective numerical error analysis requires tight bounds to be placed upon data values.

It is concluded that *approximate* fixed point is generally the most useful arithmetic capability to provide that will complement integer and floating point facilities. However, Ada fixed point also provides some exact operations such as addition and subtraction, and these are invaluable, for example for the manipulation of intervals of time.

5.1.3 Overview of Numerics in Ada

The facility for numerics is based upon the idea that a numeric variable has an *abstract value*. The set of values of a numeric type will be a subset of the set of real numbers. Computation with integers is exact. Computation with fixed point and floating point is approximate: the former with an *absolute* bound on the error, the latter with a *relative* bound. These approximate types are called the *real* types since they can be thought of as approximations to the mathematical concept of the real numbers.

The semantics of each numeric operation is determined by the type of its operands. The facility for numerics is based upon three types that cannot be named in a program (and hence are said to be anonymous – no variable of such a type can be declared). These types are referred to as *universal_integer*, *universal_real*, and *universal_fixed*. Any specific type in a given implementation is a partial representation of a universal type.

(1)   *universal_integer*

The type *universal_integer* is an integer type with a range large enough to encompass every conceivable integer type of the implementation. Integer literals are of type *universal_integer*.

(2)   *universal_real*

The type *universal_real* is a real type with a precision that is high enough to encompass any implemented real type. Real literals are of type *universal_real*.

(3)   *universal_fixed*

The type *universal_fixed* is introduced as the result type of the unscaled fixed point operations of multiplication and division to be detailed later. It is essentially a type for intermediate results. The *universal_fixed type* has a finer delta than any implemented fixed point type.

The mapping of these universal types onto the implementation-dependent types is described below.

(1) *Integer types.*

There is an implementation-dependent type INTEGER, defined in the package STANDARD. The range of type INTEGER reflects the properties of the underlying hardware, in that the most efficiently handled integer size is used, with a range symmetric about zero (apart from possibly one extra negative value – see RM 3.5.4(7)). It would have been possible to have designed a language that had no predefined type such as INTEGER, but this would have meant that in order to obtain a type that would give as large a range of integer values as possible without losing efficiency, the programmer would have had to use language facilities that were highly system dependent. So to avoid this dependence, it is desirable to have a predefined type that maps onto the integer type that is most efficiently handled by the target computer.

Additionally, an implementation may provide types LONG_INTEGER and SHORT_INTEGER with larger and smaller ranges than INTEGER. The user can define an integer type by stating the required range; this defines a subtype of a type derived from one of these predefined types – the predefined type being suitably selected by the implementation. The most positive and most negative integer values that are supported by an implementation are SYSTEM.MAX_INT and SYSTEM.MIN_INT respectively.

(2) *Floating point types*

The implementation-defined types FLOAT, LONG_FLOAT (and so on) can be thought of as copies of the type *universal_real* but with restricted relative accuracy. These types are predefined so as to approximate closely to the intrinsic floating-point types of the target computer. The user may define other floating point types in terms of these machine types, or simply by stating the required precision; in the latter case this defines a subtype of a type derived from one of the predefined types – the predefined type being suitably selected by the implementation.

A hardware floating point representation has two independent parameters – the length of the mantissa and the range of the exponent. The mantissa length defines the *relative* accuracy, and the exponent range defines the range of the floating point values. In Ada, the user defines a floating point type by stating only the required precision, as a number of decimal digits; this defines the mantissa length. The language requires each floating point type to have an exponent range that is workable in relation to its mantissa length. In this way the two parameters are reduced to one, with a gain in simplicity for the user.

(3) *Fixed point types*

In contrast to floating point, a fixed point type has an absolute rather than a relative accuracy. This absolute bound on the errors is called the *delta*. The user can define other fixed point types by specifying the required delta, together with the range of magnitudes to be encompassed.

Constants

One finds in many programs several *constants* that parameterize the particular application. These constants have no particular type, but may be related one to another; for example the middle of a line is related to the line length. *Number declarations* are provided in Ada to express this. They allow the calculation of specific values having fixed relationships. For example:

```
LINE_LENGTH           : constant := 80;
MID_LINE              : constant := LINE_LENGTH/2;
PI                    : constant := 3.14159_26536;
RADIANS_PER_DEGREE    : constant := PI/180;
```

Without this facility, a change to the program to modify a constant would involve a search for all occurrences of the constant as well as of related constants. This would be both tedious and risky: for example the constant 40 might or might not be intended to signify half the line length, and even with a corresponding comment the process would be error prone.

The type of such a named number depends on the primaries used in the expression on the right; if these yield real values, the type of the constant is *universal_real*, if they yield integer values, the type is *universal_integer*; a mixture of real and integer values gives *universal_real*. Thus the first two examples above are of type *universal_integer* and the second two are of type *universal_real*.

A numeric literal is either an integer literal or a real literal. Thus 80 and 2 above are integer literals because they contain no decimal point, while 3.14159_26536 is a real literal. Within an expression, a numeric literal will be implicitly converted to the required type determined by the context – an integer literal to an integer type and a real literal to a real type. For example, implicit conversion is performed in these cases:

```
J : INTEGER := 2;
P : INTEGER := 4*J;
A : REAL := REAL(P) - 0.23;
```

In the second case, because J is of type INTEGER, the integer literal 4 is implicitly converted to INTEGER as an operand of the multiplication, which yields a product of type INTEGER. In the last case, the subtraction must deliver a REAL result, so P needs explicit conversion to the type REAL, but conversion of the real literal 0.23 to REAL is implicit. It should be noted that no accuracy can be lost by such implicit conversion of numeric literals – the accuracy required by the target type is always provided.

5.2 THE INTEGER TYPES

The operations predefined for the integer types are:

Operator	Meaning	Result Type
+ -	identity and negation	operand type
+ -	addition and subtraction	operand type
*	multiplication	operand type
/	integer division	operand type
mod	integer modulus	operand type
rem	remainder on integer division	operand type
**	exponentiation	operand type
abs	absolute value	operand type
= /=	equality and inequality	BOOLEAN
< <= > >=	ordering	BOOLEAN

New integer subtypes declared by imposing constraints on INTEGER inherit these operations: relational operators deliver a result of type BOOLEAN; all others deliver a result of the same type as the operands. Both operands of the binary operators must have the same type, excepting exponentiation, for which the right operand type is always INTEGER. If system-defined integer types such as LONG_INTEGER are implemented, then overloadings of the arithmetic and relational operators are defined for these types in an analogous manner; and similarly for SHORT_INTEGER, if implemented.

The user can define an integer type by specifying the range to be covered, for example

```
type PAGE_NUM   is range 1 .. 2000;
type MY_INTEGER is range -100_000 .. 100_000;
```

in which case the implementation will use whichever predefined type just encompasses this range. Thus MY_INTEGER would be implemented as (a subtype of a type derived from) LONG_INTEGER on a typical 16-bit minicomputer, but as INTEGER on a machine with larger word length. Portability of the program is thus assured, in this respect.

Furthermore, a range constraint can be applied to a type to give a subtype. The subtype has all the operations of the *base* type, but the value of any variable of the subtype must always be within the range of the subtype; in general this is checked before assigning a value to the variable. One would expect compilers to represent subtypes in the same way as types, but in special cases the compiler may be able to optimize the representation by utilizing the range constraint. Thus the subtype

```
subtype SIGN is INTEGER range -1 .. 1;
```

contains only three values, so that each value could be stored using one byte, or even two bits.

The operations **/**, **mod**, and **rem** require explanation. There is no universal agreement on the semantics of these operations for negative operand values. Because different machines perform these operations differently, it is tempting not to define them for negative values. This is the approach taken in the axiomatic definition of Pascal [HW 73]. The semantics chosen in the Ada language corresponds to division with truncation toward zero (so $(-3)/2 = -1$). This has the advantage that it preserves the identity:

```
-(A/B) = (-A)/B = A/(-B)
```

The operations **/** and **rem** are related by

```
A = (A/B)*B + (A rem B)
```

so that **rem** provides the remainder on division. As a consequence the sign of the result of the **rem** operation is therefore the same as the sign of A (hence A **rem** 10 can be negative). Also the absolute value of the result of the **rem** operation is less than the absolute value of B.

The operation **mod** on the other hand is defined so that (A **mod** B) always has the same sign as B and its absolute value is less than the absolute value of B; subject to these conditions it must differ from A by an integer multiple of B, that is, for some integer value N it satisfies the relation

```
A = B*N + (A mod B)
```

Integer exponentiation is defined only for nonnegative exponents. Hence, I**(-1) will raise CONSTRAINT_ERROR as the exponent is not positive. The operation is defined as repeated multiplication of the left hand operand. The number of multiplications is one less than the exponent value, so I**2 = I*I and I**4 = I*I*I*I.

The predefined operator **abs** yields the absolute value of its operand, and is defined for all numeric types.

5.3 THE REAL TYPES

The real types form two classes: floating point types and fixed point types. Both are approximate and are different forms of approximation to the real numbers of mathematics. With floating point types, the error in representing a mathematical value is roughly proportional to its absolute value over a large range. In contrast, the error with a fixed point value has an absolute bound, so that small values have a correspondingly large relative error.

The real type definition specifies bounds on the permitted error in the representation of values: the precision for floating point and the delta for fixed point. A floating point type declaration of the form

     type T **is digits** D;

specifies D significant decimal digits precision. It would perhaps have been more consistent to specify a bound on the relative error directly, but giving the number of significant decimal digits is more natural for the user. The use of a range constraint, in the extended form of declaration

     type T **is digits** D **range** L .. R;

signifies the construction of a subtype. The check that the values of L and R lie within the range of the base type is therefore a run-time check, and CONSTRAINT_ERROR is raised if it fails.

    A fixed point type declaration of the form

     type T **is delta** D **range** L .. R;

specifies the *delta* D, which is an absolute bound on the permitted error. Here a bound specified in decimal digits would have been inappropriate, and too coarse, for a binary machine. In this case the range constraint is not optional since an unbounded range would imply an infinite number of values; the declaration is illegal if no predefined base type exists that accommodates the range and delta.

    The predefined operations provided for floating and fixed types differ in detail in order to reflect correctly the handling of error bounds within a computation. The accuracy constraints determine parameters to a semantic model for the real types which is used to bound errors on the predefined operations. This is described below in section 5.3.3.

Attributes

Ada provides three classes of predefined attributes for real types:

(1)   those also associated with other scalar types (such as 'FIRST and 'LAST),

(2)   those specific to the guaranteed properties of a real type (such as 'DIGITS), and

(3)   those associated with machine-dependent properties (such as 'MACHINE_RADIX).

There are several predefined attributes that apply to both classes of real types. For each such type R, R'FIRST and R'LAST are values of type R that bound all the values of R. The integer value R'MANTISSA gives the number of binary places for the mantissa (floating point) or magnitude (fixed point) in the abstract representation for the type. R'SMALL and R'LARGE are values of type *universal_real* which are respectively the smallest positive nonzero value and the largest positive value in the abstract representation.

5.3.1 Floating Point Types

The following operators are defined for the predefined floating point type FLOAT:

Operator	Meaning	Result Type
+ -	identity and negation	operand type
+ -	addition and subtraction	operand type
*	multiplication	operand type
/	division	operand type
**	exponentiation by an integer	type of left operand
= /=	equality and inequality	BOOLEAN
< <= > >=	ordering	BOOLEAN

Both operands of the binary operators +, -, *, / and of the relational operators must have the same type. If system-defined floating point types such as LONG_FLOAT are implemented, then overloadings of the arithmetic and relational operators are defined for these types in an analogous manner.

The operators = and /= could have been excluded because their semantics is of doubtful validity, since the representation is approximate. Given a precision of 6 digits, then equality could either mean equality of representation (which would typically be of higher precision) or equality only to 6 digits. If the former semantics were chosen then equality would be implementation dependent. Moreover, since some implementations may use a higher precision for temporary values than for declared objects, it would be possible after the assignment

```
X := (Y + Z);
```

to have

```
X /= (Y + Z)
```

If the latter semantics were chosen, then equality would be computed as *approximately* equal. This would lead to the anomaly that equality would no longer be transitive, that is, it would be possible that

```
X = Y and Y = Z and X /= Z
```

The decision has been to allow equality since it is defined for all other types. The user must be aware that the implemented precision is used, that is, the values X and Y are equal only if their representations are identical, and that in consequence code may not be portable. (The situation is no better with other languages.)

The exponentiation operation for floating point operands is defined by repeated multiplication in the same way as with integers. For a negative exponent, the value is the reciprocal of the value with the positive exponent. The exponent is of type INTEGER.

The predefined attribute R'DIGITS yields the value (of type *universal_integer*) that appears as the accuracy constraint that gives the precision of the type or subtype R.

As explained earlier, the precision of the predefined types FLOAT, LONG_FLOAT, and so on, is defined by the implementation. The user may define other floating point types directly in terms of their precision and range, in which case an appropriate one of the predefined types is selected by the compiler and the user-defined type is a subtype of a type derived from this predefined type. Alternatively, the user may define types derived from the predefined types by reducing the precision requirement and constraining the range. Thus in practice, at the machine level, there will be only one or two implemented precisions. As for other constraints, the range constraints and the precision reductions are checked by the compiler.

Defining floating point types directly in terms of their precision and range is preferable for portability. In this case the types are mapped on the nearest applicable machine implemented precision. As an example consider the type declarations

```
type MY_SHORT_FLOAT  is digits 6;
type MY_FLOAT        is digits 8;
type MY_LONG_FLOAT   is digits 10;
```

On a machine for which the implemented precision provides 7 digits for FLOAT and 14 for LONG_FLOAT these declarations have the same effect as

```
type MY_SHORT_FLOAT  is new FLOAT digits 6;
type MY_FLOAT        is new LONG_FLOAT digits 8;
type MY_LONG_FLOAT   is new LONG_FLOAT digits 10;
```

On another machine, for which the implemented precisions provide 8 digits for FLOAT and 16 for LONG_FLOAT, these declarations have the same effect as

```
type MY_SHORT_FLOAT  is new FLOAT digits 6;
type MY_FLOAT        is new FLOAT digits 8;
type MY_LONG_FLOAT   is new LONG_FLOAT digits 10;
```

If a range constraint is included in the type declaration, then a check is made that the range inherited from the implemented type will cover the range specified. If the check fails then CONSTRAINT_ERROR is raised.

To summarize, the language provides a direct and simple mechanism for achieving efficient use of the available precisions predefined by a given implementation.

Example:

As an illustration of the direct use of the predefined types FLOAT and LONG_FLOAT, consider the following typical library function:

```
function DOT_PRODUCT(X,Y : FLOAT_VECTOR) return FLOAT is
   SUM : LONG_FLOAT := 0.0;
begin
   for I in X'RANGE loop
      SUM := SUM + LONG_FLOAT(X(I)) * LONG_FLOAT(Y(I));
   end loop;
   return FLOAT (SUM);
end DOT_PRODUCT;
```

If the machine has an instruction that forms the double length product from two single length operands, it is fairly simple for a peephole optimizer to use this instruction in the inner loop (rather than expand each operand and multiply).

Multiple precisions

If an application requires floating point computation with multiple precisions, then two means can be used to achieve this: the use of subtypes, and the use of types.

(1)   *Use of Subtypes*

To use subtypes, a type must be declared with the largest required precision, for example

```
type MY_REAL is digits 20;
```

Then variables or subtypes can be declared:

```
X : MY_REAL;     -- digits 20
Y : MY_REAL digits 15;
subtype SHORT_REAL is MY_REAL digits 10;
Z1, Z2, Z3 : SHORT_REAL;
```

The operations on MY_REAL are defined for all variables with that base type (X, Y, Z1, Z2, Z3). Hence it is not possible to provide an overloaded SQRT function just for SHORT_REAL. Similarly, the error analysis is dependent on the operators for the type MY_REAL.

An optimizing compiler may be able to use single length data representation for each variable, but this depends on the variables being invisible to other compilation units and on the ability of the compiler to establish that the semantics will be preserved.

Note that the declaration of Y is also an implicit assertion that the precision of MY_REAL is at least 15 digits. This could be useful for defensive programming in large systems. For example, if in a later revision of the program the precision of the type MY_REAL is reduced by more than 5, then the compiler will give a warning message upon recompilation of the declaration of Y (or at least cause CONSTRAINT_ERROR to be raised).

(2) *Use of Types*

To use types, each distinct class of numbers would have a different type, with a precision appropriate to the task being performed. Security is better than with the use of subtypes, but all conversions must be explicit. On the other hand, converting the program for use on another target computer is simple and efficient. This is because each type is mapped separately using only as much precision as necessary. Of course, the efficiency is also high for the initial application computer as well, since even a nonoptimizing compiler will map each type onto the appropriate hardware type.

Both cases above assume that the programs have been written well using named types or subtypes. Direct use of FLOAT and LONG_FLOAT is absent, so that no assumption has been made about the precisions of these types. For a discussion of the construction of mathematical libraries in Ada, and of how one can parameterize with respect to different precisions, see [SWKW].

5.3.2 Fixed Point Types

The definition of the fixed point types is more difficult, for several reasons. First, the representation cannot be determined until both the range and delta are known. These two parameters determine the width required in bits and the position of the decimal (binary) point. Having determined these, the representation is fixed and the operations can be defined. The second problem is that the type resulting from multiplication and division is *universal_fixed*. Since no operations are available on the type *universal_fixed*, a product or a quotient must be explicitly converted to the required type (or subtype).

In a fixed point type declaration, the value following **delta**, and the two range bounds (which must be provided) are of any real type but must have a value determined at compilation time, that is, given by a static expression. In a subtype declaration, the delta value must not be less than that of the type, and the range constraint values must be within the values of the type.

To illustrate the representation of fixed point values, consider for example the type declaration

    type F is delta 0.01 range -100.0 .. 100.0;

We assume the target machine to be a 16-bit minicomputer using two's-complement arithmetic. Assuming that no length clause has been given for F'SMALL, the implemented range would use the next power of two above 100 to encompass the stated range, and would be (-128 .. 127), which needs 7 bits of magnitude (and 1 sign bit) before the decimal point. Similarly 7 bits are required after the decimal point to give error bound ≤ 0.01. Hence 15 bits are required (sign, 7 above decimal point, 7 below decimal point), leaving one spare bit which can conveniently be at the bottom of the word to provide a (fortuitous) *guard bit* (that is, precision beyond what is needed).

This representation is clearly the most efficient in terms of space, since F'SMALL is a power of 2. A different representation is obtained by specifying an arbitrary real number S for F'SMALL in a length clause

   for F'SMALL **use** S;

In this case each value of the type is an exact integer multiple of S, and the predefined attribute F'SIZE will tell how many bits are in fact used to store it. S must not exceed F'DELTA.

The predefined attribute R'DELTA for a fixed point type or subtype R has a value of type *universal_real* which is that given in the accuracy constraint of the type or subtype.

Given two fixed point types F and G (and using I to denote INTEGER) then we have the following operations:

Operator	Meaning	Operand Types Left	Right	Result Type
+ -	identity and negation		F	F
+ -	addition and subtraction	F	F	F
*	integer multiplication	F	I	F
*	integer multiplication	I	F	F
*	fixed multiplication	F	G	*universal_fixed*
/	fixed division	F	G	*universal_fixed*
/	fixed division by integer	F	I	F
= /=	equality and inequality	F	F	BOOLEAN
< <= > >=	ordering	F	F	BOOLEAN

Fixed point operators = and /= are permitted for the same reason as for floating point.

Defining the semantics of these operations in terms of the permitted rounding error requires care. The basic source of error is the representation of constants and intermediate results. If EPSILON is half the delta of F (that is, EPSILON = F'DELTA/2), then a constant C is represented by a machine value C1 such that

```
C - EPSILON ≤ C1 ≤ C + EPSILON
```

The operations above that yield a result type *universal_fixed* obey a similar inequality:

```
X, Y : F;

X*Y - EPSILON ≤ F(X*Y) ≤ X*Y + EPSILON
X/Y - EPSILON ≤ F(X/Y) ≤ X/Y + EPSILON
```

where the upper and lower limits are calculated mathematically (and the result is assumed to lie within the range of F). A value C is representable without error if C1 = C. Computations with such values are exact, except for division and fixed point multiplication. Note that integer multiplication is essentially repeated addition, it can overflow but cannot lose accuracy. Note also that integer multiplication by a floating point value is not permitted, since this is not equivalent to repeated addition. In this case the integer operand must be explicitly floated. The user could define this operation if required.

The operations of fixed multiplication and division are essentially in two parts. First, the accurate product or quotient is formed (that is, a result of the *type universal_fixed* is obtained). Second, the result must be converted before being assigned to any variable or being used in further computation. This conversion may imply a loss of accuracy due to the representation in the destination type: since the fixed point operands are essentially just scaled integers, the accurate product will in fact be another scaled integer, but the accurate quotient must be treated as a ratio of integers. The operation of fixed division by an integer operates in an analogous way and is merely provided to avoid excessive explicit type conversions. A real literal is not allowed as an operand of fixed multiplication or division, since there is not a unique fixed point type to which to convert it; this situation can be resolved by an explicit conversion, or better, by using a declared constant – which simplifies program maintenance.

To understand the computational aspects it is simplest to consider a decimal machine and model. Take a word as being a sign and three digits (SDDD), and consider the following declaration

```
type NORMAL is delta 0.001 range -0.999 .. 0.999;
```

This type requires all of the word with the representation S.DDD (that is, the point next to the far left of the word). Consider also

```
type LARGE is delta 10.0 range -800.0 .. 800.0;
```

This would ordinarily be implemented as (SDDD.), with one guard digit. Finally, consider

```
type MEDIUM is delta 0.1 range -9.0 .. 9.0;
```

This would have the representation (SD.DD) with one guard digit. We can illustrate the use of these types as follows

```
X      : NORMAL;
L1, L2 : LARGE;
C : constant MEDIUM := 2.3;

X := 0.3333;                 -- last digit lost on conversion to
                             -- NORMAL Now |X - 0.3333|< NORMAL'DELTA,
                             -- (mathematically)

X := X + 0.1;                -- 0.1 needs no qualification as the left
                             -- operand specifies the type
                             -- (NORMAL) of 0.1

X := 2*X;                    -- Now X = 0.866

X := X/2;                    -- equivalent to X := NORMAL(X/2.0),
                             -- that is, integer division avoids
                             -- qualification

X := NORMAL(C*X);            -- the constant is represented as 2.30
                             -- The machine evaluates
                             -- 2.30*0.433 = 0.99590 (six-digit
                             -- answer) and then rounds the result
                             -- to 0.996, which is stored in X. Note
                             -- that rounding is needed (no guard
                             -- digit for NORMAL).

L1 := 700.0;                 -- the .0 is necessary: no implicit
                             -- conversion of an integer literal
                             -- to a fixed point type

L1 := LARGE(X*L1);           -- calculates 700.0*0.996 = 697.20,
                             -- rounds to 697.0 (assuming the
                             -- guard digit for LARGE)
...
L1 := LARGE(X*L1) + L1;      -- conversion is necessary, and serves
                             -- to emphasize rounding before addition

L2 := LARGE(X*L1) + 100.0;   -- conversion is necessary

if L1 > X then               -- not legal: L1 and X must have the
                             -- same type

if L1 > LARGE(L2 * X) then   -- legal: explicit conversion
```

The user can perform accurate computation with fixed point by ensuring that only exactly representable values are used. In fact, the only source of error is the implied rounding of constants and conversion (which is necessary for multiplication and division).

Example:

A frequent calculation in some numerical applications is the smoothing of an input sequence by means of a running average:

```
OLD_VAL, NEW_VAL : F;
...
OLD_VAL := 0.9 * OLD_VAL + 0.1 * NEW_VAL;
```

To program this in Ada using fixed point, the types of the products and constants on the right hand side must be specified, that is:

```
K1 : constant FRACTION := 0.9;
K2 : constant FRACTION := 0.1;

OLD_VAL := F(K1 * OLD_VAL) + F(K2 * NEW_VAL);
```

An error analysis reveals that a small error in the constant K1 will cause a much larger error in OLD_VAL after successive iterations (thus a constant value of 10.0 as input converges to 9.09 if 0.9 is replaced by 0.89 for K1). This increase in error occurs when the sum of the two constants is not *exactly* 1.0. To avoid this cumulative effect, one can omit the larger constant and write the following:

```
OLD_VAL := OLD_VAL + F(K2 * (NEW_VAL - OLD_VAL));
```

Example:

As another illustration of the use of fixed point, consider the following function for computing the average of an array of components:

```
type F is ...              -- some fixed point type
type INDEX is range 1 .. 100;
type FIXED_VECTOR is array (INDEX) of F;
```

```
function AVERAGE(A : FIXED_VECTOR) return F is
   NUM_ITEMS : constant INTEGER := INDEX'LAST;
   type SUMF is delta F'DELTA
      range NUM_ITEMS*F'FIRST .. NUM_ITEMS*F'LAST;
   SUM : SUMF := 0.0;
begin
   for I in A'RANGE loop
      SUM := SUM + SUMF(A(I));
   end loop;
   return F(SUM/NUM_ITEMS);
end;
```

Here, the type SUMF has a greater range than F to accommodate the larger potential range of values. The explicit conversion inside the loop does not lose accuracy, but the final division potentially will lose accuracy. If type F requires nearly a full word, then the type SUMF will be double length. It is very difficult to write an algorithm to obtain the average which avoids double length. Since the size of the array is involved in the type SUMF, this size must be known at compilation time.

5.3.3 A Semantic Model for Approximate Computation

Programming languages do not conventionally define the semantics of floating point arithmetic. However, in Ada, with declarations controlling the accuracy of data types, it is highly desirable to do so. A proposal of W. S. Brown [Br 78] makes it possible to describe a model which is both clean in structure and realistic (that is, it describes the actual behavior of floating point arithmetic units). In this section, a brief overview is given of the model as needed by the language.

For each type, an abstract representation is defined. The abstract representation of each nonzero number x takes the form of a sign, a mantissa, and an integer exponent. Thus for the binary representation we have

$$x = \pm\ m\ *\ 2{**}n$$

where

$$1/2 \leq m < 1$$

that is, the number is *normalized*: the most significant binary digit is always 1. For example, a mantissa of length 3 allows representation of only the following mantissa values (using the notation for based literals):

```
2#0.100#, 2#0.101#, 2#0.110#, 2#0.111#
```

The relative precision here varies from 1 in 4 to 1 in 7; in general, mantissa length B guarantees precision of only 1 in 2**(B-1), although near to 1 the precision is nearly 1 in 2**B. Hence to guarantee D decimal digits precision requires B to be one more than the least integer greater than D*log(10)/log(2). If for example we declare

type F is digits 6;

then the mantissa will have 21 binary digits, that is, F'MANTISSA = 21. If the smallest value of the exponent is -84 and the largest is 84 (the values required by Ada in this case – see below) then

```
F'SMALL = 2#0.1#e-84
F'LARGE = 2#0.11111_11111_11111_11111_1#e84.
```

We do not assume that numbers are represented in this fashion, merely that numbers having the numeric values given above are representable in the machine. Brown now develops axioms for the representable numbers and the behavior of a machine number that is bounded by an interval whose endpoints are representable numbers. These axioms allow the use of higher precision than specified in the declaration, which is essential in Ada, since the implemented precision will typically be greater than the declared precision.

The Ada version of the Brown model for floating point works as follows:

(1) From the decimal precision specified (F'DIGITS) the corresponding number of binary places is determined, being F'MANTISSA.

(2) The *model numbers* are those with F'MANTISSA binary places and an exponent in the range

```
-4*F'MANTISSA .. 4*F'MANTISSA.
```

(3) The *safe numbers* are those with F'MANTISSA binary places and a potentially larger exponent range limited by the hardware.

The model numbers guarantee workable properties including a reasonable range of values – their definition is machine-independent: hence the term *model*. The safe numbers allow one to exploit the larger exponent range that many machines provide. Safe numbers have the same properties as model numbers and include the model numbers but their range is machine-dependent.

For fixed point types, a similar representation is chosen without an exponent. In this case for the binary representation of each nonzero number x we use:

```
x = ± M * small
```

where M is now an integer, whose length B defines its range 1 .. 2**(B-1), and small is the smallest positive representable value (corresponding to M=1). Axioms (not treated by Brown) can now be given which reflect the exact nature of some operations and the approximate nature of others. In addition, because of the obvious correspondence between the abstract representations of all approximate types, conversions can be defined.

These conversions and some use of subtypes can result in weaker error bounds than those of the type. Consider:

```
type F is digits 6;        -- 21 bits
X : F;
Y : F digits 5;            -- 18 bits
```

The accuracy constraint in the declaration of Y implies loss of precision in the subtype. Thus the statement Y := X; allows an implementation to lose the three least significant binary digits on the assignment. A subsequent assignment X := Y; will then mean that the last three bits of X are undefined (that is, the interval that bounds the value of X is larger than that given by the type).

Example:

Consider the fixed point type:

```
type F is delta 0.01 range -100.0 .. 100.0;
```

To discuss the semantics, we again write model numbers in the form of based numbers, thus:

```
64 = 2#100_0000.0000_000#
```

Then

```
F'FIRST     = -2#110_0100.0000_000#          = -100.0
F'LAST      = 2#110_0100.0000_000#           = 100.0
F'MANTISSA  = 14
F'SMALL     = 1/128 = 2#000_0000.0000_001#   = 0.0078125(<0.01)
F'LARGE     = 255 + 127/128 = 2#111_1111.1111_111# = 255.9921875
-- F'DELTA is not a model number
-- F'FIRST and F'LAST are model numbers in this
-- example but this need not always be the case.
```

Now consider the representation of 2.1, as in the declaration:

```
Z : F := 2.1;
```

The value is bounded by the two consecutive model numbers

```
2 + 12/128 = 2#000_0010.0001_100# = 2.09375
2 + 13/128 = 2#000_0010.0001_101# = 2.1015625
```

of the type F, which therefore define the smallest model interval that bounds Z. On a 20-bit machine, Z is likely to be represented by the machine value (using the same notation) of

```
2.10009765625 = 8602/4096 = 2#000_0010.0001_1001_1010#
```

The error analysis of ordinary computation proceeds similarly. Take:

```
Z := Z + 2.0;
```

Here 2.0 is a model number (and hence is represented exactly). So as a result, the bounds for Z are now 4.09375 and 4.1015625. If the operands are not model numbers, then the bounds for the result of the operation are computed as the closest model numbers that are guaranteed to enclose all possible results, for all possible values in the model intervals associated with the operands. Thus after

```
Z := Z + Z;
```

we shall get new bounds 8.1875 and 8.203125 for Z, so the model interval associated with Z has doubled in size.

The logic with fixed point multiplication and division is slightly different. Take

```
Z := F(X * Y);
```

Here X and Y are of any fixed point types, not necessarily type F, but of course Z must be of type F for the rules for assignment compatibility. The logic of multiplication (and similarly with division) is as follows. X and Y are computed in the ordinary way, and associated with each of their values will be a corresponding bounding model interval. The multiplication is then performed with essentially arbitrarily high precision. One can think of this intuitively in terms of giving a double length result. This arbitrarily accurate result is then converted to type F; in consequence some accuracy may well be lost, and in any case a bounding model interval will be dependent upon the characteristics of the fixed point type F. This result is then assigned, of course, to the variable Z in this case.

The reason why multiplication and division work in this way, is because the resulting values cannot be constrained to lie within the same range and delta as of the type of the operands. Hence it is essential that these operations allow the result to be *rescaled*. This is done in two stages: by calculating a result with an essentially arbitrarily high precision, and then by explicit conversion to a fixed point type.

5.4 IMPLEMENTATION CONSIDERATIONS

Fixed point types can be represented on most machines with one or two machine words. Implementations should not support fixed point types in excess of this length if credible performance is required (and cannot be provided). Note that the predefined type DURATION requires 23 bits of accuracy (plus one sign bit), because the reference manual requires that intervals of at least twenty milliseconds be accommodated, as well as an interval of up to a day. Such an implementation would be as efficient in time and space as conventional assembler coding (assuming a good register allocation algorithm). As with subranges of integers, tight packing is possible, and this could result in a major advantage over floating point.

Good performance depends largely upon the proper specification of the range and delta. For machines with limited arithmetic shifts, a value in a range that excludes negative values could have its scale converted by the use of logical shifts. All type conversions with fixed types could be accomplished with simple arithmetic shifts and masking. All the operations are likewise straightforward.

With real types there is a problem about the end points of the range with a range constraint. Ordinarily, such values would be in the set of values permitted. However, a fixed point range 0.0 .. 1.0 on a two's complement machine would not usually want to include 1.0. To avoid giving ranges as 0.0 .. 0.999999999, it seems best not to require that nonzero end values be within the specified range. See the wording in RM 3.5.9(6) for details.

A *lazy* implementation of numeric types which could be used by a diagnostic compiler is as follows. Every value is stored in long floating point format together with a flag indicating if it is integer or real. The long format must be sufficiently long to encompass the longest integer, fixed point and floating point types supported by the implementation. Operations can now be applied to these values, the flag being used to ensure that integer results are correctly rounded to integers (if the floating point hardware does not give integer results from integer values). This implementation method is clearly inefficient, especially for fixed point types, which are often used as a method of avoiding expensive floating point. However, it illustrates the concept of the abstract value and the fact that the operators have the same meaning for each type.

Although it is theoretically feasible, it is not practical to implement floating point types as fixed point quantities. This is because of the potentially large dynamic range of floating point values – a floating point mantissa length B would need $small = 2**(-5*B)$ and hence fixed point mantissa length 9*B.

With the real types, the language does not specify rounding or truncation, since either choice could be excessively expensive on some machines. The user can control its effect by increasing the digits or decreasing the delta in the type declaration, but should note that a small decrease in the delta could require going from 1 word to 2 words, with consequent performance degradation. With multiplication and division, rounding may be required in order to preserve the relational inequalities. Exact conversion can only occur between integer types (although many other conversions may not require any rounding). No conversions are significantly more troublesome than are integer to real and real to integer in (say) Algol 60.

Consider a function ROOT for taking the square root of an argument, where the argument and the result are of type FRACTION:

```
type FRACTION is delta D range 0.0 .. 1.0;
```

By declaring the fixed point quantities X and Y to have a type with larger delta:

```
type SIXTEEN is delta 16.0*D range 0.0 .. 16.0;
X, Y : SIXTEEN;
```

one can then take the square root of X by

```
Y := SIXTEEN(4 * ROOT(FRACTION (X/16)));
```

and here the division by 16 is a shift that corresponds to the converse of the FRACTION type conversion and hence produces no code (assuming reasonable peephole optimization). (Note that the literals 4 and 16 are integers; real literals would not be allowed here.)

The body of ROOT (for argument range 0.5 to 1) could be:

```
function ROOT(X : FRACTION) return FRACTION is
   HALF : constant FRACTION := 0.5;
   APPROX : FRACTION := 0.7;        -- a starting value
begin
   while abs(APPROX - FRACTION(X/APPROX)) > FRACTION'DELTA loop
      APPROX := FRACTION(HALF * (APPROX + FRACTION(X/APPROX)));
   end loop;
   return APPROX;
end ROOT;
```

The machine dependence is largely restricted to the declaration of FRACTION, whose range relative to the accuracy would reflect the word length of the machine. Note that since the declared range is 0.0 .. 1.0 the algorithm may give values equal to 1.0 for arguments near 1.0. This would cause overflow on a two's complement machine. The check for negative arguments is implicit in the type definition.

In evaluating an expression at compilation time, the identification of the operators must be performed. Then expressions involving only literals, constants, other evaluated expressions and predefined operators can be evaluated. The accuracy of real arithmetic may here be different from that of the target machine, although both are within that specified in the type declarations.

The efficient implementation of some mathematical algorithms requires access to the component parts of a floating point value. For instance, a square root routine typically starts by estimating a value by dividing the exponent by 2. We therefore need to be able to access and update the exponent. This can elegantly be done in Ada by the use of a record type and associated record representation clause defining the internal structure of the floating point value, and then using UNCHECKED_CONVERSION to convert between the floating point type and the record type. Such operations are best performed by subprograms in the mathematical library; in this way the implementation dependent operations can be encapsulated so that they are hidden from the normal user.

The above example illustrates the essential dilemma between efficiency and portability that intrudes into certain sensitive areas of numerical computation; there are occasions where the demands for a very efficient implementation outweigh those for complete portability. The facilities in Ada enable the non-portable parts to be readily identified and encapsulated so that a proper balance between the conflicting aims can be obtained.

5.5 CONCLUSION

The aim of the design is to provide the full range of numeric facilities within a secure system of types. This has been achieved by a combination of two techniques.

Firstly, use is made of the ability in the language to define new types derived from an existing type, from which the new types inherit properties. The convenience of the derived type mechanism in Ada is that it provides a simple method of ensuring a high degree of portability. If the user declares a new type (therefore derived from a machine type), this type is distinct from other types in the program. This distinction ensures that type conversions are explicit and that a quite different representation could be used on other machines.

Secondly, the precision of numerical representation and the bounds on results of computation are strictly controlled: With the model developed by Brown, it is possible to define an axiomatic system which gives the minimal properties of approximate computation. These minimal accuracy properties could be exploited by a diagnostic or program analysis system to ensure that the algorithm being used is appropriate. The axiomatic system is realistic in the sense that it can (and must) be applied to existing floating point implementations.

The numeric types available to the programmer are derived from those defined in the implementation. This guarantees that the efficiency of the resulting code is directly related to that of the implementation, which, in the case of floating point, could be hardware, firmware, or software. Fixed point types are not predefined in the standard environment, but acquire their properties on declaration. However, in terms of code generation these properties involve little more than what is required for the integers and hence the performance should be high.

Portability cannot be entirely guaranteed by the language because it is not possible for a program to be completely isolated from dependence on the underlying hardware. However, such dependence is limited to the attributes of the predefined numeric types, and properties of the implemented real types that cannot be derived from the axiomatic system – such as the radix of the underlying floating point representation.

To conclude, the numeric types in Ada provide facilities clearly needed by the envisaged applications. A rigorous axiomatic system is available to handle approximate computation. Most importantly, a good balance between portability and efficiency has been achieved.

6. Access Types

6.1 INTRODUCTION

The notion of access type encompasses the concept of objects that are dynamically created during the execution of a program. In general, neither the number of such objects, nor their names, can be fixed in advance.

The inclusion of such a feature in a language raises what are traditionally some of the most difficult issues in language design, and indeed in programming. Accordingly, the first section of this chapter is devoted to an overview of these issues. This will serve as background for an exposition of the approach adopted in Ada.

6.2 OVERVIEW OF THE ISSUES

The main problems usually encountered with access types fall into two categories:

- Conceptual aspects

- Reliability, efficiency, and implementation.

We first discuss these problems and then define the desirable goals for a formulation of access types.

6.2.1 Conceptual Aspects

The objects of a program can be classified into two categories: *static* objects and *dynamically allocated* objects.

Static objects are declared in a program and are containers for values. Each static object has a simple name that is used to denote either the container or the value, depending on the context where the name appears. The simple name of a static object is defined by its declaration. For example, an object declared within a procedure is created by the elaboration of the object declaration and exists until the end of the procedure. Such objects are said to be static since their lifetime is determined by the static (textual) structure of the program.

In contrast, the creation of dynamically allocated objects occurs dynamically, by the execution of so-called *allocators*, and is not directly related to the program structure. In general, the number of dynamically allocated objects is not easy to predict and it will not be possible to define their names by declarations. Hence what is returned by the execution of an allocator is an *internal name* – not an identifier – and therefore it cannot be used explicitly in the text to denote the newly allocated object.

To deal with this problem, one usually defines by declaration a number of *indirect* names that may be used to access the different dynamically allocated objects at successive stages of execution. The internal names of the allocated objects will be the values of these declared indirect names. For this reason, indirect names are called *access objects* in Ada and throughout the remainder of this chapter (they have been called *pointers* or *reference variables* in other languages). An access object can be a declared variable or a component of a declared variable (and hence static); but it can also be a component of some dynamically created object. Internal names are called *access values* in Ada. To emphasize the difference between names and internal names, we say that a name *denotes* an object whereas we say that an access value *designates* an object.

Four important consequences follow from the fact that access objects contain internal names:

(a) The same internal name may be contained in several access objects, with the consequence that they provide access to the same dynamically allocated object.

(b) Access objects may be used to describe relations, in particular, relations that change over time.

(c) Since the internal name contained in an access variable may vary with successive stages of the program execution, a given dynamically allocated object may become inaccessible: A dynamically allocated object is accessible as long as its internal name is contained by a declared access object, or if its internal name is contained by an access object that is itself a component of a dynamically allocated object that is still accessible, and so on.

(d) Since an access object does not contain any internal name prior to its first allocation or assignment, there must be a special null value corresponding to no internal name (**none** in Simula, **nil** in Algol 68 and Lisp, **null** in Ada). This value is also required for describing partial relations.

Sharing and the possibility of inaccessibility are thus two of the classical difficulties of access types. A third classical difficulty is the well-known problem of *dereferencing*: Considering the name of an access object, this name may stand for several different things:

- The name of the (static) access object.

- The content of the access object (that is, its value: an internal name).

- The content of the dynamically allocated object that is designated by this internal name.

The first two possibilities (name or content) also exist for static objects. Most languages (Bliss being an exception) have the same notation in the two cases, and make a distinction by context. The third possibility, however, only exists for access objects, and the solutions offered by programming languages are very diverse.

Two issues arise:

- For assignments, it must be clear whether the assignment refers to the access objects (access assignment), or to the dynamically allocated objects they designate (value assignment). This distinction is essential and has been treated differently in most languages.

- For component selection, that is, for denoting a component of a dynamically created record, there is no possible ambiguity. Nevertheless some languages have chosen to make dereferencing explicit even in this case.

The diversity of the solutions adopted by several languages is a clear indication of the conceptual difficulties involved. We illustrate this diversity with the example below, where X and Y are access variables and AGE is a component of the dynamically allocated record object (For the Algol 68 formulation, T is assumed to be the *mode* of the record values; the Simula example extends the possibilities offered for texts).

language	*access assignment*	*value assignment*	*component selection*
Simula	X :- Y;	X := Y;	X.AGE
Algol 68	X := Y;	T(X) :=Y;	X.AGE
Pascal	X := Y;	X^:= Y^;	X^.AGE
Ada	X := Y;	X.all := Y.all;	X.AGE

A final conceptual difficulty in defining access types is the notion of constant access objects. Suppose an access object is declared to be constant. Several alternative interpretations could be given for such a declaration.

(1) The access value (an internal name) is constant. This means that it always designates the same dynamically allocated object. The value of the latter, however, could vary.

(2) The access value can vary, but it may only be used to read the components of a designated object.

(3) The access value is constant and it may only be used to read the components of the designated object. Note, however, that we cannot infer that the dynamically allocated object designated by such a constant is itself constant, since other variables may designate the same dynamically allocated object.

Some languages, including Mary and Lis, have provided different syntaxes for all three forms of constant semantics. The first meaning, however, is the one that is most consistent with what is done for other types. Consider the analogy with an index:

```
subtype INDEX is INTEGER range 1 .. 9;
MEDIAN : constant INDEX := (INDEX'FIRST + INDEX'LAST)/2;
TABLE  : array (INDEX) of COLOR := (others => WHITE);
```

In this formulation we use the index MEDIAN to refer to the median value of the table: TABLE(MEDIAN). Now, the fact that MEDIAN is constant only means that we always refer to this component; it does not mean that assignment to this component is forbidden.

6.2.2 Reliability, Efficiency, and Implementation Issues

When a dynamically allocated object becomes inaccessible, the corresponding space may (at least theoretically) be reclaimed for other uses without any risk. This operation, classically called *garbage-collection*, has been used in languages such as Lisp, Simula, and Algol 68.

Unfortunately, there is no method of garbage collection that is generally suitable to real-time applications. The method used in most Lisp implementations is to allocate storage continuously until the available space is exhausted, and then reclaim inaccessible objects by a complete traversal of all allocated structures. This implies that the execution of an allocator can suddenly initiate garbage collection, thereby causing a large and unpredictable overhead. Moreover, as the available storage becomes increasingly fragmented by accessible objects, garbage collection could be triggered ever more frequently, causing rapid degradation of performance.

Another method is to maintain *reference counts* with each allocated object: an object is inaccessible if its reference count is zero. This fails with cyclic structures, where a non-zero reference count does not necessarily imply accessibility. It also causes implementation problems, since the reference count of an accessed object must be decremented whenever a declared access object that designates it passes out of scope – either in the normal course of execution or as a result of an exception. Access objects are therefore associated with *finalization* actions, with all their attendant difficulties. However, even if this method were fully implemented it would not solve the problem: the unpredictable overhead has merely been transferred to the *deallocation* operation.

A third method is to perform garbage collection periodically by a parallel process of lower priority. Provided the synchronization problems can be solved, this provides the least unsatisfactory solution for real-time use. Its major defect is that, under conditions where the transaction rate is high, the lower-priority processes may become starved, so garbage collection might not be done often enough to maintain a satisfactory pool of free storage.

For these reasons several languages in the systems programming area (including Lis and Euclid) try to achieve better control over storage management for dynamically allocated objects. This means that such languages offer the opportunity to define the workings of object allocation within the language itself. Similarly they admit an explicit deallocation statement which can also be defined within the language itself.

Such operations usually cannot be written with the full degree of compilation-time checking that is provided by types, though the Ada generics facility permits a greater degree of safety than is found in many other languages. In addition, the availability of explicit deallocation introduces the possibility of *dangling* access values: the program might deallocate a dynamically allocated object that is still accessible by other paths – its internal name still being contained by other access variables.

Confronted with this dilemma between reliability and efficiency, a possible answer is to choose reliability and accept the possibility that access types might not be used in programs that are time-critical. However, there are cases where access types should be used, precisely because the application considered is time-critical. We illustrate this point with the following example:

Assume that we need to compute the sum of the elements of a circular list. A formulation using an array might look as follows:

```
type INDEX is range 1 .. 1000;

type ITEM is
   record
      SUCC, PRED : INDEX;
      CONTENT    : INTEGER;
   end record;

TABLE : array (INDEX) of ITEM;
HEAD, NEXT : INDEX;
SUM : INTEGER;
```

The algorithm for adding the contents of the successors of HEAD may be written as a while loop:

```
SUM  := 0;
NEXT := TABLE(HEAD).SUCC;
while NEXT /= HEAD loop
   SUM  := SUM + TABLE(NEXT).CONTENT;
   NEXT := TABLE(NEXT).SUCC;
end loop;
```

Clearly, the above formulation attempts to use index values in order to express relations, and does not achieve this with quite the elegance and readability offered by access variables. The main point, however, is that the index computation involved in accessing the array element TABLE(NEXT) at each iteration may be a drawback, especially on small computers where multiplication is rather slow.

The alternative formulation with access objects (declarations omitted) is given below:

```
SUM := 0;
NEXT := HEAD.SUCC;
while NEXT /= HEAD loop
   SUM := SUM + NEXT.CONTENT;
   NEXT := NEXT.SUCC;
end loop;
```

This solution is more readable – it does not require mention of names such as TABLE that are irrelevant to the logic of the algorithm – and also more efficient since no index calculation is involved.

In general, when access variables are used, address computations will be done only once, at the time of dynamic allocation. Thereafter access values can only be assigned to access objects or used to access the dynamically allocated objects. This however does not involve address computations. On the other hand, when indices are used, address computations must be redone for every access.

6.2.3 Goals For a Formulation of Access Types

As shown by the previous example, one of the advantages of access variables is efficiency. As a consequence we must be able to use them in time-critical applications. In this case, however, we must provide a form of access variable that does not result in garbage collection with the associated costs and unpredictability. Naturally this does not exclude the possibility of more elaborate storage management strategies in applications that are not time-critical.

The needs of efficiency being thus satisfied, it remains that reliability should be a major goal in the formulation of access types, especially in view of the conceptual difficulties they raise. Hence a safe formulation of access types should have several important properties:

- There must be a **null** value for access objects. Since **null** designates no object, any attempt to denote a component of this nonexistent object should raise the exception CONSTRAINT_ERROR (the null value cannot be dereferenced). On many computers checking for such attempts is achievable without any run-time cost if the internal value of **null** corresponds to some protected address.

- Access variables should be typed (as in Simula or Pascal) so that one access variable can designate only objects of one type.

- There should be a basic operation – the allocator – that dynamically creates an object and delivers an access value designating this object (its internal name). On the other hand, there should be no operation for explicit deallocation of a dynamically allocated object (to avoid dangling access values).

- There should be a clear distinction between access types and other types. In particular, there should be no possibility for an access value to designate a static variable (again, to avoid dangling access values).

6.3 PRESENTATION OF ACCESS TYPES

The presentation of the properties of access types in Ada. will cover the following topics:

- How to declare access types

- The collection of dynamically allocated objects implied by the declaration of an access type

- How to declare access variables and constants

- How to allocate a dynamically allocated record object

- Component and value assignments

- Recursive access types

- Subprograms with parameters belonging to an access type

- Storage management for a collection of dynamically allocated objects

6.3.1 Declaration of Access Types and Subtypes

An access variable, like any other variable in Ada, has a type, which is in this case an access type. The example below shows a declaration of a record type followed by the declaration of an access type:

```
type PERSON(SEX : GENDER := F) is
  record
    AGE : INTEGER range 0 .. 123;
    ...
  end record;

type PERSON_NAME is access PERSON;
```

In this example, PERSON is declared as a record type, and static variables of this type can be declared as usual. The access type PERSON_NAME is declared as a type whose values provide access to dynamically allocated record objects of type PERSON.

It is of course possible to copy the value of a dynamically allocated PERSON into a static variable of this type and vice versa. Note, however, that there is no way for an access variable of type PERSON_NAME to designate a static variable of type PERSON.

The type of the dynamically allocated objects can be any type. For example it can be an array type, as in

```
type ALPHA is access STRING;
```

It is possible to declare a subtype of an access type, and this will mean that the constraints defined by the subtype declaration are imposed on the dynamically allocated objects. Thus the subtype ALPHA_LINE defined below corresponds to dynamically allocated strings of 80 characters:

```
subtype ALPHA_LINE is ALPHA(1 .. 80);
```

6.3.2 Collections of Dynamically Allocated Objects

Conceptually it is important to realize that each access type declaration implicitly defines a *collection* for dynamically allocated objects. The actual collection will be built during program execution as allocators are executed. Its lifetime cannot be longer than that of the program unit in which the access type definition is provided.

Collections in Ada are implicit and cannot be named (unlike those in Lis and Euclid). The collections associated with different access types are always disjoint, so that dynamically allocated objects designated by access variables that do not have the same type are guaranteed to be in different collections.

6.3.3 Access Variables, Allocators, and Access Constants

Access variables are declared in the usual way and may be initialized in their declaration, for instance with the value of some other previously declared access variable or with the special value null representing no internal name. For safety reasons, access variables that are not explicitly initialized are implicitly initialized with this null value. Hence all variables declared in the example below have this initial value:

```
YOU, HIM, HER : PERSON_NAME;      -- implicit initialization to null
SOMEONE : PERSON_NAME := null;    -- explicit initialization to null
```

An allocator creates a dynamically allocated object and assigns its internal name to an access variable:

```
YOU := new PERSON'(SEX => F, AGE => 30, ... );
                                  -- all components, as usual
```

The above allocator includes a qualified aggregate, with the name of the type of the dynamically allocated object – the so-called *designated type* – and with the aggregate defining the initial value of this object.

The constraints applicable to a dynamically allocated object are established when the allocator is evaluated and cannot be modified during the lifetime of the dynamically allocated object. In the case of a dynamically allocated array, this means that the bounds of such an array cannot be modified. Consider

```
MESSAGE : ALPHA := new STRING'(1 .. 45 => ' ');
```

It is certainly possible to modify the character values of the string designated by MESSAGE, but the bounds of this string remain those that are set at allocation time (here 1 and 45). Similarly, for a type with discriminants, the discriminant values established at allocation time cannot be modified:

```
type TEXT(SIZE : LENGTH) is
  record
    POS  : LENGTH := 0;
    DATA : STRING(1 .. SIZE);
  end record;

type TEXT_NAME is access TEXT;

BUFFER : TEXT_NAME;
...
BUFFER := new TEXT'(SIZE => 50, POS => 0, DATA =>(1 .. 50 => '*'));
```

The discriminant SIZE, once initialized by the allocator, cannot be changed thereafter (not even by a whole record assignment to the dynamically allocated record object). As a consequence, only the size actually required by the dynamically allocated object need be allocated.

Another possibility is to provide a constraint in the allocator without otherwise initializing the dynamically allocated object. For a discriminant constraint, the corresponding discriminants are initialized. Examples of such allocators are given below:

```
MESSAGE := new STRING(1 .. 90);     -- index constraint
HIM     := new PERSON(SEX => M);    -- discriminant constraint
BUFFER  := new TEXT(SIZE => 40);    -- discriminant constraint
```

Declarations of access constants are given in the usual way. The access value (an internal name) contained by an access constant cannot be changed. Consider, for example, the constant declarations:

```
YOU_NOW : constant PERSON_NAME := YOU;

DAY_NAME : constant array (1 .. 7) of ALPHA :=
            (new STRING'("MONDAY"),
             new STRING'("TUESDAY"),
             new STRING'("WEDNESDAY"),
             new STRING'("THURSDAY"),
             new STRING'("FRIDAY"),
             new STRING'("SATURDAY"),
             new STRING'("SUNDAY") );
```

The constant YOU_NOW contains the internal name of the dynamically allocated record designated by YOU at the time of the initialization. It means that YOU_NOW will always contain this access value even if YOU is updated at a later time. On the other hand, components of the person designated by this constant can be modified (aside from the discriminant) by assignments such as

```
YOU_NOW.AGE := 31;      -- or indirectly by
YOU.AGE := 31;
```

Similarly, the array DAY_NAME is a constant array, hence its components are constant access values obtained from allocators. But this does not mean that the strings designated by these constants are themselves constant, and it would not be possible for a compiler to perform the string allocations statically (at compilation time) unless their invariability can be deduced on other grounds: for example, if this array were local to a package body in which it is read but never updated.

6.3.4 Component Selection, Indexed Components, and Value Assignments

In the previous example, the contents of YOU is the internal name of a dynamically allocated record object. The usual syntax of component selection is used, as if YOU were the record object itself (this means that *dereferencing* is implicit for component selection):

```
YOU.AGE     -- a component that has the type INTEGER
YOU.SEX     -- a component that has the type GENDER
```

Similarly, we can use the normal selection syntax to designate the entire (dynamically allocated) record object. Thus YOU.all is an object of type PERSON such that the following conditions are true:

```
YOU.all.SEX = YOU.SEX
YOU.all.AGE = YOU.AGE
...
```

This notation can also appear in an allocator, as in the assignment statement

```
HER := new PERSON'(YOU.all);
```

Finally the same notation may be used for value assignments. Remember that if YOU and HER contain internal names of dynamically allocated record objects, then after the assignment

```
YOU := HER;
```

the two access variables contain the same internal name. In contrast, the value assignment for copying the value of the dynamically allocated record designated by HER into the dynamically allocated record designated by YOU – without necessarily altering the access values – is written

```
YOU.all := HER.all;
```

Such value assignments are always possible between dynamically allocated record objects without variants. With variants, they are legal only if the discriminants of the objects are identical. This must be checked (usually at execution time), and the exception CONSTRAINT_ERROR is raised if the check fails.

Indexed components for arrays denoted by access types are written exactly as in the case of statically denoted arrays (this means that dereferencing is also implicit for indexing). Thus we can write

```
MESSAGE(1)  := '*';
MESSAGE(11 .. 16) := DAY_NAME(1)(1..6);
MESSAGE(21 .. 27) := "MORNING";
```

Note, finally, that the notation X.**all**, denoting the dynamically allocated object designated by X, can be used for all dynamically allocated objects, whether they are records, arrays, scalars, or task objects.

6.3.5 Recursive Access Types

The type of a record component can be an access type. This opens up the possibility of *recursive* access types, where a dynamically allocated object in a given collection has components designating other dynamically allocated objects in the same collection. The declaration of recursive access types will usually involve an *incomplete* type declaration. As an example, consider the following variation of the type PERSON_NAME:

```
type PERSON(SEX : GENDER := F);   -- Incomplete declaration of
                                  -- PERSON                      (1)
type PERSON_NAME is access PERSON; -- Access type declaration    (2)
type PERSON(SEX : GENDER := F) is -- Full declaration of PERSON  (3)
   record
      AGE    : INTEGER range 0 .. 123;
      FATHER : PERSON_NAME(SEX => M); -- Component declaration    (4)
      MOTHER : PERSON_NAME(SEX => F); -- Component declaration    (5)
      SPOUSE : PERSON_NAME;           -- Component declaration    (6)
      ...
   end record;
```

The incomplete declaration allows a linear reading of the example: We first learn about the existence of a type called PERSON, so that at (2) we can understand what "**access** PERSON" means. We then learn what the type PERSON is in full. Without the incomplete declaration (1), the access type declaration (2) would be illegal. Similarly, we could not reverse the order of declarations (2) and (3) because then (3) would be illegal: we need to know what a PERSON_NAME is in order to understand the component declarations at (4), (5), and (6).

Having declared objects of this type, we can establish relations between them, and these relations can evolve dynamically. For example

```
HENRY_VIII   : PERSON_NAME(M) := new PERSON(SEX => M);
ANNE_BOLEYN  : PERSON_NAME(F) := new PERSON(SEX => F);
JANE_SEYMOUR : PERSON_NAME(F) := new PERSON(SEX => F);
...
HENRY_VIII.SPOUSE   := ANNE_BOLEYN;
ANNE_BOLEYN.SPOUSE  := HENRY_VIII;
...
HENRY_VIII.SPOUSE   := JANE_SEYMOUR;
JANE_SEYMOUR.SPOUSE := HENRY_VIII;
```

Note in particular that such recursive structures may include cycles: for example

    HENRY_VIII.SPOUSE.SPOUSE

designates the same object as the access variable

    HENRY_VIII

itself.

This kind of *recursion* in access type declarations may involve more than one access type. In such cases it is necessary to provide an incomplete declaration for each type whose name is mentioned before the occurrence of its full declaration. This is shown by the following pair of access types:

```
type CAR;                          -- Incomplete declaration of CAR

type PERSON(SEX : GENDER := F); -- Incomplete declaration of PERSON

type CAR_NAME is access CAR;
type PERSON_NAME is access PERSON;

type CAR is
  record
    OWNER : PERSON_NAME;
    SERIAL_NUMBER : POSITIVE;
  end record;

type PERSON(SEX : GENDER := F) is
  record
    ...
    VEHICLE : CAR_NAME;
    ...
  end record;
```

6.3.6 Access Objects as Parameters

Like other variables, access variables can be passed as parameters, and the parameter modes have their usual meaning. For functions, the parameters must be **in** parameters (as must all parameters of functions) but this does not prevent assignment to local access objects. As an example consider the declarations for the lists of section 6.2.2, above.

```
type PLACE;
type LIST is access PLACE;

type PLACE is
  record
    SUCC, PRED : LIST;
    CONTENT    : ITEM;
  end record;
```

A function CARDINAL that counts the elements in a given circular list can be written as follows:

```
function CARDINAL(HEAD : LIST) return NATURAL is
  -- The head is not counted as a list element
  -- For an empty list, HEAD.SUCC = HEAD.PRED = HEAD

  NEXT  : ITEM := HEAD.SUCC;
  COUNT : NATURAL := 0;
begin
  while NEXT /= HEAD loop
    NEXT  := NEXT.SUCC;
    COUNT := COUNT +1;
  end loop;
  return COUNT;
end;
```

Moreover, assignment to the object designated by an **in** parameter, or to a component of that object, is also permitted.

As an example, consider the procedure given below:

```
procedure DIVORCE(P : in PERSON_NAME) is
begin
  P.SPOUSE.SPOUSE := null;
  P.SPOUSE := null;
end;
```

Although P is an **in** parameter, assignment to P.SPOUSE is permitted.

6.3.7 Storage Management for Access Types

Unless specified otherwise, the collection of dynamically allocated objects associated with an access type will be allocated in a global heap and may be garbage-collected in some implementations. For time-critical applications, however, it is possible to provide a *length clause* that specifies an upper bound for the space needed by the collection of a given access type. This space can then be reserved globally when the length clause is elaborated. Subsequently, when leaving the innermost block, subprogram, or task that encloses the access type declaration, the space occupied by the collection may be reclaimed since the contained objects cannot any longer be accessible.

```
for CAR_NAME'STORAGE_SIZE use -- no more than 2000 cars
    (2000*CAR'SIZE) / SYSTEM.STORAGE_UNIT;
```

The expression provided after the reserved word **use** is the size in storage units of the storage area to be reserved for the collection of dynamically allocated cars designated by values of the type CAR_NAME. Given an estimate of the maximum number of cars to be allocated (here 2000), the size in bits is obtained by multiplying this number by the value of the attribute CAR'SIZE; the size in storage units is then obtained by dividing the result by the size in bits of a storage unit (SYSTEM.STORAGE_UNIT). Note that this storage area does not limit the storage for persons designated by values of the type PERSON_NAME, in spite of the fact that each CAR has a component of this type.

A collection for which such a length clause has been given behaves like a static array as far as storage allocation is concerned. The objects are allocated within this static storage area by allocators; and the whole collection can be reclaimed globally under the same conditions as for an array declared at the place of the access type declaration. The exception STORAGE_ERROR is raised if the space reserved is insufficient for an allocation.

If we want to ensure that garbage collection is never performed by the run-time system, the following pragma must be used

```
pragma CONTROLLED(CAR_NAME);
```

Such collections may be allocated either on the stack or on the heap. They have several advantages. In terms of storage management they have a cost comparable to that of arrays. In addition they offer both the notational advantages and the addressing efficiency of access variables. Finally, if an application wants to perform its own deallocation, it can do so by means of a generic instantiation of a predefined generic library procedure, as follows:

```
procedure FREE is
new UNCHECKED_DEALLOCATION(OBJECT => CAR, NAME => CAR_NAME);
```

The resulting procedure FREE has a parameter profile corresponding to the following specification:

```
procedure FREE(X : in out CAR_NAME);
```

The execution of a call such as FREE(MY_CAR); will assign the null value to MY_CAR, and establish that the storage occupied by the object designated by MY_CAR can be reclaimed. This form of deallocation is said to be *unchecked* since no check will then be done to ensure that there are no *dangling* accesses to the same object. The use of this form of deallocation may therefore be justified by efficiency, but it presents some danger, and so programs that use it must be written with great care.

7. Derived Types

7.1 INTRODUCTION

The basic mechanisms for defining a new type are by enumeration and by composition from existing ones; certain operations are automatically introduced by such definitions, for example the basic operations that are inherent in indexing, component selection, and the formation of aggregates. Another way of defining a type is by means of a private type declaration.

A third possibility is provided by the language: A type COPY is said to *derive* its characteristics from those of another existing type MODEL if it is declared as

```
type COPY is new MODEL;
```

This form of declaration is useful whenever a type is to have the same characteristics as another type, (and possibly some additional ones). The type MODEL is said to be the *parent* type, and COPY is said to be a *derived* type – derived from the parent type. Although the derived type COPY and its parent type MODEL have similar characteristics, they are nevertheless distinct types.

The following topics are some of the major uses of derived types:

- Simple strong typing

- The explanation of numeric types

- The ability to define new types that have numeric literals

- The construction of private types

- Achieving transitivity of visibility

- Change of representation

After an informal introduction to derived types, these major uses are discussed in what follows. It will be shown that all these uses rely on a unique ability, namely the ability to introduce a distinct type with similar properties.

7.2 INFORMAL INTRODUCTION TO DERIVED TYPES

Given some useful type, the derivation mechanism offers a simple way of creating other types that are distinct *copies* of this type. Consider for example the types:

```
type SCALAR is digits 8;

type COLOR is (VIOLET, INDIGO, BLUE, GREEN, YELLOW, ORANGE, RED);

package METRIC is
   type COORDINATE is
      record
         X : SCALAR := 0.0;
         Y : SCALAR := 0.0;
         Z : SCALAR := 0.0;
      end record;

   function "+" (LEFT, RIGHT : COORDINATE) return COORDINATE;
   function "-" (LEFT, RIGHT : COORDINATE) return COORDINATE;

   procedure INVERT(A : in out COORDINATE);
end METRIC;
```

By derivation we can create the following new types:

```
type MASS   is new SCALAR;
type LENGTH is new SCALAR;
type AREA   is new SCALAR;


type DYE is new COLOR;

type HUE is new COLOR;

type POINT  is new METRIC.COORDINATE;
type FORCE  is new METRIC.COORDINATE;
type VECTOR is new METRIC.COORDINATE;
```

The motivation for creating new types that are copies of existing types will be examined in later sections. For the time being let us review the properties of such types – obtained by derivation. In each case, the derived type is a copy of its parent type. This has several implications concerning the type class, the set of values, the applicable operations, and overloading.

Type Class:

The derived type belongs to the same class as its parent type. Thus DYE is an enumeration type since COLOR is an enumeration type; similarly, POINT is a record type since COORDINATE is a record type.

Set of Values:

The set of values of the derived type is a copy of the set of values of its parent type. Thus we have a set of seven values for the type DYE – exactly as for the parent type COLOR. There is a one-to-one correspondence between the two sets of values; but these two sets are nevertheless distinct: it would not be possible to assign a value of type DYE to a variable of type COLOR.

Basic Operations:

The basic operations for the derived type are as for the parent type. For example, if component selection is available for the parent type, it is available for the derived type. Thus selection of the component Y (by dot notation) is available for the type POINT since it is available for the type COORDINATE; similarly aggregates exist for both types and they use the same notation.

Attributes:

Attributes are basic operations, so the previous rule applies: If an attribute is available for the parent type, it is available for the derived type. Thus the attribute FIRST is available for the type MASS since it is available for the type SCALAR: the attribute FIRST for the type MASS yields a value of type MASS; the attribute FIRST for the type SCALAR yields a value of type SCALAR. The (implicit) declarations of these two attributes are in fact as follows (this is NOT legal Ada):

```
function SCALAR'FIRST return SCALAR; -- for the type SCALAR
function MASS'FIRST   return MASS;   -- for the type MASS
```

Implicit Conversions of Numeric Literals:

Implicit conversions of numeric literals are also basic operations. Hence there exists an implicit conversion of any real literal (such as 1.54) to the type MASS since there exists such a conversion for the type SCALAR (the parent type of MASS).

Enumeration Literals:

If a given enumeration literal exists for the parent type, there is a corresponding enumeration literal – with the same identifier – for the derived type. Thus there is the enumeration literal INDIGO for the type DYE since there is an enumeration literal INDIGO for the type COLOR. The (implicit) declarations of these two enumeration literals are in fact as follows:

```
function INDIGO return COLOR;    -- for the type COLOR
function INDIGO return DYE;      -- for the type DYE
```

Thus each literal yields a value of the corresponding type: as we know already there is a correspondence between the indigo value of COLOR and that of DYE, but they are distinct values belonging to distinct types.

Predefined Operations:

For each predefined operation of the parent type there is a corresponding predefined operation of the derived type. For example we have the addition:

```
function "+" (LEFT, RIGHT : SCALAR) return SCALAR;
```

for the type SCALAR and hence the corresponding additions for the derived types:

```
function "+" (LEFT, RIGHT : MASS)   return MASS;
                                        -- for the type MASS
function "+" (LEFT, RIGHT : LENGTH) return LENGTH;
                                        -- for the type LENGTH
function "+" (LEFT, RIGHT : AREA)   return AREA;
                                        -- for the type AREA
```

Derivable Operations:

For a type declared in the visible part of a package, each subprogram that has a parameter or result of the type and is declared within the visible part of this package is *derivable*. This means that corresponding operations are derived by the derived type. For example, the package METRIC defines an addition, a subtraction, and a procedure INVERT for the type COORDINATE; and hence the corresponding subprograms are derived for the type POINT:

```
function "+" (LEFT, RIGHT : POINT) return POINT;
function "-" (LEFT, RIGHT : POINT) return POINT;
procedure INVERT(A : in out POINT);
```

Note that these derived operations are obtained by *systematic* substitution of the name of the derived type for the name of the parent type.

(We will say more about the effect of these derived subprograms after we have presented explicit conversions.)

Explicit Conversions:

The above description shows that a derived type is very much like its parent type. They are nevertheless distinct types. Thus with the declarations

```
C : COLOR := INDIGO;
D : DYE   := VIOLET;
H : HUE   := RED;
```

assignments such as the following are illegal

```
D := H;    -- Illegal: a hue value cannot be assigned to a dye
C := D;    -- Illegal: a dye value cannot be assigned to a color
```

These assignments are not allowed because we are dealing with distinct types and distinct sets of values. However, there is a one-to-one correspondence between these sets of values and, for this reason, the language provides *explicit conversions* between corresponding values. For example

```
DYE(H)
```

is an explicit conversion of the value of H – of type HUE – into the corresponding value of type DYE: here it will yield the RED value of the type DYE, and so the following assignment is legal

```
D := DYE(H);
```

Type conversions between types that are derived directly or indirectly from each other (or from a common parent type) usually do not result in any run-time executable code. Such conversions are also involved (implicitly) in the derivation of a derivable operation. Consider for example the procedure INVERT:

```
procedure INVERT(A : in out COORDINATE) is
begin
   A.X := - A.X;
   A.Y := - A.Y;
   A.Z := - A.Z;
end;
```

and the derivation of the procedure

```
procedure INVERT(A : in out POINT);
```

The effect of this derived operation is obtained by application of the parent procedure, but conversion of the parameter to the parent type is assumed to take place before the call, and conversion back to the derived type is assumed to take place after the call. Thus for a variable P of type POINT, the call

```
INVERT(P);
```

has the same effect as

```
declare
  use METRIC;
  K : COORDINATE;
begin
  K := COORDINATE(P);   -- convert to parent type
  METRIC.INVERT(K);     -- call parent procedure
  P := POINT(K);        -- convert back to derived type
end;
```

or simply

```
METRIC.INVERT(METRIC.COORDINATE(K));
```

but this form does not show the conversion back.

Here again these conversions usually do not result in any run-time executable code but they are needed to explain the use of the procedure METRIC.INVERT, which is only applicable to the type METRIC.COORDINATE.

Overloading considerations:

A final point to consider with derived types is overloading. Derivation creates several overloaded entities. Thus we have

- Overloaded aggregates. For example, for the types METRIC.COORDINATE and POINT, the aggregate: (X => 1.0, Y => 2.0, Z => 1.5)

- Overloaded enumeration literals. For example, for the types COLOR, DYE, and HUE, enumeration literals such as VIOLET, INDIGO, and so on.

- Overloaded subprograms. For example, the procedure INVERT for the types POINT, FORCE, and METRIC.COORDINATE. Similarly, the operator "+" for these types, for the type SCALAR, and for the types derived from SCALAR.

As usual, overloaded entities are identified by the context. Thus there is no ambiguity in the following cases:

```
C := INDIGO;    -- the INDIGO of the type COLOR
D := INDIGO;    -- the INDIGO of the type DYE
```

Qualification can be used when the context is not sufficient for the determination of the meaning of an overloaded construct. For example the following comparison is ambiguous (and admittedly somewhat pathological):

```
if (X => A, Y => B, Z => C) = (X => U, Y => V, Z => W) then
                                                -- ambiguous
```

But this ambiguity can be resolved by qualification of one or of both aggregates:

```
POINT'(X => A, Y => B, Z => C) = (X => U, Y => V, Z => W)
```

or

```
POINT'(X => A, Y => B, Z => C) = POINT'(X => U, Y => V, Z => W)
```

or

```
(X => A, Y => B, Z => C) = POINT'(X => U, Y => V, Z => W)
```

We next review major classes of use of derived types.

7.3 SIMPLE STRONG TYPING

Given some useful type, the derivation mechanism offers a simple way of creating other types that are distinct *copies* of this type. The usual motivation for such type replication is to keep the two value spaces well separated and, thus, to achieve a simple form of strong typing. We illustrate this idea by an example due to Erhard Ploedereder and Helmut Hummel. Consider a useful type for counting currency:

```
type CURRENCY is delta 0.01 range 0.0 .. 1.0E6;
```

and assume that we have forced an exact representation of decimal values by means of the representation clause:

```
for CURRENCY'SMALL use CURRENCY'DELTA;
```

From this type we can derive the usual types:

```
type DOLLAR is new CURRENCY;    -- three
type FRANC  is new CURRENCY;    -- distinct
type MARK   is new CURRENCY;    -- types
```

The motivation for having these distinct types is well-known to every traveller, namely not to mix the different currencies. So we could now declare

```
MY_MONEY, YOUR_MONEY : DOLLAR;
ARGENT       : FRANC;
TASCHENGELD : MARK;
```

and the usual constants

```
CENT     : constant DOLLAR := 0.01;
CENTIME : constant FRANC   := 0.01;
PFENNIG : constant MARK    := 0.01;
```

By virtue of these declarations, we can write assignments such as

```
YOUR_MONEY   := 1*CENT;
TASCHENGELD := 50*PFENNIG;
MY_MONEY     := YOUR_MONEY;
```

All are legal and this can be checked by an Ada compiler at compilation time. Similarly an Ada compiler will detect at compilation time any of the following misuses:

```
ARGENT    := YOUR_MONEY;    -- Illegal!
MY_MONEY := TASCHENGELD;    -- Illegal!
```

What this example illustrates is that we have provided type declarations that reflect the common-sense view that having one "centime" is not the same as having one "pfennig". Although both correspond to an abstract value of "0.01", we consider that they belong to different value spaces. Note that this would not be achieved if we had declared our variables as

```
MY_MONEY, YOUR_MONEY, ARGENT, TASCHENGELD : CURRENCY;
```

since this would allow mixing different currencies in an uncontrolled manner. Distinguishing the value spaces was also the main reason for having typed constants for CENT, CENTIME, and PFENNIG. Using a named number such as

```
ONE_UNIT : constant := 0.01;
```

would indeed be misleading in this case: After the assignments

```
ARGENT    := ONE_UNIT;
MY_MONEY := ONE_UNIT;
```

it would be wrong to believe that these two variables have the same value since an implicit conversion of the *universal_real* value 0.01 has taken place for each assignment: to the type FRANC in the case of ARGENT and to the type DOLLAR in the case of MY_MONEY.

So we have different currencies but we can exchange them. For example we can assume a range of conversion rates:

```
type CONV_RATE is delta 0.0001 range 1.0 .. 2000.0;
-- for converting from the stronger currency
for CONV_RATE'SMALL use CONV_RATE'DELTA;
```

and define the function

```
function EXCHANGE(A : MARK) return FRANC is
   MARK_TO_FRANC : constant CONV_RATE := 3.20;
begin
   return FRANC(MARK_TO_FRANC * CURRENCY(A));
end;
```

and thereafter write

```
ARGENT := EXCHANGE(TASCHENGELD);
```

which has exactly the intended effect of converting TASCHENGELD from marks to francs before assigning the result to ARGENT.

Note that the return statement of the function EXCHANGE includes two successive explicit conversions. First

```
CURRENCY(A)
```

yields the number of currency units that correspond to the value of A. Then, after multiplication by the mark to franc rate, this number is converted to the type FRANC:

```
FRANC(MARK_TO_FRANC*CURRENCY(A))
```

Thus if the value of A is equal to 2.0, this means that we have 2.0 marks; the conversion CURRENCY(A) yields 2.0 units of currency; the multiplication by MARK_TO_FRANC yields 6.40_0000 units – conceptually units of currency; and the final conversion converts them into 6.40 francs. We could have written it – equivalently – as

```
FRANC(MARK_TO_FRANC*A)
```

but this would fail to show the conversion into the more neutral type CURRENCY as an important conceptual intermediate step. Each of the above conversions is purely on the conceptual level – helping to make the intent more explicit – but will not result in any run-time executable code.

Note that we could write this example – without derivation – in the following manner:

```
type DOLLAR is delta 0.01 range 0.0 .. 1.0E6;
type FRANC  is delta 0.01 range 0.0 .. 1.0E6;
type MARK   is delta 0.01 range 0.0 .. 1.0E6;
```

But this formulation would hide the fact that these three types are currencies with the same delta and range, and for which certain currency-specific functions could be declared, such as interest:

```
package FINANCIAL is
    type CURRENCY is delta 0.01 range 0.0 .. 1.0E6;
    for CURRENCY'SMALL use CURRENCY'DELTA;
    type RATE is delta 0.01 range 0.0 .. 10.0;
    for RATE'SMALL use RATE'DELTA;

    function INTEREST(A : CURRENCY; R : RATE) return CURRENCY;
    ...
end;

package body FINANCIAL is
    ...
    function INTEREST(A : CURRENCY; R : RATE) return CURRENCY is
    begin
       return CURRENCY(A*R);
    end;
    ...
end FINANCIAL;
```

With this variation, and assuming the derived types to be declared as follows:

```
type DOLLAR is new FINANCIAL.CURRENCY;
type FRANC  is new FINANCIAL.CURRENCY;
type MARK   is new FINANCIAL.CURRENCY;
```

we can now use the functions INTEREST derived for each of these types from the corresponding function defined for the common parent type:

```
MY_MONEY := MY_MONEY + INTEREST(MY_MONEY, 0.10);
ARGENT   := ARGENT + INTEREST(MONNAIE, 0.15);
```

To conclude on this first example, it shows that derived types can be used to achieve program reliability and readability in quite a simple manner – hence the name simple strong typing. We will see later in this chapter (and in chapter 13) that generic units can often (but not always) be used to achieve similar goals. However generic solutions will usually involve much more *machinery* and, in consequence, are less likely to be used in simple situations such as the currency example.

Note also that derivation will allow the construction of hierarchies of derived types. Thus having the predefined type

```
type STRING is array(POSITIVE range <>) of CHARACTER;
```

we can derive the types

```
type LINE is new STRING(1 .. 140);
type CARD is new STRING(1 .. 80);
```

Moreover we can further derive the following types

```
type CONTROL_CARD is new CARD;
type PROGRAM_CARD is new CARD;
type DATA_CARD   is new CARD;
```

These definitions ensure that objects of type LINE are not accidentally mixed with objects of type CARD. However, they can both be converted to the type STRING by means of appropriate conversions. Also we have defined three distinct types, derived from the type CARD, and we can define distinct operations for them. For example we may want to define certain subprograms that are applicable to control cards but not to program cards, or vice versa.

From a purist point of view one could argue that the use of derived types in many of these examples does not achieve *total* reliability. For example, with the derivations of SCALAR in

```
type LENGTH is new SCALAR;
type AREA   is new SCALAR;
```

the multiplication that is derived for LENGTH is the following multiplication, which is not useful:

```
function "*" (LEFT, RIGHT : LENGTH) return LENGTH;
```

However, we can always define – explicitly – the function

```
function "*" (LEFT, RIGHT : LENGTH) return AREA is
begin
   return AREA(SCALAR(LEFT)*SCALAR(RIGHT));
end;
```

Furthermore, should we fear the misuse of the inherited multiplication, we can always hide it by the following declaration:

```
function "*" (LEFT, RIGHT : LENGTH) return LENGTH is
begin
   raise DIMENSION_ERROR;
end;
```

But in many cases, we will not even bother to introduce such additional definitions: There are many ways in which we are trying to improve program reliability, and types are but one of them. The fact that any specific mechanism does not achieve one hundred percent safety does not mean that this mechanism should be neglected. Thus by declaring the derived type

```
type MASS is new SCALAR;
```

we have ensured that masses are not assigned to lengths by accident. However we will leave it to the programmer to avoid improper uses such as multiplication of masses. Actually, having written

```
KILO : constant MASS := 1.0;
...
LOAD : MASS := 3.0*KILO;
```

a programmer is not likely to write

```
LOAD := LOAD*LOAD;
```

which (although legal in Ada) would not make much sense: the careful choice of names makes such errors unlikely – and easily detectable by code inspection, whether by the same or by another programmer.

We have already seen examples in which we were quite willing to have a type declaration be no more than a first order characterization of the data. Thus when defining dates we did not bother to take into account short and long months – not to mention leap years: Although such a formulation would be possible, we felt that the added complexity was not justified. The same reasoning will often apply to the use of derived types: they provide a simple mechanism for achieving a first level of safety. Being simple, this mechanism is more likely to be used than heavier mechanisms. Thus derived types will *encourage* the use of types for logical structuring.

We next consider other examples of the use of derived types for simple strong typing. Let us first review possible derivations of the type COORDINATE defined in the package METRIC in section 7.2:

```
type BASE_COORD  is new METRIC.COORDINATE;
type LOCAL_COORD is new METRIC.COORDINATE;
```

By this we achieve some security since coordinates of the two systems cannot be mixed inadvertently. When changing coordinate systems, an important property of derived types can be used, namely, the ability to perform explicit conversions. Thus, using the "+" operator defined on coordinates, we can program a change of base as follows:

```
declare
  B, D : BASE_COORD;
  L    : LOCAL_COORD;
begin
  ...
  B := D + BASE_COORD(L);
end;
```

Another example (due to Etienne Morel) comes from the design of an Ada compiler, using a software managed virtual memory. A single package is in charge of this management of virtual addresses:

```
package VIRTUAL_ADDRESS_MANAGER is
  type VIRTUAL_ADDRESS is private;
  function ADDRESS(LOCATION : MEMORY_ADDRESS)
                  return VIRTUAL_ADDRESS;
  function ADDRESS(LOCATION : VIRTUAL_ADDRESS)
                  return MEMORY_ADDRESS;
...
private
  type VIRTUAL_ADDRESS is
    record
      BASE   : SEGMENT;
      OFFSET : DISPLACEMENT;
    end record;
end VIRTUAL_ADDRESS_MANAGER;
```

In various parts of the compiler, data structures are accessed by means of virtual addresses. Type derivation is used as follows:

```
type SYMBOL_VA is
        new VIRTUAL_ADDRESS_MANAGER.VIRTUAL_ADDRESS;
type NODE_VA is
        new VIRTUAL_ADDRESS_MANAGER.VIRTUAL_ADDRESS;
```

With derivation, the ADDRESS functions are inherited by these types so that the same functions, defined in a single package, are used for all these types – this single package remains the single interface with the virtual memory system. But the most important property of this solution is the security that is achieved: it is not possible to assign (by mistake) a SYMBOL_VA value to a variable whose type is NODE_VA: Although these two types are conceptually similar (being derived from the same parent), they are nevertheless distinct types.

Our last example of simple strong typing (due to Robert Firth) illustrates an ability similar to the Simula hierarchical type composition (although it is admittedly less powerful).

Let us assume that we have defined a private type CREDIT_CARD and the corresponding basic operations. We can then derive the types

```
type PERSONAL_CARD is new CREDIT_CARD;
type BUSINESS_CARD is new CREDIT_CARD;
```

and then define certain operations on personal_cards but not on business_cards and vice versa. This enables the definition of a system that has some security against inadvertent misuse. Clearly it does not cover the case of intentional forgery since explicit conversions are possible.

The above comment is characteristic of many uses of derived types for simple strong typing:

- The mechanism is very simple to use.

- The protection offered is against inadvertent misuse – heavier mechanisms would be required against intentional forgery.

The previous forms of strong typing can almost be obtained by the use of generic instantiation instead of derivation:

```
generic
package METRIC is
   type COORDINATE is
     record
        X : SCALAR;
        Y : SCALAR;
        Z : SCALAR;
     end record;
   ...
end;

package BASE  is new METRIC; use BASE;
package LOCAL is new METRIC; use LOCAL;

subtype BASE_COORD  is BASE.COORDINATE;
subtype LOCAL_COORD is LOCAL.COORDINATE;
```

Generic instantiation almost achieves what is needed but one may regret the need to use a more elaborate feature of the language: generic program units. In many teaching strategies this feature would only be encountered at the advanced level. Hence it is not really satisfactory that the user should be confronted with this degree of difficulty (on top of verbosity) for such a simple situation.

Moreover, the major drawback of the generic solution is that conversions between BASE_COORD and LOCAL_COORD are not possible, whether explicitly or implicitly, in the generic formulation. To achieve such conversion would require writing functions such as the following:

```
function TO_BASE(A : LOCAL_COORD) return BASE_COORD is
begin
   return BASE_COORD'(X => A.X, Y => A.Y, Z => A.Z);
end;
```

This solution is far from satisfactory from a maintenance point of view, since the conversion has to be expressed by duplication of the *structure* within the aggregate. In particular, it has to express the structural correspondence on a component-by-component basis. Any change in the definition of the type COORDINATE would therefore require revision of the text of these conversion functions.

The approach taken for conversions is far simpler in the case of derivation: if a type is derived from another one, then it is immediately known that the two types have the same structure – by construction. Hence there is no need to detect structural similarity.

Another approach in the case of the type SCALAR would be to copy the type definition. Thus assuming a range constraint for illustration:

```
D : constant := 8;
L : constant := 0.0;
U : constant := 1.0E6;

type SCALAR is digits D range L .. U;
```

we may just provide *identical* type definitions:

```
type MASS   is digits D range L .. U;
type LENGTH is digits D range L .. U;
```

This copying technique works in the case of numeric types, in particular for explicit conversions. However there are methodological objections to the fact that the *sameness* is hidden. In order to understand that the two types are similar we have to compare D, L, and U. But the intention does not appear. Actually there could be situations where these same constants D, L, and U are used in a third type by accident. Conversely, there are situations where we want two types to be similar although their range need not be the same.

The superiority of the derivation approach for copying comes from the fact that the intention is made *explicit* by *naming* the parent type, even if the derived type has a different range:

```
type VELOCITY is new SCALAR range ... ;
```

7.4 THE EXPLANATION OF NUMERIC TYPES

The explanation of numeric types is based on the use of derived types. A type declaration such as

    type REAL is digits 8 range -1.0E30 .. 1.0E30;

is explained as being equivalent to the following succession of declarations

    type *hidden_real* is new *predefined_floating_point_type*;
    subtype REAL is *hidden_real* digits 8 range *hidden_real* (-1.0E30) ..
                                          hidden_real (1.0E30);

This means that REAL is a subtype of a type *hidden_real* obtained by copying a predefined floating point type. The selection of this predefined type is done by the compiler; the type chosen must support the precision required – here it must have at least 8 digits; furthermore it must support at least the range required. The fact that this selection is performed by the compiler ensures portability: the programmer need not know which floating point type is actually used.

   The role played by derivation in this explanation is to provide a distinct replica of the floating point type. Thus if we write

    type MY_REAL is digits 8;

we are sure of getting a new type. In particular this means that REAL and MY_REAL are distinct types.

   The reason to consider REAL as a subtype of *hidden_real* is that for operations on values of this type, the compiler may generate code that corresponds to one of the hardware floating point types: range checks are used for assignments but not for intermediate results in expressions.

7.5 THE ABILITY TO INHERIT LITERALS

With derivation, it is possible to define new types that inherit the implicit conversions of numeric literals but have different operations.

   For example, modulo arithmetic can be declared by means of a type derived from an integer type. Modulo operations that hide the inherited operations can be declared, yet integer literals can still be used.

7.6 THE CONSTRUCTION OF PRIVATE TYPES

For the construction of private types, derived types provide an easy and unambiguous way of distinguishing the operations of the private type from those of the type used for its representation (that is, the type declared by the full type declaration). The relevant aspects are: (1) the fact that the parent and the derived type are distinct types; (2) the fact that explicit conversions between the two types exist.

Consider for example the case where an operation specified for a private type is implemented in terms of an operation of the type that is used for representing the private type:

```
package LOCKSMITH is
   type KEY is private;
   procedure GET_KEY(K : out KEY);
   ...
   function "<" (X, Y : KEY) return BOOLEAN;
private
   type KEY is new CHARACTER;
   ...
end;
```

The user need not know that keys are implemented as characters, but he is provided with the operator "<" to order keys. This operator is implemented as the comparison of the corresponding characters:

```
package body LOCKSMITH is
   ...
   function "<" (X, Y : KEY) return BOOLEAN is
   begin
      return CHARACTER(X) < CHARACTER(Y);
   end;
   ...
end LOCKSMITH;
```

The function first converts the parameters X and Y into characters and then compares them using character comparison. (Note that X < Y would not work: it would be a recursive call.)

A more general example of this problem is provided by the following schema

```
package P is
   type T is private;
   function F(X : T) return T;
private
   type T is new REP;
   -- there exists a function F operating on REP
end P;
```

In order to implement the function F on T by means of that on REP we first convert the parameter to the type REP; then convert the result back to type T.

```
package body P is
   ...
   function F(X : T) return T is
   begin
      return T(F(REP(X)));
   end;
   ...
end;
```

Without derivation, a solution can be developed using one-component records:

```
package P is
   type T is private;
   function F(X : T) return T;
private
   type T is
      record
         VALUE : REP;
      end record;
end;
```

```
package body P is
   ...
   function F(X : T) return T is
   begin
      return T'(VALUE => F(X.VALUE));
   end;
   ...
end;
```

The function F is applied to the single component of the parameter; then a one-component aggregate is returned as the function result. The drawback of this solution is its lack of symmetry. Thus, compare

    return T(F(REP(X)));

with

    return T'(VALUE => F(X.VALUE));

Instead of the succession of two conversions – to REP and then back to T – we have now the succession of component selection (X.VALUE) and of aggregate construction T'(VALUE => ...). Note that there are already cases where the language requires one-component records (for implicit initializations). For the remaining cases, however, the solution with derived types is more elegant.

7.7 ACHIEVING TRANSITIVITY OF VISIBILITY

When a derived type is declared, a new type is thereby obtained that is a *copy* of an existing parent type. The new type derives some operations from the parent type and these derived operations are implicitly declared at the point of declaration of the derived type. This ability to declare a copy of a type can be used to achieve *transitivity of visibility*. This term will be explained by the following examples. Consider a generic package

    generic
       ...
    package BASE **is**
       type T **is private**;

       function F(X : T) **return** T;
       function G(X : T) **return** T;
       ...
       function H(X : T) **return** T;
       ...
    end;

Consider now an application of this package, and let us assume that we now want to build higher-level operations on top of those of BASE. This can be achieved as follows:

```
with BASE;
package HIGHER_LEVEL is
   package NEW_BASE is new BASE(...);

   type T is new NEW_BASE.T;
   -- this derived type declaration implicitly declares:

   -- function F(X : T) return T;
   -- function G(X : T) return T;
   ...
   -- function H(X : T) return T;

   -- now we declare additional operations on T:

   procedure P(X, Y : in out T);
   ...
   procedure R(X : T);
end;
```

Consider finally a user procedure

```
with HIGHER_LEVEL; use HIGHER_LEVEL;
procedure USER is
   ...
end;
```

Within the body of USER the operations directly available on T are the functions F, G, ..., H, and the procedures P, ..., R. The functions are directly visible, without having to write

```
use NEW_BASE;
```

It is in this sense that derivation has achieved *transitivity* of visibility.

To further emphasize the point, consider a nongeneric formulation of the above problem

```
package BASE is
   ...
end;

with BASE;
package HIGHER_LEVEL is
   type T is new BASE.T;
   -- implicit declaration of F, G, ... , H

   procedure P(X, Y : in out T);
   ...
   procedure R(X : T);
end;
```

Because of the transitivity achieved by derivation, the procedure USER does not have to mention

```
with BASE; use BASE;
```

The package BASE can thus be considered as a lower-level package ignored by the user.

Note that the controlled transitivity achieved by derivation would not be obtained by subtypes. Consider for example:

```
with BASE; use BASE;
package HIGHER_LEVEL is
   subtype T is BASE.T;
   procedure P(X, Y : in out T);
   ...
   procedure R(X : T);
end;
```

The effect of the use clause "use BASE;" is not transitive. This means that its effect covers the package HIGHER_LEVEL itself but not packages that mention HIGHER_LEVEL in their context clause.

Another alternative for achieving transitivity is to use renaming as shown in the example below:

```
with BASE;
package HIGHER_LEVEL is
  package NEW_BASE is new BASE(...);
  subtype T is NEW_BASE.T;

  function F(X : T) return T renames NEW_BASE.F;
  function G(X : T) return T renames NEW_BASE.G;
  ...
  function H(X : T) return T renames NEW_BASE.H;

  procedure P(X, Y : in out T);
  ...
  procedure R(X : T);
end;
```

The main disadvantage of this alternative approach is that it involves considerable rewriting and therefore suffers from the maintenance problems that are inherent in manual copying: any change in the specification of the operations of the type T would have to be repeated in the renaming declarations. Hence the renaming alternative is not very appealing.

7.8 CHANGE OF REPRESENTATION

The design of Ada adheres to the principle of a single representation per type, with the consequence that two types must be declared if there is a need for two different representations. Again in this situation, derivation is used to produce a second type that is a logical *copy* of its parent type, the only difference between the two types being the representation. Consider for example the parent type:

```
type PARENT(D : BOOLEAN := TRUE) is
  record
    A : INTEGER;
    case D is
      when TRUE =>
        U : INTEGER;
        V : INTEGER;
      when FALSE =>
        W : REAL;
    end case
  end record;
```

From a logical point of view, derivation will produce a copy of the parent type:

```
type COPY is new PARENT;
```

This means that COPY and PARENT have the same components, including discriminants, and components that are declared in variants. Having two types, we can specify two (different) representations; for example:

```
for PARENT use
   record
      -- a sparse representation that optimizes
      -- efficiency of access to components
   end record;

for COPY use
   record
      -- a compact representation
      -- to be stored on secondary storage
   end record;
```

For change of representation we can exploit the fact that the two types are derived from each other and use explicit conversion:

```
declare
   C : COPY;
   P : PARENT;
begin
   READ_FROM_DISK(C);
   P := PARENT(C);        -- convert to PARENT form
   OPERATE_EFFICIENTLY_ON (P);
   C := COPY(P);          -- convert back to COPY form
   WRITE_TO_DISK(C);
end;
```

or simply:

```
declare
   C : COPY;
begin
   READ_FROM_DISK(C);
   OPERATE_EFFICIENTLY_ON(PARENT(C));
   WRITE_TO_DISK(C);
end;
```

Aside from derivation, there is actually no satisfactory way to achieve this change of representation. Consider for example the alternative of copying (whether manually or with text editors) the type definition of PARENT when defining the type COPY:

```
type COPY(D : BOOLEAN := TRUE) is
   record
      A : INTEGER;
      case D is
         when TRUE =>
            U : INTEGER;
            V : INTEGER;
         when FALSE =>
            W : REAL;
      end case;
   end record;
```

To achieve change of representation, we must first realize that the obvious idea – component-by-component assignment – will not work:

```
P.D := C.D;      -- Illegal!
P.A := C.A;
case C.D is
   when TRUE =>
      P.U := C.U;
      P.V := C.V;
   when FALSE =>
      P.W := C.W;
end case;
```

This is the equivalent of the code that will be generated by a compiler for the conversion for change of representation. But it cannot be written directly by the programmer since direct assignment to a discriminant is not allowed: discriminant values may only be changed by whole record assignments. Therefore, the solution to the above problem is to write:

```
case C.D is
   when TRUE =>
      P := (TRUE, C.A, C.V, C.U);
   when FALSE =>
      P := (FALSE, C.A, C.W);
end case;
```

This solution is wordy and again requires a manual copy of the record structure; it is therefore likely to create errors (such as interchanging U and V above – did you spot it?). Furthermore, it suffers from the maintenance problems that are inherent in any solution that requires text duplication. Thus if the type definition is ever extended, corresponding changes need to be performed in the above case statement. Their complexity – and hence the likelihood of error – will increase with the size of the record type definition.

Note finally that defining the type PARENT in a generic package and creating copies by generic instantiation is not a solution to our problem: All instantiations would result in types that have the same representation, and conversions between such types would not be available.

7.9 CONCLUSION – ACHIEVING COPIES IN ADA

Three main classes of entity are found in Ada programs:

(1) Objects

(2) Types

(3) Program units

The last class consists mainly of subprograms and packages. Nominally, it also includes tasks; although in certain respects tasks are closer to types and objects.

For each class of entity, the language provides a copying mechanism; that is, a mechanism by which we can create distinct replicas having similar properties:

	class of entity	*replication mechanism*
(1)	objects	object declaration
(2)	types	type derivation
(3)	program units	generic instantiation

Clearly, there are limits to this analogy since each replication mechanism is adapted to the class of entities to which it applies.

The replication mechanism offered by generic units is very powerful and can be used to replicate the contents of program units. Thus in section 7.3 it was shown that some aspects of type replication (not all, however) could be achieved by generic instantiation of a package that included the model type.

The generality of generic units certainly runs against a saying often heard in programming language design that *there should be only one way of doing a given thing.* Generic instantiation can even be used to achieve object replication, but it would be carrying matters to extremes to conclude from this that no simpler way should be provided. Consider thus

```
generic
package CREATE is
   OBJECT : INTEGER;
end;
```

and now we can replicate objects by generic instantiation:

```
package A is new CREATE;      -- creates A.OBJECT
package B is new CREATE;      -- creates B.OBJECT
...
package Z is new CREATE;      -- creates Z.OBJECT
```

But (obviously) replication of objects could be achieved in a simpler manner:

```
A : INTEGER;
B : INTEGER;
...
Z : INTEGER;
```

The awkwardness of the above example should be an indication of the limitations of the *only one way* principle. (Note also that we are in an inescapable circular situation since both ways imply an object declaration.) Generic instantiation can be used to replicate objects but it is not the most natural way. Similarly, although generic instantiation can be used to replicate types, derivation is a more natural and direct way.

To summarize this point, the design of Ada has provided replication mechanisms for each of the three main classes of entity: objects, types, and program units. Each of these mechanisms is adapted to the corresponding class of entity: it provides the *natural* way of replicating the corresponding entities. Being specialized, these mechanisms can also take advantage of specific aspects of the entities concerned. In the case of generic units these specific aspects correspond to parameterization. In the case of derived types the specific aspects correspond to the allowed explicit conversions.

Six major situations have been reviewed in which copying a type provides a natural solution for the problem considered:

- Simple strong typing

- Numeric types

- New types inheriting literals

- Construction of private types

- Transitivity of visibility

- Change of representation

The common characteristic of the above six situations is that in each of them there is a need to introduce a type that is a *copy* of another type. Without derivation, a variety of solutions and palliatives, most of them only partially satisfactory, would be required to solve these six problems. Furthermore many of these palliatives would involve manual copying and therefore raise severe issues of maintenance and configuration control. With derivation a unique – and elegant – mechanism is used to solve what is inherently a unique problem: the replication of a type.

8. Subprograms

Subprograms can be functions or procedures. The form of these program units is quite traditional, following from Algol 60. Nevertheless the design of a subprogram facility raises several issues in terms of the organization of the program text, the definition of the parameter mechanism, and the nature of functions. These issues are discussed in separate sections.

8.1 SUBPROGRAM DECLARATIONS AND SUBPROGRAM BODIES

The textual presentation of subprogram bodies is largely classical, as shown in the following example:

```
procedure PUSH(E : in ELEMENT; S : in out STACK) is
  -- local quantities could be declared here
begin
  if S.INDEX = S.SIZE then
    raise STACK_OVERFLOW;
  else
    S.INDEX := S.INDEX + 1;
    S.SPACE(S.INDEX) := E;
  end if;
end PUSH;
```

However, Ada allows the subprogram declaration to be separated from the subprogram body. For example, the subprogram declaration

```
procedure PUSH(E : in ELEMENT; S : in out STACK);
```

may appear grouped with other subprogram, variable, constant, and type declarations in a given declarative part, while its body may appear later, in the list of bodies of the declarative part.

The declaration consists of the *subprogram specification* followed by a semicolon.

The main reason for permitting such separation is readability. If the body and the specification appear together (as in Algol 60), the potentially large body is mixed with the smaller interface specification. The specification provides the information needed to call the subprogram; it may be hard for the reader to find, especially when examining a program with a large number of subprograms spread over several pages of text. In addition, an isolated variable declaration between two large subprograms is a well-known source of error in Algol 60 (the neglected variable may hide an outer variable that is in consequence never used – see 3.2).

These inconveniences are avoided in Ada. All bodies must be grouped at the end of a declarative part without any variable declaration in between them. Furthermore the user is provided with the ability to regroup subprogram declarations within a small space of text, so as to provide an immediate overview of all subprograms that are local to a given program unit. The split of the subprogram declaration from its body is merely a convenience for large subprograms; but it is a necessity for subprograms declared in the visible part of a package, and for subprograms that are mutually recursive. However, requiring a split in all cases, including small subprograms, would add only verbosity without compensating advantages. In Ada, the decision to split is therefore left to the programmer, except in the cases just mentioned where it is necessary.

Although this decision is left to the programmer, no semantic problems are involved since the information provided by the subprogram declaration is repeated in full in the subprogram body, and the two specifications must agree.

8.2 PARAMETER MODES

In a subprogram call, each formal parameter is associated with a corresponding actual parameter. Actions performed by the subprogram body on a formal parameter will result at the place of the call in actions on the associated actual parameter: Thus a formal parameter may permit reading the value of the associated actual parameter, updating this value, or both. Such reading and updating rights are specified by the *mode* of the formal parameter.

Three parameter modes are provided in Ada: they are the modes **in**, **in out**, and **out**. The properties of formal parameters of each of these modes are summarized in the table given below. The second column indicates the nature of the formal parameter: constant or variable. The third column indicates the reading and updating rights:

Mode	*Nature*	*Rights*
in	Constant	Only Reading
in out	Variable	Both Reading and Updating
out	Variable	Only Updating

This definition of parameter modes offers an abstract view of parameter passing. It can be expressed as a contract regarding the data flow between the caller and the subprogram:

Mode	Requirement
in	The caller must supply a value
in out	The caller must supply a value
	The subprogram must return a value
out	The subprogram must return a value

In principle, two different mechanisms can be used to implement this abstract view of parameter passing.

The first possibility is parameter passing *by copy*. At the start of each call, copy the value of the actual parameter into the associated formal parameter, if the mode is **in** or **in out**. Then, after normal completion of the subprogram body, copy the value of the formal parameter back into the associated actual parameter, if the mode is **in out** or **out**.

The second possibility, called parameter passing *by reference*, is to arrange that, throughout the execution of the subprogram call, each reading or updating of the formal parameter is treated as reading or updating of the associated actual parameter.

The problems associated with each of these mechanisms are reviewed first, and then the Ada solution is presented.

8.2.1 Efficiency Issues of Parameter Passing Mechanisms

Which of the two mechanisms of parameter passing (by reference or by copy) is more efficient depends on the case considered. For large objects, the by-reference mechanism is often more efficient. On the other hand, for objects that are smaller than the storage units of the target machine, copy will usually be more efficient. Furthermore copy may be the only possible mechanism between different addressing spaces in distributed systems.

The problem of reference to small objects is indeed severe and may be illustrated by the problem of reading and updating parameters that are boolean components of records. Although such components have the same type (BOOLEAN) there is no guarantee that they will always be found in the same bit position within a record.

Achieving parameter passing by reference would then require that, with each boolean formal parameter, there be an implicit subprogram (a *thunk*) for reading the value of the corresponding actual parameter; and similarly, another thunk for updating. This is somewhat complex and inefficient.

Some languages, such as Pascal, have tried to avoid the problem by forbidding the association of a formal reference parameter with an actual that is a component of a packed record or array; and by adopting otherwise a unique default representation for all small objects: one addressable storage unit per small object (even for boolean components). The problem with this solution is that, for all practical purposes, it would force programmers to use representation clauses in too many cases: the default representation chosen by the compiler would often be too costly, except on machines with small storage units. Moreover, this restriction would mean that the legality of a program would depend on the presence or absence of representation clauses or packing pragmas, which Ada avoids (see Chapter 15).

A further problem arises with parameter passing by reference with respect to the checking of constraints. To illustrate the problem consider the following declarations:

```
subtype NATURAL is INTEGER range 0 .. INTEGER'LAST; -- predefined
SUM : NATURAL := 200;
...
procedure REDUCE(AMOUNT : in out INTEGER) is
   DECREMENT : NATURAL;
begin
   -- compute DECREMENT
   ...
   AMOUNT := AMOUNT - DECREMENT; -- (1)
   if AMOUNT < 0 then
      AMOUNT := 0;
   end if;
end;
```

Now consider the procedure call statement

```
REDUCE(SUM);
```

If parameter passing were by reference, it would not be possible to complete the assignment at (1) in the case where AMOUNT became negative, since it would violate the constraint on SUM; hence the exception CONSTRAINT_ERROR would have to be raised by this statement. This, however, would require passing range constraint information as a run-time descriptor for such procedure calls, in order to allow these constraint checks within the procedure body. Alternatively, if we assume that the constraint applicable to the formal parameter is that specified by the subtype of the formal parameter, then by-reference is not possible and all parameter passing must be by copy.

8.2.2 The Effect of Parameter Passing Mechanisms for Access Types

A difficulty of a different nature arises for parameter passing by reference in the case of access types. Consider for example a procedure to delete a given element from a list (see section 6.3.6):

```
type PLACE;
type LIST is access PLACE;

type PLACE is
  record
    SUCC    : LIST;
    PRED    : LIST;
    CONTENT : ITEM;
  end record;
...

E : LIST;
procedure DELETE(L : in LIST) is
begin
  L.SUCC.PRED  := L.PRED;
  L.PRED.SUCC  := L.SUCC;
  L.SUCC       := null;
  L.PRED       := null;
end;
```

This is the conventional way of deleting an element from a doubly-linked list, and a call such as

```
DELETE(X);
```

will work regardless of whether parameter passing is achieved by reference or by copy. Consider however the procedure call

```
DELETE(E.PRED);
```

where we assume the list to be in the following state before the call:

place:	A	B	C	D	E	F
successor:	B	C	D	E	F	...
predecessor:	...	A	B	C	D	E

If parameter passing is by copy, we achieve the desired effect of deleting D (the predecessor of E) and we obtain the state

place:	A	B	C	D	E	F
successor:	B	C	E	null	F	...
predecessor:	...	A	B	null	C	E

If parameter passing is by reference, then the formal parameter L will refer to the object E.PRED. The first assignment will have the expected effect of establishing E.PRED = C. But this means that the remaining statements will operate on C (rather than D) and will not achieve what we want: the second assignment will achieve B.SUCC = D; and the last two assignments will unlink C (rather than D), leaving the list in a state of chaos:

place:	A	B	C	D	E	F
successor:	B	D	null	E	F	...
predecessor:	...	A	null	C	C	E

One possible reaction to this example is to consider that parameter passing by reference is legitimate for access types, and that we are just confronted with an incorrect program. Our preferred viewpoint is rather to consider that access types are already unique in that the programmer is permitted explicitly to manipulate references and construct aliases: This is the purpose of access types, and a programmer using such types is asserting that he wishes to take control of all references and aliases. Accordingly, the parameter passing should not generate extra references and aliases of which the programmer is unaware; therefore, all parameter passing for access types should be by copy.

A final problem with parameter passing by reference is that this mechanism will be almost impossible to achieve (or at least, very costly) on distributed systems and whenever we deal with systems with multiple address spaces.

8.2.3 The Effect of Parameter Passing Mechanisms for Composite Types

In *normal* situations the effect of a program does not depend on whether parameter passing for array and record types is by reference or by copy. The only situations where there might be a difference in effect correspond to:

- Certain cases in which the execution of a subprogram is abandoned as a result of an exception.

- Certain cases in which there are multiple access paths to a given variable.

These situations are reviewed below. The subject of multiple access paths is further subdivided into a discussion of *aliasing* in sequential programs, and a discussion of *shared variables* in parallel programs.

Exceptions

If the execution of a subprogram is abandoned as the result of an exception not handled locally, then the final value of an actual parameter that is associated with a formal parameter of mode in out may depend on the parameter passing mechanism: If by copy, the final value will still be the initial value before the call. If by reference, the final value may be this initial value, or any value assigned to the formal parameter during the execution of the subprogram (before the exception was raised). In either case, the final value is guaranteed to have the subtype of the actual parameter.

At the cost of more elaborate run-time treatment of exceptions, it would certainly be possible to copy back current values in the case of termination by an exception. But this complication is not worth the effort. Consider for example:

```
procedure P(X : in out COMPOSITE_TYPE) is
begin
   ...            -- (1)
   X := ... ;
   ...            -- (2)
end ;
   ...
P(A);
```

If the execution of P is abandoned as a result of an exception, then the caller may obtain information about the nature of the exception by means of appropriate handlers:

```
begin
   P(A);
exception
   when ERROR =>
      -- the exception raised was ERROR
   when CONSTRAINT_ERROR =>
      -- the exception raised was CONSTRAINT_ERROR
   when others =>
      -- the exception raised is other than the above two
end;
```

On the other hand, the caller does not usually know whether the exception was raised during (1) or (2) or even during the assignment to the formal parameter X. Consequently the difference resulting from choosing a reference rather than a copy mechanism is of the same order as the uncertainty that already exists about the exact point where the exception is raised. In addition, when a user writes P(A) where the parameter mode is **in out** (and even more so if the mode is **out**), then he expects the value of A to be changed. So it does not matter much if this value is changed during the call or only at the end. If the user wants to reuse the previous value of A in the case that P is terminated by an exception, the only logical way to do so is to assign its value to another variable before the call.

Note finally that if it is important to guarantee that the initial value is not modified if an exception is raised, then this is best achieved by the procedure body itself. One possibility is to compute first whatever needs to be changed but perform the change itself only at the end of the procedure, so that no change occurs if an exception is raised before the end. Another possible style involves the use of exception handlers for expressing last wishes:

```
procedure P(X : in out COMPOSITE_TYPE) is
begin
   ...
exception
   when others =>
      -- restore initial value of X
      raise;
end;
```

Aliasing

If aliasing is used then the results may differ between reference implementations and copy implementations. For example consider

```
A : STRING(1 .. 8)  := "AAAAVVVV";
B : STRING(1 .. 12) := "111122223333";

procedure MODIFY(S : in out STRING) is
begin
   if S'LENGTH >= 8 then
      S(S'FIRST .. S'FIRST + 3) := "-**-";
      S(S'FIRST + 4 .. S'FIRST + 7) := A(1 .. 4);
   end if;
end;
...
MODIFY(B);     -- leaves B = "-**-AAAA3333"
MODIFY(A);
```

The call of MODIFY for the string B will deliver the expected result. Consider however what happens when A is passed as actual parameter. Since A is referred to directly within the body of MODIFY, we now have two possible access paths to A, the second being via the formal parameter S. In this case of aliasing the effect of the procedure will depend on the mechanism used for parameter passing: the final value of A will be "-**-AAAA" by value, and "-**--**-" by reference.

The same trick could actually be used (facetiously) to discover which mechanism is used for parameter passing:

```
MODE : STRING(1 .. 4) := "COPY";
procedure FIND_MECHANISM(S : in out STRING) is
begin
   MODE := "REF ";
   if S = "COPY" then
      PUT("MECHANISM IS COPY");
   else
      PUT("MECHANISM IS REFERENCE");
   end if;
end;
...
FIND_MECHANISM(MODE);
```

although an implementation is in fact free to use different mechanisms for different calls.

In both examples, the effect obtained by reference is somewhat pathological: In the first example, normally we would like the first assignment to S not to affect A and the subsequent assignment to S. So whereas for efficiency reasons we might prefer an implementation by reference, the copy mechanism provides us with a simpler model for understanding programs and therefore for developing reliable programs.

Whereas aliasing between a formal parameter and a global variable may reasonably be assumed to be unintentional, aliasing is not necessarily undesirable. In particular, aliasing between formal parameters may in many cases be deliberate. Consider for example a procedure for vector addition

```
procedure ADD(A : in out VECTOR; B : in VECTOR) is
begin
   if A'FIRST = B'FIRST and A'LAST = B'LAST then
      for N in A'RANGE loop
         A(N) := A(N) + B(N);
      end loop;
   end if;
end;
...
V : VECTOR(1 .. 100) := ...;
```

Then for a call such as

```
ADD(V, V);
```

although we have a case of aliasing between formal parameters within the body of ADD, since both A and B refer to V, the effect of the procedure does not depend on whether reference or copy is used for the implementation of parameter passing.

To conclude the discussion on this subject it appears that for certain cases of aliasing, different effects will be obtained for parameter passing by reference and by copy. These cases, however, represent poor programming practice, and do not provide a sound basis for deciding language semantics.

Shared Variables

The language rules state that the execution of a program is *erroneous* if a shared variable that is updated by a given task between two synchronization points is also read or updated by another task between these two synchronization points (hence asynchronously). The effect of such erroneous execution is unpredictable. This indeterminacy will be further revealed by differences in the parameter passing mechanism. Consider for example

```
SHARED : COMPOSITE_TYPE; -- a shared variable
...
procedure LIST(X : in COMPOSITE_TYPE);
...
LIST(SHARED);
```

The code of the procedure LIST will rely on the fact that the formal parameter is constant: in particular this means that reading a component of the formal parameter at different times and places within this procedure must always yield the same value. This is obviously achieved (whether the actual parameter is a shared variable or not) if parameter passing is by copy. If however parameter passing is by reference, and the actual parameter is a shared variable asynchronously updated by another task, then this invariability is no longer guaranteed.

Here again, the indeterminacy is inherent in the asynchronous access to the shared variable: it is further revealed by differences in parameter passing mechanism, but these differences are not the primary cause.

8.2.4 The Ada Solution for Parameter Passing

Before describing the parameter passing mechanisms, consider first the interpretation of the subtype that is declared for a formal parameter.

- In the case of a scalar type, the constraint applicable to the formal parameter is always that imposed by the subtype of the formal parameter.

- In the case of an array or record type, the constraint on the formal parameter is inherited from the corresponding actual parameter (if the declaration of the formal specifies a constraint, then the actual constraint must be the same).

In implementation terms, the above subdivision reflects the fact that run-time descriptors for constraints are never passed to subprograms in the case of scalar types (see the example AMOUNT in section 8.2.1). On the other hand the constraint information is always passed in the case of composite types:

- For arrays, the bounds are passed and can be interrogated within subprograms by means of array attributes.

- For records with discriminants, the discriminants are part of the value. Furthermore, the value of the CONSTRAINED attribute is passed.

The allowed mechanisms follow from the above considerations.

(a) For scalar types, and for all modes, all parameter passing must be achieved by copy. The same treatment applies to access types, for the reasons given in the previous section.

(b) For record and array types, the language does not specify whether parameter passing is achieved by reference or by copy. Furthermore, the execution of a program is *erroneous* if its effect depends on which mechanism is selected by the implementation.

In *normal* situations the semantics of a program will not be affected by whether parameter passing for composite types is implemented by reference or by copying: We have seen that the indeterminacy resulting from the parameter passing mechanism only matters where there is already a higher degree of indeterminacy (shared variables and exceptions) and where aliasing is used to achieve dubious effects: In both cases the language rules therefore state that the execution of the program is erroneous.

For private types parameter passing is as for the type declared by the corresponding full type declaration. Finally for task types the mechanism never matters, since a task object always designates the same task.

During this design we considered, and rejected, several alternatives to this abstract formulation of the parameter passing modes. For example, an implementation-oriented formulation of modes could be defined in terms of the mechanisms involved: copy or reference. However, if the same capabilities are to be offered this leads to yet more modes (constant by copy, constant by reference, variable by copy before and after, variable by reference, result by copy, result by reference). Although only a subset of them might be provided, it is critical for reliability and efficiency to be able to pass an array by reference and nevertheless deny the right to modify its components. Apart from its complexity, such a formulation would force the programmer to think in terms of (and be aware of) the representation of objects, and would therefore compromise portability.

We consider the formulation of the parameter passing modes **in, in out**, and **out** in terms of their abstract behavior to be much simpler and therefore preferable.

8.3 PARAMETER PASSING NOTATIONS

Two notations for parameter passing need to be considered. The usual positional notation is almost universal. However, with more than three or four parameters it is hard to follow the text. Following the Lis language, and common usage in many control languages, Ada permits an alternative notation of parameter passing in which the associations are specified on a name basis (see also [Fr 77] and [Har 76]). Placing the formal parameter on the left and the corresponding actual parameter on the right of a parameter association provides more readable procedure calls. For example:

```
CREATE(FILE => MY_FILE, NAME => "FINALTEXT.FEB.15");
```

Where long parameter lists are common and have default values, as in the job control area, this form of named parameter association provides especially high readability. It may be used in conjunction with the default value facility available for an **in** parameter if no explicit value is provided within the call. For example, a simulation package may declare the procedure ACTIVATE as follows:

```
procedure ACTIVATE (PROCESS : in PROCESS_NAME;
                    AFTER   : in PROCESS_NAME := NO_PROCESS;
                    WAIT    : in DURATION     := 0.0;
                    PRIOR   : in BOOLEAN      := FALSE);
```

As shown in this declaration, the parameter PROCESS must be provided in all calls (because no default expression is given). On the other hand the parameters AFTER, WAIT and PRIOR may be omitted. Thus the two following calls of ACTIVATE are equivalent:

```
ACTIVATE(PROCESS => X, AFTER => NO_PROCESS,
                       WAIT => 0.0, PRIOR => FALSE);
ACTIVATE(PROCESS => X);
```

Clearly in many contexts the order of parameters is either highly conventional (as for coordinate systems) or immaterial (as in MAX(X,Y)). Hence Ada admits both conventions. The classical positional notation may be used whenever the programmer feels that named parameters would add verbosity without any gain in readability.

The two notations may also be combined, with positional parameters appearing first; that is, once naming is used the rest of the call must use naming. This allows the default value mechanism to be used even when positional notation is desirable, as in the following examples from graph plotting and simulation:

```
MOVE_PEN(X1, Y1, LINE => THICK);
MOVE_PEN(X2, Y2, PEN => UP);


ACTIVATE(X);
ACTIVATE(X, AFTER => Y);
ACTIVATE(X, WAIT => 50*SECONDS, PRIOR => TRUE);
```

As shown in this last example, the named notation may be used in conjunction with the default parameters to provide a high degree of expressivity and readability. For the activate primitive in Simula, this could only be achieved at the expense of predefined syntax.

Finally the default parameter facility can be used in conjunction with overloading, thereby allowing further possibilities. These are illustrated by the declarations of PUT in the generic package INTEGER_IO:

```
procedure PUT (FILE  : in FILE_TYPE;
               ITEM  : in NUM;
               WIDTH : in FIELD       := DEFAULT_WIDTH;
               BASE  : in NUMBER_BASE := DEFAULT_BASE);

procedure PUT (ITEM  : in NUM;
               WIDTH : in FIELD       := DEFAULT_WIDTH;
               BASE  : in NUMBER_BASE := DEFAULT_BASE);
```

Given the declarations

```
F : FILE;
N : NUM;
```

we can issue the following procedure calls for output on the file F:

```
PUT(F, N, 10, 8);                       -- width 10, octal base
PUT(F, N, WIDTH => 10, BASE => 8);      -- more explicitly
PUT(F, N);                              -- default width, decimal base
```

We can also issue similar calls for output on the current default output file:

```
PUT(N, 10, 8);
PUT(N, WIDTH => 10, BASE => 8);
PUT(N);
```

Overloading and default parameters are complementary: In theory, we could achieve the desired flexibility of procedure calls by means of overloading, but this would require a procedure declaration for each possible form of call (eight instead of two in the above example). On the other hand default parameters provide a concise – and thereby convenient – formulation. But – as the above example shows – if we want to omit the first parameter without using named associations, this will have to be achieved by overloading.

The example of the two PUT procedures further illustrates that the default expressions need not be static: DEFAULT_WIDTH and DEFAULT_BASE are variables. Another example of the dynamic computation of default expressions is provided by the following procedure ADMISSION: Admission requires a key, a new one being allocated by default in the absence of an explicit one:

```
procedure ADMISSION(K : in KEY_NAME := new KEY);
```

8.4 FUNCTION SUBPROGRAMS

The purpose of a function is to calculate a value. This is the conventional mathematical meaning of a function. Small functions to access complex data structures are an essential feature of structured programming: Not only do they hide irrelevant parts of the data structure but they provide a cleaner interface to the outside world.

Although the mathematical origin of the function concept is clear, its incorporation into a programming language can lead to several different formulations depending on what operations are allowed on variables. Different levels of restriction can be considered, leading to different concepts of function:

(1) Reading global variables is not allowed.

(2) Reading global variables is allowed but updating them is not.

(3) Reading and updating global variables is allowed.

The first level corresponds to the mathematical notion of function; there are no implicit parameters in the guise of global variables, and two function calls with the same arguments always deliver the same result. However the class of cases in which such functions can be used is rather limited.

The second level has interesting mathematical properties that can be used for code optimization. For example, if F is such a function then for evaluation of an expression such as

```
F + F
```

the function need only be called once. However this kind of function would not be allowed to perform input-output (since this is a side-effect), and instrumentation (by update of a global counter upon each call) would not be possible.

The third level allows functions such as random number generators or *memo functions*, which modify the global environment. Such functions do not have the aforementioned properties. If for example RANDOM is such a function, then 2*RANDOM is not necessarily equal to RANDOM + RANDOM.

In an earlier version of Ada – the Green language – we attempted to provide a formulation of functions that corresponds to the second level, but experimenting with this concept has shown that this would exclude many *benevolent* side-effects. For example, it led to the imposition of limitations on access variables (since the invocation of an allocator is a kind of side-effect). Furthermore, checking for functionality could require reconsideration of the text of separately compiled compilation units.

These conceptual and implementation difficulties led to the present more pragmatic definition, which corresponds to the third level.

The only limitation imposed in Ada on functions is that the mode of all parameters must be in: it would not be logical to allow **in out** or **out** parameters for functions in a language that excludes nested assignments within an expression.

This means that optimization of expressions such as F + F will be achieved only when the compiler can conclude that there are no side-effects that matter.

For multiple calls of functions within an expression, Ada follows an approach of **collaterality** as described in section 3.8. This means that the language does not define in which order to call F, G, and H in an expression such as

```
F + G + H
```

The language rules state that this evaluation must be done in some order – that is, not in parallel – but this order is not defined by the language, so that the meaning of a program for which this order matters is not defined.

This semantics reflects a pragmatic view of side-effects, once expressed by Brian Higman [Hi 63]:

The plain fact of the matter is (1) that side-effects are sometimes necessary, and (2) programmers who are irresponsible enough to introduce side-effects unnecessarily will soon lose the confidence of their colleagues, and rightly so.

9. Packages

9.1 MOTIVATION

Packages allow the programmer to define groups of logically related items. They cover a wide variety of uses, ranging from collections of common declarations to groups of subprograms and encapsulated data types.

The ability to package declared entities – such as variables, types, subprograms, and even other packages – provides the basis for a powerful structuring tool for complex programs. Moreover, a package permits clear separation between information that is usable by the rest of the program, and other information that must remain purely internal to the package. The internal information is hidden, and thereby protected from deliberate or inadvertent use by other programmers. This serves not only to localize the effect of internal errors to the package itself, but also to make it easier to replace one implementation of (the services offered by) a package by another. Packages are thus an essential tool for program modularity, supporting program verification and information hiding as advocated by Parnas [Pa 71].

Facilities for modularization have appeared in many languages. Some of them – such as Simula, Clu, and Alphard – provide dynamic facilities which may entail large run-time overhead. The facility provided in Ada is more static – in the spirit of previous solutions offered in Lis, Euclid, Mesa, and Modula. At the same time it retains the best aspects of solutions in earlier languages such as Fortran and Jovial.

We shall first discuss packages informally by means of examples, and then go on to discuss a number of important technical issues addressed during the design of Ada.

9.2 INFORMAL INTRODUCTION TO PACKAGES

We recognize three general kinds of modularization that can be achieved by different forms of package:

(1) *Named collections of entities:*

Logically related constants, variables, and types, that are to be used in other program units.

(2) *Groups of related subprograms:*

Logically related functions and procedures that share internal data, types, and subprograms. This form of package corresponds to what is commonly called a *software package*. By extension, the same term is used in Ada for all three forms.

(3) *Encapsulated data types – Private types:*

Definition of new types and associated operations in such a way that the user does not know (and need not care) how the operations are implemented.

The essential difference between these three forms is in the amount of information hiding that is provided. The package can be viewed as a *wall* surrounding the enclosed declarations, thereby separating them from the rest of the program. One may then imagine a *window* in the wall, through which (depending on its size) some or all of the declarations are exposed. For the three kinds of package we have:

(1) *Named collections of entities:*

The package exposes all of its declarations (all declarations can be seen through the window).

(2) *Groups of related subprograms:*

The package exposes the declarations of the externally usable subprograms (only these can be seen through the window) but hides their implementations and the declarations of the shared internal entities.

(3) *Encapsulated Data Types – Private types:*

The package exposes the type name and the declarations of applicable operations but hides all details of structure, representation, and implementation of the operations. Several related types may be encapsulated in the same package.

There is no critical linguistic difference between these three forms, and intermediate degrees of hiding exist. However, to present the ideas simply, we shall discuss the three forms separately with appropriate examples.

9.2.1 Named Collections of Entities

The most traditional use of named collections of entities is for variables that serve as communication areas accessed by several program units. As an example, in a simple graphics application, the following package declaration may be provided:

```
package PLOTTING_DATA is
    PEN_UP : BOOLEAN := TRUE;

    CONVERSION_FACTOR,
    X_OFFSET, Y_OFFSET,
    X_MIN,    X_MAX,
    Y_MIN,    Y_MAX    : REAL;

    X_VALUE : array(1 .. 500) of REAL;
    Y_VALUE : array(1 .. 500) of REAL;
end PLOTTING_DATA;
```

The elaboration of this package consists of the elaboration of its constituent variable declarations. Elaboration takes place in the context where the package declaration appears textually. Thus, in terms of the lifetime of the constituent variables such as PEN_UP and Y_VALUE, everything happens as if their declarations were inserted in the place of the declaration of the package PLOTTING_DATA.

The constituent variables are not, however, automatically visible outside the package: steps must be taken to render them visible. In any context where the package is itself visible, it is possible to acquire visibility (by selection) of such a variable by an expanded name, written with the *dot notation*. For example, we could write statements such as

```
PLOTTING_DATA.PEN_UP := TRUE;
PLOTTING_DATA.X_VALUE(10) := PLOTTING_DATA.X_MIN;
```

In the expanded name PLOTTING_DATA.PEN_UP, the variable PEN_UP is visible by selection after the dot following PLOTTING_DATA: in this sense the dot notation opens up the visibility of one variable at a time. It is also possible to acquire direct visibility of all these variables at once by means of a *use clause* such as

```
use PLOTTING_DATA;
```

The effect of the use clause is that all variables declared within the package become directly visible (unless they would conflict with other names already visible). The simple name, and the meaning, of each variable is then as defined in the package. For example, the previous statements can be rewritten more concisely as follows:

```
declare
   use PLOTTING_DATA;
begin
   PEN_UP := TRUE;
   X_VALUE(10) := X_MIN;
end;
```

This simple form of package corresponds closely to the notion of a *named common* block in Fortran. There are however three crucial differences between this use of packages and Fortran named common blocks:

(1) A package can be declared in any nested block or program unit (and will of course be written at a place from which it is visible by all program units that need to use the encapsulated declarations). By contrast, in Fortran all named common blocks are effectively global to the main program.

(2) Storage reservation for a package (and hence the start of the lifetime of constituent variables) need not happen before the elaboration of the package declaration. Thus, for a package that is local to a procedure, this storage reservation may be performed when the procedure is called. By contrast, the storage space for a Fortran named common block is normally reserved throughout the entire program execution.

(3) The entities declared in a package are defined only once: in the context of the package declaration. Within the scope of the declaration, it is then possible to acquire visibility of that entire set of entities, in as many program units as necessary, merely by mentioning the name of the package in a use clause (even in the case of separately compiled units). For Fortran named common blocks, on the other hand, the specification must be replicated in its entirety in each subroutine that needs to use one of the common declarations. The need to replicate information in this fashion is generally recognized as a violation of the principles of modularity, as an inconvenience, and as a potential source of serious error.

A similar use of named collections of entities is for groups of constants. For example:

```
package METRIC_CONVERSIONS is
   CM_PER_INCH : constant := 2.54;
   CM_PER_FOOT : constant := 12*CM_PER_INCH;
   CM_PER_YARD : constant := 3*CM_PER_FOOT;
   KM_PER_MILE : constant := 1.609_344;
end METRIC_CONVERSIONS;
```

More generally, in a typed language, groups of entities are likely to include logically related types, along with constants and variables, as shown in the following example:

```
package WORK_DATA is
    type DAY is (MON, TUE, WED, THU, FRI, SAT, SUN);
    type HOURS_SPENT is delta 0.25 range 0.0 .. 24.0;
    type TIME_TABLE is array (DAY) of HOURS_SPENT;

    WORK_HOURS : TIME_TABLE;
    NORMAL_HOURS : constant TIME_TABLE :=
            (MON .. THU => 8.25, FRI => 7.0, SAT|SUN => 0.0);
end WORK_DATA;
```

In all three examples we achieve the same effect: the elaboration of the package *creates* the corresponding entities (whether they be constants, variables, or types). But these entities are not automatically externally visible: external visibility is obtained only by an expanded name (dot notation) or by a use clause. Thus in a context that has a use clause for WORK_DATA we may declare variables of type HOURS_SPENT, update the array WORK_HOURS, and read the constant NORMAL_HOURS.

```
declare
    use WORK_DATA;

    TODAY : DAY;
    HOURS : HOURS_SPENT;
begin
    -- compute HOURS and TODAY
    ...
    if HOURS > NORMAL_HOURS (TODAY) then
        HOURS := 2*HOURS - NORMAL_HOURS(TODAY);
    end if;
    WORK_HOURS (TODAY) := HOURS;
end;
```

9.2.2 Groups of Related Subprograms

The second major use of packages is for the creation of named groups of related subprograms. For example, we may want to have a package of mathematical functions (such as SIN, COS, LOG, and EXP) for the reason that a user needing one of them is very likely to need the others too. Moreover, the functions may share common subprograms that should not be directly accessible to the user.

Declaring such functions within a package (say MATH_FUNCTIONS) is certainly preferable to having them be predefined functions in the standard environment. Thereby, a user who is not dealing with numerical computations does not have to refer to MATH_FUNCTIONS, and his *name space* – the set of names that must be remembered

– will not be congested by names that are useless to him or restricted by names that he might wish to use differently.

We next consider a package for table management – an example that will enable us to point out other important possibilities. It is made of two parts: The first part is the package specification and its structure is as follows:

```
package TABLE_MANAGER is
   -- the visible part
end TABLE_MANAGER;
```

The package specification defines the visible part of the package; that is, the declarations that become directly visible in a context that has a use clause for TABLE_MANAGER. In the present case, this user interface consists of the declaration of the type ITEM and of the three procedures INSERT (to insert an item into the table), RETRIEVE (to retrieve the first item from the table), and DISPLAY (to display the current contents of the table), as shown below:

```
package TABLE_MANAGER is
   type ITEM is
      record
         -- the components of each item
      end record;

   procedure INSERT    (NEW_ITEM   : in   ITEM);
   procedure RETRIEVE (FIRST_ITEM : out ITEM);
   procedure DISPLAY;
end TABLE_MANAGER;
```

The second part of the package is the package body. This encloses the hidden part of the package: none of the entities contained therein is visible outside the package (the only entities that can be made visible by expanded names or by use clauses are those of the visible part). The structure of the package body is as follows:

```
package body TABLE_MANAGER is
   -- hidden data and subprogram bodies
begin
   -- statements for initialization
end TABLE_MANAGER;
```

In the formulation of this package body given below, each item is put in a cell: hence we have the declaration of a local type called CELL. The table itself is a local variable, called TABLE and declared as an array of cells. The fact that this declaration is local to the package body ensures that reading and updating of the table is possible only from within this body. The table is initialized by the statements at the end of the package body, and its value can be read and updated by the subprogram bodies that appear within the package body. Finally the package body contains the bodies of the procedures INSERT, RETRIEVE, and DISPLAY, as well as two local functions.

```
package body TABLE_MANAGER is

    type CELL is ... ;                        -- a local type
    subtype INDEX is ... ;                    -- a local subtype
    TABLE : array (INDEX) of CELL;            -- a local variable

    function NEXT return INDEX is             -- a local function
    begin
      -- computes the index to the next cell
    end;

    function STORE(N : ITEM) return CELL is   -- a local function
    begin
      -- returns a cell containing N
    end;

    procedure INSERT(NEW_ITEM : in ITEM) is
    begin
      TABLE(NEXT) := STORE(NEW_ITEM);
    end;

    procedure RETRIEVE(FIRST_ITEM : out ITEM) is
      ...
    end;

    procedure DISPLAY is
      ...
    end;
begin
    -- statements for the initialization of TABLE
end TABLE_MANAGER;
```

The two parts of a package (the package specification and the package body) are always distinct. They need not even be textually contiguous, and may indeed be compiled separately. In this way the contents of a package body are not only hidden *logically*, but can also be hidden *physically* (as discussed in section 9.3.3 below).

Another example of a package containing a type declaration and functions defining operations for this type is a variation of the package RATIONAL_NUMBERS given in the Reference Manual (section 7.3). The specification of this package is as follows:

```
package RATIONAL_NUMBERS is
   type RATIONAL is
      record
         NUMERATOR   : INTEGER;
         DENOMINATOR : POSITIVE;
      end record;

   function EQUAL(X, Y : RATIONAL) return BOOLEAN;

   function "/" (X : INTEGER; Y : POSITIVE) return RATIONAL;
      -- to construct a rational number

   function "+" (X, Y : RATIONAL) return RATIONAL;
   function "-" (X, Y : RATIONAL) return RATIONAL;
   function "*" (X, Y : RATIONAL) return RATIONAL;
   function "/" (X, Y : RATIONAL) return RATIONAL;
   ...
end;
```

The type RATIONAL is declared within the visible part of the package. In a context that contains a use clause for RATIONAL_NUMBERS it is possible to declare variables of type RATIONAL and to apply the operators "+", "-", "*", "/", and the function EQUAL to them. The operator "/" with integer arguments allows rational values to be written in the conventional form. For example:

```
declare
   use RATIONAL_NUMBERS;
   A : RATIONAL := 3/31;
   B : RATIONAL := 7/100;
   C : RATIONAL;
begin
   ...
   C := A*B;
   C := C + 5/17;
   ...
end;
```

Consider for example the initialization of A with 3/31. The "/" operation must be applicable to integer literals and yield a value of type RATIONAL. The only one to do so is the construction declared in the visible part with two parameters, one of type INTEGER and one of type POSITIVE. Hence the integer literals 3 and 31 are implicitly converted to the respective type and the construction is applied. The body of this function will be provided in the package body. For example, it could be written in the following way, which involves no arithmetic and is exact:

```
function "/" (X : INTEGER; Y : POSITIVE) return RATIONAL is
begin
   return RATIONAL'(NUMERATOR   => X;
                    DENOMINATOR => Y);
end "/";
```

Note also that a user could also write a rational value directly, as an aggregate:

```
C := C + RATIONAL'(NUMERATOR => 5, DENOMINATOR => 15);
```

Hence, with this formulation, it remains possible to operate directly on the components of a rational number and to construct rational values as record aggregates. This could be considered a weakness of the formulation. For instance, the algorithms used for all the operations on rational numbers may maintain them in a canonical form (where no further reduction is possible); but users could create noncanonical rationals by operating directly on the record components. The third form of package, presented in the next section, deals with such issues.

9.2.3 Private Types

In the previous examples of packages, we have ensured, by declaring them within the package body, that entities properly local to a package could not be affected by any outside program unit; entities were either public (if declared in the visible part) or totally hidden (if declared in the package body).

Private types cater for situations in which we want the name of a type to be public, but the knowledge of the internal properties to be available only to the subprogram bodies contained in the package body. This encapsulation is achieved by declaring the type name (alone) within the visible part – since the type name is to be available to users of the package – but at the same time specifying the type to be *private*; the full definition of the type (showing its structure) is then provided following the visible part.

As an example of the use of private types, consider the following skeleton of the declaration of an input-output package:

```
package SIMPLE_IO is
  type FILE_NAME is private;

  NO_FILE : constant FILE_NAME;

    procedure CREATE (FILE : out  FILE_NAME; NAME : in STRING);
    procedure READ   (ITEM : out  INTEGER;   FILE : in FILE_NAME);
    procedure WRITE  (ITEM : in   INTEGER;   FILE : in FILE_NAME);
private
  type FILE_NAME is new INTEGER range 0 .. 50;
  NO_FILE : constant FILE_NAME := 0;
end SIMPLE_IO;
```

In the visible part given above, the type FILE_NAME is declared as private. External to the package it is possible to declare variables of the type FILE_NAME, but the properties of objects of this type are kept private. Hence the only things a user can do with file names is assign them to other file-name variables, compare them for equality, obtain them by calling the procedure CREATE, or pass them as parameters to the procedures READ and WRITE.

The full definition of the private type FILE_NAME and that of the *deferred constant* NO_FILE are given in the private part (the declarations at the end of the package, between the reserved words **private** and **end**). A package body for the above package is sketched below:

```
package body SIMPLE_IO is
  type FILE_DESCRIPTOR is
    record
      ...
    end record;
  DIRECTORY : array (FILE_NAME) of FILE_DESCRIPTOR;
  ...
  procedure CREATE (FILE : out FILE_NAME; NAME : in STRING) is
    ...
  end;
  procedure READ (ITEM : out INTEGER; FILE : in FILE_NAME) is
    ...
  end ;
  procedure WRITE (ITEM : in INTEGER; FILE : in FILE_NAME) is
    ...
  end;
begin
    -- initialization of DIRECTORY and other local objects
end SIMPLE_IO;
```

Within the body, file names are integers indexing an internal directory which is declared as an array. However, an external user of the package cannot use this internal information: for example, an external user cannot perform arithmetic on file names, since the arithmetic operators for the type FILE_NAME can be used only inside the package.

With the above definition of the type FILE_NAME, it remains possible for users to assign file names, and also to compare file names for equality and inequality. For the following variation of the previous package, even these operations are denied:

```
package SAFE_IO is
   type FILE_NAME is limited private;

   procedure CREATE (FILE : in out FILE_NAME; NAME : in STRING);
   procedure CLOSE  (FILE : in out FILE_NAME);

   procedure READ  (ITEM : out INTEGER; FILE : in FILE_NAME);
   procedure WRITE (ITEM : in  INTEGER; FILE : in FILE_NAME);
   FILE_ERROR : exception;
private
   type FILE_INDEX is range 0 .. 50;
   NOT_CREATED : constant FILE_INDEX := 0;
   type FILE_NAME is
      record
         INDEX : FILE_INDEX := NOT_CREATED;      -- default value
      end record;
end SAFE_IO;
```

Even the operations of assignment and equality comparison are not available for a *limited private* type. Therefore, the user of package SAFE_IO can only:

- Declare variables of type FILE_NAME.

- Pass these variables as actual parameters to the operations defined by the package SAFE_IO – the procedures CREATE, CLOSE, READ, and WRITE.

The user can of course define other procedures that operate on objects of type FILE_NAME, provided the above restrictions are observed. For example, it is possible to write the following procedure

```
procedure TRANSFER_ITEM(SOURCE, DESTINATION : in FILE_NAME) is
   ITEM : INTEGER;
begin
   READ  (ITEM, SOURCE);
   WRITE (ITEM, DESTINATION);
end;
```

Since neither assignment nor comparison of file names is possible, defining a constant NO_FILE would not be very useful in this formulation. The only safe way to ensure that files are always initialized is to provide a default value, as we have done in the full declaration of FILE_NAME. This allows the package body to control the consistency of all operations: CREATE can check that the file has not already been created; READ and WRITE can check that the file has been created; and CLOSE can reset the internal value to NOT_CREATED. The exception FILE_ERROR can be raised by the body if any of these checks fails. Note that in this variation of the package, the file parameter mode for CREATE has been changed to **in out**, in order to allow this procedure to check whether the file has already been created, and to avoid overwriting an existing file name.

The prohibition of assignment, in this formulation, is quite essential if we want the package body to be in full control of active files. Let us assume, for example, that the package body maintains a count of active files as the difference between the number of (correct) calls of CREATE and the number of (correct) calls of CLOSE. If assignment were allowed, it would be possible to call CLOSE twice for the same file value (having copied this value into another variable), and this count would then not be reliable.

For the more classical examples of encapsulated data types (from the current literature), the reader is referred to chapter 12 of this document (a generic definition of the type queue) and to section 12.4 of the Reference Manual (a generic definition of the type stack).

9.3 TECHNICAL ISSUES

The design of packages involves nearly all aspects of the language. The most significant in this context are

- Visibility control and information hiding

- Relation to separate compilation

- Initialization of packages

- Availability of the properties of types defined within packages

- Initialization of objects of private types.

- Private types with discriminants

Other aspects will be discussed in the chapters on program structure and visibility, tasking, separate compilation, and generic units.

9.3.1 Visibility Control and Information Hiding

The visibility rules of Algol 60, as embodied in its so-called block structure, are quite natural for programs of moderate size and have been adopted by most subsequent languages, including Ada: any declaration is visible throughout the block for which it is given, including nested inner blocks, unless hidden by declarations local to those blocks. However this simple structure is insufficient for the reliable construction of large programs since more precise control over the visibility of declarations is then needed. For example, with the above rule, a variable that is used by several subprograms must be declared outside their bodies, although it has no relevance to other parts of the program. This variable will then be visible to all users of these subprograms, and unprotected from accidental or malicious access.

Packages give the programmer precisely the kind of control needed. The details of the visibility rules are discussed in chapter 11 on program structure; in this chapter we concentrate on characteristics that are essential for visibility control and information hiding.

In the definition of a package, the visible part states which declarations are potentially visible outside the package. (This identifies the *window* in the above-mentioned *wall*.) It is possible for other program units to see whatever is in the visible part; but they do not see it automatically. Within these program units, this visibility is achieved either by use clauses or by expanded names written in the form known as dot notation.

Thus visibility of the identifiers declared in the visible part is controlled by the user. Names declared in the visible part of a package do not spontaneously invade (and *pollute*) the name space of the rest of the program. Visibility of the identifiers declared in the package body is even more tightly controlled: they are visible only within the package body – in particular, within the body of any subprogram declared in the visible part.

The other essential characteristic of packages in Ada is the textual separation of the interface – those declarations that are relevant to users of the package – from the implementation. In an Ada package, these declarations are textually separated from the rest of the text: they form what is called the visible part of the package. This textual separation is a significant advantage for readability and for information hiding.

Other languages such as Euclid and Modula have used a formulation based on an *export list* that mentions all identifiers that constitute the interface. This means that in order to know the properties of these identifiers, the human reader must scan through the entire text of the module to find the declarations of entities listed in the export list. This is a tedious operation and is, as we shall see, a breach of *information hiding* principles, since it involves reading parts of the text that should be of no concern (and should not even be available) to the user.

There are good reasons for hiding the text of a package body from its users. An obvious one is confidentiality: a software producer supplying the services of a given package may want to protect his investment by not showing the package implementation (at least, not in source form). Another reason to hide the text of a package body from its users is to establish the normal producer-consumer contractual relationship that exists for other commercial products. It is the package specification that should be considered as the *contract* between the producer and the users. The included procedure specifications already form a (minimal) syntactic contract, but these may be supplemented by some explanation of their intended effect. In the present state of the art such explanation must perforce take the form of comments. In the future, however, it could consist of statements of some more formal specification language such as Anna [KBL 80].

Letting a user read the implementation would create the danger that he might derive some additional implicit assumptions from an analysis of the current implementation: assumptions that are not explicit in the contract. The producer of a package is bound only by the contract, and is therefore free to deliver later releases of the package that might not satisfy any such implicit assumptions of the user.

The textual separation between the package specification and the package implementation provides an easy solution to this problem. The user will be provided with the source text of the package specification, and no more.

9.3.2 Guaranteeing Software Components

In an industry of software components, users are likely to request some guarantee against malfunction, as is usual for buyers of components in other industries. The problem of proving software components is certainly not an easy one; but we can show that packages lead to a reduction in its difficulty. Consider, for example, the above table management package and the steps that would have to be taken to convince oneself that it was operating correctly. To begin with we have to define a consistent state for the package: for example, we can define the table to be consistent if it contains all the items that have been inserted but not yet retrieved, and only these. We first have to show that the table is consistent initially: that is, after execution of the initialization statements. Then we have to show that if the table is consistent before the use of any one of the services offered (the three procedures promised in the visible part), it will still be consistent after the execution of that procedure.

In order to do this, our analysis need only consider the text of the corresponding procedure: the table cannot be updated directly from outside the package since it is not visible there.

Without packages, the table would have to be global and we would have no protection against direct update of the table by users (whether the update is intentional or by accident). The previous consistency argument would then be considerably more complex since it would be necessary to inspect the text of all programs that use any of the three procedures and check that these programs do not directly update the value of the table: The amount of text to be checked could be an order of magnitude larger than the text of the package itself.

With the package concept – with the separation between the interface and the implementation; and with the protection of whatever is local to the package body – servicing software components becomes similar to servicing components in other industries: If a user reports a malfunction of the operations of a package, we know that we have only to check within the package to establish the reality and cause of any malfunction (and to make repairs as needed). The package body effectively acts as a sealed container.

9.3.3 Influence of Separate Compilation on the Design of Packages

The essential role of packages is for *logical* modularity. In addition, they also play an important role for the *physical* modularity that is achieved by separate compilation. These two aspects of program modularization lead to slightly different (although not conflicting) requirements.

For logical modularity the interface defined by the visible part of a package is sufficient. This information is needed for physical modularity too, but the physical interface also requires the availability of the additional information that is contained in the private part.

This extra information is needed by compilers for the treatment of variables that are declared in one compilation unit but whose type is a private type declared in a different compilation unit. The difference essentially concerns storage allocation: knowledge of the amount of storage needed for such variables is necessary for selecting the machine instructions used for operations on the variables; this code selection is not a decision that could be postponed until the program is complete (that is, until linkage editing time).

The reasons for this are found in the architectures of our current computing machines. These generally provide *code abstractions* that are bound at execution time, in the form of subprograms invoked by the call instruction. It is therefore possible to defer the binding of the bodies of such abstractions until link time, or even later. However, current machines do not provide similar *data abstractions*: every instruction that operates on a datum must be aware of its representation, and that representation must therefore have been bound at the moment the instruction was generated; that is, at compilation time. A more flexible architecture – evolved perhaps from today's *tagged architectures* – would indeed allow data representation choices to be deferred until link time, or even later.

The declaration of a private type therefore does not in itself provide enough information for storage allocation and other operations. The full declaration of the type is needed, and so is any representation clause that the user wants: storage allocation will therefore require the information provided by the private part. Note that placing this information in the package body would not be satisfactory since it would create unnecessary dependences of other compilation units on this body, with the consequence that changes in the algorithms provided in the body would require recompilation of these other compilation units, even in the absence of change to the full type declaration.

The one case where full type information can indeed be deferred until the package body is the case where the private type is implemented as an *access* type:

```
package MINIMAL is
   type OPAQUE is private;
private
   type HIDDEN;                    -- nothing more required
   type OPAQUE is access HIDDEN;
end MINIMAL;
```

In the above example, the full definition of HIDDEN can indeed be deferred until the package body. The reason, of course, is that nearly all current machines have a *uniform* addressing structure, so that an access value always looks the same regardless of what it is designating. (The language Modula-2 provides opaque types in essentially the form of this example.)

To summarize, the logical interface corresponds to the visible part; the physical interface corresponds to the complete package specification, that is, to both the visible part and the private part.

As long as a package specification is not changed, the package body that implements it can be defined and redefined without affecting other units that use this specification as an interface to the package. Hence it is possible to compile a package body separately from its package specification.

9.3.4 Initialization of Packages

Each package declaration results in a single package which is created when the declaration is elaborated. At that time, the space needed for any object declared in the package is allocated, and any initialization specified in such an object declaration is performed.

More elaborate initializations can be included in the sequence of statements following the (optional) reserved word **begin** in the package body, in particular, initializations that require the execution of statements and not just expressions in object declarations. The execution of this (optional) sequence of statements completes the elaboration of the package. Any exception handler provided at the end of these statements applies to exceptions raised during their execution.

When several copies of a given package are needed, the solution is to use instead a related form of program unit called a generic package (see Chapter 13). In this case the specification includes a generic formal part and individual packages (instances of the generic unit) are created by generic instantiation.

9.3.5 Note on Visibility

If a use clause is provided within a given program unit, it opens up the visibility of the visible part of each package mentioned by the clause. However this effect is not transitive.

Thus, if the clause

```
use FIRST_LAYER;
```

is given in the visible part of a package SECOND_LAYER, it does not mean that units containing the clause

```
use SECOND_LAYER;
```

will also see FIRST_LAYER. If we want the above use clause also to provide visibility of certain entities declared in FIRST_LAYER, then this can often be achieved explicitly, by renaming declarations. Consider for example

```
package FIRST_LAYER is
   type T is private;
   procedure P(X : T);
   ...
   E : exception;
end FIRST_LAYER;
```

Suppose now that the package SECOND_LAYER defines additional operations for the type T in terms of the operations supplied by FIRST_LAYER, and that we want to make T, P, and E available to all users of the package SECOND_LAYER without an explicit use FIRST_LAYER clause. This can be achieved as follows:

```
package SECOND_LAYER is
   subtype T is FIRST_LAYER.T;
   procedure P(X : T) renames FIRST_LAYER.P;
   -- additional operations defined by SECOND_LAYER
   ...
   E : exception renames FIRST_LAYER.E;
end SECOND_LAYER;
```

Note that a similar effect can be achieved by making T a derived type instead of a subtype:

```
type T is new FIRST_LAYER.T;
```

This latter form could be used if we wanted to prevent operations defined by another package for objects of type FIRST_LAYER.T from being used at the same time as those defined by the package SECOND_LAYER: the only operations that may be applied to the derived type are those inherited from FIRST_LAYER and those defined in SECOND_LAYER.

9.3.6 Availability of the Properties of Types Defined Within Packages

It is important to define which of the properties of a type declared in the visible part of a package can be made available outside the package (for example, within another program unit that mentions the package in a use clause). In Ada the answer to this question is quite simple: the only available properties are those declared in the visible part.

In the first place, consider the declaration of a type other than a private type, say a record type. If such a declaration is given in the visible part of a package, then the record type is potentially available – without restriction – to outside program units. In particular, such units can declare variables and invoke basic operations of this type (such as component selection and aggregates) in full knowledge of the data structure specified by the type.

For a type declared as *private*, on the other hand, the visible part provides only the type name, and the specification of the subprograms applicable to objects of this type – these are the only operations applicable to objects of the type, apart from assignment and comparison for equality and inequality (which are available unless the private type is *limited*), and attributes such as 'SIZE and 'ADDRESS (which are always available).

Within a package body the characteristics of a private type are available as if the type were not private. For example, if the type is a record type, its components can be denoted with the usual syntax of selected components. Some precautions must be taken when one of the visible operations of the type is defined in terms of an existing operation with the same name. As an example consider the skeleton of the package KEY_MANAGER given in the Reference Manual (section 7.4.2):

```
package KEY_MANAGER is
   type KEY is private;
   ...
   function "<" (X,Y : KEY) return BOOLEAN;
private
   type KEY is new NATURAL;          -- full type definition of KEY
   ...
end;

package body KEY_MANAGER is
   ...
   function "<" (X,Y : KEY) return BOOLEAN is
   begin
      return INTEGER(X) < INTEGER(Y);
   end "<";
end KEY_MANAGER;
```

Within the package body, the full definition of the type KEY is known. The operation "<" declared in the visible part is a (perfectly legal) redeclaration of the operation "<" that is predefined for the type INTEGER (the base type of NATURAL). Thus, with the declarations

```
U, V : KEY;
```

within the body of the package, the relation

```
U = V
```

refers to the predefined operation "=" of the type INTEGER, whereas the relation

```
U < V
```

refers to the operation "<" defined within the package itself (in this case, of course, it does not matter since this redefinition is equivalent to the inherited operation). It should be noted that within the body of the function "<" itself, the relation

```
X < Y
```

would be a recursive call of the function "<". Hence conversion must be used to invoke the operation "<" defined on integers, as shown:

```
INTEGER(X) < INTEGER(Y)
```

To summarize, the availability of properties of types declared in a package can be deduced from purely textual considerations: outside units see only the visible part and consequently can use only properties defined there; on the other hand, the package body can use all properties, including those defined by the full type declaration for a private type.

9.3.7 Initialization of Objects of Private Types

The elaboration of an object declaration results in the reservation of space for the corresponding object, whether the type of the object is private or not. The initialization of an object whose type is a private type could be achieved in the object declaration itself by assigning to it the value of a deferred constant or the value returned by a function; for a limited private type, it could only be achieved by a procedure call statement – hence not in the object declaration. However, there are cases where we want the components of an object whose type is private to satisfy some invariant as soon as the object is created, although initialization of other components may not be needed. This is achieved by means of initialization of record components. Consider the following package declaration:

```
package ALL_ABOUT_STACKS is
   type STACK is limited private;

   procedure PUSH (E : in  ELEMENT; S : in out STACK);
   procedure POP  (E : out ELEMENT; S : in out STACK);
private
   type INDEX is range 0 .. 1000;
   type STACK is
      record
         TOP   : INDEX := INDEX'FIRST;
         SPACE : array (INDEX) of ELEMENT;
      end record;
end ALL_ABOUT_STACKS;
```

For any declaration of an object of type STACK, the component TOP is initialized to the minimum INDEX value. Thus, the stack invariants are satisfied as soon as the declaration of a stack object has been elaborated (another example was shown in section 9.2.3 above, with the initialization of file names in the package SAFE_INPUT_OUTPUT).

9.3.8 Private Types with Discriminants

A final facility provided by Ada combines the concepts of private types and types with discriminants. This is the ability to define a private type with discriminants. Here is an example: it is a formulation of the familiar *dimensioned units* problem inspired by an earlier formulation due to Paul Hilfinger.

The package DIMENSIONED_UNITS defines a private type that represents a set of numerical values with physical dimensions. These dimensions are appropriate powers of mass, length, and time; so each object has a value and a set of indices giving its dimensionality. Objects may change their values, but they must not change their dimensionality. One possible solution (presented elsewhere) is to use derived types to separate objects of different dimensionality; this however does not permit general expressions involving mixed dimensions to be written, such as

```
E = M * (C**2)
```

Another solution is to use a private type with discriminants:

```
package DIMENSIONED_UNITS is

   type UNIT(M, L, T : INTEGER) is private;

   subtype MASS   is UNIT(M => 1, L => 0, T => 0);
   subtype LENGTH is UNIT(M => 0, L => 1, T => 0);
   subtype TIME   is UNIT(M => 0, L => 0, T => 1);
   subtype SCALAR is UNIT(0, 0, 0);

   KILO   : constant MASS;
   METER  : constant LENGTH;
   SECOND : constant TIME;

   function "*" (LEFT : FLOAT; RIGHT : UNIT) return UNIT;
   function "*" (LEFT, RIGHT : UNIT) return UNIT;
   function "/" (LEFT, RIGHT : UNIT) return UNIT;
   ...
   DIMENSION_ERROR : exception;
private
   type UNIT(M, L, T : INTEGER := 0) is
     record
        V : FLOAT;
     end record;
   KILO   : constant MASS   := (M => 1, L => 0, T => 0, V => 1.0);
   METER  : constant LENGTH := (M => 0, L => 1, T => 0, V => 1.0);
   SECOND : constant TIME   := (M => 0, L => 0, T => 1, V => 1.0);
end DIMENSIONED_UNITS;
```

The user of this package may then declare entities such as:

```
subtype VELOCITY is UNIT(M => 0, L => 1, T => -1);
subtype ENERGY   is UNIT(M => 1, L => 2, T => -2);

C : constant VELOCITY := 300_000_000.0 * (METER/SECOND);

function REST_ENERGY(M : MASS) return ENERGY is
begin
   return M*C*C;
end;
```

The implementation of the package will contain subprogram bodies such as:

```
function "*" (LEFT, RIGHT : UNIT) return UNIT is
begin
   return (M => LEFT.M + RIGHT.M,
           L => LEFT.L + RIGHT.L,
           T => LEFT.T + RIGHT.T,
           V => LEFT.V * RIGHT.V);
end;
```

The dimensions must be visible because the user, when declaring an object, must be able to specify its dimensionality. But the type must be private because the operations must check the dimensionality of their operands, and so must all be controlled by the package DIMENSIONED_UNITS.

9.4 SUMMARY AND CONCLUSION

A simple approach was taken for the package facility of Ada. Packages provide the ability to encapsulate information. When defining a package, the programmer simply states the visible information and provides its implementation as a separate text – the package body. The information contained in a package body is not (directly) available outside the package body. Thus, packages support information hiding as well as control of visibility.

The package facility is central to the definition of private data types: it provides complete control over the available operations for such types. Moreover, packages can be separately compiled and the language also provides a parameterized form of package, called a generic package.

All of these aspects are in many respects fundamental for program development. Packages are used to construct libraries containing common pools of data and types, application packages, and complete systems.

10. Separate Compilation and Libraries

10.1 INTRODUCTION

Separate compilation of program units is a practical necessity. Its basic goals are to permit the separation of large programs into simpler, more manageable parts, and to create libraries of program units. Separate compilation helps to reduce compilation costs and to simplify the development and management of program corrections and modifications.

For large projects involving several programmers, separate compilation permits program texts to be separated physically in a way that reflects the division of work and responsibilities. Once the common interface between two parts has been agreed upon and recorded, the two parts can be developed and compiled separately. The fact that the common interface is a physically separate text guarantees that separate recompilation of either part does not invalidate the common interface.

The physical separation of program texts may be viewed as a support facility for the structured programming concept of refinement. It may also be used to conceal the text of a subprogram body from users who are only allowed to call the subprogram. Such concealment may be justified either for reasons of confidentiality or in order to prevent the user from inferring implicit properties or making assumptions regarding the functioning of the subprogram. Finally this physical separation facilitates the construction of libraries and reusable software components.

It is appropriate at this stage to introduce the distinction between *independent* and *separate* compilation (following J.J. Horning). Independent compilation has been achieved by most assembly languages and also by languages such as Fortran and PL/1. Compilation of individual modules is performed independently in the sense that the modules have no way of sharing knowledge of properties defined in other modules.

Independent compilation is usually achieved with a lower level of compile-time checking of consistency between units than is possible within a single compilation unit. In consequence, independent compilation came into disrepute and was rejected by safety-minded early typed language definitions such as Algol 68 and Pascal. Fast compilation of the complete program was often advocated by promoters of these languages as a safe alternative to independent compilation. However, fast compilation has its limits, and it fails to answer the needs of confidentiality and libraries.

Separate compilation, on the other hand, reconciles type-checking safety and the pragmatic reasons for compiling in parts. It is based on the use of a *program library* which contains a record of previous compilations of the units that form a program. It has been developed in the language Sue and in later languages such as Lis, Jossle, Mesa and later extensions of Pascal and Algol 68. We next discuss its properties in terms of what is provided in Ada.

When a program unit is submitted to the compiler, the compiler also has access to the program library and is therefore able to perform the same level of checking (in particular type checking) whether a program is compiled in many parts or as a whole. It is the existence of the program library that makes the compilation separate but not independent.

Using the general information available in the program library, the compiler will be able to assist the user in organizing recompilations. In particular, it will be able to display information about the current state of the compilation of a program that is divided into several compilation units: which separate program units have been compiled, and which need to be recompiled because of prior recompilations.

It is thus for reasons of safety and utility that Ada offers a powerful facility for separate compilation. Two additional criteria have been followed in this design, namely simplicity of use and simplicity of implementation.

Separate compilation being a user-oriented facility, it should be simple to understand and use. Consequently it should not introduce other concepts than those required by the nature of separate compilation. Scope rules and the general form of separately compiled program units should be similar to those of other program units.

In addition, separate compilation should be implementable simply and efficiently. The additional work required for separate compilation should stay within reasonable limits, since one of the goals is to save overall compilation and recompilation time.

10.2 PRESENTATION OF THE SEPARATE COMPILATION FACILITY

A complete program is a collection of compilation units submitted to the compiler individually or in batches (called compilations). A compilation unit is either a *library* unit or a *secondary* unit. A library unit can be:

- a package declaration

- a subprogram declaration

- a generic declaration or instantiation

A secondary unit, as the name indicates, is always related to another compilation unit: A secondary unit can be the body of a library unit –

- a package body

- a subprogram body

- the body of a generic unit

– or, as we shall see later, a secondary unit can be a *subunit* of another compilation unit (the latter being either a library unit or another secondary unit).

Each compilation unit may have a *context clause* at the beginning, containing *with clauses* that mention the names of other library units that the compilation unit needs. Thus, although compilation units can be submitted individually to a compiler, they can depend on each other – as indicated by with clauses. For this reason the compilation units that form a given program are said to belong to a *program library*.

Traditionally, one distinguishes two main styles of program development: top-down (or hierarchical) program development and bottom-up program development. The separate compilation facility provided in Ada supports both styles, as well as intermediate forms.

10.2.1 Bottom–Up Program Development

In this style of program development we may have programmers developing libraries of generally usable packages.

Each generally usable package can be separately compiled and therefore made available in the program library. The specification and the package body (if any) can both be compilation units, and they can be submitted either in the same or in different compilations (each compilation is a succession of compilation units).

Some of these packages do not depend on any outside information, except perhaps that of the predefined environment (the package STANDARD, which defines types such as BOOLEAN and INTEGER). The package declarations for METRIC_CONVERSIONS and WORK_DATA given in Chapter 9 fall into this category.

More generally, packages may depend on information that is defined by other packages of the program library. For example an application – level input-output package may depend on a more basic input-output package; similarly a surveying package could depend on this application-level input-output package and on another package that defines trigonometric functions.

As an example of a compilation unit that depends on other library units consider the following procedure, which presents a (naive) solution of quadratic equations. The compilation unit starts with the *context clause*:

```
with TEXT_IO, REAL_OPERATIONS; use REAL_OPERATIONS;
```

The with clause specifies that the packages TEXT_IO and REAL_OPERATIONS are both needed. The use clause for the latter package achieves direct visibility of the entities declared in its visible part – the type REAL, the (nested) package REAL_IO, and the function SQRT:

```
with TEXT_IO, REAL_OPERATIONS; use REAL_OPERATIONS;
procedure QUADRATIC_EQUATION is
   A, B, C, D : REAL;
   use REAL_IO;      -- To see GET and PUT for the type REAL
   use TEXT_IO;      -- To see PUT for strings, and NEW_LINE
begin
   GET(A); GET(B); GET(C);
   D := B**2 - 4.0*A*C;
   if D < 0.0 then
      PUT("IMAGINARY ROOTS.");
   else
      PUT("REAL ROOTS : X1 = ");
      PUT((-B - SQRT(D))/(2.0*A));
      PUT (" X2 = ");
      PUT((-B + SQRT(D))/(2.0*A));
   end if;
   NEW_LINE;
end QUADRATIC_EQUATION;
```

Although the programmer who wrote QUADRATIC_EQUATION might think he had finished at this stage, the *complete* program includes more than this single procedure. Thus, it is not going to work unless the program library already contain the packages REAL_OPERATIONS and TEXT_IO on which QUADRATIC_EQUATION depends. Otherwise the function SQRT supplied by the package REAL_OPERATIONS would not be visible; nor would similarly the procedures GET and PUT supplied by REAL_IO within REAL_OPERATIONS and by TEXT_IO.

Realizing that this program might be generally usable, the programmer may decide to encapsulate it within a package, perhaps along with other similar procedures:

```
with REAL_OPERATIONS; use REAL_OPERATIONS;
package EQUATION_SOLVER is
   procedure QUADRATIC_EQUATION;
   procedure LINEAR_EQUATION;
   -- other procedures needing real operations
   -- in their declaration
end;

with TEXT_IO;
package body EQUATION_SOLVER is

   procedure QUADRATIC_EQUATION is
      -- same text as before
   end;

   procedure LINEAR_EQUATION is
      -- reads a linear equation, solves it, prints results
   end;
   ...
end EQUATION_SOLVER;
```

Note that the context clause for REAL_OPERATIONS is needed for the body as well as for the declaration of the package EQUATION_SOLVER, but need not be repeated for the body since the context clause of a package declaration applies also to the corresponding package body. However, TEXT_IO is needed only by the body, so it would introduce unwanted dependences to mention it in the context clause of the package declaration.

A program that uses this package is shown below:

```
with EQUATION_SOLVER; use EQUATION_SOLVER;
procedure EXERCISE is      -- solves 10 quadratic equations
begin
   for I in 1 .. 10 loop
      QUADRATIC_EQUATION;
   end loop;
end EXERCISE;
```

The procedure EXERCISE need only mention the package EQUATION_SOLVER in its context clause. It need not (and should not) mention the packages REAL_OPERATIONS and TEXT_IO, which are actually needed by the package body of EQUATION_SOLVER, since EXERCISE does not contain direct calls to subprograms defined in either REAL_OPERATIONS or TEXT_IO.

Note also that a library unit may be a generic unit. Instances of such generic compilation units can be obtained as usual:

```
with DIRECT_IO;
procedure TREAT_ITEMS is
    type ITEM is ...
    package ITEM_IO is new DIRECT_IO (ELEMENT_TYPE => ITEM);
    ... -- use of the input-output procedures for objects of type ITEM
end TREAT_ITEMS;
```

Here a use clause for the generic package DIRECT_IO would be illegal; one for the instance ITEM_IO may appear after the instantiation.

Finally, a library unit may be an instance of another (generic) library unit:

```
with DIRECT_IO;
package FLOAT_IO is new DIRECT_IO(FLOAT);
```

10.2.2 Hierarchical Program Development

The other style of program development is called hierarchical or top-down, as used in programming by stepwise refinement [Wi 71, Wo 72]. The top level provides a formulation of the program in terms of operations that are to be supplied by the next lower level. Each such operation is then further defined in terms of operations of another lower level, and so on. In support of this style of program development, Ada offers the possibility of having compilation units that are *subunits* of other compilation units.

We illustrate subunits by means of a variant of the example of section 10.2.1 of the Reference Manual. Assume that we are developing the procedure TOP in a top-down fashion. The top level of definition is given by the following compilation unit:

```
procedure TOP is

   type REAL is digits 10;
   NEXT : REAL;

   procedure TRANSFORM(U : in out REAL);

   package TABLE is
      procedure INSERT(X : in REAL);
      function  FIRST return REAL;
      procedure DISPLAY;
   end;

   package body TABLE is separate;    -- stub of TABLE

   procedure TRANSFORM(U : in out REAL) is separate;
                                         -- stub of TRANSFORM

begin    -- TOP
   ...
   TRANSFORM(NEXT);
   ...
   TABLE.INSERT(NEXT);
   TABLE.DISPLAY;
   ...
end TOP;
```

The specifications of the procedure TRANSFORM and of the package TABLE are given as usual. Hence the statements of TOP can be expressed in terms of these units and can invoke the procedure TRANSFORM and the subprograms INSERT, FIRST, and DISPLAY that are defined by the package TABLE. However, the *proper body* of TRANSFORM (and TABLE) is separately compiled and is not, therefore, provided as part of the text of TOP. In each case a body *stub* has been given at the place where the proper body would appear if it were not separately compiled. The role of the stub is to inform the compiler that the proper body is to be found elsewhere – as a separately compiled *subunit*. Without the stub, the compiler would issue an error message; with the stub, it is told to expect that sooner or later a subunit such as the following will be submitted:

```
separate (TOP) procedure TRANSFORM(U : in out REAL) is
   use TABLE;
begin
   ...
   U := FIRST;
   ...
end TRANSFORM;
```

Although separately compiled, TRANSFORM still has visibility of the identifiers that are declared within TOP. For example it sees the type REAL and the package name TABLE. This dependence is reflected by the presence of

    separate(TOP)

at the start of the subunit. This indicates that TOP is the *parent* unit of the procedure TRANSFORM; the parent unit is the program unit that contains the stub that announces the subunit. Similar considerations apply to the separately compiled body of the package TABLE:

    separate (TOP) package body TABLE is
       -- some local declarations of TABLE followed by

    procedure INSERT(X : REAL) is
    begin
       -- sequence of statements of INSERT
    end;

    function FIRST return REAL is
    begin
       -- sequence of statements of FIRST
    end;

    procedure DISPLAY is separate;   -- stub of DISPLAY
    end TABLE;

In this case the package body contains the proper bodies of the procedure INSERT and the function FIRST, but another stub in the case of the procedure DISPLAY, which is thus a subunit of TABLE:

    with TXT_IO;
    separate (TOP.TABLE) procedure DISPLAY is
    begin
       -- sequence of statements of DISPLAY
    end DISPLAY;

Note that the name of the parent unit must be given in full, starting with the ancestor library unit TOP, in order correctly to identify TABLE. There could be other subunits called TABLE in the same program library (although not for the same ancestor TOP).

Note also that it is possible to provide a with clause for a subunit, as for any compilation unit. In this example, assuming that DISPLAY is the only procedure performing input-output, the dependence on TEXT_IO is conveniently localized to that procedure (instead of creating a more global dependence at the level of TOP or at that of TABLE).

Subunits can be declared at the outermost level of another unit or subunit. This creates the possibility of an hierarchy of program subunits depending on a given compilation unit. This hierarchy is no different from the nesting hierarchy in ordinary program units. In particular, the visibility rules are the same and a subunit can depend on dynamic information. For example, consider

```
separate (TOP) procedure TRANSFORM(U : in out REAL) is
   use TABLE;
   SQUARE : REAL := U ** 2;
   procedure UPDATE is separate;
begin
   ...
end TRANSFORM;
```

Access to the local variable SQUARE is still possible within UPDATE, exactly as if the body of UPDATE were textually nested at the place of the stub.

```
separate (TOP.TRANSFORM) procedure UPDATE is
begin
   -- access to SQUARE is possible
end UPDATE;
```

It should be clear that these two methods of introducing compilation units are not mutually exclusive and can be used in combination. For example, a general purpose package may be split into subunits in order to facilitate its development, compilation, and subsequent recompilation.

10.2.3 Compilation Order

Compilation units may be compiled separately, but this does not mean that compilations can be submitted in an arbitrary order, since units are not independent. In particular we have seen that the context clause of one unit may mention the name of another unit, and that some units are subunits of other units. These two forms of dependence and the usual dependence of a body on the corresponding specification determine a partial ordering of compilations:

- A compilation unit must be compiled after all units that are named by its context clause.

- A secondary unit that is a subprogram body or a package body must be compiled after the library unit that provides the corresponding subprogram specification or package specification.

- A secondary unit that is a subunit must be compiled after its parent unit.

These rules are rules of common sense and they must be enforced by an Ada Compiler. These order relations are summarized below in the case of the procedures

QUADRATIC_EQUATION and TOP. The notation "A <-- B" is used to indicate that A must
be compiled before B.

```
Specification of REAL_OPERATIONS <-- Body of REAL_OPERATIONS
Specification of REAL_OPERATIONS <-- QUADRATIC_EQUATION

Specification of TEXT_IO <-- Body of TEXT_IO
Specification of TEXT_IO <-- QUADRATIC_EQUATION
Specification of TEXT_IO <-- DISPLAY

TOP <-- TABLE      <-- DISPLAY
TOP <-- TRANSFORM <-- UPDATE
```

It should be clear that these relations only define a partial ordering of compilations.
For example:

- The bodies of the packages REAL_OPERATIONS and TEXT_IO are two secondary units
  that can be compiled in either order. Furthermore QUADRATIC_EQUATION can be
  compiled either before or after either of these secondary units.

- The subunit TABLE can be compiled before or after TRANSFORM, indifferently. Similarly the relative order of compilation of TABLE with respect to UPDATE, of TRANS-
  FORM with respect to DISPLAY, and of DISPLAY with respect to UPDATE, are all
  undefined.

Of course, in order to execute the program, it is necessary that all compilations be
completed: an Ada compiler or library manager will report an error if this is not the
case.

Note that although the body of TRANSFORM includes a use clause that mentions
TABLE, this has no influence on compilation order: the only information that TRANSFORM
may obtain about TABLE is that given by the declaration of TABLE, and this declaration
is part of the (common) parent unit TOP; hence the use clause will not affect the subunit
TABLE – which is a package body. No use clause will ever affect compilation order.

10.2.4 Recompilation Order

Similar considerations apply in the case of recompilation. If we change the definition of
some entity, then any compilation unit that used the previous definition is now obsolete
and must be recompiled.

In principle, this rule could be applied to individual declarations. However, for
the sake of compiler simplicity, Ada compilers are only required to consider that the
quantum of change is the (re)compilation of a whole compilation unit. Thus any change
to a package specification is assumed to affect any compilation unit that mentions this
package in a with clause. Similarly any change to a parent unit is assumed to affect
all its subunits. With this simplifying assumption, the rules defining the need for
recompilations follow directly from the above-defined order relations.

- After recompilation of the declaration of REAL_OPERATIONS the body of REAL_OPERATIONS and the procedure QUADRATIC_EQUATION must be recompiled.

- After recompilation of the declaration of TEXT_IO (if that is even possible) the body of TEXT_IO, the procedure QUADRATIC_EQUATION, and the subunit DISPLAY must be recompiled.

- The subunit DISPLAY must be recompiled after the recompilation of its parent TABLE; similarly the subunit UPDATE after recompilation of TRANSFORM; and all of TABLE, DISPLAY, TRANSFORM, and UPDATE after recompilation of TOP.

In principle, a compiler that included a librarian facility for source texts could compare the old text of a compilation unit with the new text and keep track of changes on an individual basis. Thus it could detect that although a given package specification had been recompiled, the modification did not actually affect other compilation units that used this package but did not use the modified part. Such a compiler could then optimize by cutting short the process and not recompiling those other units – simply marking them as no longer obsolete, realizing that the recompiled dependent unit would deliver the same results as the previous one.

The above optimization is not imposed on all Ada compilers: given the ability separately to compile a package or subprogram specification and the corresponding body, the simple strategy (using a compilation unit as quantum) should not in practice require many more recompilations than strictly necessary.

Note, in this respect, that the language design has carefully avoided unnecessary *textual dependence*. For example, the fact that a context clause is associated with a subunit rather than with a body stub is quite important. Consider the alternative:

```
procedure EXAMPLE is
    ...
    -- The following is not in Ada:

    with TEXT_IO;          -- Illegal in this position
    procedure P(X : INTEGER) is separate;

    with REAL_OPERATIONS;   -- Illegal in this position
    procedure Q(Y : REAL) is separate;
    ...
end EXAMPLE;
```

Assume that in some later revision of this program, TEXT_IO needs to be used also within the body of Q. Then if context clauses were provided with the stubs as shown, it would be necessary to modify the stub of Q and hence to recompile the text of the EXAMPLE. However since the stub of P is also provided there – this is the textual dependence – a compiler using the simple strategy would not notice that the stub of P was unmodified, and would have to recompile P as well.

While we recognize that future compilers might adopt more ambitious schemes, the Ada design has carefully avoided any feature that would be incompatible with the simple strategy. Given this careful avoidance of unnecessary textual dependences the number of recompilations can be kept quite close to the actual minimum.

10.2.5 Execution of a Main Program

Prior to the execution of a main program such as TOP or QUADRATIC_EQUATION, any library unit that is used directly or indirectly by this main program must be elaborated. For example, the package declarations of TEXT_IO and REAL_OPERATIONS are elaborated before control is passed to QUADRATIC_EQUATION; furthermore, any other library unit that is used by these packages or by their bodies must also be elaborated before control is passed to QUADRATIC_EQUATION.

The order of elaboration of these library units is not fully defined but must be consistent with the partial ordering defined by the dependences.

10.2.6 The Pragma ELABORATE

In most cases, the Ada library manager can choose any elaboration order consistent with the unit dependences, and the resulting program will always have the same effect. However, in some cases further control over elaboration order is required. Here is an example.

Suppose we have a package specification PRINT that uses the package SIMPLE_IO of Chapter 9. The specification might look like this:

```
with SIMPLE_IO; use SIMPLE_IO;
package PRINT is
   DATA, RESULTS : FILE_NAME;
   ...
end;
```

and the package body will of course say something like:

```
CREATE(RESULTS, "Results");
```

This creates the partial orderings

```
Specification of SIMPLE_IO   <-- Body of SIMPLE_IO
Specification of SIMPLE_IO   <-- Specification of PRINT
Specification of PRINT       <-- Body of PRINT
```

Note that (so far) there is no ordering relation between the *body* of SIMPLE_IO and the specification or body of PRINT. However, PRINT calls SIMPLE_IO.CREATE. CREATE presumably changes the local object DIRECTORY in the body of SIMPLE_IO. And DIRECTORY is initialized – set into its first consistent state – by the elaboration of the body of SIMPLE_IO. For this sequence of events to work, we *must* elaborate the body of SIMPLE_IO before any call of SIMPLE_IO.CREATE.

To express this kind of dependence, Ada introduces the pragma ELABORATE. It may be used immediately following a context clause, and may take as arguments any of the library units referred to by the context clause. Its meaning is that the *body* of the referenced unit must be elaborated *before* the elaboration of the referencing unit.

In the case above, the user would write

```
with SIMPLE_IO;
pragma ELABORATE(SIMPLE_IO);
use SIMPLE_IO;
package PRINT is
   ...
end;
```

This creates a new partial ordering

```
Body of SIMPLE_IO <-- Specification of PRINT
```

which ensures that any use of the services of SIMPLE_IO occurs *after* the state variables have been initialized. Of course, the program is illegal if no consistent order is possible.

10.3 METHODOLOGICAL IMPACT OF SEPARATE COMPILATION

The ability to compile separately a package specification and the corresponding package body has important methodological consequences for program development and maintenance. For example, it allows a team of programmers to agree upon a common interface and to define it by one or more package specifications. This being done, the package bodies, and any other unit that uses the common interface, can be developed in parallel and compiled in an arbitrary order.

A package specification contains all the declarations that need to be seen by any unit that uses the services of the package. The corresponding package body may be modified and recompiled without the need for recompilation of the units that use the services of the package. As long as the operations promised by the visible part are correctly achieved, the user will not be affected by changes to the package body. Another version of the package body, using a different technique, may be substituted without affecting the user.

This ability to compile a package specification and the corresponding package body separately is an extension of the idea of encapsulation. Since users are not affected by the contents of the package body – provided it is correct – there is no need to show them the source text of the package body: all they need is the corresponding object code.

Separate compilation of package bodies may thus be used to achieve *physical hiding*. This will be useful for confidentiality purposes. It will also help to prevent users from reading the algorithms and inferring implicit properties and making assumptions that might not be satisfied by later implementations. In this sense, separately compiled package bodies provide good support for the policy of restricted flow of information advocated by Parnas [PA 71].

10.4 THE PROGRAM LIBRARY

The program units that form a given Ada program are said to belong to what is called a *program library*. A program library may contain only the units necessary for a single *main* program, but it may also contain the units of several main programs, especially in the case of related projects. Finally it may contain generally usable packages and the predefined units.

Associated with each program library there must be a file that records information relative to the compilations that have already been done. In particular, this file must contain *symbol tables* for separately compiled package specifications. It must also record compilation dates and dependence relations between compilation units: this information is used by the compiler for checking compilation order and for deciding which compilation units are affected by given recompilations.

When submitting a compilation unit to the compiler, the programmer provides:

- the source text of the compilation unit, and

- the name of the program library to which the unit is to belong.

It is this second item – the program library – that makes the compilation separate but not independent: The compiler uses the information contained in the program library to perform type checking across compilation units exactly as it normally would within a single compilation unit. The effect of the compilation is as usual (the production of listings, object codes, messages, and so on), but it also results in an update of the program library (an update of compilation dates, the recording of new or updated symbol tables, and so on).

For each Ada program we consider a single program library. In practice a given program library will often be formed from components obtained from other program libraries. The means for transferring components from one library to another are not properly within the domain of the Ada language but rather within that of its possible support environments [DoD 80]. The following facilities are expected:

Library creation

There should be commands for creating the program library of a given program, or of a given family of programs.

Inclusion of library units

There should be a command to include a unit of one library within another library. This process is similar to what is traditionally done for transferring the object code of a software component; in particular it can imply either making a copy or creating a new access path to a single (shared) copy. The only difference is that for Ada compilation units the information transferred includes descriptive information such as symbol tables, compilation dates, and dependence relations on other software components, and checks are made that no Ada rule is violated.

After its inclusion, a unit should be indistinguishable from other units of the library. Inclusion of a given compilation unit may require further inclusion of other compilation units that are needed by the given unit.

Deletion of library units

Conversely there should be a command to delete a unit from a given library.

Completion check

There should be a command by which a user states that the program is considered to be complete: all units should have been compiled by that time. The compiler will check that this is the case and issue appropriate error messages otherwise.

Status checks

There should be commands to display global information about the current state of the program library: which units have been compiled, which subunits have never been compiled, which units need to be recompiled, and so on.

Completion and status checks are quite useful since a library may contain obsolete units at intermediate stages of the program development.

Since the compiler is able to detect the need for recompilations, it could conceivably do these automatically upon detection of such a need. However, changes are often done for several units at the same time. A compiler that performed recompilations after each change might perform more recompilations than necessary unless it had global knowledge of all changes submitted.

Assume for example that the specifications of the packages A and B were modified. If all units that see A were automatically recompiled, then if some of them also see B, they would be recompiled a second time after the compilation of B.

Hence it is certainly preferable to let the user manage the recompilations. However, this means that tools for displaying the current status of compilation units of a program should be provided. Similarly it means that the user should be able to state that a program is complete and let the compiler check that this is actually the case.

10.5 THE IMPLEMENTATION OF SEPARATE COMPILATION

The Ada separate compilation facility can be implemented at a reasonable cost for the simple strategy where the quantum of change recognized by the compiler is the compilation or recompilation of a single unit. The model described below is similar to the technique used in compilers for the Lis language.

10.5.1 Principle of Separate Compilation

As mentioned before, the Ada separate compilation facility involves a program library that records information on compilation units and on dependence relations between them.

The library file associated with the program library can be organized as a collection of records: one for each compilation unit. If a compilation unit includes declarations that are potentially visible from other compilation units, the corresponding record must contain a description of these declarations – commonly called a symbol table. This need arises in the following cases:

- Any library unit: The symbol table describes the specification of the package, subprogram, or generic unit.

- Any compilation unit that has subunits: The symbol table describes the declarative environment of each stub.

These symbol tables are produced and managed by the compiler. For the compilation of a given unit, the compiler must first retrieve the symbol tables that describe the current context, and then assemble them as appropriate. In other words, the compiler must construct an integrated symbol table that describes visibility for the compilation unit as if the program were not split into separate texts.

In order to perform this task it is useful to consider the following *forest* structure (a collection of genealogical trees), which reflects the declaration of units and subunits:

(a)   Each library unit is a root.

(b)   The parent unit of a subunit is the compilation unit that contains the corresponding body stub.

This structure is necessary for the determination of visibility rules. Hence it must be recorded in the library file and updated as new body stubs are encountered, and as new units are compiled.

Finally, for each compilation unit, the list of library units that are mentioned by its context clause must be kept. The forest structure will help for determining the symbol tables to be retrieved, for checking the validity of context clauses and for determining the recompilations that need to be done as a consequence of previous recompilations. Naturally, the compiler may also use this information to assist the user with recompilations.

To check for required recompilations, the compiler may use a system of *time-stamping* that reflects the order in which compilations are submitted: a unique compilation *date* is associated with the symbol table of each compilation unit.

10.5.2 Details of the Actions Performed by the Compiler

The following major actions must be performed during the compilation of a compilation unit:

Determination of the compilation context

The context clause is analyzed and the name of the compilation unit is recognized. Using the full name of the subunit (given after the reserved word **separate**), the genealogy of a subunit can be found: its parent, grandparent, and so on up to the ancestor library unit. A combined with clause is formed by merging the with clauses of the genealogy.

Checking the validity of the compilation context

Any unit mentioned by a context clause must be a library unit.
      The following checks must be performed:

- In the genealogy, each subunit must have been compiled after its parent.

- Each compilation unit of the genealogy must have been compiled after any library unit mentioned by its context clause.

- Each library unit mentioned by the combined context clause must still be valid: A compilation unit is no longer valid if its context clause names a library unit that is no longer valid or that has been compiled after the compilation unit itself.

Compilation may proceed only if all these checks succeed. Otherwise diagnostics, a list of required recompilations, and a recommended recompilation order may be printed by the compiler.

Table loading

The symbol tables of the library units named by the merged with clause may now be assembled. For a subunit the constitution of the current context also involves nesting the declarative parts of the units of the genealogy – layer by layer, from the ancestor to the immediate parent.

This table assembly may involve establishing some links between the individual symbol tables, since they may refer to each other (for example, an identifier declared in a given package may be of a type declared in another package).

Update of the forest structure, table unloading

At the end of the compilation of a compilation unit, the date of compilation must be updated. For a library unit, and for a unit that contains body stubs (and therefore has subunits), a new symbol table must be stored in the library file in a suitable format. Newly declared subunits must be entered in the forest. If a new library unit is compiled, a root must be added to the forest.

The forest structure can be used to mark units that have become invalid as a consequence of the current compilation and for which recompilation will therefore be needed.

10.5.3 Treatment of Package Bodies

For a given package, the two disjoint units (specification and body) must be viewed as defining complementary aspects of the same logical entity. Consequently it will be convenient for the user to have a single object module, and not two. In order to achieve this effect the code produced during the compilation of the package specification, if any, may be kept in some intermediate form in the record that is associated with the package in the program library. Later, when compiling the package body, this initial code may be recovered and the compilations may proceed as if the two units were concatenated. (The code produced for the specification must still be retained, in case the body is recompiled.)

10.5.4 Summary of the Information Contained in a Library File

The library file contains a representation of the forest structure discussed above. Each node of a tree corresponds to a subunit, except the root, which is always a library unit. A node contains:

- The name of the unit or subunit.

- Its nature: subprogram, package, generic unit, or task unit.

- Its compilation date and that of the associated unit body, if there is one.

- The list of library units mentioned in the context clause.

- A symbol table, if the compilation unit is a library unit and in any case if it includes body stubs (has subunits).

- Possibly, a boolean component indicating need for recompilation.

The record for a given node is created either when the stub for a subunit is analyzed (and then initialized in the state *recompilation needed*), or during compilation in the case of a library unit. This record is updated during compilations. The record for a subunit may be deleted from the library file upon recompilation of the parent unit if this unit no longer has a corresponding body stub.

Each individual symbol table should be kept in a format that simplifies establishment of the relations between different symbol tables when they are assembled. As an example, consider the two following packages:

```
package D is
  type T is ...
  ...
end D;

with D;
package E is
  use D;
  X : T;
  ...
end E;
```

Given the symbol table entry for the declaration of X, it must be possible to find the symbol table entry for its type T.

If internal references are used to represent such relations, they must be relocated when the symbol tables are assembled. Methods involving relocation information, or a mapping into virtual memory can be used to support this table assembly.

Note, finally, that symbol tables may be transferred from the library file of one program to that of another program. The internal structure adopted for symbol tables should permit this.

10.6 SUMMARY AND CONCLUSION

To summarize the Ada separate compilation facility:

- The compilation units of a program form a program library. Library units can be declarations of packages, subprograms or generic units, or generic instantiations. The bodies of library units are separately compiled secondary units.

- Subunits of other compilation units can be defined by means of body stubs. These subunits are separately compiled.

- The visibility rules applicable to compilation units are the usual visibility rules, as complemented by with clauses. The order of compilation and recompilation is governed by these rules.

Separate compilation has been designed as a user-oriented facility that supports the traditional forms of program development. It can be implemented at reasonable cost, as evidenced by the previous sections and by previous languages supporting a similar separate compilation facility such as Lis and Mesa. The type rules are enforced across separate units to the same degree as within a given unit, and the information contained in a program library can be used to check that the compilation of a given unit does not use information from other units that have become obsolete in the meantime.

Finally, one of the motivations of separate compilation is the creation of software libraries. This is supported by Ada. By far the most useful library units should be packages and generic packages. Ada permits their use with the same degree of safety as for internal units.

It is expected that library packages will be used for the encapsulation of type definitions, for common constants and data, and for shared declarations. The fact that these library items are already compiled program units, rather than source texts, offers a degree of safety not found in languages that provide merely independent compilations.

Other compilation units will be used for the creation of user packages such as input-output packages, to be found in libraries. The ability to compile a package specification separately from the corresponding package body provides the possibility of separating the interface of a package from its implementation. Thus it supports information hiding and reliability to an extremely high degree.

11. General Program Structure – Visibility and Overloading

11.1 INTRODUCTION

Central to the definition of Ada is a concern for the general structure of a program, the rules defining the visibility of identifiers at various points of a program, and the facilities offered for separate compilation. A major goal in this design was to give the programmer precise control over his name space: the set of names that he may define and use. It is important to be able to introduce new names without having to bother about possible conflicts with existing names. This requires the ability to control the inheritance of names that are defined in other contexts. As mentioned in chapter 9, the notion of package is essential to achieve this kind of control. Another goal was to provide the same visibility rules for all program units, whether they are separately compiled or not.

The subjects of general program structure and visibility rules are connected in many ways – in particular because of the possibility of nesting program units. They also interact with the facilities offered for separate compilation. This chapter will discuss program structure and visibility in that order, and also the related subject of overloading.

11.2 PROGRAM STRUCTURE

The overall structure of an Ada program text (a compilation unit) is similar to that of an Algol 60 or Pascal text: it appears as a nested structure of program units – subprograms, packages, task units, and generic units – and block statements.

Nesting is achieved through declarative parts: A declarative part may contain bodies of program units, and each of these may in turn contain a declarative part; furthermore, a sequence of statements may contain a block statement that contains a declarative part.

A key question in the definition of program structure is that of the purpose of nesting. Clearly, nesting has been used in Algol 60 and Pascal in relation to visibility. In these languages, two units are written in the context of the same declarative part if they are to share the visibility of some common outer entities.

Is this, however, the only purpose of nesting? If it were, a logical conclusion would be the systematic unnesting of units that do not share any common visibility.

We consider this view to be too extreme. Units that do not have any visibility dependence may nevertheless be maintained together in a nested text structure for the benefit of the logical exposition of the program. There is an analogy with an encyclopedia, whose material is organized into nested subjects: It is the knowledge of this organization that enables the easy retrieval of a given subject.

Systematic unnesting of units that do not share any common visibility would produce a sequence of small units – not unlike a sequence of Fortran subprograms. Finding a given unit in such a sequence is difficult unless aided by a directory or by some convention such as alphabetical ordering. Reading the program may also be difficult since the structure of the text does not reflect the logical organization and the logical connections.

For these reasons, the ability to nest units has been retained in Ada along with the ability to control visibility that is afforded by packages and use clauses. Thus an Ada program appears as a collection of nested declarative regions. A given declarative region may include the declarations of inner program units, in which case it will also include the bodies of these program units. Each of these bodies again defines a declarative region which may in turn declare other inner program units.

In general it is possible to provide the definition of program units – especially packages – in two textually distinct parts:

(a) the specification, which defines the logical interface (between definition and use) of the program unit

(b) the body, which describes a particular realization of the specification.

This possibility has far reaching implications, in that it provides a single basis for achieving several different objectives, notably textual clarity, abstraction, and separate compilation.

We first illustrate this ability in the case of a procedure. Consider for instance the procedure declaration:

procedure PUSH(E : **in** ELEMENT; S : **in out** STACK);

This declaration contains the name of the procedure and the specification of the mode and type of each formal parameter. This is the information needed to specify the interface of PUSH, both syntactically and semantically, at least with regard to type checking. From this point of view the declaration conveys all one needs to know in order to call the procedure PUSH. The declaration could be augmented by comments specifying pre-conditions and post-conditions and any exception that might be raised by PUSH.

Obviously, however, this formulation of PUSH is incomplete in that it does not define an implementation of the procedure. The latter is provided by a procedure body:

```
procedure PUSH(E : in ELEMENT; S : in out STACK) is
begin
  if S.INDEX = S.SIZE then
    raise STACK_OVERFLOW;
  else
    S.INDEX := S.INDEX + 1;
    S.SPACE(S.INDEX) := E;
  end if;
end PUSH;
```

These two constructs – the declaration and the body – jointly define the procedure. In cases where the advantages of separate specification are not essential, the procedure declaration may be omitted. In any case, the specification of the parameters must always be given in the body for reasons of readability, and also because of the possibility of overloading: there could be push procedures for items, integers, and so on.

A similar separation is provided for packages. A package declaration provides the interface to the user: the visible part. For example, the declaration of a SIMPLE_IO package is provided as follows:

```
package SIMPLE_IO is
  type FILE_NAME is limited private;
  procedure CREATE(FILE : out FILE_NAME);
  procedure READ  (ELEM : out INTEGER; F : in FILE_NAME);
  procedure WRITE (ELEM : in  INTEGER; F : in FILE_NAME);
private
  type FILE_NAME is new INTEGER range 0 .. 50;
end SIMPLE_IO;
```

This declaration provides the user with the specification of the name of a type – FILE_NAME – and also with the specification of the associated procedures CREATE, READ, and WRITE. This constitutes the logical interface of the package.

The package implementation is always provided as a textually distinct package body as shown in the sketch below:

```
package body SIMPLE_IO is
  type FILE_DESCRIPTOR is
    record
      -- components of each file descriptor
    end record;
  DIRECTORY : array (FILE_NAME) of FILE_DESCRIPTOR;

  -- other local constants, variables and subprograms

  procedure CREATE(FILE : out FILE_NAME) is
    ...
  end CREATE;
  procedure READ(ELEM  : out INTEGER; F : in FILE_NAME)
            is ... end READ;
  procedure WRITE(ELEM : in INTEGER;  F : in FILE_NAME)
            is ... end WRITE;
end SIMPLE_IO;
```

As in the case of procedures, the package declaration and the package body jointly define the package considered. For pragmatic reasons (a package declaration is generally much larger than a procedure declaration), the package body does not repeat the information contained in the package declaration; furthermore packages cannot be overloaded and so there is no problem of identification.

A similar separation is also used for task units and for generic units.

11.3 VISIBILITY RULES

The visibility rules provided in Ada combine Algol-like inheritance rules with an ability to control the set of names that can be used within a given context. This ability follows from the naming conventions and the facilities offered by packages and use clauses. A renaming capability is also provided.

We first discuss the basic visibility model, then the naming conventions, use clauses, and renaming.

11.3.1 Basic Visibility Model

The search for simple and uniform scope rules has led to the adoption of a traditional approach: an identifier that is declared immediately within a given declarative region is directly visible within inner (nested) declarative regions.

The term *declarative region* in the above rule refers to a portion of the program text which includes a major group of declarations. For example a declarative region is formed by a block statement, by a subprogram, or by any other program unit (a package, a task unit, or a generic unit); similarly a declarative region is formed by a record type declaration. Thus the basic rule is essentially that of Algol 60. The only extensions to this rule are related to packages and to separate compilation.

The fundamental reason for selecting this liberal approach is the pragmatic assumption that names declared together are normally meant to be used together. Consider, for instance, the skeleton

```
procedure P is
   type T is ... ;        -- type declaration
   V : T;                 -- variable declaration
   procedure Q;           -- procedure declaration

   ...

   procedure Q is
      ...
   begin
      ...
   end Q;
begin
   ...
end P;
```

It can be assumed that the names T, V and Q are defined in the same context (the declarative part of P) because they are intended to be used together – here in the sequence of statements of P. Extending this reasoning to inner program units means for instance that the names T, V, and possibly Q are also visible within the body of Q, so that this body may be directly defined in terms of these names. This suggests the assumption that entities declared in the same context have mutually dependent definitions.

One alternative considered was to designate certain program units such as procedures and packages as being always *closed*: Closed units would not automatically inherit the visibility of outer declarative regions, so that some form of explicit *import directive* would be required in order for names declared in outer regions to become visible within closed units. This was ultimately deemed unacceptable because it led to clutter and to long name lists in many common cases.

The following example illustrates the useless redundancy of the directive "*sees* T, C, L", where the procedures P_1 through P_N are obviously meant to work with T, C and L.

```
-- the following is not an Ada text

package D is
  type T is ... ;
  C : constant T := ... ;

  procedure P_1 ( ... );
  procedure P_2 ( ... );
  ...
  procedure P_N( ... );
end D;

package body D is
  L : T;

  -- note: "sees T, C, L" is not legal in Ada

  procedure P_1( ... ) sees T, C, L is ... end P_1;
  procedure P_2( ... ) sees T, C, L is ... end P_2;
  ...
  procedure P_N( ... ) sees T, C, L is ... end P_N;
end D;
```

Early experience with the Euclid language, in which such an approach was taken, shows that the danger of long name lists is not to be underestimated. Because of transitivity, Euclid import lists can get very long. The danger is then – as evidenced by experience with "named COMMON" in Fortran programs – that programmers tend to use the same import lists in all program units, for fear of omitting something. In any case, long name lists are usually skipped when reading, and this defeats their very purpose. The classical argument developed by Dijkstra [Di 72], about our inability to deal with a large number of entities at the same time, also applies to long – and therefore unstructured – name lists.

The only way to avoid this form of text clutter is to make automatic inheritance the default rule. The argument is that the textual embedding of declarations is already a strong indication of potential dependence. The systematic inclusion of additional import directives does not usually provide much information that may usefully be exploited by the translator, and it is likely to distract readers – and writers – of programs.

It was found, moreover, that whether a given syntactic category should be an open scope or a closed scope was a highly subjective question. The answer may vary from one use to another, depending on the size of a particular program unit, the depth to which it is nested, the probability of subsequent recompilation, and so on.

It seems clear, therefore, that the syntax of the language should not arbitrarily impose a decision in this regard. For this reason we have adopted the following approach:

- All syntactic constructs that introduce declarations normally inherit the identifiers of outer (enclosing) contexts.

- A set of declarations can be encapsulated in the visible part of a package: the visibility of these declarations is then acquired in other contexts by means of use clauses.

11.3.2 Naming Conventions: Expanded Names and Use Clauses

Since classical inheritance of identifiers from outer declarative regions is the default rule, redeclaration of identifiers is possible, with the effect of hiding the outer definitions within the inner region.

Some of the difficulties with identifier redeclarations disappear if the names of the corresponding entities can be written as *expanded names*: using the dot notation. Consider, for example, the type T declared immediately within the procedure P above, and assume that the same identifier were reused for a declaration given within the body of Q. The type name could still be written as P.T in the inner unit (exploiting the fact that the identifier P is visible there); this expanded type name may thus be used in qualified expressions and wherever the need to denote the type arises.

The use of expanded names is also the general rule for denoting an identifier declared within a package, when outside of the package itself. Thus, outside the package SIMPLE_IO, the identifier CREATE declared in the visible part of this package can be denoted by the expanded name SIMPLE_IO.CREATE, in spite of the fact that CREATE is not directly visible there.

As an additional syntactic convenience, a *use clause* may be given in a declarative part. A use clause mentions the names of one or more packages and its effect is to achieve direct visibility of any identifier declared in the visible part of one of the packages, exactly as if the identifier were declared at the place of the package concerned. For a given identifier, however, this effect is only achieved in the absence of any conflicting identifier. For example, in a region that includes the use clause

```
use D, E;
```

the identifier I is an acceptable abbreviation for D.I provided that this identifier is declared in D and is not hidden by an intervening redeclaration of I, and provided also that the package E does not contain an identifier I in its visible part. In all cases of redeclaration or conflict, the intended name must be given in full, as an expanded name.

These rules are illustrated by the following example:

```
procedure DEMO is
package D is
   T, U, V : BOOLEAN;
end D;
                              -- (1)
procedure P is
                              -- (2)
   package E is
      B, W, V : INTEGER;
   end E;
                              -- (3)
   procedure Q is
      T, X : REAL;
                              -- (4)
   begin
      ...
   declare
      use D, E;
   begin
      -- the name T means Q.T, not D.T
      -- the name U means D.U
      -- the name B means E.B
      -- the name W means E.W
      -- the name X means Q.X
      -- the name V is illegal:it must be written either D.V or E.V
      ...
   end;
   end Q;
begin
   ...
end P;
begin
   ...
end DEMO;
```

In deciding which names are visible within the sequence of statements of the block statement we apply the following two-step rule:

(a) First we inherit the names declared in outer regions and not redefined. Thus we inherit the names D and P, the names E and Q declared within P, and the names T and X declared within Q.

(b) Then we consider the entities that may be made directly visible by means of use clauses. In the above example this means the entities that are declared in the visible parts of D and E. We retain names that appear in only one of these packages and that do not conflict with a name introduced in the step (a). Hence the names retained here are U, B, W.

One consequence of these rules is that the position of use clauses does not matter. Thus the same effect would be achieved in the above example if the clause "use D;" were given at any of the points (1), (2), (3), or (4); and the clause "use E;" were given at any of the points (3) or (4).

Another consequence is that a name that is made directly visible by a use clause cannot hide another name. This is quite essential for maintainability reasons. Assume, for example, that the specification of the package D were modified to include the declaration of some new entity called X. This should normally have no effect on the procedure Q. In particular, the inner reference to X should retain its previous meaning and should hence mean Q.X both before and after the modification. (Note that we have only reduced the magnitude of this general problem, since a later introduction of W within D would conflict with the W of E; the full solution lies in maintenance tools.)

A similar maintainability argument led us to reject a *unique visibility* rule; that is, a rule forbidding redeclaration of identifiers that were already visible. If redefinition of identifiers were not allowed, the later introduction of some entity named X in the declaration list of P would force textual modification of an inner procedure such as Q, which should normally be unaffected by this change.

Note that use clauses may be viewed as one possible form of the import directives mentioned in section 11.3.1. However, the items listed in use clauses can only be names of packages, and the risk of long use lists is correspondingly reduced. Naturally, effective modularization will depend upon the user writing packages in such a way that related definitions are in the same packages; related definitions will usually be required together.

11.3.3 Visibility Rules for Record Types

A record type definition introduces a new declarative region. Hence component identifiers may be freely chosen. For each selected component, the visibility of the corresponding component is opened by the dot that follows the name of the record object that contains the selected component.

As with Pascal, variants within a record do not introduce new declarative regions. Hence the component names of each variant must be distinct from those of every other variant, even if they are semantically equivalent as far as the programmer is concerned. The reason for not introducing a new declarative region with each variant can be seen from the following example:

```
type T(COMPACT : BOOLEAN := TRUE) is
  record
    case COMPACT is
      when TRUE  => VALUE : FLOAT;
      when FALSE => VALUE : LONG_FLOAT;   -- illegal redeclaration
    end case;
  end record;

R : T;
```

A selected component such as R.VALUE would have to be treated as a conditional expression, dependent on the discriminant, possibly delivering results of alternative types.

11.3.4 Renaming

A renaming capability is offered in Ada. As an example consider

```
declare
  L : PERSON renames LEFTMOST_PERSON;
  R : PERSON renames TO_BE_PROCESSED(NEXT);
begin
  L.AGE := L.AGE + 1;
  R.AGE := R.AGE - 1;
  if L.BIRTH < R.BIRTH then
    L.RANK := L.RANK + 1;
  else
    R.RANK := R.RANK + 1;
  end if;
end;
```

The renaming declarations of L and R are used to introduce new local names for the outer variables LEFTMOST_PERSON and TO_BE_PROCESSED(NEXT). In the sequence of statements of the block, L and R may be used as convenient names of the variables that they denote. Here the renaming facility is used for purposes similar to the Pascal *with statement* – as a convenient alternative for frequently used long names. However, components of renamed records are still denoted with the syntax of record components so they cannot be confused with variables bearing the same name as the components.

In addition to the notational advantage, such a renaming declaration avoids reevaluating the access path to the record variable for each component selection, and may allow more efficient code to be generated.

Renaming declarations are also permitted for subprograms, packages, and exceptions. In addition, subtype declarations can be used to achieve the effect of renaming for types:

```
function "*" (LEFT, RIGHT : VECTOR) return REAL renames DOT_PRODUCT;
procedure READ(V : out ELEM) renames PROTECTED_VARIABLE.READ;
package TM renames TABLE_MANAGER;
DATA_ERROR : exception renames IO_EXCEPTIONS.DATA_ERROR;
```

The ability to rename turns out to be very convenient when working with packages that are developed independently by different groups of programmers. Being independently developed, such packages may well declare the same identifiers. If later these packages are both mentioned by a use clause in a given region, it may often be convenient to resolve name conflicts by renaming rather than by using dot notation whenever these identifiers appear. For example consider:

```
package TRAFFIC is
   type COLOR is (RED, AMBER, GREEN);
   ...
end TRAFFIC;

package WATER_COLORS is
   type COLOR is (WHITE, RED, YELLOW, GREEN, BLUE, BROWN);
   ...
end WATER_COLORS;

declare
   use TRAFFIC, WATER_COLORS;
   subtype SIGNAL is TRAFFIC.COLOR;
   subtype TINT   is WATER_COLORS.COLOR;
   LIGHT : SIGNAL;
   SHADE : TINT;
   ...
begin
   ...
end;
```

The subtypes SIGNAL and TINT effectively rename the corresponding types and are unambiguous within the block, whereas COLOR would be ambiguous.

Because of the possibility of overloading, it will often suffice to rename conflicting type names: names of subprograms will in consequence be resolved by the overloading rules. The renaming facility can also be used to provide a name more appropriate to the context of its use. For instance, the author of a sort routine may call his version QUICKSORT2 whereas SORT may be better (and less cumbersome) throughout the application.

11.4 OVERLOADING

In Ada, every use of a simple name or operator symbol is understood with reference to an (explicit or implicit) declaration of the name or symbol. In the case of types, variables, and constants, at most one such declaration can be visible at any one point in the program. In the case of subprograms, enumeration literals, and entries, however, several declarations may be simultaneously visible. An occurrence of a subprogram name, such as PUT or "*", may therefore refer to one of several simultaneously visible declarations. The name or operator symbol is then said to be *overloaded*.

11.4.1 Overloading of Operators

The overloading of operators is a situation familiar also in other languages, and it illustrates the main reason for the existence of overloading in Ada. Consider, for example:

```
I, J, K : INTEGER;
X, Y, Z : REAL;
```

It is then possible to write the statements

```
K := I*J;
Z := X*Y;
```

in which the operator symbol "*" refers in the first statement to

function "*" (LEFT, RIGHT : INTEGER) **return INTEGER;**

and in the second statement to

function "*" (LEFT, RIGHT : REAL) **return REAL;**

The functions that implement integer multiplication and floating multiplication are represented by the same symbol because they are different implementations of the same abstract operation: the operation of multiplication.

The overloading of predefined operators has been a feature of programming languages ever since FORTRAN. But Ada also permits users to define new data types, for example COMPLEX or RATIONAL. Since much of the power of the language comes from its extensibility, and since proper use of that extensibility requires that we make as little distinction as possible between predefined and user-defined types, it is natural that Ada also permits new operations to be defined, by declaring new overloadings of the operator symbols. Therefore, since the operation of abstract multiplication applies to complex and rational numbers, one would expect to see

```
function "*" (LEFT, RIGHT : COMPLEX)  return COMPLEX;
function "*" (LEFT, RIGHT : RATIONAL) return RATIONAL;
```

whereby the programmer can multiply rational or complex numbers using the familiar mathematical notation. The ability to coin descriptive names is an important part of good programming, and it is therefore desirable that a programming language give the programmer as much freedom as possible in the choice of names. Moreover, the use of familiar notation in new contexts is a very powerful descriptive tool: it is an example of the principle of analogy. The ability of an Ada programmer to overload operators upon new types allows the principle of analogy to be used in programming. Further examples of this principle are:

```
function "*" (LEFT, RIGHT : VECTOR) return SCALAR;
function "*" (LEFT, RIGHT : MATRIX) return MATRIX;
```

In practice, it is unlikely that two quite different overloadings, such as the two declarations of "*" above, will be defined together. It is more likely that each will be defined in its own package – in this case, one package might be called VECTOR_OPERATIONS and the other SCALAR_OPERATIONS. Similarly, rational multiplication might well be defined in a package

```
package RATIONAL_ARITHMETIC is

   type RATIONAL is private;

   function "+" (RIGHT : RATIONAL) return RATIONAL;
   function "-" (RIGHT : RATIONAL) return RATIONAL;

   function "+" (LEFT, RIGHT : RATIONAL) return RATIONAL;
   function "-" (LEFT, RIGHT : RATIONAL) return RATIONAL;
   function "*" (LEFT, RIGHT : RATIONAL) return RATIONAL;
   function "/" (LEFT, RIGHT : RATIONAL) return RATIONAL;

   function "**" (LEFT : RATIONAL; RIGHT : INTEGER) return RATIONAL;

   function "/" (LEFT : INTEGER; RIGHT : POSITIVE) return RATIONAL;
   ...
private
```

```
    type RATIONAL is
      record
        NUMERATOR    : INTEGER;
        DENOMINATOR : POSITIVE;
      end record;

    end RATIONAL_ARITHMETIC;
```

In this package, a new type is defined, together with the complete set of applicable operations. The programmer defining the type is free to use the traditional operator symbols for the new type, and to give them a meaning analogous to their meaning with other types. There is no need to worry about other meanings (declarations) that might occur in other packages defining other types: the Ada overloading facility permits the package RATIONAL_ARITHMETIC to be defined as an independent software component.

These operations could be used thus:

```
CM_PER_INCH : constant RATIONAL := 254/100;
                                        -- by international decree!
function INCH_TO_CM(INCHES : RATIONAL) return RATIONAL is
begin
    return INCHES * CM_PER_INCH;
end;
```

Note that, by an analysis similar to the one given in section 9.2.2, we can identify the "/" operation in the expression "254/100" as being the function that takes one integer and one positive number, and yields a rational result.

11.4.2 Overloading of Names

Several languages beside Ada, such as Algol 68, permit operator symbols to be overloaded. Ada however also permits subprogram names to be overloaded, for exactly the same reasons. Consider for example

```
    procedure PUT(X : in STRING);
    procedure PUT(X : in INTEGER);
```

This allows a programmer to write

```
    PUT("The value of X is: ");
    PUT(X);
```

The abstract operation PUT applies indifferently to both strings and integers; it is there-fore appropriate that the same name be used in both cases. Observe that this is in accord with the conventions of natural language:

"Put the book on the shelf"
"Put the cat out"

which does not have separate words for putting books and putting cats.

Ada does not permit the overloading of variables or constants. This again is in accordance with traditional habits of thought: we seem far more willing to accept potentially ambiguous names for operations than for things. Thus, mathematicians typically write

```
I1 + I2        -- integers
X1 + X2        -- floating-point values
V1 + V2        -- vectors
M1 + M2        -- matrices
Z1 + Z2        -- complex numbers
```

where all the addition operations are written "+" but their operand types are distin-guished by a systematic nomenclature. It seems to be a convention of our language that *verbs* are generic but *nouns* are specific; Ada reflects this by permitting operations to be overloaded but – normally – not operands. Thus, Ada allows (and we find normal)

```
procedure SERVE(S : SOUP);
procedure SERVE(F : FRUIT);     -- permitted overloading
```

but does not allow (and which we would find abnormal)

```
OF_THE_DAY : SOUP;
OF_THE_DAY : FRUIT;            -- not a legal overloading!
```

11.4.3 Overloading of Literals

Literals stand for values. However, in a strongly-typed language, it must be possible to associate a type with every value, and so in some sense a literal should imply a type. This creates difficulties in two cases: first, when different values, of different types, by chance are represented by the same literal; and secondly, when *the same* conceptual value belongs to more than one type.

Enumeration Literals

The first case is called *homography*: two conceptually different values have the same symbol. It may be illustrated by

```
package PALETTE is
   type COLOR is (RED, ORANGE, YELLOW, GREEN, ... );
   procedure PUT(X : COLOR);
   ...
end;

package BOTANY is
   type FRUIT is (APPLE, ORANGE, BANANA, KIWI, ... );
   procedure PUT(X : FRUIT);
   ...
end;

package ORNITHOLOGY is
   type APTERON is (MOA, KIWI, OSTRICH, ... );
   procedure PUT(X : APTERON);
   ...
end;
```

In no sense is a KIWI fruit the same as the flightless KIWI bird: the homography is an accident of language.

A programming language should not *forbid* such homography: it would be unreasonable to force the author of PALETTE to change the word ORANGE merely because it was a fruit; and indeed Ada never forbids a programmer from defining a locally unambiguous name. But it is a separate design decision whether to permit overloading of such names.

Ada permits overloading of enumeration literals; this is in accord with the idea that an enumeration literal resembles a parameterless function. Hence the following is legal:

```
with BOTANY, ORNITHOLOGY;
use BOTANY, ORNITHOLOGY;
procedure P is
   FRUIT_OF_THE_DAY : FRUIT   := KIWI;
   BIRD_IN_THE_HAND : APTERON := KIWI;
   ...
end;
```

Resolution is exactly as for parameterless functions: in the above declarations the required type is evident from the context.

This rule also permits character literals to be used in more than one type:

```
type ASCII  is ( ... , 'A', 'B', 'C', ... );
type EBCDIC is ( ... , 'A', 'B', 'C', ... );

AC : ASCII  := 'A';
EC : EBCDIC := 'B';
```

Numeric Literals

The numeric literals, however, illustrate the second case. In the following:

```
X : FLOAT      := 1.0;
Y : LONG_FLOAT := 1.0;
```

the two occurrences of "1.0" stand for *the same* abstract value – unity – but in two different physical representations, and hence, in Ada, associated with two different types. It would be possible to view "1.0" as an overloaded literal – overloaded on all real types. Ada however takes a different view, that we believe corresponds more closely to our intuition. It regards real literals as being all of one type, the type *universal_real*, and introduces an *implicit conversion* to the required numeric type. The declarations above are therefore interpreted as

```
X : FLOAT      := FLOAT(1.0);
Y : LONG_FLOAT := LONG_FLOAT(1.0);
```

The alternative view – that the literals should be considered to be overloaded on all numeric types – would lead to some anomalies, of which the most annoying would perhaps be that

```
if 1 < 2 then ...
```

would be ambiguous: would we mean to invoke the "<" of type INTEGER or that of type LONG_INTEGER? The Ada view avoids such difficulties.

Observe by contrast that, if ASCII and EBCDIC are both visible, then

```
if 'A' < '0' then ...
```

will indeed be rejected as ambiguous, and rightly so, since the relation means different things in ASCII and EBCDIC.

11.5 OVERLOAD RESOLUTION

When an overloaded name or symbol occurs, the language translator must determine which of several possible definitions is meant. This process is called *overload resolution*, and it must naturally rely on information from the context in which the name occurs. In defining the language, the rules for overload resolution need to be established, and these rules must make clear two things:

- what is the *context* from which information is to be taken

- what information may be used

As an example of the former question, consider the fragment

```
for I in MIN(A,B) .. MAX(C,D) loop
```

and how we might resolve the overloaded function MIN.

(a) consider only the context MIN(A,B); that is, the function and its actual parameter list;

(b) consider the context MIN(A,B) .. MAX(C,D), including the fact that the result types of the two calls must be the same;

(c) consider the context for I in MIN(A,B) .. MAX(C,D), including the fact that the result types must be the same, and must be of a discrete type.

As an example of the latter question, consider a call of CREATE, from the package SIMPLE_IO of section 9.2.3

```
CREATE(FILE => OUTFILE, NAME => "Results");
```

and what information we should use to determine which CREATE is being invoked:

(d) there are two actual parameters

(e) their types are FILE_NAME and STRING

(f) their formal names are FILE and NAME

(g) since "Results" is a string literal, the mode of the NAME parameter must be in

We shall consider these two issues in turn.

11.5.1 Context of Overload Resolution

It might appear that the simplest overload resolution rule is to use *everything* – all information from as wide a context as possible – to resolve the overloaded reference. This rule may be simple, but it is not helpful. It requires the human reader to scan arbitrarily large pieces of text, and to make arbitrarily complex inferences (such as (g) above). We believe that a better rule is one that makes explicit the task a human reader or a compiler must perform, and that makes this task as natural for the human reader as possible.

The contexts to be used in overload resolution are given explicitly in RM 8.7. They correspond, we believe, to the natural program fragments that both writer and reader will regard as conceptual units. For example, the controlling expression of a **for** loop is such a unit: it represents a bounded, ordered iteration over a set of discrete values. Accordingly, the resolution process considers (a), (b), and (c) above: both bounds of the range, and also the fact of its discreteness. We can therefore resolve

```
for F in ORANGE .. KIWI loop
```

in the way that we believe the human reader would: as an iteration over fruits.

As another example, consider the case statement

```
case BIRD_IN_THE_HAND is      -- (1)
   when KIWI =>               -- (2)
      ...
      -- imagine a lot of text here
   when ORANGE =>             -- (3)
      ...
   ...
end case;
```

The case expression and the values in the case alternatives must of course all have the same type. However, Ada requires the case expression, on line (1), to be resolved *first*, before considering the case arms. This is because, otherwise, the human reader would have to scan an arbitrarily large amount of text in order to understand the very first line of the case statement. This would violate our convention (sanctioned by both Ada and natural usage) of linear readability. With the Ada rule, the reader *knows* at point (2) that KIWI is an APTERON, and knows at point (3) that ORANGE is an error.

11.5.2 Information Used to Resolve Overloading

A more difficult issue is, what information should be taken from the context of resolution? Since the main purpose of overloading is to allow analogous operations on different types to be given the same name, resolution clearly must consider type information. The other information available is the order, names, and modes of the parameters, the presence of defaults, and the result type.

The rationale behind the Ada position is threefold. First, the rules should be convenient for, and comprehensible to, the human reader and writer: this must override any consideration of compiler simplicity. Secondly, the rules should allow natural programming conventions to be followed with unsurprising results. Thirdly, the information used should be readily observable in the program text, and not highly implicit.

Overloaded Operations

It seems best to consider first the overloading of operations. The natural use of operator symbols is in infix notation, where clearly the *order* of the parameters matters, but the formal names do not. And Ada therefore uses the one, and not the other. Thus, given

```
function "-" (LEFT : TIME; RIGHT : DURATION) return TIME;
```

then an expression such as

```
MIDNIGHT - 10*MINUTE
```

is interpreted as subtracting a DURATION from a TIME (assuming the declaration of MIDNIGHT as a variable of type TIME, and MINUTE as a constant of type DURATION), but

```
10*MINUTE - MIDNIGHT
```

will fail: the operands are in the wrong order.

However, Ada does not permit these overloadings:

```
function "-" (LEFT, RIGHT : INTEGER) return INTEGER;
function "-" (MINUEND, SUBTRAHEND : INTEGER) return INTEGER;
```

because, even if we did happen to remember the traditional names of the operands, we would never use them in an invocation of the "-" operator. The formal names will never be seen at the point of call, and so cannot be considered in overload resolution.

Since operations are functions, the parameter mode must always be in and so is irrelevant to the resolution. There remains only the question of the result type.

Some languages, such as Algol 68, do not use the result type of an operation to assist in overload resolution. This has the advantage that it leads to an implementation of overload resolution by a single bottom-up traversal of the expression. But is this admitted convenience for the compiler writer accompanied by any benefit for the human programmer?

There are few cases in conventional mathematics where an abstract operation may yield two different types of result, but these cases are significant. One example is the distinction between *scalar* product and *vector* product. It is surely desirable to allow

```
function "*" (LEFT, RIGHT : VECTOR) return SCALAR;
function "*" (LEFT, RIGHT : VECTOR) return MATRIX;
```

since otherwise one hapless programmer will have to abandon infix notation completely, and the other will have to fight for his monopoly over the "*" symbol.

As another example, consider the rational constructor

```
function "/" (LEFT: INTEGER; RIGHT: POSITIVE) return RATIONAL;
```

defined above. It is hard to imagine any better way of writing

```
ALMOST_PI := 355/113;
```

But this requires the ability to overload "/" on the result type.

We conclude that the use of the function result type in overload resolution is methodologically the better choice, and one that enhances the freedom of the programmer to write natural, comprehensible expressions.

Overloaded Names

Named procedures and functions, called by conventional prefix notation, present a rather different issue. This is because Ada permits both positional and named parameter association, for the reasons given in section 8.3. Moreover, procedure parameters may take one of three modes: **in, in out, out**; and **in** parameters may be defaulted. Potentially, all this information is available for overload resolution.

To resolve overloading, Ada uses the formal names but not the modes; that is, (d), (e) and (f) above, as described in RM 6.6. The reason is simple: the programmer may write the formal names explicitly in the call statement, but has no means of indicating the modes at the place of the call (since all parameter associations use "=>"). Hence, the formal names can be made explicit, but the modes are always implicit, and the natural action is to use explicit information where given, but to avoid using implicit information that the human reader might have difficulty in deducing.

11.5.3 Ambiguity

An overloaded name is potentially ambiguous. In practice, even with the best programming style, actual ambiguities will sometimes arise, in the form of expressions that cannot be resolved. The most common reason is accident: two packages are jointly used; each defines a consistent set of names; but there is a clash of names. For example, consider the packages PALETTE and BOTANY defined above. One cannot find fault with these packages individually, but then

```
with PALETTE, BOTANY;
use  PALETTE, BOTANY;
procedure P is
  ...
  PUT(ORANGE);
  ...
end P;
```

contains an ambiguous call of PUT – one that is ambiguous even when all available information is used.

Clearly, the programmer must provide more information. There are two sorts of information that Ada permits one to provide: information about the source of a name, and information about its type. To illustrate the former, consider

```
BOTANY.PUT(ORANGE);
```

This is clearly unambiguous, since only one PUT is defined in package BOTANY. Ada dot notation can always be used to give information about the source that provides the name, and, if the package in question has been properly written, this information should suffice. Indeed, this property is essential if packages are to be generally useful software components, since it guarantees that a properly-constructed package can be used by anyone, regardless of what other packages they may need.

To illustrate how type information can be given, consider

```
PUT(FRUIT'(ORANGE));
```

This also is unambiguous: ORANGE is a FRUIT, and so the PUT that puts fruits is intended. Since type names cannot be overloaded, and since all expressions can be qualified, this method also ensures overload resolution.

By either of these methods, the user who by accident encounters an ambiguity can make the intended meaning explicit.

12. Generic Units

12.1 INTRODUCTION

Generic units are a general form of parameterized program units. As with other parameterization mechanisms, the primary purpose is factorization, resulting in a reduction in the size of the program text while also improving maintainability, readability, and efficiency.

Parameterization by generic units is a natural extension of subprogram parameterization. When otherwise identical actions differ by a particular value or variable, these actions may be encapsulated in a subprogram where the value or variable appears as a parameter. Having thereby *factored out* the common part, the text becomes smaller and easier to read; and clerical errors, resulting from accidental lack of identity among the copies, are eliminated. Moreover, compilers can take advantage of this commonality to produce more compact code.

Traditional parameterization mechanisms are usually in terms of values and variables. But the same factorization arguments apply when two otherwise identical program units differ by some other property, such as a type.

A classical example is provided by stacks. In Ada, stacks would typically be formulated as a private type, encapsulated with its associated operations within a package. Although one may want to have stacks of integers and stacks of real numbers, it is clear that neither the stack algorithms, nor the proof of their correctness, depends upon the type of the items to be stacked. However, the typing rules will not allow the writing of a single procedure to deal with items that are either integer or real values: if this were allowed, there would be no way to guarantee that a given stack does not contain intermixed integer and real values. Hence another parameterization mechanism is needed to express the intent that, although all items of a stack have the same type, we may want to specify this type independently for individual stacks: this parameterization mechanism is what is provided by the *generic formal part* of a generic unit.

Generic units are parameterized program units (for example, generic packages) for which parameters can be types and subprograms as well as values and variables. Replication of text can thereby be avoided, yielding better readability and maintainability. In addition, compilers may use their knowledge of type representations to achieve certain optimizations; for example, reusing the same code for stacks of integers and reals if the same number of bits is used for the mapping of values of these types. Seen in this light, the generic facility provides a natural complement to strong typing, minimizing the unnecessary duplication of both source text and object code.

One of the commonest applications of any generic facility is factoring out dependences on particular types. Several earlier languages have accordingly introduced language features to accommodate this sort of parameterization. By far the most powerful is that provided by the language EL 1; however, this generality is achieved at the cost of *interpreting* types in a fully dynamic fashion, which is incompatible with the efficiency and security criteria imposed in the present context.

Languages such as Simula, Clu, and Mary offer a reasonably elegant approach to this problem, but all require that all objects be handled by reference. This introduces additional overhead – namely, indirect access – even in cases where this generality is neither needed nor wanted. To some degree, type discriminants and variants (such as in Euclid and Ada) or type unions (such as in Algol 68) provide a possible approach when the alternative types are known in advance; similarly the language CS-4 provides a limited facility that may only be used in conjunction with predefined types. Neither approach offers the flexibility that is required when the definition of new data types is viewed as the rule rather than the exception.

A review of the shortcomings of existing mechanisms that allow types to be used as parameters showed that it was inappropriate to introduce overly elaborate language features solely for this purpose, principally because the same effect (and many others as well) can be essentially achieved by far simpler means using traditional macro-expansion techniques – although in a context-sensitive manner. The problem then reduced to integrating this well-established approach into the framework of a high-order language at reasonable cost.

In Ada, the more sophisticated sorts of parameterization are accommodated by generic program units, which are a restricted form of context-sensitive macro facility. The main objectives in providing this particular mechanism have been:

- to allow an additional degree of freedom in factorization without sacrificing efficiency;

- to allow compilers to take advantage of this factorization to minimize the size of the code;

- to preserve the security that is present for ordinary, unparameterized program units; in particular, the degree of compilation-time error checking.

12.2 INFORMAL PRESENTATION OF GENERIC UNITS

A generic unit is a program unit: it is either a generic subprogram or a generic package. The declaration of a generic unit starts with a generic formal part which defines compilation-time generic formal parameters; the generic formal part is followed by a subprogram declaration (for a generic subprogram) or by a package declaration (for a generic package).

A generic subprogram is not an ordinary subprogram: for example it cannot be called; it is rather a *template* for all (ordinary) subprograms that can be obtained by associating specific actual parameters with the generic formal parameters. Similarly a generic package is a template for (ordinary) packages.

A specific program unit that corresponds to a given template is created by a declaration called a *generic instantiation*. This has the effect of creating a named *instance*. In the case of a subprogram, for example, this named instance can then be called in the usual way. Thus, apart from parameterization, generic declaration is for nongeneric program units what a type declaration is for data objects:

	data objects	*program units*
defining the template:	type declaration	generic declaration
defining an instance:	object declaration	generic instantiation

12.2.1 Generic Formal Parts

A generic formal part starts with the reserved word **generic** and includes declarations of generic formal parameters. These can be formal objects (variables and constants, as in the case of parameters of subprograms); but they can also be generic formal subprograms and generic formal types. For example, the generic formal part

```
generic
   type ITEM is private;
```

declares the generic formal type ITEM. We find this generic formal part in the declaration of the following generic procedure:

```
generic
  type ITEM is private;
procedure EXCHANGE(LEFT, RIGHT : in out ITEM);

procedure EXCHANGE(LEFT, RIGHT : in out ITEM) is
  OLD_LEFT : constant ITEM := LEFT;
begin
  LEFT  := RIGHT;
  RIGHT := OLD_LEFT;
end;
```

In this example, LEFT and RIGHT are the ordinary (that is, nongeneric) parameters: each procedure obtained by instantiation of this template will have these parameters, which are subject to dynamic replacement. In contrast, the type ITEM given in the generic formal part is a generic formal parameter which is to be substituted for at compilation time. This generic parameter may appear in the body of the generic subprogram; here it is used in the declaration of the constant OLD_LEFT.

12.2.2 Generic Instantiations

A generic instantiation creates an instance of a generic unit by replacement of the generic parameters. A generic instantiation is a declaration and it associates a name with the corresponding instance. Usually, there will be several different instantiations of a given generic unit:

```
procedure SWAP_INT   is new EXCHANGE(ITEM => INTEGER);
procedure SWAP_CHAR  is new EXCHANGE(ITEM => CHARACTER);
procedure SWAP_COLOR is new EXCHANGE(ITEM => COLOR);
```

Each resultant program unit is an ordinary procedure, applicable to actual parameters of the corresponding type. The resulting procedure specifications are as follows:

```
procedure SWAP_INT   (LEFT, RIGHT : in out INTEGER);
procedure SWAP_CHAR  (LEFT, RIGHT : in out CHARACTER);
procedure SWAP_COLOR (LEFT, RIGHT : in out COLOR);
```

In each case, the name of the generic procedure has been replaced by the name given in the instantiation, the formal type by the actual type, and everything else remains the same – the names and modes of the formal parameters of the instantiation are the same as those of the generic procedure.

The fact that these procedures are obtained by generic instantiation does not preclude overloading of their names:

```
procedure SWAP is new EXCHANGE(ITEM => INTEGER);
procedure SWAP is new EXCHANGE(ITEM => CHARACTER);
procedure SWAP is new EXCHANGE(ITEM => COLOR);
```

Calls of these procedures will be as usual; for example:

```
SWAP(I, J);            -- for integers
SWAP(SHADE, TINT);     -- for colors
```

In general, a generic instantiation for a procedure has the form

> **procedure** *identifier* **is**
> **new** *name* [(*generic_association* {, *generic_association*})];

The syntax of generic associations is similar to that of parameter associations for subprogram calls. Note that both named associations and positional associations are possible, as usual. Thus our previous example can be written equivalently in positional form as:

```
procedure SWAP is new EXCHANGE(INTEGER);
procedure SWAP is new EXCHANGE(CHARACTER);
procedure SWAP is new EXCHANGE(COLOR);
```

A program unit obtained by generic instantiation can be viewed as a copy of the corresponding generic unit where each formal parameter has been replaced by the corresponding actual parameter. For example, the declaration of SWAP_INT produces a procedure equivalent to

```
procedure SWAP_INT(LEFT, RIGHT : in out INTEGER) is
   OLD_LEFT : constant INTEGER := LEFT;
begin
   LEFT  := RIGHT;
   RIGHT := OLD_LEFT;
end;
```

A generic instantiation need not appear in the same declarative part as the corresponding generic declaration – it may appear at any point where the name of the generic unit is visible.

The rule followed for the identification of names within a generic unit is similar to that used for subprograms: All non-local identifiers of the body of a generic unit are identified in the context of the *generic declaration*. In contrast, the actual parameters given in the generic associations must be interpreted in the context of the *generic instantiation*.

Note that this rule differs from a simple textual substitution. In the latter case all identifiers, including non-local ones, would be interpreted in the context of the instantiation. Hence it would not be possible in general to obtain the effect of generic program units by a simple (context-free) macro facility; and this was our reason for referring to *context-sensitive* macro expansion, earlier in the introduction.

To summarize, the generic parameter names (and the name of the unit itself) are the only unresolved identifiers in the body of a generic program unit. For any generic instantiation, replacements must be provided for all generic parameters. These replacements are to be interpreted in the context of the instantiation.

12.2.3 Private Types as Generic Formal Types

In the simple EXCHANGE example presented so far, very little information is needed about the type given as a generic parameter: within the body of this generic procedure, the only operation assumed available for objects of the type is assignment. Hence this template can be applied to any type for which assignment is available; that is, to any type except a limited type.

In general when a generic formal type is specified as being *private*, no operations are assumed to be available aside from assignment, the predefined comparison for equality and inequality, and certain attributes such as SIZE. Furthermore, if the generic formal type is declared as *limited private*, then not even assignment and the comparison for equality and inequality are available.

For such types – whether limited or not – each operation that is used within the generic body must be specified by another generic formal parameter, namely, a generic formal subprogram. As an example, consider the generic function:

```
generic
   type ELEM is limited private;
   with function "*" (LEFT, RIGHT : ELEM) return ELEM;
function SQUARING(X : ELEM) return ELEM;

function SQUARING(X : ELEM) return ELEM is
begin
   return X * X;
end;
```

Since nothing is known a priori about the type ELEM, it would not be possible to write X * X if the specification of "*" were not provided explicitly by a generic formal parameter (this specification is prefixed by the reserved word **with** to distinguish it syntactically from the generic function itself and thus to show that we are still in the generic formal part):

```
with function "*" (LEFT, RIGHT : ELEM) return ELEM;
```

Instances of SQUARING are created by supplying the corresponding actual parameters. For example, for the instantiation

```
function SQUARE is new SQUARING(INTEGER, "*");
```

the operation "*" used in the body is the operation defined as

```
function "*" (LEFT, RIGHT : INTEGER) return INTEGER;
```

that is, the normal integer multiplication. Thus the generic instantiation produces a function body equivalent to the following:

```
function SQUARE(X : INTEGER) return INTEGER is
begin
   return X * X;
end;
```

Of course, other instantiations are possible. For example, we may want to use SQUARING for matrices, to extend the existing component-by-component multiplication

```
function MULT(X, Y : MATRIX) return MATRIX;
```

Thus with the generic instantiation

```
function SQUARE is new SQUARING(ELEM => MATRIX, "*" => MULT);
```

we obtain a function that performs component-by-component squaring of a matrix.

12.2.4 Other Forms of Generic Formal Types

Types are by far the most useful form of generic formal parameter. For this reason, the language provides (beyond formal private types) forms of formal type that correspond to major families of types in Ada. Many of these formal types appear as type patterns formed with the *box* symbol. For example:

```
type BASE  is (<>);         -- discrete
type INT   is range <>;     -- integer
type FIXED is delta <>;     -- fixed point
type MASS  is digits <>;    -- floating point
```

In each case, the box symbolizes what is not there, what is left unspecified. So for example, the type INT will stand for any integer type, with any possible range; the type BASE will stand for any discrete type, whether an enumeration or an integer type.

Each formal type specifies minimum requirements for the corresponding actual types, and the specification and body of the generic unit can rely on these minimal assumptions. For example, for a formal type such as BASE, we can count on the availability of all properties of discrete types:

- assignment: :=

- comparison for equality and inequality: = /=

- ordering relations: < <= > >=

- attributes: FIRST, LAST, SUCC, PRED, ...

- use for array indexing

Similarly for a formal type such as INT we can count on the availability of all properties of discrete types, and also on the additional properties of integer types:

- binary adding operators: + -

- unary adding operators: + -

- multiplying operators: * / mod rem

- highest precedence operators: ** abs

For a given instantiation, the actual type will have to satisfy the minimum requirements established by the formal type. Thus any enumeration type and any integer type will match the formal type BASE; on the other hand, only an integer type will match the formal type INT (not an enumeration type).

As an example, consider the treatment of sets. In Pascal, sets are dealt with by means of a specific language feature. In Ada a specific feature is unnecessary since sets can be defined by a generic package:

```
generic
  type BASE is (<>);        -- any discrete type
package ON_SETS is
  type SET is array (BASE) of BOOLEAN;

  EMPTY : constant SET := (BASE => FALSE);
  FULL  : constant SET := (BASE => TRUE);

  type SEQUENCE is array (POSITIVE range <>) of BASE;

  function SET_OF(S : SEQUENCE) return SET;
  function "+" (LEFT : SET; RIGHT : SET)  return SET;  -- set union
  function "+" (LEFT : SET; RIGHT : BASE) return SET;
                                          -- element insertion
  -- other set operations:
end ON_SETS;
```

The declaration of the formal type BASE requires the actual type to be discrete and we are clearly using this assumption when using BASE as index subtype for the type SET; and similarly when using BASE as a choice for the aggregates that give the values of EMPTY and FULL.

We can now use ordinary set operations with a chosen discrete type by instantiation of this generic package. For example, for the enumeration type:

```
type DAY is (MON, TUE, WED, THU, FRI, SAT, SUN);
```

we can create the instance

```
package DAY_SETS is new ON_SETS(BASE => DAY);
```

and then

```
use DAY_SETS;
S : SET;
...
S := SET_OF((SUN, TUE, WED));
S := S + SAT;
...
S := S + SET_OF((MON, THU));
```

The actual parameter of SET_OF is a SEQUENCE – an array of values of the base type, indexed by the positive numbers 1, 2, and 3 – and the function constructs the corresponding set. The next statements then use set addition. A sketch of the generic body is given below:

```
package body ON_SETS is
  ...
  function SET_OF(S : SEQUENCE) return SET is
    RESULT : SET := EMPTY;
  begin
    for N in S'RANGE loop
      RESULT(S(N)) := TRUE;
    end loop;
    return RESULT;
  end;

  function "+" (LEFT : SET; RIGHT : SET) return SET is
  begin
    return LEFT or RIGHT;
  end;

  function "+" (LEFT : SET; RIGHT : BASE) return SET is
    RESULT : SET := LEFT;
  begin
    RESULT(RIGHT) := TRUE;
    return RESULT;
  end;
  ...
end ON_SETS;
```

On top of these type patterns with boxes we can construct other type patterns by means of array type definitions and access type definitions. For example, a generic sorting procedure could be specified as:

```
generic
  type ITEM  is private;
  type INDEX is (<>);
  type ROW   is array (INDEX range <>) of ITEM;
  with function "<" (LEFT, RIGHT : ITEM) return BOOLEAN;
procedure SORT(R : in out ROW);
```

An instantiation would have to meet the minimum requirements established by this generic formal part. For example, consider:

```
type MEETING is ...          -- some record type
type AGENDA  is array (DAY range <>) of MEETING;
function LESS_IMPORTANT(X, Y : MEETING) return BOOLEAN;

procedure ORDER is
   new SORT(ITEM  => MEETING,
            INDEX => DAY,
            ROW   => AGENDA,
            "<"   => LESS_IMPORTANT);

MY_WEEK : AGENDA(MON .. FRI);
   ...
ORDER(MY_WEEK);
```

The matching types are clearly shown by the named parameter associations. Consider for example the definition of the formal type ROW:

array (INDEX range <>) of ITEM;

After replacing ITEM by MEETING, and INDEX by DAY, we obtain the type definition

array (DAY range <>) of MEETING;

which is exactly the way AGENDA is defined, so that AGENDA matches ROW correctly. Similarly, the function LESS_IMPORTANT matches the operator "<", once we have replaced ITEM by MEETING.

The types used in this example are certainly not the usual types we find in ordinary programming, and yet the instantiation works because we have limited our required assumptions to the minimum. We did not assume anything about ITEM, apart from the ability to assign, which is needed for sorting; the only assumption that we made about the index type was that it was discrete (assuming an integer type would have been overspecification); finally we assumed the existence of an order relation for ITEMS. Had we assumed more than is strictly needed (for example, real items, integer indices) the instantiation would have failed.

12.2.5 Default Parameters

Default values can be defined for generic parameters that are subprograms. Thus an alternative form of definition for SQUARING might be

```
generic
   type ELEM is private;
   with function "*" (LEFT, RIGHT : ELEM) return ELEM is <>;
function SQUARING(X : ELEM) return ELEM;

function SQUARING(X : ELEM) return ELEM is
begin
   return X * X;
end;
```

The specification of the formal function "*" indicates, by means of a box, that a corresponding actual parameter need not be present in instantiations of the generic function SQUARING. For example, we can write:

```
function SQUARE is new SQUARING(INTEGER);
```

As usual, the box stands for what is missing – in this case it is a function whose specification is obtained by replacing ELEM by INTEGER:

```
function "*" (LEFT, RIGHT : INTEGER) return INTEGER;
```

and since there is such an operation for the type INTEGER, this integer multiplication is used – by default – in place of the actual parameter.

This form of default corresponds to very good programming practice: We have a natural notation, such as "*" for multiplication, and we expect users to make natural use of this notation. With this form we can specify the box for the corresponding formal parameter so that instantiations will select by default the "natural" operation.

Naturally, we can always override the default by providing an explicit actual parameter:

```
function SQUARE is new SQUARING(ELEM => MATRIX, "*" => MULT);
```

There is another form of default, which names the default actual subprogram; for example:

```
with procedure STEP(X : in out INTEGER) is INCREMENT;
```

where the procedure INCREMENT is a procedure visible at the place of the formal parameter declaration, and whose profile matches that of the formal procedure:

```
procedure INCREMENT(N : in out INTEGER);
```

For this second form of default, the actual parameter is to be found in the context of the generic declaration, whereas in the case of the box, the default was to be found in the context of the generic instantiation.

12.3 THE USE OF GENERIC UNITS

This section contains a number of examples illustrating the use of generic units.

12.3.1 Examples of Generic Functions

The following program fragment defines a generic function POWER to raise the value of an object of a type T to its nth power. This exponentiation is defined by repeated multiplication, and the corresponding multiplication operation must be supplied as a generic actual parameter.

```
generic
   type ELEM is private;
   with function OPER(LEFT, RIGHT : ELEM) return ELEM;
function POWER(E : ELEM; N : POSITIVE) return ELEM;

function POWER(E : ELEM; N : POSITIVE) return ELEM is
   RESULT : ELEM := E;
begin
   for J in 2 .. N loop
      RESULT := OPER(RESULT, E);
   end loop;
   return RESULT;
end POWER;
```

This generic function can be used to define exponentiation for types for which a multiplication operation is known. For example:

```
function "**" is new POWER(ELEM => RATIONAL, OPER => "*");
function "**" is new POWER(ELEM => MATRIX, OPER => MULT);
```

Each of these declarations defines an overloading of the operator **, obtained by generic instantiation. For example, the first declaration defines a function with the following specification:

```
function "**" (E : RATIONAL; N : POSITIVE) return RATIONAL;
```

It can be used to exponentiate rational numbers by repeated application of the multiplication operation defined for this type. Note also that the generic function can be used to apply any meaningful operation repeatedly, for example multiplication of a rational by a positive integer performed by repeated addition:

```
function "*" is new POWER(ELEM => RATIONAL, OPER => "+");
```

or repeated catenation of strings:

```
function "*" is new POWER(ELEM => STRING, OPER => "&");
RULER : constant := "!----+----" * 5;
```

so that

```
RULER = "!----+----!----+----!----+----!----+----!----+----"
```

The generic function body can be expressed more briefly in the following recursive form:

```
function POWER(E : ELEM; N : POSITIVE) return ELEM is
begin
  if N = 1 then
    return E;
  else
    return OPER(POWER(E, N - 1), E);
  end if;
end;
```

which eliminates the local declaration and is thus easier to maintain.

We next consider a variation of the preceding generic function, repeatedly applying a unary operation:

```
generic
  type ELEM is private;
  with function NEXT(X : ELEM) return ELEM;
function INVOLUTION(E : ELEM; N : NATURAL) return ELEM;

function INVOLUTION(E : ELEM; N : NATURAL) return ELEM is
  RESULT : ELEM := E;
begin
  for J in 1 .. N loop
    RESULT := NEXT(RESULT);
  end loop;
  return RESULT;
end INVOLUTION;
```

or the briefer recursive form:

```
function INVOLUTION(E : ELEM; N : NATURAL) return ELEM is
begin
  if N = 0 then
    return E;
  else
    return NEXT(INVOLUTION(E, N - 1));
  end if;
end;
```

This generic function can be used to apply any unary function repeatedly, for example, to produce the *n*th successor or predecessor of an enumeration value

```
function SUCC is new INVOLUTION(ELEM => COLOR,
                               NEXT => COLOR'SUCC);
function PRED is new INVOLUTION(ELEM => COLOR,
                               NEXT => COLOR'PRED);
```

Again, these generic instantiations declare functions, whose specifications are:

```
function SUCC(E : COLOR; N : POSITIVE) return COLOR;
function PRED(E : COLOR; N : POSITIVE) return COLOR;
```

Similar functions can be instantiated to find the *n*th successor or predecessor of an item in a list, where the successor and predecessor are defined by the unary functions:

```
function SUCC(X : LIST) return LIST is
begin
  return X.SUCC;
end;
```

```
function PRED(X : LIST) return LIST is
begin
  return X.PRED;
end;
```

```
function SUCC is new INVOLUTION(ELEM => LIST, NEXT => SUCC);
function PRED is new INVOLUTION(ELEM => LIST, NEXT => PRED);
```

Note that these involutions overload (but do not hide) the functions SUCC and PRED. Actually, the immediate successor of an element can be obtained in three ways:

```
X.SUCC        -- using the component SUCC
SUCC(X)       -- the unary function
SUCC(X,1)     -- the involution
```

12.3.2 An Example of a Generic Package

A discussion of generic units would probably not be complete without a presentation of the treatment of either stacks or queues. Since the example of stacks has already been given in the Reference Manual, we shall give here a formulation of queues.

Here is the specification of the generic package QUEUE_OF:

```
generic
   -- the formal parameters are:
   type ITEM is private;    -- the type of the items in the queues
   MAX_LENGTH : in POSITIVE := 400;
                            -- the maximum length for all the queues
package QUEUE_OF is
   type LENGTH is new INTEGER range 1 .. MAX_LENGTH;
   type QUEUE(SIZE : LENGTH := MAX_LENGTH) is limited private;
      -- the only operations that will be available on queues are
      -- the operations declared in this visible part:
   procedure ADD(X : in ITEM; Q : in out QUEUE);
                  -- adds an item to a queue
   procedure REDUCE(Q : in out QUEUE);
                  -- removes the first item from the queue
   function EMPTY(Q : in QUEUE) return BOOLEAN;
                  -- returns TRUE if the queue is empty
   function FRONT(Q : in QUEUE) return ITEM;
                  -- returns the first item of the queue (not removed)

   OVERFLOW, UNDERFLOW : exception;
                  -- raised when illegal operations are attempted
   private        -- this part will not be available to users
   type VECTOR is array(LENGTH range <>) of ITEM;
   type QUEUE(SIZE : LENGTH := MAX_LENGTH) is
      record
         POOL       : VECTOR(1 .. SIZE);
                              -- the queued items in a circular list
         COUNT     : NATURAL := 0; -- their number
         IN_INDEX  : LENGTH  := 1; -- position of next in
         OUT_INDEX : LENGTH  := 1: -- position of next out
      end record;
   end QUEUE_OF;
```

The package body provides the bodies of the functions and procedures promised in the specification:

```
package body QUEUE_OF is
  function NEXT(Q : in QUEUE; INDEX : in LENGTH) return LENGTH is
    -- returns the position that follows INDEX in queue Q
  begin
    return (INDEX mod Q.SIZE) + 1;
  end NEXT;

  procedure ADD(X : in ITEM; Q : in out QUEUE) is
    -- adds item X at the end of queue Q,
    -- or raises OVERFLOW if Q is full
  begin
    if Q.COUNT < Q.SIZE then
      Q.POOL(Q.IN_INDEX) := X;
      Q.IN_INDEX := NEXT(Q, Q.IN_INDEX);
      Q.COUNT := Q.COUNT + 1;
    else
      raise OVERFLOW;
    end if;
  end ADD;

  procedure REDUCE(Q : in out QUEUE) is
    -- removes the first item from queue Q,
    -- or raises UNDERFLOW if Q is empty
  begin
    if Q.COUNT > 0 then
      Q.OUT_INDEX := NEXT(Q, Q.OUT_INDEX);
      Q.COUNT := Q.COUNT - 1;
    else
      raise UNDERFLOW;
    end if;
  end REDUCE;

  function EMPTY(Q : in QUEUE) return BOOLEAN is
    -- returns TRUE if Q is empty
  begin
    return Q.COUNT = 0;
  end EMPTY;
```

```
      function FRONT(Q : in QUEUE) return ITEM is
        -- returns the first item in queue Q
        -- but does not remove it
      begin
        if Q.COUNT > 0 then
          return Q.POOL(Q.OUT_INDEX);
        else
          raise UNDERFLOW;
        end if;
      end FRONT;

  end QUEUE_OF;
```

Having defined QUEUE_OF, it is now possible to instantiate two packages that deal respectively with queues of integers and queues of reals:

```
  package ANY_INT_QUEUE is
    new QUEUE_OF(ITEM => INTEGER, MAX_LENGTH => 200);

  package ANY_REAL_QUEUE is
    new QUEUE_OF(ITEM => REAL);   -- default maximum length
                                  -- where the type REAL is any
                                  -- properly declared real type
```

In effect, these two declarations have created two packages (two ordinary nongeneric packages). In the present case, a compiler may be able to reuse the same code for the procedures of the two packages if reals and integers are represented with the same number of bits.

A block dealing with real queues may appear as below:

```
  declare
    use ANY_REAL_QUEUE;
    QA : QUEUE(SIZE => 100);
    QB : QUEUE(SIZE => 200);
  begin
    ADD(3.14, QA);
    ...
    if FRONT(QA) = FRONT(QB) then
      REDUCE(QA);
      ADD(FRONT(QB) + 1.0, QA);
    end if;
    ...
  end ;
```

With the use clause for ANY_REAL_QUEUE, the type QUEUE is made directly visible and can be used to declare the queues of reals QA and QB.

A slight difficulty exists if we want to use both ANY_REAL_QUEUE and ANY_INT_QUEUE in the same block, since both declare a type QUEUE. The name conflict can be resolved by the use of expanded names for the type names:

```
declare
    use ANY_REAL_QUEUE, ANY_INT_QUEUE;
    QC : ANY_REAL_QUEUE.QUEUE(SIZE => 50);
    QD : ANY_INT_QUEUE.QUEUE(SIZE => 40);
begin
    ...
    ADD(3.0E5, QC);
    REDUCE(QD);
    ...
    ADD(15, QD);
    ...
end;
```

Using expanded names for the type names will usually be sufficient (repeated use can be avoided by declaring corresponding subtypes). Thereafter, subprograms (such as ADD) appear as overloaded subprograms, and no confusion is possible. For example, the expanded specifications of ADD correspond to

```
procedure ADD(X : in REAL;    Q : in out ANY_REAL_QUEUE.QUEUE);
procedure ADD(X : in INTEGER; Q : in out ANY_INT_QUEUE.QUEUE);
```

In the case of the exceptions OVERFLOW and UNDERFLOW, overloading is of no help and either expanded names or renaming declarations must be used.

A final word on these two exceptions: the bodies of ADD, REDUCE, and FRONT are written so that no damage occurs to the queue if either exception occurs. In consequence it is possible to provide a local handler for these exceptions:

```
declare
  use ANY_REAL_QUEUE, ANY_INT_QUEUE;
  subtype INT_QUEUE is ANY_INT_QUEUE.QUEUE;
                  -- INT_QUEUE defined as an abbreviation
  INTQ_ERROR : exception renames ANY_INT_QUEUE.OVERFLOW;
  QA : INT_QUEUE(SIZE => 100);
  ...
begin
  ...
  ADD(3, QA);
  ...
exception
  when INTQ_ERROR =>
      -- actions to be performed if QA overflows.
end;
```

12.3.3 A Generic Package with Tasks

The parameterization mechanism provided by a generic unit applies to all entities nested within the generic unit. Thus it can be used to parameterize a task type – indirectly. As an example consider the buffering interposed between a producer and a consumer (the example of section 9.12 of the Reference Manual). This might be reformulated as a task type defined within a generic package where the type of the buffered items as well as the size of the buffer in question have been factored out as generic parameters.

```
generic
  type ITEM is private;
  SIZE : POSITIVE := 400;
package ON_BUFFERS is
  task type BUFFER is
    entry READ(C : out ITEM);
    entry WRITE(C : in ITEM);
  end;
end ON_BUFFERS;
```

```
package body ON_BUFFERS is
  type LENGTH is new INTEGER range 1 .. SIZE;
  type VECTOR is array (LENGTH range <>) of ITEM;
  task body BUFFER is
    POOL   : VECTOR(1 .. SIZE);
    COUNT  : NATURAL := 0;
    IN_INDEX, OUT_INDEX : LENGTH := 1;
  begin
    loop
      select
        when COUNT < SIZE =>
          accept WRITE(C : in ITEM) do
            POOL(IN_INDEX) := C;
          end;
          IN_INDEX := (IN_INDEX mod SIZE) + 1;
          COUNT := COUNT + 1;
      or
        when COUNT > 0 =>
          accept READ(C : out ITEM) do
            C := POOL(OUT_INDEX);
          end;
          OUT_INDEX := (OUT_INDEX mod SIZE) + 1;
          COUNT := COUNT - 1;
      or
          terminate;
      end select;
    end loop;
  end BUFFER;
end ON_BUFFERS;
```

A task equivalent to that given in the Reference Manual is obtained by the generic instantiation:

```
package CHARACTER_BUFFERING is
  new ON_BUFFERS(ITEM => CHARACTER, SIZE => 100);
```

followed by the declaration of a task object:

```
A_BUFFER : CHARACTER_BUFFERING.BUFFER;
```

Use of the generic formulation permits the same strategy to be employed in a variety of different applications; for example:

```
package MESSAGE_BUFFERING is
   new ON_BUFFERS(ITEM => MESSAGE, SIZE => BACKLOG);
```

where MESSAGE is assumed to be a previously declared type and BACKLOG yields an estimate for a reasonable buffer size.

It is interesting to observe that the logic of the queuing strategy, shown by the example in the previous section, and that of the buffering strategy, presented above, are in many respects identical. The essential difference between the two approaches is that overflow and underflow are treated as exceptions in the former case, whereas in the latter case they merely result in some parallel task waiting until it can proceed.

12.3.4 A More Complicated Example

A final example, involving binary trees, is presented to illustrate the use of different kinds of generic units in combination. A frequently encountered data type like binary trees is best encapsulated within a package, where the types of the leaves and nodes can be factored out as generic parameters. A straightforward definition of the (recursive) data structure in question might then be formulated as follows:

```
generic
   type LEAF_TYPE is private;
   type NODE_TYPE is private;
package BINARY_TREES is
type FORM is (INTERMEDIATE, TERMINAL);

   type TREE(KIND : FORM);
   type LINK is access TREE;

   type TREE(KIND : FORM) is
      record
         case KIND is
            when TERMINAL =>
               LEAF : LEAF_TYPE;
```

```
        when INTERMEDIATE =>
            NODE  : NODE_TYPE;
            LEFT  : LINK;
            RIGHT : LINK;
        end case;
    end record;

-- specifications of standard operations on binary trees

end BINARY_TREES;
```

A number of standard operations associated with binary trees would normally be in-cluded within the generic package given above; for simplicity, they will not be detailed here. Instead, we shall illustrate the typical ways in which binary trees are processed. These generally involve a recursive traversal (or *walk*) of the tree in one of a few char-acteristic orders (namely, prefix order, infix order, or postfix order). These orders can be expressed as generic operations.

The commonest of these orders is used in the example below. This is the *postfix walk*, where a certain operation is applied to each leaf, while another operation is applied to each node, as well as to the results of previously processed left and right branches. The desired generic function might be defined within the package BINARY_TREES as follows:

```
generic
    type RESULT is private;
    with function LEAF_ACTION(L : LEAF_TYPE) return RESULT;
    with function NODE_ACTION(N : NODE_TYPE;
                              L, R : RESULT) return RESULT;
function POST_WALK(T : LINK) return RESULT;

function POST_WALK(T : LINK) return RESULT is
begin
    case T.KIND is
        when TERMINAL =>
            return LEAF_ACTION(T.LEAF);
        when INTERMEDIATE =>
            return NODE_ACTION(N => T.NODE,
                               L => POST_WALK(T.LEFT),
                               R => POST_WALK(T.RIGHT));
    end case;
end POST_WALK;
```

Note that the recursive invocations of POST_WALK within this function cause no confusion (or infinite loop during instantiation) since, within an instantiation of a generic function body, the name of the generic function refers to the name of the current instantiation.

A number of useful utility functions on binary trees follow the pattern of a postfix walk. Some of these might well be included within the package BINARY_TREES itself. For example, given the functions ONE, SUM, SUM_PLUS_ONE, and MAX:

```
function ONE(L : LEAF_TYPE) return INTEGER is
begin
  return 1;
end;

function SUM(N : NODE_TYPE; L, R : INTEGER) return INTEGER is
begin
  return L + R;
end;

function SUM_PLUS_ONE(N : NODE_TYPE; L, R : INTEGER) return INTEGER
is
begin
  return L + R + 1;
end;

function MAX(N : NODE_TYPE; L, R : INTEGER) return INTEGER is
begin
  if L < R then
    return R;
  else
    return L;
  end if;
end;
```

– where a dummy parameter of node type or leaf type has been provided in order to match the generic functions – then the usual tree functions COUNT, DEPTH, and WIDTH are obtained by generic instantiation:

```
function COUNT is new POST_WALK(RESULT => INTEGER,
                               LEAF_ACTION => ONE,
                               NODE_ACTION => SUM_PLUS_ONE);
    -- the number of leaves and nodes

function DEPTH is new POST_WALK(RESULT => INTEGER,
                               LEAF_ACTION => ONE,
                               NODE_ACTION => MAX);
    -- the length of the longest path from root to leaf
```

```
function WIDTH is new POST_WALK(RESULT => INTEGER,
                               LEAF_ACTION => ONE,
                               NODE_ACTION => SUM);
   -- the number of leaves
```

The advantages of using the generic facility in this fashion to formulate a basic pattern for several similar definitions are obvious. Another application of such definitions involves the use of binary trees to represent simple arithmetic expressions, where the leaves are integer values and the nodes correspond to the usual operators:

```
type OPERATOR is (ADD, SUB, MUL, DIV);
```

The appropriate definition can be obtained by instantiating the generic package

```
package EXPRESSION_TREES is
   new BINARY_TREES(LEAF_TYPE => INTEGER,
                    NODE_TYPE => OPERATOR);
```

In an application, a use clause would be provided for this package and, to introduce a name more appropriate to the application, the tree type would be renamed by a subtype declaration:

```
use EXPRESSION_TREES;
subtype EXPRESSION is EXPRESSION_TREES.TREE;
```

One may then introduce the specific operations associated with the type of tree in question. The most obvious is the evaluation function

```
function EVAL(E : EXPRESSION) return INTEGER;
```

This, however, exactly follows the pattern of a postfix walk, and may therefore be obtained directly by instantiation:

```
function EVAL is new POST_WALK(RESULT => INTEGER,
                              LEAF_ACTION => VALUE,
                              NODE_ACTION => INTERPRET);
```

where the requisite definitions of VALUE and INTERPRET are as follows:

```
function VALUE(I : INTEGER) return INTEGER is
begin
   return I;
end;
```

```
function INTERPRET(OP : OPERATOR; L, R : INTEGER) return INTEGER is
begin
  case OP is
    when ADD => return L + R;
    when SUB => return L - R;
    when MUL => return L * R;
    when DIV => return L / R;
  end case;
end ;
```

Once again, the desired function is obtained by merely providing the appropriate operations for each leaf and node, while the details of the recursive tree walk are encapsulated within the generic function POST_WALK.

The binary tree example of this subsection presents a rather sophisticated structure, namely a generic recursive function (the function is recursive but there is of course no recursive instantiation), the declaration of which is itself nested within a generic package! While this example shows why such complicated formulations are occasionally desirable (see also [VH 75]), a word of warning is in order with regard to generic packages. Dependence between generic units in the form of mutual instantiation is not allowed since such a structure could yield an infinite loop during instantiation:

```
generic
  ...
package A is
  ...
end;

generic
  ...
package B is
  ...
end;

package body A is
  ...
  package NEW_B is new B( ... ); -- THIS ALONE IS LEGAL
  ...
end A;
package body B is
  ...
  package NEW_A is new A( ... ); -- BUT NOT TOGETHER WITH THIS!
  ...
end B;
```

12.4 RATIONALE FOR THE FORMULATION OF GENERIC UNITS

The generic facility is expected to serve for the construction of general-purpose parameterized packages. Whereas such packages are likely to be utilized by large classes of users, it should be realized that fewer programmers will actually be involved in writing generic packages. Accordingly, we have tried to design a facility that can be almost ignored by the majority of users. They must indeed know how to instantiate a generic package, and this is fairly easy. On the other hand, they need not be familiar with the rules and precautions necessary for writing generic units.

A major simplification, in this respect, is achieved by adopting an approach based on a context-dependent extension of the traditional techniques of macro-expansion. This solution has the advantage of introducing only a minimum of additional features. It is well implementable within the state of the art, and it provides the flexibility required by the applications.

This approach has important consequences for the specification of generic formal parameters. The other major simplifying assumptions made in the language concern the requirement for explicit instantiation, and the specification of formal operations applicable to formal types. These issues will be discussed separately below.

12.4.1 Explicit Instantiation of Generic Units

The requirement that instantiation be explicit greatly simplifies the compilation of program units obtained by generic instantiation.

The approach taken here clearly distinguishes between the *instantiation* of a program unit, obtained from a generic unit, and the *invocation* of the resulting program unit – calling a subprogram, using a package. Thereby it emphasizes the contrast between translation-time substitution of generic actual parameters and execution-time passage of actual parameters to subprograms. Explicit instantiation provides a well-defined locus for the point of instantiation and also for reporting any errors arising from inconsistent substitution. The resultant program unit can be invoked subsequently as often as required, with the same degree of power and security as for any other non-generic program unit; this is a consequence of the fact that a program unit obtained by generic instantiation is indistinguishable from the same program unit defined explicitly at the point of instantiation.

An alternative solution considered was implicit instantiation. For the purpose of the discussion of the complexity of implicit instantiation, consider the following generic function (which is actually just a different way of writing the power function given in a previous section):

```
generic
  type ELEM is private;
  with function "*" (LEFT, RIGHT : ELEM) return ELEM;
function POWER(E : ELEM; N : POSITIVE) return ELEM;

function POWER(E : ELEM; N : POSITIVE) return ELEM is
begin
  if N = 1 then
    return E;
  else
    return E * POWER(E, N - 1);
  end if;
end POWER;
```

If implicit instantiation were provided, then for:

```
R : RATIONAL;
I : INTEGER;
```

exponentiation could be applied without prior explicit instantiation. Thus:

```
POWER(R , 5)
POWER(I , 5)
```

would both be legal. The actual type used for ELEM would be implicitly inferred from the actual parameter associated with E in each call – that is, RATIONAL for R, INTEGER for I.

Implicit instantiation would complicate the rules for the identification of overloaded subprograms. If a version of POWER were defined directly within the package RATIONAL_NUMBERS itself:

```
function POWER(E : RATIONAL; N : INTEGER) return RATIONAL;
```

then this explicit definition would hide the generic definition in an application such as POWER(R, 5). Thus the generic definition would be visible for some types and hidden for others. This added complexity would reflect on compilers, and also on program readability.

Another problem would arise for the identification of POWER in the body of the generic unit itself: would this be a recursive implicit instantiation or a recursive call of the same instance? In the simple example considered, it could be easily interpreted as a recursive call. However, in general, it is not at all clear that the problem can always be resolved by a static analysis of the program (unless restrictions are adopted). A sufficient condition to guarantee that no generic operation will ever require an unbounded number of implicit generic instantiations during execution has been given in [BJ 78]. However such checks require a quite complex analysis of the program.

In conclusion, implicit instantiation is still a research subject. The only solution within the current state of the art is explicit instantiation and this is therefore the solution chosen for Ada.

Explicit instantiation certainly requires more writing on the part of the user, but it provides better awareness of the instances that are created and thus contributes to reliability and readability. In addition, it offers distinct advantages in terms of efficiency, since compilers can easily identify the existing instantiations and, in some cases, achieve optimizations such as sharing of code among several instantiations of the same generic unit.

12.4.2 Generic Formal Parameters: The Contract Model

As stated earlier, a user instantiating a given generic package should be able to ignore the details of the generic body completely. In particular, if any error is made in instantiating a generic unit, the error should be reported to the user in terms of the generic instantiation itself – not in terms of the internals of the generic body. This requirement influences the form used for specifying generic formal parameters.

Consider by analogy what is done for subprograms. For a normal – that is, non-generic – procedure, specification of parameters permits independent checks of the procedure body on the one hand, and of the procedure calls on the other hand. Both must conform to the formal parameter specifications and these legality checks can be done *independently*: the procedure specification is a sort of *contract* between the procedure body and the corresponding procedure calls.

The specification of generic formal parameters must achieve the same degree of independence:

(a) For a given generic body, it should be possible to check that its text is consistent with respect to the formal parameter specifications.

(b) For a given generic instantiation, it should be possible to check that the actual parameters are consistent with respect to the formal parameter specifications.

(c) The precision of the formal parameter specifications should be sufficient to guarantee that if the checks (a) and (b) are successful, then the corresponding instantiations produce legal program units.

The solution adopted to achieve these goals is to require that all operations of a generic formal type be determinable from its specification:

● For a formal type specified as limited private, no operation is assumed available (apart from certain attributes: see RM 7.4.2). Hence any operation that is applied to an object of the formal type within the generic unit must be provided as an explicit generic formal parameter.

- For a formal type specified as private (not limited), the same holds except that assignment and the predefined comparison for equality and inequality are available.

- For a generic formal type declared as a type pattern with a box, the operations of the corresponding kind of type are available: they are implicitly declared. For example, the floating point operators are available for any generic formal type defined by **"digits <>"**. Any other operation must be provided explicitly by a generic formal parameter.

When the body of a generic unit is being checked, the generic formal part thus provides the information required for the identification of all operations. When a given instantiation is being checked, the demands of the generic formal part must be met and incorrect actual parameters can be reported. These two checks can be performed independently. Furthermore, if errors exist in an instantiation, error messages can be formulated in terms of the generic formal part, which is necessarily known, rather than in terms of the details of the generic body, which might be separately compiled and hidden.

Consider for example the generic formal part given for the generic function **POWER**:

```
generic
   type ELEM is private;
   with function "*" (LEFT, RIGHT : ELEM) return ELEM;
function POWER(E : ELEM; N : POSITIVE) return ELEM;
```

The operation **"*"** is explicitly provided as a generic parameter, along with the type **ELEM** itself. The parameter E and the result of the function **POWER** are both specified as being of this formal type. Thereafter the identification of the **"*"** appearing within the generic body:

```
function POWER(E : ELEM; N : POSITIVE) return ELEM is
begin
   if N = 1 then
      return E;
   else
      return E * POWER(E, N - 1);
   end if;
end POWER;
```

within the expression E * POWER(E, N-1) can be done as usual – it refers to the **"*"** declared in the generic formal part. Similarly the recursive call of **POWER** can be correctly identified (since implicit instantiation is not allowed). Hence the generic body can be completely checked.

Similarly a generic instantiation such as

```
function "**" is new POWER(ELEM => MATRIX, "*" => MULT);
```

can be fully checked: Consider the function specification obtained by substituting in the generic formal function the name MULT for the designator "*", and the actual type MATRIX for the formal type ELEM:

function MULT(LEFT, RIGHT : MATRIX) **return** MATRIX;

Then the instantiation is correct if there is – in the context of the instantiation – a function MULT with this parameter and result profile – the only allowed difference being for the names of the parameters (LEFT and RIGHT). Conversely, consider:

function "**" **is new** POWER(ELEM => RATIONAL, "*" => "not");

                                                        -- ILLEGAL!

This generic instantiation can be reported as incorrect since there is no operation **not** corresponding to the specification

function "not" (LEFT, RIGHT : RATIONAL) **return** RATIONAL; -- ILLEGAL!

An alternative considered in this design was the *implicit inference* of operations of a formal type. The reasons for rejecting this alternative are similar to those leading to the rejection of implicit instantiation. With implicit inference of operations, the previous example could be rewritten as:

generic
    type ELEM **is** private;
function POWER(E : ELEM; N : POSITIVE) **return** ELEM;

and we would be left with the problem of identifying the "*" operation used in the body. For a given instantiation, say with the type RATIONAL, should the "*" operation be identified as a global operation in the context of the generic declaration or in the context of the generic instantiation? The two alternatives might lead to different results.

Note also that a statement such as

return E * E * E;

would be ambiguous in the presence of several overloadings of "*"; for example:

function "*" (X, Y : RATIONAL)   **return** RATIONAL; -- (1)
function "*" (X, Y : RATIONAL)   **return** INTEGER; -- (2)
function "*" (X : INTEGER; Y : RATIONAL) **return** RATIONAL; -- (3)

One possible interpretation would identify both operations with definition (1); another interpretation would identify the first "*" with (2) and the second with (3).

In general, the specifications of the identified operations could be quite different from instantiation to instantiation depending on the operations visible in the context of the instantiation. None of this can happen with an explicit specification of the formal operation "*".

To summarize, implicit inference of operations, based on the instantiation, would introduce awkward context-dependence and would require complete rechecking of the generic body for each instantiation. This last consequence would be particularly unfortunate, since generic bodies could not be checked (and proved correct) independently of the context. It would defeat the goal stated initially, since some error messages would have to be stated in terms of what is done within the generic body.

Note that none of the problems of implicit inference based on the instantiation arise with the implicit specification of formal operations that exists for type patterns with boxes. Consider for example

```
generic
   type ELEM is digits <>;
function SQUARING(X : ELEM) return ELEM;

function SQUARING(X : ELEM) return ELEM is
begin
   return X * X;
end;
```

Here the declaration of the formal type has the effect of providing implicit declarations for the operators of floating point types. Thus we have an implicitly declared formal function

```
function "*" (LEFT, RIGHT : ELEM) return ELEM;
```

so that identification of the "*" used in the generic body is done solely in terms of the generic specification.

The Ada solution permits independent checking of generic units and of generic instantiations. Hence it largely fulfills our goal of permitting the user to ignore the internal details of the generic units instantiated in his programs.

One limitation of the contract model concerns the ability to declare unconstrained objects. Consider a variant of the formulation of the generic procedure EXCHANGE:

```
generic
   type ITEM is private;
procedure EXCHANGE(LEFT, RIGHT : in out ITEM);

procedure EXCHANGE(LEFT, RIGHT : in out ITEM) is
   TEMPORARY : ITEM;
begin
   TEMPORARY := LEFT;
   LEFT := RIGHT;
   RIGHT := TEMPORARY;
end;
```

Then an instantiation with an unconstrained array type such as

```
procedure SWAP is new EXCHANGE(ITEM => STRING);
```

will not work since a declaration of an unconstrained variable of type STRING (here TEMPORARY) would not be allowed. The same problem would arise if the actual type were a type with discriminants that must be constrained. Note on the other hand that the problem does not exist for constants – as in the original formulation:

```
OLD_LEFT : constant ITEM := LEFT;
```

This limitation means that some instantiations may be rejected on the grounds that the body requires the ability to declare unconstrained objects of the formal type. We have considered this consequence to be preferable to an increase in the complexity of the syntax.

Another limitation concerns representation clauses. It is illustrated by the following example:

```
generic
   type T is private;
package OCTETS is
   type R is
      record
         A : T;
      end record;
   for R'SIZE use 8;
end;
```

since any instantiation with a type such that T'SIZE > 8 will fail. Again, such cases are considered sufficiently abnormal not to warrant any special language rule.

To conclude this section on formal types let us note that Ada provides formal types for all classes of type except record and task types. The major reason for this is that it is not clear that reasonable criteria for matching exist for these type classes – criteria that would be consistent with the degree of type checking performed elsewhere, yet at the same time have a good probability of being usable for many actual record types and task types.

12.4.3 Default Generic Parameters

As stated before, all operations applicable to a formal type must be specified explicitly in the generic formal part. Nevertheless, in order to keep generic instantiations as simple as possible, a facility for specifying default values for generic parameters is offered, as it is for normal subprograms.

In many cases, such defaults will actually be expressed by boxes. For example, the generic formal part of the generic function POWER can be rewritten as follows:

```
generic
    type ELEM is private;
    with function "*" (LEFT, RIGHT : ELEM) return ELEM is <>;
```

This parallels exactly the treatment of in parameters with default values for subprograms. The default parameter is optional, and an instantiation such as

```
function "**" is new POWER(RATIONAL);
```

is taken as equivalent to the generic instantiation

```
function "**" is new POWER(ELEM => RATIONAL, "*" => "*");
```

where the actual operation "*" should have the specification

```
function "*" (name_1, name_2 : RATIONAL) return RATIONAL;
```

and the instantiation is legal if there is such a "*" operation for the type RATIONAL, whatever may be the parameter names. For the same reason

```
function "**" is new POWER(BOOLEAN);
```

would be an error, since no such operation exists for the type BOOLEAN (assuming no explicit definition). Again, the generic body and the generic instantiations can be checked independently. Furthermore, the default can always be overridden by providing an explicit parameter as in

```
function "**" is new POWER(VECTOR, MULT);
```

To summarize, the necessity to be able to check a generic body independently of its generic instantiations (an important user requirement) forces all operations applicable to a formal type to be specified, explicitly or implicitly, by the generic formal part. This could increase the number of generic parameters that must be supplied and could hence lead to a heavy syntax of generic instantiations. However, defaults can be specified for these operations, thus restoring much of the simplicity while losing none of the security.

In most applications it should be possible to have only types as mandatory parameters and to provide defaults for all operations. This is consistent with the goal stated in the introduction, that writing a generic unit may well require some care, but using it ought to be extremely simple.

13. Tasking

13.1 INTRODUCTION

Tasking is an important aspect of many embedded systems and this importance was clearly recognized in the Steelman requirements. However tasking seems to have been neglected in most languages currently in production use for such systems. One reason has clearly been a lack of confidence in the many different facilities put forward for the control of parallelism. Semaphores, events, signals and other similar mechanisms are clearly at too low a level. Monitors, on the other hand, are not always easy to understand and, with their associated signals, perhaps seem to offer an unfortunate mix of high-level and low-level concepts. It is believed that Ada strikes a good balance by providing facilities that are not only easy to use directly but can also be used as tools for the creation of mechanisms of different kinds.

The basic textual concept in Ada is that of a task, which in form is closely analogous to a package. Tasks are automatically executed in parallel with the unit in which they are declared, and their termination similarly follows the scope structure. Task types enable the declaration of a dynamic number of tasks with similar properties. This facility, when used in conjunction with access types, allows flexible control over the number of tasks in a system and the manipulation of task identities.

Communication and synchronization are both achieved using the concept of a rendezvous between a task issuing an entry call and a task accepting the call by an accept statement. An entry call is similar to a procedure call except that the calling and called tasks are distinct and synchronized.

Timing control is provided by the delay statement together with a package that defines operations on times and dates.

Great power is provided by the select statement, which enables a task to respond to several different possible entry calls. Variants of the select statement provide timed-out and conditional communication in a natural manner. Interrupts may be handled by a representation clause associated with a particular entry.

This chapter comprises two main parts. The first describes the tasking facilities and illustrates their use with examples. This is followed by a brief historical survey of parallel processing mechanisms, which puts the Ada concepts into perspective.

13.2 PRESENTATION OF THE TASKING FACILITY

This section introduces the tasking facilities, defines them generally, and illustrates them by means of examples. After a presentation of tasks and their associated hierarchy, we describe rendezvous, entry calls, and accept statements. The discussion continues with select statements, timing, timed and conditional communication, and interrupts. Task types and families of entries are then described, and the presentation concludes with the use of these concepts for scheduling.

13.2.1 Tasks : Textual Layout

A task is a textually distinct program unit which may be executed concurrently with other tasks. It is very similar in form to a package. Indeed the major difference between a package and a task is that the former is merely a passive construct whereas a task may be active.

Like the package, a task may be declared within any declarative part (except the visible part of another task) and similarly comprises two distinct pieces of text. These are the specification, which describes its external appearance, and the body, which describes its internal behavior. These two parts will often be juxtaposed in the text, but need not be, and indeed need not even be compiled together. We shall now consider the details of these two parts, showing in particular how they differ from the corresponding parts of packages.

The specification defines the interface of the task to the outside world by the declaration of entries in the task, in much the same way as the specification of a package contains declarations of types, objects, subprograms, and so on, which define its external interface. Entry declarations have a similar form to procedure declarations and are called in a similar manner, but they are executed in a different manner, as will be described in a moment.

Note carefully that a task specification may contain only entry declarations and any associated representation clauses or pragmas. Unlike a package, it may not contain the declarations of types, objects, subprograms or other entities. The reasons are mainly methodological (emphasizing that a task provides parallelism whereas a package provides visibility control), but there would also be difficulty in implementation if other entities were allowed, since there would be problems of existence and prevention of access if the task were not active. On the other hand, of course, a package specification may not contain the declarations of entries.

The following is an example of the specification of a task:

```
task LINE_TO_CHAR is
   entry PUT_LINE (L : in LINE);
   entry GET_CHAR (C : out CHARACTER);
end;
```

The body of a task has a form similar to that of a package and comprises a declarative part and a sequence of statements. The body of the above example has the following outline.

```
task body LINE_TO_CHAR is
   BUFFER : LINE;
begin
   -- sequence of statements
end;
```

The full details of the body of this example are deferred until section 13.2.4.

13.2.2 Task Execution

Before describing the detailed statements associated with tasks, it is important that the reader understand the underlying concept of a task, its activation and execution, and the concept of a master. We describe this in terms of a model which should be considered to be only illustrative and applies to the simple form of task declaration described above; the extension to task types is outlined in 13.2.9.

We distinguish between the *execution* of a task and the text of a task. An execution of a task is a dynamic parallel activity whereas the text is merely a passive description of some code. The main program can be considered to be called by an anonymous task whose execution is created by the underlying system.

When an execution enters a unit that contains task object declarations, the elaboration of each declaration creates a further task execution. There is therefore a one-to-one correspondence between task executions and the elaboration of task object declarations, and we can loosely refer to the task execution by the name of the corresponding task declaration.

Although each elaboration of a task declaration only gives rise to one execution, nevertheless there may be several such parallel executions corresponding to different coexisting elaborations of the declaration. This would occur for example if a task were declared through the use of task types which are described below.

It should also be realized that a subprogram does not in any sense belong to any particular task. If it is within the body of a task that has no subtasks (and is not passed as an actual generic parameter), then it can only be called by the enclosing task. On the other hand, if it is declared in the same declarative part as several tasks, then it can obviously be called by all these tasks.

The *master* of a task is the innermost task, block, subprogram, or library package that contains its declaration (other packages are excluded because they merely affect the visibility and not the scope of data). A task is said to *depend* on its master.

The reader should note that the RM introduces the concept of an hierarchical set of masters of a task. For didactic purposes we here use the term master to mean the direct master. It should also be noted that the rules for tasks declared via access types are somewhat different: they are described in section 13.2.9.

A task automatically commences execution when its master reaches the **begin** following the task declaration. Task execution is a two-stage process. The first stage, known as *activation*, consists of the elaboration of the declarative part of the task body, whereas the second stage consists, of course, of the execution of its statements. During the activation stage the master is not allowed to proceed. If several tasks are declared in a unit then their activations and subsequent execution occur in parallel and moreover each task commences its execution as soon as it has finished its own activation. However, it is only when the activation of all the tasks is complete that the master can continue with the execution of the statements following the **begin**, in parallel with the new tasks.

The reason for treating task activation in this way concerns exceptions. An exception raised by the elaboration of a declarative part is not handled at that level but propagated. So an exception raised by the elaboration of the declarative part of a task (that is, by its activation) cannot be handled by the task and has to be propagated to the master. In order that such an exception not be asynchronous, the master remains suspended at the **begin** until all activations are complete. It should be added that even if two or more tasks raise exceptions during activation, then only one exception is received by the suspended master. Furthermore, the single exception is always **TASKING_ERROR**, irrespective of the nature and number of the original exceptions. This is because it would be almost impossible for the master to handle more than one exception anyway, and the single exception then clearly has to be of a neutral nature – it would be unreasonable to choose one of the originating exceptions in preference to another.

Task termination is also a two-stage process. This is a consequence of an important rule that a unit cannot be left until all dependent tasks are terminated. This rule ensures that objects declared in a unit and therefore visible to local tasks cannot disappear while there exists a task that could access them.

A unit is said to be *completed* when it reaches its final **end**. It then waits, if necessary, until all dependent tasks are terminated before itself becoming terminated. Of course, if a unit has no dependent tasks then it becomes completed and terminated at the same time.

For example consider the following procedure P containing the tasks T1 and T2.

```
procedure P is

    task T1 is
      -- specification of T1
    end;

    task T2 is
      -- specification of T2
    end;

    task body T1 is
      -- body of T1
    end;

    task body T2 is
      -- body of T2
    end;
begin
    -- T1, T2 made active here
    ...
    -- P waits for T1, T2 here
end;
```

The tasks T1 and T2 automatically commence activation when P reaches its begin, and P waits at that point until activation of both tasks is complete. All three (that is, P, T1 and T2) may then execute in parallel. When P reaches its final **end**, it again waits until both T1 and T2 have terminated, if they have not already done so.

It is possible to force the termination of a task by the use of the abort statement. Thus

```
    abort T1, T2;
```

will force tasks T1 and T2 to become completed as well as any other tasks that depend on T1 and T2. The actual mechanism is a little complex. Briefly, the abort statement places a task in an abnormal state, which then leads to it becoming completed as soon as possible. Complications arise because of the possibility of the task being engaged in a rendezvous. The completion of an aborted caller is delayed until the rendezvous is completed and the called task is not affected (this permits the reliable programming of service tasks); on the other hand, if the called task is aborted then the caller receives the exception TASKING_ERROR.

Note that the behavior of the abort statement is formulated in terms of *completing* tasks rather than *terminating* them. This is because a parent task cannot be terminated until its dependent tasks are terminated, and if one of those is the caller in a rendezvous with a third party then its termination will be delayed. Thus completion of the tasks is the best that can be individually enforced and their termination will then automatically occur in the usual way.

The abort statement is very disruptive but seems a necessary means of last resort to deal with a rogue task. For example, it is not possible to leave a unit while dependent tasks are active, and so an exception handler in a unit might need to abort all local tasks.

Although unconditional and immediate termination is the desirable semantics for an abort statement, nevertheless as explained above problems in a rendezvous lead to a formulation in terms of completion. Apart from this, the abort statement is severe. All dependent tasks are also aborted since their names will become unreachable after the abort. Furthermore an aborted task is removed from any entry queue on which it may have been placed as the result of calling an entry. This possibility demands care in the use of the COUNT attribute (see 13.2.5).

The abort statement is provided for emergency use only. Its ill-considered use will severely hinder program understanding and validation.

The status of a task may be interrogated by two attributes. Thus T'TERMINATED is TRUE if the task T has terminated; T'CALLABLE is TRUE if its entries are callable, that is, unless the task is abnormal, completed, or terminated.

The above discussion was presented in terms of several tasks executing in parallel. Whether or not this *physically* occurs depends upon the hardware. In a multiprocessor system true parallel execution may occur, whereas in a single processor system only one task at a time can really be executing. In any case a scheduler is required in order to allocate the *ready* tasks to the one or more processors. The scheduling algorithm is deliberately not defined in complete detail, but a task can be given a static priority by a pragma. The basic rule regarding priority is

"If two tasks with different priorities are both eligible for execution and could sensibly be executed using the same physical processors and other processing resources, then it cannot be the case that the task with the lower priority is executing while the task with the higher priority is not."

This rule requires preemptive scheduling. Note that the phrase *could sensibly be executed* refers to situations such as distributed systems where a high priority task may not be physically able to execute on some processors. Thus preemption is only required for processing resources that the high priority task can use.

Priorities are provided as a tool for indicating relative degrees of urgency and on no account should their manipulation be used as a technique for attempting to obtain mutual exclusion.

Task types are discussed in section 13.2.9.

13.2.3 Visibility Rules

The usual visibility rules are applicable to tasks. As a consequence several tasks may share global variables and it is the programmer's responsibility to ensure their integrity; problems arising from optimization whereby the value of a variable is temporarily held in a register may be overcome by the pragma SHARED. Of course the primary means of communication between tasks is not through the sharing of global variables (which should be done with caution) but by the use of the rendezvous as described in the next section. However to disallow shared variables seems to be a constraint that would be unwise in some critical circumstances.

13.2.4 Entries and the Accept Statement

As we have seen, the specification part of a task may contain the declaration of entries. Externally an entry looks like a procedure, has parameters of mode **in**, **in out** or **out**, and is called in the same way. The difference lies in the internal behavior. In the case of a procedure the calling task executes the procedure body itself, and the procedure body can be executed immediately. In the case of an entry the corresponding actions are executed by the task owning the entry, not by the calling task. Moreover these actions are only executed when the called task is prepared to execute a corresponding accept statement. In fact the calling and called tasks may be thought to meet together in a *rendezvous*. We will illustrate this by completing the example introduced earlier.

```
task LINE_TO_CHAR is
  entry PUT_LINE(L : in LINE);
  entry GET_CHAR(C : out CHARACTER);
end;

task body LINE_TO_CHAR is
  BUFFER : LINE;
begin
  loop
    accept PUT_LINE(L : in LINE) do
      BUFFER := L;
    end PUT_LINE;
    for I in LINE'RANGE loop
      accept GET_CHAR(C : out CHARACTER) do
        C := BUFFER(I);
      end GET_CHAR;
    end loop;
  end loop;
end;
```

The accept statement looks somewhat like a procedure body. It can be thought of as a body to be executed where it stands, in much the same way as a block can be thought of as an inline procedure without parameters.

The accept statement repeats the formal part of the entry declarations, both in order to emphasize the parameters and to permit unambiguous identification of an **accept** with the correct, possibly overloaded, entry. The formal part is then followed by the statements to be executed during the rendezvous.

There are two possibilities for a rendezvous, according to whether the calling task issues the calling statement such as

```
LINE_TO_CHAR.PUT_LINE(MY_LINE);
```

before or after a corresponding accept statement is reached by the called task. Whichever task gets there first waits for the other. When the rendezvous is achieved, the appropriate parameters of the caller are passed to the called task (note that actual parameters are evaluated when the entry call is issued, not when the rendezvous occurs). The caller is then temporarily suspended until the called task completes the statements embraced by **do ... end**. Any out parameters are then passed back to the caller and finally both tasks again proceed independently of each other.

It should be observed that the rendezvous is named in one direction only. The calling task must know the name of the entry, and this is specific to the called task. Thus the calling task must know the called task. The called task on the other hand will accept calls from any task. Thus we have a many-to-one pattern of communication. As a consequence of this, each entry potentially has a queue of tasks calling it. This queue is processed in a strictly first-in-first-out manner, and each rendezvous at an accept statement removes just one item from this queue.

The behavior of the task LINE_TO_CHAR should now be clear. It contains an internal buffer which may hold a line of characters. The task alternately fills the buffer by accepting a call of PUT_LINE, and then empties it by accepting successive calls of GET_CHAR. Calls of the entries can only be processed when the corresponding accept statement is reached. Thus many different tasks could be held up calling PUT_LINE. They are only accepted one at a time in accordance with the groups of calls of GET_CHAR. Again note that the buffer may be emptied by several different tasks calling GET_CHAR. Indeed several tasks could be suspended on calls of GET_CHAR until a task issues a call of PUT_LINE.

It should be carefully observed that at any one time a task can be queuing only in one place (one position in one entry queue). This is because a task can naturally only be calling one entry at a time.

This example could therefore be used to provide a simple buffering mechanism between a producer and a consumer task:

```
task CONSUME_CHAR;
task PRODUCE_LINE;

task body PRODUCE_LINE is
  MY_LINE : LINE;
begin
  loop
    -- fill MY_LINE from somewhere
    LINE_TO_CHAR.PUT_LINE(MY_LINE);
  end loop;
end;

task body CONSUME_CHAR is
  MY_CHAR : CHARACTER;
begin
  loop
    LINE_TO_CHAR.GET_CHAR(MY_CHAR);
    -- do something with MY_CHAR
  end loop;
end;
```

In the task LINE_TO_CHAR there is only one accept statement corresponding to each entry. This need not necessarily be the case, as later examples will show. Moreover if there are several accept statements corresponding to one entry then their sequences of statements may differ. We see here a sharp distinction between entries and procedures. All calls of a procedure execute the same body whereas calls of entries need not. This is because procedure bodies do not change state between successive calls, and so the normal case is that all calls do the same thing; whereas tasks continue to execute between calls of their entries, and so may need to do different things each time. In this respect an entry call is analogous to a coroutine transfer.

As general programming practice, the body of the accept statement between **do** and **end** should not contain unnecessary statements; otherwise the calling task will be needlessly held up. As a consequence, it will often be the case that the accept body will contain only the code that accesses the entry parameters; additional code as may be necessary to update the task's state variables to reflect the status of its callers can then follow the accept body.

An accept statement may have no **do ... end** part. This will usually, but not necessarily, be the case when the entry has no parameters.

As a didactic example, the following task implements a binary semaphore for protecting critical sections:

```
task SEMAPHORE is
  entry P;
  entry V;
end;

task body SEMAPHORE is
begin
  loop
    accept P;
    accept V;
  end loop;
end;
```

A critical section is then bracketed thus

```
SEMAPHORE.P;
-- critical section
SEMAPHORE.V;
```

In this case the rendezvous merely provides synchronization and no data is transferred.

An accept statement must be in the body of the task concerned, and not within any inner subprogram, package or task. This ensures that it can only be executed by the task that owns the corresponding entry.

If an entry is renamed, it is renamed as a procedure. This preserves the uniform user interface. A minor distinction between entries and subprograms is that it is not possible to have an entry function. Finally it should be remarked that there also exist so-called families of entries. These are discussed in 13.2.10.

13.2.5 The Select Statement

The accept statement enables a task to wait for some event to happen, and the happening of the event is in our notation indicated by the calling of the corresponding entry. To wait until several such different events have all happened merely requires a sequence of accept statements. To wait for one only of several alternative possible events is not easy, and for this purpose we introduce the select statement. As will become evident, the select statement has great expressive power.

The select statement has some analogy with the case statement, and in its simplest form allows one of several alternative accept statements to be obeyed.

As an example, suppose we wish a variable to be accessible to many tasks, but nevertheless wish to prevent more than one task at a time from accessing it. Moreover suppose we wish to provide facilities to read the variable and to write a new value to it. The following task provides the entries READ and WRITE for this.

```
task PROTECTED_VARIABLE is
   entry READ (V : out ITEM);
   entry WRITE(E : in ITEM);
end;

task body PROTECTED_VARIABLE is
   VARIABLE : ITEM;
begin
   loop
     select
       accept READ(V : out ITEM) do
         V := VARIABLE;
       end;
     or
       accept WRITE(E : in ITEM) do
         VARIABLE := E;
       end;
     end select;
   end loop;
end PROTECTED_VARIABLE;
```

A call of READ outputs the value of the variable to the parameter V. A call of WRITE inputs the value of the expression E passed as parameter into the variable.

The select statement allows the task to accept either READ or WRITE. On entry to the select statement, if neither a READ nor a WRITE has been called, the task waits for the first of either and then obeys the appropriate accept statement. If one has already been called then that call is immediately accepted. If however both entries have already been called (obviously by two or more other tasks) then one of the alternatives is chosen *arbitrarily*.

In the more general case each alternative may include a *guarding* condition. These conditions are all evaluated at the beginning of the select statement, and only those alternatives whose guards are true are considered in the subsequent selection. An absent guard is of course considered to be true. If all guards are false, so that no alternative can be considered, then it is an error (unless there is an else part as described later in this section) and the PROGRAM_ERROR exception is raised. An alternative whose guard is true (or absent) is said to be *open*. An alternative whose guard is false is said to be *closed*. The guard is written as a Boolean expression preceded by the word **when** and followed by "=>", in the same manner as other preconditions in Ada.

It should also be noted that each alternative may also include further statements following the rendezvous body of the accept. These additional statements are executed in the normal way after the rendezvous has been completed.

The following example of a bounded buffer illustrates the use of guards.

```
task BUFFER is
   entry READ (V : out ITEM);
   entry WRITE(E : in ITEM);
end;

task body BUFFER is
   SIZE                  : constant := 10;
   POOL                  : array (1 .. SIZE) of ITEM;
   IN_INDEX, OUT_INDEX : INTEGER range 1 .. SIZE := 1;
   COUNT                 : INTEGER range 0 .. SIZE := 0;
begin
   loop
      select
         when COUNT < SIZE =>              -- not full
            accept WRITE(E : in ITEM) do
               POOL(IN_INDEX) := E;
            end;
            IN_INDEX := IN_INDEX mod SIZE + 1;
            COUNT := COUNT + 1;
      or
         when COUNT > 0 =>                 -- not empty
            accept READ(V : out ITEM) do
               V := POOL(OUT_INDEX);
            end;
            OUT_INDEX := OUT_INDEX mod SIZE + 1;
            COUNT      := COUNT - 1;
      end select;
   end loop;
end BUFFER;
```

The variables IN_INDEX and OUT_INDEX index the ends of the currently used part of the buffer and COUNT indicates how many items are in the buffer. Note how obvious the guards are. A READ can only be accepted when the buffer is not empty, and a WRITE can only be accepted when the buffer is not full. The reader is invited to compare the readability of the solution presented here with the example written in other languages in section 13.3.2.

It should be noted that the updating of the values of IN_INDEX, OUT_INDEX and COUNT is not done within the rendezvous. This allows the calling task to continue as soon as possible, but does not cause any problem of potential interference because these objects are local to BUFFER and so cannot be seen by any external task.

In many situations it is desirable to enforce a protocol on the use of entries. This can be done by placing the task within a package body and then providing access to the entries via procedures declared in the package specification. This technique also illustrates the point that a package provides visibility control whereas a task provides parallelism.

As an example consider an extension of the task PROTECTED_VARIABLE, which allows several tasks to READ simultaneously but only one to WRITE, and then only when no tasks are reading. It is written as a package READER_WRITER containing a task CONTROL.

```
package READER_WRITER is
   procedure READ (V : out ITEM);
   procedure WRITE(E : in ITEM);
end;

package body READER_WRITER is
   VARIABLE : ITEM;

task CONTROL is
   entry START_READ;
   entry STOP_READ;
   entry WRITE(E : in ITEM);
end;

task body CONTROL is
READERS : NATURAL := 0;
begin
   accept WRITE(E : in ITEM) do
      VARIABLE := E;
   end;

   loop
      select
         accept START_READ;
         READERS := READERS + 1;
      or
         accept STOP_READ;
         READERS := READERS - 1;
      or
         when READERS = 0 =>
            accept WRITE(E : in ITEM) do
               VARIABLE := E;
            end;
      end select;
   end loop;
end CONTROL;
```

```
      procedure READ(V : out ITEM) is
      begin
        CONTROL.START_READ;
        V := VARIABLE;
        CONTROL.STOP_READ;
      end;

      procedure WRITE(E : in ITEM) is
      begin
        CONTROL.WRITE(E);
      end;

   end READER_WRITER;
```

In this example READ and WRITE are procedures and not entries. However, since entries are called in the same way as procedures, the effective interface from the point of view of the caller remains unchanged. Of course the compiled calling code may be different, but this need not concern the user.

This example also illustrates the use of more than one accept statement corresponding to the internal entry WRITE (in this particular example the bodies are the same, but this need not be the case). It shows that a task can be viewed as a sort of *coroutine*, where entry calls can achieve different actions depending on the current point of execution of the task.

We now consider a further elaboration of this example that gives a better distribution of priority between readers and writers. Normally writers have priority over readers, and a new reader should not be permitted to start if there is a writer waiting.

Moreover, all waiting readers at the end of a write should have priority over the next writer. In order to program this strategy we use the attribute E'COUNT of an entry E, which denotes the number of tasks waiting in the queue for the entry. The use of this attribute requires some care as explained below. We illustrate this point by means of two different formulations of this problem. In the first formulation the declaration

```
   STILL_WAITING : INTEGER := 0;
```

is added to the declarative part of the body of CONTROL and the statement part now becomes as follows:

```
   begin
      accept WRITE(E : in ITEM) do
        VARIABLE := E;
        STILL_WAITING := START_READ'COUNT;
      end;
```

```
loop
  select
    when WRITE'COUNT = 0 or STILL_WAITING > 0 =>
      accept START_READ;
      READERS := READERS + 1;
      if STILL_WAITING > 0 then
        STILL_WAITING := STILL_WAITING - 1;
      end if;
  or
    accept STOP_READ;
    READERS := READERS - 1;
  or
    when READERS = 0 and STILL_WAITING = 0 =>
      accept WRITE(E : in ITEM) do
        VARIABLE := E;
        STILL_WAITING := START_READ'COUNT;
      end;
  end select;
end loop;
end;
```

In this formulation, STILL_WAITING is the number of readers still waiting of those who were waiting when the previous write finished.

The first-in-first-out queue discipline is necessary for the correct working of this example. At the end of each write, the number of readers waiting is noted in STILL_WAITING. A reader is accepted if there are still old readers waiting to be served, or if nobody is waiting to write; hence the test of STILL_WAITING in the guard of **accept** START_READ and the decrement of STILL_WAITING after the body of START_READ. Similarly, the guard of **accept** WRITE ensures that a new writer is only served if there are neither current readers nor old readers still waiting.

The above formulation should be treated with caution. Thus consider what happens if one of the waiting readers is aborted while in the queue on the entry START_READ, and after the value of START_READ'COUNT has been assigned to STILL_WAITING. The value of STILL_WAITING will then become inconsistent and the next writer will be further delayed until a new reader arrives.

This illustrates a general danger with using the COUNT attribute in guards, since any task that has issued an entry call can be aborted between the evaluation of COUNT and the execution of an accept statement based on the value of COUNT.

We will now reformulate the above example by introducing the else part of the select statement. A select statement may contain an else part following the various possibly guarded alternatives. The else part cannot be guarded. If all guards are false, or an immediate rendezvous is not possible, then the else part is obeyed. If there is an else part then PROGRAM_ERROR cannot arise.

In the reformulated example, STILL_WAITING is no longer required and the main loop now becomes as follows:

```
loop
  select
    when WRITE'COUNT = 0 =>
      accept START_READ;
      READERS := READERS + 1;
  or
      accept STOP_READ;
      READERS := READERS - 1;
  or
    when READERS = 0 =>
      accept WRITE(E : in ITEM) do
        VARIABLE := E;
      end;
      loop
        select
          accept START_READ;
          READERS := READERS + 1;
        else
          exit;
        end select;
      end loop;
  end select;
end loop;
```

After accepting a WRITE the task loops, accepting as many START_READs as can immediately be processed. Of course the behavior is marginally different, but the general objective is satisfied. The loop ought also to follow the initial WRITE, but because of the constraints on the position of an accept statement it cannot be placed in a procedure.

It should be observed that none of the above solutions to this problem is satisfactory if the calling tasks are aborted. They have been introduced in order to illustrate various features of Ada and not as solutions to the classic readers and writers problem.

It is worth noting that the entries in the various alternatives need not be distinct (although they usually will be). If two or more prove to be the same then the usual rule of arbitrary selection applies. This may be felt surprising. One motivation here is the fact that if several alternatives are open, one of them is chosen arbitrarily and there is hence no reason to disallow the same entry in two alternatives. Another motivation is the existence of families of entries. If E(I) and E(J) were two entries and they had to be different, then a tedious runtime check would be necessary. The rule thus allows different actions to be programmed in a simple way on the same entry but according to different guards.

Note that the guards are all evaluated at the start of the select statement only. The alternative semantics of evaluating a guard only when an entry is called was considered and rejected. The problem concerns the indivisibility of evaluating the guard and accepting the call together. One could not afford to make the guard evaluation indivisible, and so it would be possible for the calling task to be aborted during the guard evaluation. This would cause havoc if the guard proved to be true.

Guard evaluation at the start of the select statement could be criticized on the grounds that the value of a guard may be changed by another task before an alternative is chosen. This is not a good argument since even if the guard were evaluated when the corresponding alternative is chosen, there is no guarantee that it might not be immediately changed. In either case there is a danger with the use of asynchronously modifiable guards (such as those containing COUNT, CLOCK, and so on). Note that in practice most guards are local to the task that contains the select statement. In addition they are most often very simple. Consequently several optimizations of guard evaluation are possible.

The rule for choosing one of the open alternatives has been stated to be *arbitrary*. This should be interpreted as meaning that it is not defined by the language but is rather left to the implementation to choose an appropriate efficient algorithm. However, the algorithm used should not be unduly predictable, and any program that relies on a particular algorithm is not portable. Thus one could not assume for instance that the alternatives were taken in some order. If a uniform strategy is desired, then it must be programmed by using appropriate guarding conditions.

The need for the else part has been adequately demonstrated by earlier examples. It should be observed that the select statement allows a server to choose between different accept statements. There is no corresponding mechanism for a caller to choose between the first of several calls. This is because of a fundamental design decision: a task can be on at most one queue at a time. The main motivation for this decision is simplicity and efficiency of implementation.

13.2.6 Timing

Timing facilities are provided by the delay statement and the predefined package CALENDAR.

The delay statement holds up execution of the task for at least the specified time interval. Thus:

```
delay 2.0;
```

The expression following **delay** is of the predefined fixed point type DURATION, and gives the interval in seconds. The type DURATION is a fixed point type so that the addition of durations can be done without systematic loss of accuracy. The sum of two fixed point model numbers is always a model number; this is not so with a floating point type. However, the use of a real type rather than an integer type allows convenient literals for fractions of a second.

The user can declare constants such as

```
MINUTES : constant := 60.0;
```

and then naturally write

```
delay 6 * MINUTES;
```

The predefined package CALENDAR (see RM 9.6) provides the type TIME (which is a combined time and date), access to the clock, and various operations on times and durations.

The type TIME is private so that each implementation can choose an appropriate internal structure. The current time is provided by the function CLOCK, of type TIME, which returns its result in an indivisible manner, thereby avoiding difficulties around midnight. The individual components, year, month, day, and duration since midnight, can then be obtained from a TIME by various selector functions. Appropriate overloadings of +, -, and the relational operators allow the addition, subtraction, and comparison of times and durations.

As an example of the use of the package CALENDAR, the following text calls the procedure ACTION at almost regular intervals without cumulative drift.

```
declare
  use CALENDAR;
  INTERVAL  : constant DURATION := 10 * MINUTES;
  NEXT_TIME : TIME := CLOCK + INTERVAL;
begin
  loop
    delay NEXT_TIME - CLOCK;
    ACTION;
    NEXT_TIME := NEXT_TIME + INTERVAL;
  end loop;
end;
```

13.2.7 Timed and Conditional Communication

A delay statement may occur instead of an accept statement within an alternative of a select statement, and may have a guard in the usual way. Such a delay statement may be used to provide a time-out for the select statement. If no rendezvous has occurred within the specified interval then the statement list following the delay statement is executed. Of course if a rendezvous occurs before the interval has expired, then the delay is canceled and the select statement is executed normally.

As an example we can consider a task to drive a chain printer. If the printer does not receive any printing order for ten seconds, then the chain has to be stopped. Once it has stopped, a further print request will cause it to restart but a one-second delay must take place before printing commences.

```
task PRINTER_DRIVER is
   entry PRINT(L : LINE);
end;

task body PRINTER_DRIVER is
   CHAIN_GOING : BOOLEAN := FALSE;
   BUFFER      : LINE;
begin
   loop
      select
         accept PRINT(L : LINE) do
            BUFFER := L;
         end;
         if not CHAIN_GOING then
            -- start the chain
            delay 1.0;
            CHAIN_GOING := TRUE;
         end if;
         -- print the line
      or
         when CHAIN_GOING =>
            delay 10.0;
            -- stop the chain
            CHAIN_GOING := FALSE;
      end select;
   end loop;
end;
```

A select statement may have several alternatives starting with a delay statement. This extends the general rule that the entries in the different alternatives need not be distinct. If there are several open delay alternatives then the one with the shortest delay is chosen.

A select statement is not allowed to have delay alternatives as well as an else part; the else part would always take precedence anyway. Moreover, at least one alternative must have an accept statement.

Further variations on the select statement allow entry calls to be conditional or to be timed out. These take the form

```
select
   T.E( ... );      -- entry call
else
   -- statements to be obeyed if call
   -- not immediately accepted
end select;
```

and

```
select
   T.E( ... );      -- entry call
or
   delay EXPRESSION;
   -- statements to be obeyed if call
   -- not accepted within specified duration
end select;
```

respectively.

It should be noted that such select statements do not allow the possibility of calling one of several entries (by analogy with obeying one of several accept statements). To do so would violate the principle that a task may not be on two or more entry queues at the same time.

The timed and conditional forms of entry call are provided because of their convenience. Such features can be programmed using agent tasks and the abort statement, but only with some difficulty if race conditions are to be avoided.

Timed entry calls present difficulties which **are** similar to, but less severe than, those associated with abort statements. For example, a task may be removed from an entry queue because the call timed out, and thereby invalidate a decision based on the value of the COUNT attribute. However such dangers can be overcome by hiding the task in a package so that all entry calls are via a procedure.

13.2.8 Interrupts

Hardware interrupts can be handled by interpreting them as external entry calls. A representation clause is used to link the entry to the interrupt, thus:

```
task DEVICE_DRIVER is
    entry IO_DONE;
    ...
    for IO_DONE use at 4;
end;
```

The value following **at** is of type ADDRESS (as explained in section 15.6.1), and interpreted in a machine-dependent manner. For example, it could be a physical address, an index into a table of records, or a binary number representing encoded information.

The interrupt is processed when the task owning the entry performs a rendezvous by using a corresponding accept statement:

```
accept IO_DONE;
```

The behavior regarding multiple interrupts and masking depends on the implementation, but may be compared to the various forms of entry calls. Interrupts that are queued correspond to normal calls, whereas interrupts that are lost if not immediately processed correspond to conditional entry calls.

The hypothetical task that makes the entry call behaves as if it had a priority higher than that of any user task. It then follows from the normal priority rules that interrupts get obeyed immediately, provided of course that the handling task is waiting at the corresponding accept statement.

An interrupt may provide control information via one or more in parameters of the entry. Clearly an entry associated with an interrupt cannot have out or in out parameters because there is no real calling task to whom to pass the values.

13.2.9 Task Types

It is often important to have many similar tasks, and also to be able to create them in a dynamic manner. This can be done with task types.

A task type declaration is similar to a single task declaration except that **type** follows **task** in the specification. Thus

```
task type T is
  entry E( ... );
  ...
end;

task body T is
  ...
end T;
```

This just creates a template. Actual tasks are then created, as are other objects, by an object declaration

```
X : T;
```

or through an access type and an allocator

```
type REF_T is access T;

RX : REF_T := new T;
```

Tasks so declared become active at the **begin** following their declaration, or at the end of the allocator in the case of accessed tasks. The termination rules are as before except that accessed tasks are dependent on the unit containing the access type definition rather than the allocator; this accords with the normal scope rules for objects created by an allocator.

Task objects can be used in structures in the usual way; thus tasks may be components of arrays and records. Task types are limited types; this is because a task object is permanently bound to the created task and so assignment would make no sense. However, task identities can be manipulated by the use of access types.

An important application of task types is in the creation of *agents*. A simple example is provided by the following messenger task type.

```
task type MESSENGER is
  entry DEPOSIT (X : in ITEM);
  entry COLLECT (X : out ITEM);
end;
```

```
task body MESSENGER is
   STORE : ITEM;
begin
   accept DEPOSIT(X : in ITEM) do
      STORE := X;
   end;
   accept COLLECT(X : out ITEM) do
      X := STORE;
   end;
end MESSENGER;
```

A messenger is a carrier of an ITEM. It is given to him by a call of DEPOSIT and retrieved by a call of COLLECT. Note that a messenger dies after a single use.

Such a messenger can be used to solve the problem of a customer asking for a service and wishing to do other things while waiting for the result. The essence of the solution is for the customer to leave with the server the address of a messenger who will later communicate with the customer. In the following solution the service consists of repairing an item. The repaired item is passed back to the customer via the messenger. Note the need for the access type

```
type AGENT is access MESSENGER;
```

The server and customer are as follows:

```
task SERVER is
   entry REPAIR(X : ITEM; A : AGENT);
end;

task body SERVER is
   JOB       : ITEM;
   THE_AGENT : AGENT;
begin
   loop
      accept REPAIR(X : ITEM; A : AGENT) do
         JOB       := X;
         THE_AGENT := A;
      end;
      -- doing the repair of the item JOB
      THE_AGENT.DEPOSIT(JOB);
   end loop;
end SERVER;
```

```
task CUSTOMER;

task body CUSTOMER is

   MY_ITEM  : ITEM;
   MY_AGENT : AGENT := new MESSENGER;
begin
   ...
   SERVER.REPAIR(MY_ITEM, MY_AGENT);
   ...
   MY_AGENT.COLLECT(MY_ITEM);
   ...
end CUSTOMER;
```

The agent task serves two very important purposes. First it enables the customer and server to be *decoupled*. This means that the customer can do other things while the server does the repair, and equally the server does not have to wait for the customer to collect the item before dealing with the next customer. Second, and perhaps more important, it enables the customer to be of an arbitrary task type by factoring off the required entry DEPOSIT. Without the agent the customer would have to have the entry DEPOSIT, and this would in fact mean that all customers would have to be of the same task type; this would, of course, be intolerable.

A natural use of task types occurs when there are several copies of a piece of physical equipment, and a distinct but similar task is required to drive each one. Thus suppose we have ten line printers and wish to drive each one by a distinct task such as PRINTER_DRIVER of section 13.2.7.

We could declare a task type with specification

```
task type PRINTER_DRIVER is
   entry PRINT(L : LINE);
end;
```

The task body would be as before. We could then declare an array of tasks thus

```
PRINTER : array (1 .. 10) of PRINTER_DRIVER;
```

A particular task is then designated by indexing the array in the usual way and so an entry could be called thus

```
PRINTER(I).PRINT(MY_LINE);
```

It is often convenient to rename an entry in such circumstances so that calls are abbreviated. Thus:

```
procedure PRINT_6 (L : LINE) renames PRINTER(6).PRINT;
```

The introduction of task types in Ada gives much additional capability especially since, in conjunction with access types, the number of such tasks can be dynamically determined quite independently of the block structure. Objects of task types can also be used to implement abstract data types.

Task types are valuable in handling certain task identification problems, as illustrated by the agent mechanism described above; this avoids introducing anonymous untyped task variables which would have raised complex problems of run-time type checking.

Another important use that would have been made of such anonymous task variables can be covered by other existing language concepts. It corresponds to the case of a server that needs to be able to recognize its customers. In such a case limited private types provide a facility whereby a key may be created and handed to a task on its first request. On later requests the task shows the key, thus enabling the server to recognize the owner. The private type mechanism prevents forgery of the key. There is a risk that keys will get reused in the future, since a normal mechanism would be to represent each new key as the next integer. This risk is no more than that associated with remembered task activation variables and indeed can be minimized to any required degree by using a key composed of a record of several integers. Thus using just two 16-bit words a new key can be issued every second for 136 years without duplication.

13.2.10 The Terminate Alternative

It will have been noticed that many of the examples of server tasks have had bodies containing endless loops. This means of course that it would never be possible to leave the unit on which such a task depended. An entry could be added which, when called, terminated the task, and this could then be called prior to quitting the unit. However, this would often be inconvenient. Moreover, the existence of task types and the use of tasks as objects, and especially as a means of implementing private types where the active nature of the private type is hidden from the user, makes such a technique most unsatisfactory.

In order to cope with such circumstances, a special form of select alternative may be used which automatically has the required effect. Thus a select statement can take the form

```
select
   accept A( ... )
      ...
or
   accept B( ... )
      ...
or
   terminate;
end select;
```

The terminate alternative is taken if the unit on which the task depends has completed, and all sibling and dependent tasks are terminated or similarly able to select a terminate alternative. In such a situation all the tasks are dormant and could not be called, and so they can all become terminated together.

13.2.11 Families of Entries and Scheduling

The key to designing parallel tasks in Ada lies in the realization that queues are associated with entries and only entries and that such queues are handled in a strictly first-in-first-out manner. In many situations it is convenient to be able to dissect a queue into several subqueues. This can be done by using a family of entries, which is very like a one-dimensional array.

A family of entries is declared by adding a discrete range to the entry name in the declaration. Thus

```
entry TRANSFER(1 .. 200)(D : DATA);
```

declares a family of 200 entries each of which has the parameter D.

A particular entry is called by the use of an index as expected

```
TRANSFER(I)(DATA_VALUE);
```

In a corresponding accept statement, the particular member has to be indicated by appending an actual index to the family name. It is then followed by the formal parameter list, if any, in the usual way.

```
accept TRANSFER(I)(D : DATA) do
   ...
end TRANSFER;
```

Our example is that of scheduling a queue of requests for data transfers to or from a moving-head disk. In order to minimize head movement the requests are grouped into separate queues for each track and all the requests for a particular track are serviced together. It would be possible to consider each track as a separate physical entity demanding its own task. We would then use an array of tasks. However, the tracks are not independent. The disk head can serve only one track at a time and so the parallelism obtained by using many tasks is not necessary. Instead the transfers are handled by a single slave task with a family of entries. There is an entry for each track so that the queues are independent. A separate task controls the arm movement and the choice of track for the slave task. The two tasks are embedded in a package as usual.

```
package DISK_HEAD_SCHEDULER is
   type TRACK is range 1 .. 200;
   type DATA is ...    -- other parameters of transfer
   procedure TRANSMIT(TN : TRACK; D : DATA);
end;

package body DISK_HEAD_SCHEDULER is
   type DIRECTION is (UP, DOWN);
   INVERSE : constant array (DIRECTION) of DIRECTION :=
                             (UP => DOWN, DOWN => UP);
   STEP    : constant array (DIRECTION) of INTEGER range -1 .. 1 :=
                             (UP => 1, DOWN => -1);
   WAITING : array (TRACK) of INTEGER := (TRACK => 0);
   COUNT   : array (DIRECTION) of INTEGER := (DIRECTION => 0);
   MOVE    : DIRECTION := DOWN;
   ARM_POSITION : TRACK := 1;

   task CONTROL is
      entry SIGN_IN(T : TRACK);
      entry FIND_TRACK(REQUESTS : out INTEGER;
                       TRACK_NO : out TRACK);
   end;

   task TRACK_MANAGER is
      entry TRANSFER(TRACK)(D : DATA);
   end;

   procedure TRANSMIT(TN : TRACK; D : DATA) is
   begin
      CONTROL.SIGN_IN(TN);
      TRACK_MANAGER.TRANSFER(TN)(D);
   end;

   task body TRACK_MANAGER is
      NO_OF_REQUESTS : INTEGER;
      CURRENT_TRACK  : TRACK;
   begin
```

```
    loop
      CONTROL.FIND_TRACK(NO_OF_REQUESTS, CURRENT_TRACK);
      while NO_OF_REQUESTS > 0 loop
        accept TRANSFER(CURRENT_TRACK)(D : DATA) do
          -- do actual I/O
          NO_OF_REQUESTS := NO_OF_REQUESTS - 1;
        end TRANSFER;
      end loop;
    end loop;
  end TRACK_MANAGER;

  task body CONTROL is
  begin
    loop
      select
        when COUNT(UP) + COUNT(DOWN) > 0 =>
          accept FIND_TRACK(REQUESTS : out INTEGER;
                     TRACK_NO : out TRACK) do
            if COUNT(MOVE) = 0 then
              MOVE := INVERSE(MOVE);
            else
              ARM_POSITION := ARM_POSITION + STEP(MOVE);
            end if;
            while WAITING(ARM_POSITION) = 0 loop
              ARM_POSITION := ARM_POSITION + STEP(MOVE);
            end loop;
            COUNT(MOVE) := COUNT(MOVE) -
                            WAITING(ARM_POSITION);
            REQUESTS := WAITING(ARM_POSITION);
            TRACK_NO := ARM_POSITION;
            WAITING(ARM_POSITION) := 0;
          end FIND_TRACK;
      or
```

```
            accept SIGN_IN(T : TRACK) do
              if T < ARM_POSITION then
                COUNT(DOWN) := COUNT(DOWN) + 1;
              elsif T > ARM_POSITION then
                COUNT(UP) := COUNT(UP) + 1;
              else
                COUNT(INVERSE(MOVE)) := COUNT(INVERSE(MOVE)) + 1;
              end if;
              WAITING(T) := WAITING(T) + 1;
            end SIGN_IN;
          end select;
        end loop;
      end CONTROL;
  end DISK_HEAD_SCHEDULER;
```

The user indicates his requests by calling the procedure TRANSMIT. This in turn calls the entry SIGN_IN in the task CONTROL which records the request. The user then waits on the call of TRANSFER until the slave task TRACK_MANAGER is ready to perform transfers on the track concerned.

The slave task TRACK_MANAGER calls the entry FIND_TRACK in order to determine which track should be handled next. CONTROL only honors the call when there are requests outstanding (COUNT(UP)+COUNT(DOWN) > 0). If there are requests outstanding, an extended rendezvous occurs during which the arm is moved and the data transferred to TRACK_MANAGER.

Note the accept statement within TRACK_MANAGER, which references the member CURRENT_TRACK of the family TRANSFER and so finally deals with the user who has been waiting in TRANSMIT.

It should be pointed out that the example given is purely illustrative. No genuine disk head scheduler would need to be so heavily engineered. A perfectly adequate solution is to allow only two calls to TRACK_MANAGER at a time and to sort these into the more efficient order. If a disk queue frequently exceeds two items then the system is grossly overloaded anyway and elaborate scheduling is unlikely to help.

The above example shows how a family of entries could be used to dissect a queue into subqueues. The first-in-first-out nature of the entry queue might be thought to be a severe constraint in cases where some requests may be of high priority and also in cases where later similar requests could be satisfied even though earlier ones had to wait.

The handling of requests with priorities is easily achieved by the use of separate entries for each level. A family can conveniently be used for that purpose. The following example illustrates an approach suitable for a small number of levels.

```
type LEVEL is (URGENT, MEDIUM, LOW);

task CONTROL is
  entry REQUEST(LEVEL)(D : DATA);
end;

task body CONTROL is
  ...
  select
    accept REQUEST(URGENT)(D : DATA) do
      ...
    end;
  or when REQUEST(URGENT)'COUNT = 0 =>
    accept REQUEST(MEDIUM)(D : DATA) do
      ...
    end;
  or when REQUEST(URGENT)'COUNT = 0
    and REQUEST(MEDIUM)'COUNT = 0 =>
    accept REQUEST(LOW)(D : DATA) do
      ...
    end;
  end select;
  ...
end CONTROL;
```

For a larger number of levels, this approach is obviously not satisfactory. An alternative possibility at first sight is just to scan all the values of the family thus

```
task body CONTROL is
  ...
begin
  loop
    for I in LEVEL loop
      select
        accept REQUEST(I) (D : DATA) do
          ...
        end;
        exit;
      else
        null;
      end select;
    end loop;
  end loop;
end CONTROL;
```

Unfortunately this is not satisfactory since the task will busy-wait when there are no requests outstanding.

An acceptable solution is to use a double interaction with the control task and this is best structured by placing the task inside a package as illustrated below:

```
package CONTROLLER is
   type LEVEL is range 1 .. 50;
   procedure REQUEST(L : LEVEL; D : DATA);
end;

package body CONTROLLER is
   task CONTROL is
      entry SIGN_IN(L : LEVEL);
      entry PERFORM(LEVEL)(D : DATA);
   end;
   task body CONTROL is
      PENDING : array (LEVEL) of INTEGER := (LEVEL => 0);
      TOTAL   : INTEGER := 0;
   begin
      loop
         if TOTAL = 0 then
            -- no request to be served: wait if necessary
            accept SIGN_IN(L : LEVEL) do
               PENDING(L) := PENDING(L) + 1;
               TOTAL := 1;
            end SIGN_IN;
         end if;
         loop    -- accept any pending SIGN_IN call without waiting
            select
               accept SIGN_IN(L : LEVEL) do
                  PENDING(L) := PENDING(L) + 1;
                  TOTAL := TOTAL + 1;
               end SIGN_IN;
            else
               exit;
            end select;
         end loop;
```

```
            for I in LEVEL loop
              if PENDING(I) > 0 then
                accept PERFORM(I)(D : DATA) do
                  -- satisfy the request of highest level
                end;
                PENDING(I) := PENDING(I) - 1;
                TOTAL := TOTAL -1;
                exit; --restart main loop in order to accept new requests
              end if;
            end loop;
          end loop;
        end CONTROL;

        procedure REQUEST(L : LEVEL; D : DATA) is
        begin
          CONTROL.SIGN_IN(L);
          CONTROL.PERFORM(L)(D);
        end;
      end CONTROLLER;
```

In order to service a request, a call to SIGN_IN must first be accepted, and its occurrence recorded in the global counter TOTAL, and the appropriate PENDING counter. In a second step, the appropriate entry of the family PERFORM must be accepted. CONTROL proceeds by

- waiting for the first SIGN_IN if all previous requests have been serviced;

- accepting all pending calls to SIGN_IN;

- executing the request with the highest priority;

- going back to the beginning of the loop to take care of any call to SIGN_IN that has arrived in the meantime.

We will now illustrate a very general mechanism which in effect allows the items in a queue on a simple entry to be processed in an arbitrary order. The example is of a controller for the allocation of groups of items from a set of resources. The generality is emphasized by making the package generic.

```
generic
   type RESOURCE is (<>);
package MULTI_RESOURCE_CONTROL is
   type RESOURCE_SET is array (RESOURCE) of BOOLEAN;
   procedure RESERVE(GROUP : RESOURCE_SET);
   procedure RELEASE(GROUP : RESOURCE_SET);
end;

package body MULTI_RESOURCE_CONTROL is
   EMPTY   : constant RESOURCE_SET := (RESOURCE => FALSE);
   USED    : RESOURCE_SET := EMPTY;
   WAITERS : INTEGER := 0;

   task CONTROL is
      entry FIRST   (ASKED : RESOURCE_SET; OK : out BOOLEAN);
      entry AGAIN   (ASKED : RESOURCE_SET; OK : out BOOLEAN);
      entry RELEASE (GROUP : RESOURCE_SET);
   end;

   procedure RESERVE(GROUP : RESOURCE_SET) is
      POSSIBLE : BOOLEAN;
   begin
      CONTROL.FIRST(GROUP, POSSIBLE);
      while not POSSIBLE loop
                    -- if at first you don't succeed, try, try again
         CONTROL.AGAIN(GROUP, POSSIBLE);
      end loop;
   end;

   procedure TRY(ASKED : RESOURCE_SET; OK : out BOOLEAN) is
   begin
      if (USED and ASKED) = EMPTY then
         USED := USED or ASKED;
         OK   := TRUE;    -- allocation successful
      else
         OK   := FALSE;   -- not possible, try again later
      end if;
   end;

   procedure RELEASE(GROUP : RESOURCE_SET) is
   begin
      CONTROL.RELEASE(GROUP);
   end;
```

```
      task body CONTROL is
      begin
        loop
          select
            accept FIRST(ASKED : RESOURCE_SET; OK : out BOOLEAN) do
              TRY(ASKED, OK);
              if not OK then
                WAITERS := WAITERS + 1;
              end if;
            end;
          or
            accept RELEASE(GROUP : RESOURCE_SET) do
              USED := USED and not GROUP;
            end; -- now find a user for the released resource
            for I in 1 .. WAITERS loop
              accept AGAIN(ASKED : RESOURCE_SET; OK : out BOOLEAN) do
                TRY(ASKED, OK);
                if OK then
                  WAITERS := WAITERS - 1;
                end if;
              end;
            end loop;
          end select;
        end loop;
      end CONTROL;
  end MULTI_RESOURCE_CONTROL;
```

The user requests and obtains an arbitrary group of resources by calling the procedure
RESERVE and returns resources by calling the procedure RELEASE. The procedure
RESERVE makes an immediate attempt to acquire the resources by calling the entry
FIRST. If they are not all available, OK is returned false and the request is queued by
calling AGAIN. It should be noted that FIRST is always honored promptly (except when
the controller is busy with RELEASE) whereas AGAIN is only considered when a RELEASE
occurs. Thus all requests that cannot be satisfied immediately are placed on the AGAIN
queue. It is important that these requests are not serviced on a first-in-first-out basis
but rather that when some resources are released the requests in the queue that can
then be fully satisfied should be honored. The technique is to scan the queue by doing
a rendezvous with AGAIN and to allow each user (in RESERVE) to place itself back on
the queue if it cannot get the resources it requires. In order that each user should have
only one retry the loop is controlled by the variable WAITERS. This indicates how many
tasks have called FIRST unsuccessfully and are waiting in the system. We cannot use
AGAIN'COUNT since resources might be released between a task unsuccessfully calling
FIRST and actually calling AGAIN.

The above solution is reasonably satisfactory, although not completely fair. Tasks could reenter the AGAIN queue in a slightly different order because of the *race conditions*.

However, it should be realized that the solutions in this section are not satisfactory if the tasks involved can be aborted. One general approach in such circumstances is to use agent tasks that can be relied upon. Nevertheless, entirely satisfactory solutions in such circumstances are not easily obtained. There seems to be a conflict between the intrinsic high level features of Ada and low level queue manipulation. It should be realized however that the tasking features of Ada are aimed at cooperating systems.

13.3 RATIONALE FOR THE DESIGN OF THE RENDEZVOUS FACILITIES

This section starts by briefly surveying some of the more important and older real-time primitives and their shortcomings. It then considers the concept of rendezvous and shows how this concept has influenced the design of the tasking facilities in Ada.

13.3.1 Early Primitives

The understanding of algorithmic sequential processes is based upon that of the evaluation of arithmetic and Boolean expressions, whose axioms have been well understood for centuries. However, there is no mathematical tradition upon which we can draw in order to help us to understand the behavior of cooperating sequential processes. As a consequence it has always been difficult to decide whether a particular set of real-time primitives is good or not. Many sets can be implemented in terms of each other but their relative primitiveness is often hard to perceive.

Broadly speaking the primitives (or perhaps the applications) can be divided into two categories. The first enables common data or common code to be protected from multiple usage. The second enables one task to send a message to another; this includes the degenerate case of a signal, which can be thought of as a message with no content.

One of the oldest and best known primitive sets is the *binary semaphore* described by Dijkstra [Di 68]. This consists of the two operators P and V, acting on a semaphore S which takes two values, busy and free (or equivalently true and false). The behavior of the operations is:

P(S)   If S is busy the task is suspended until S becomes free. If S is free then it is set busy and the task proceeds.

V(S)   S is set free. If there are tasks held up on a P(S) operation then one of them is allowed to proceed.

Semaphores can be used to protect data by embedding the code that accesses the data between matched calls thus:

```
P(S)                        P(S)
  -- access data              -- access data
V(S)                        V(S)

task A                      task B
```

Semaphores can also be used to signal happenings. One task waits by calling P, the other signals by calling V.

```
P(S) -- wait for B        V(S) -- signal to A

task A                    task B
```

Semaphores can therefore be used both for protection and for signalling. They also have the merit of being primitives that are both simple to describe and easy to understand. What then are their disadvantages? Briefly the problem is that for all but the simplest applications, the programming of semaphores is difficult. Programs using semaphores exhibit similar symptoms to unstructured programs using gotos. They are hard to write, understand, prove, and maintain. More specifically, typical problems are:

- One can jump around a call of P and therefore accidentally access unprotected data.

- One can jump around a call of V and accidentally leave the semaphore busy so that the system deadlocks.

- One can forget to use them.

- It is not possible to program an alternative action if a semaphore is found to be busy when attempting P.

- It is not possible to wait for one of several semaphores to be free.

- Semaphores are often visible to tasks that need not access them.

An extended form of semaphore is the *integer semaphore*. In this case the value is an integer rather than a boolean. It is particularly useful for allowing a limited number of tasks to have access to a resource. Nevertheless it has been shown that the integer semaphore can be programmed in terms of binary semaphores, and so in practice it is only marginally more useful.

Closely related to the semaphore is the *signal* or *event*. There are variations, but a typical definition would be that an event E has two states, *set* and *unset*, and the following operations upon it:

WAIT(E)   If E has not been set then the task is suspended until the event is set. If E has been set then it is unset and the task is allowed to proceed.

SEND(E)   E is set. If there are tasks waiting for E then one of them is allowed to proceed.

Clearly such an event is isomorphic to the binary semaphore. The difference lies perhaps in the intended use. Semaphores are associated with data protection, and events with indicating that something has happened. There are variations in which several events are remembered. But in all forms, events suffer from the same structuring problems as semaphores.

Various other primitives have been proposed in order to overcome the structuring difficulties of semaphores and events. However, they usually tackle only one of the application areas distinguished above (data protection and signalling). In this respect they are somewhat unbalanced.

The *critical section* has been proposed as a syntactic form equivalent to a bracketed pair of P and V operations. This prevents goto statements from bypassing one of the operations and hence overcomes some of the difficulties of semaphores. A further form, the conditional critical section, allows an alternative action to be performed if the resource represented is busy.

Critical sections do not seem to have been successful. They solve only the exclusion problem and need to be complemented with a signalling mechanism; this does not lead to the unification sought by language designers.

Many forms of message switching system have been implemented in order to give improved solutions to the signalling problem (see [BH 70, 73]). Typically they enable messages to be sent between tasks, and allow the source or destination of the message to be optionally specified. They therefore give added protection by preventing unauthorized access to messages.

Perhaps the biggest disadvantage of message systems is the need for a sizeable message controller. Message systems also seem to be of an ad-hoc nature with an apparently arbitrary set of parameters. Moreover they do not easily solve exclusion problems because of the high overhead involved.

A significant step forward was the *monitor*, first described by Brinch Hansen [BH 73,75] and by Hoare [Ho 74]. This includes the facilities of the critical section, and when combined with events (as in Modula), gives a reasonable solution to problems such as the bounded buffer. The monitor solves the exclusion problem but not the message problem. Indeed the signals in Modula still suffer from the structuring problems of semaphores.

13.3.2 The Rendezvous Concept

Another line of approach to mutual exclusion and synchronization was introduced in early computer science by Conway [Co 63] with the notion of *coroutine*, the first definition of a high-level synchronization mechanism. One of the important concepts introduced by Conway (and maybe forgotten later) is that synchronization and data transmission are two inseparable activities. Two parallel tasks need to be synchronized to exchange information – thereafter they resume their respective activities; this synchronization is known as a *rendezvous*. Two papers by Hoare [Ho 78] and Brinch Hansen [BH 78] proposed a rethink of parallel processing in terms of this concept of rendezvous and strongly influenced the design of Ada.

The difficult problem that arises here is one of making tasks known to each other. Tasks have names that identify them unambiguously. Should these names be used by tasks to synchronize with each other, or should there exist a further entity that makes both candidates for synchronization known to each other by reference to some common *channel*? These two solutions are extreme forms of *symmetric* communication; either each communicating task has full knowledge of its colleague, or it has no information at all. Both solutions appear in the literature: [Ho 78] and [Ka 74].

We rejected the channel solution in this design in order to avoid an additional language concept and the dual connection mechanism that it requires. The solution adopted in Ada, although closer to the one proposed by Hoare, is *asymmetric*: one of the two communicating tasks knows the name of the other and names it explicitly; the second task knows only that it expects some external interaction.

In order to justify the asymmetry, let us first summarize the symmetric proposal developed by Hoare and embedded in a language which has become known as CSP (Communicating Sequential Processes). In CSP, communication between tasks is seen as synchronized input-output: one task outputs data which the other inputs, and both tasks rendezvous during the transfer – that is, the first to arrive at its input or output statement waits for the other and they both then execute the I/O statements together (or apparently together) before proceeding independently. Each task names the other in the transfer. The transfer can be thought of as an assignment split into two parts with the left side in one task and the right side in the other.

As an example we shall consider a task BUFFER, to smooth variations in the speed of output of items by a producer task and input by a consumer task (given in section 13.2.5). The program is as follows:

```
BUFFER ::
  pool : (1 .. 10) item;
  inindex, outindex, count : integer;
  inindex := 1; outindex := 1; count := 0;
    * [count < 10; producer?pool(inindex) ->
      inindex := inindex mod 10 + 1; count := count + 1
    [] count > 0; consumer?more() ->
      consumer!pool(outindex);
      outindex := outindex mod 10 + 1; count := count - 1
    ]
```

The key language statements in this example are:

```
X ? Y    Input Y from task X
X ! Y    Output Y to task X
```

On each iteration the guards "count < 10" and "count > 0" are evaluated. If both guards are true then calls from either the consumer or producer are acceptable and the first such call will be waited for; if both have already made such a call and are therefore themselves waiting then a nondeterministic choice will be made; if only one has made a call then obviously that call is taken. If, however, only one guard is true then only the corresponding call can be accepted, and the other task will wait until the buffer is partially filled or emptied as the case may be. In this example both guards cannot be false and so the iterative process continues indefinitely.

In the producer case the statement

```
producer ? pool(inindex)
```

moves the item into the buffer directly. In the consumer case the statement

```
consumer ? more()
```

indicates that the consumer is ready and a subsequent

```
consumer ! pool(outindex)
```

actually does the transfer. The producer task therefore contains statements such as

```
BUFFER ! X
```

whereas the consumer task has pairs such as

```
BUFFER ! more();
BUFFER ? X
```

Note that *more()* denotes a structured value with no components and is used here as a signal.

As can be seen the program is readable, although perhaps presented in a terse style by traditional high-level language standards. However, there are two problems with CSP. One is that a (one-to-one) named correspondence is required; because of this symmetry, it is not possible to program a library routine to provide resources to arbitrary users. The other problem is that a double interaction is required for the consumer; this means that the two calls really need to be *encapsulated* by a single procedure in order to give a clean interface.

In Ada, as we have seen, naming is one-sided. Tasks can be characterized as services or as users. A user certainly needs to know the name of the service it is requesting. On the other hand, a server need not know the names of its users. Because of this asymmetry it possible to program the above library routine. As a consequence there can be queues of waiting tasks associated with each request. On each successful rendezvous just one waiting task is served.

The other important concept introduced in Ada is the notion of the *extended rendezvous*. This notion is a major breakthrough to a higher level of abstraction. In the case of the task BUFFER this overcomes the need for the double rendezvous with the consumer. This is seen by comparing the example in section 13.2.5 with that above. Thus we now have

```
BUFFER.READ(X);
```

rather than the two statements of CSP. This also illustrates the procedural form of entry call as opposed to some specialized statements. As we have seen, this enables a similar external interface to be presented, even if a change of solution demands that a procedure be replaced by an entry or vice versa.

The extended rendezvous is more disciplined since it ensures that the same task performs the interaction throughout. It is also instructive to consider the same example written in Modula using monitors as follows:

```
interface module buffer;
   define put, get;
   const poolsize = 10;
   var pool : array [1 .. poolsize] of item;
   inindex, outindex, count : integer;
   nonfull, nonempty : signal;

   procedure put (x : item);
   begin
     if count = poolsize then wait(nonfull) end;
     pool [inindex] := x;
     inindex := inindex mod poolsize + 1; count := count + 1;
     send(nonempty)
   end put;
```

```
procedure get (var x : item);
begin
   if count = 0 then wait(nonempty) end;
   x := pool [outindex];
   outindex := outindex mod poolsize + 1; count := count - 1;
   send(nonfull)
end get;
begin
   inindex := 1; outindex := 1; count := 0
end buffer;
```

The producer and consumer processes move the items by calls such as

put(x)   and   get(x)

respectively. This is satisfactory, but the internal behavior of the monitor is not nearly as clear as in CSP and Ada. The rendezvous mechanism is more disciplined than a monitor, since the accept statements appear inside a context (for example following a guard) from which information can be deduced, thereby facilitating both understanding and proof.

Perhaps the most important point about both CSP and Ada is that they offer mechanisms that are applicable to both data protection and signalling. Earlier attempts to develop features at a higher level than semaphores or events (such as message systems and monitors) seemed to solve only one problem, and by offering an unbalanced solution were not clearly better than the original simple primitives.

The rationale behind the accept statement and entry call is simply to provide a rendezvous. In some applications it is necessary that a rendezvous be achieved, whereas in others it is important for the caller not to be held up. It is much more difficult to program a rendezvous in terms of non-rendezvous primitives than vice versa. Hence the rendezvous has been chosen as the natural primitive.

It is noted that calls are accepted in simple order of arrival. The alternative of making the order depend on some parameter of the call was considered and rejected because of the difficulty of implementation, which could severely penalize the simple user. As has been demonstrated in the examples, it is possible to program different strategies when necessary.

The introduction of entries leads naturally to the unification of tasks and packages. A task encapsulates entries in the same way as a package encapsulates procedures. Moreover there is a strong analogy between on the one hand the specification, in which the entries are specified, and the body, containing the sequence that controls the critical actions, and on the other hand the corresponding subdivisions of a package with respect to the specification and bodies of procedures.

However, this unification has its limits. It proved necessary to disallow entities other than entries in the specification. As mentioned earlier, this was partly for methodological reasons and partly because of the cost of preventing access to variables of an inactive task and of implementing access on a distributed system.

The general applicability of the rendezvous concept has been confirmed by its use in other examples. This concept is well adapted to distributed systems – communication is achieved by entry calls, exchanged data is passed via parameters. From a more theoretical viewpoint, it is interesting to note that path expressions [CH 74] can be shown to be easily expressible in terms of rendezvous primitives.

13.4 PACKAGES AND TASKS

We conclude by emphasizing one strong distinction between packages and tasks, despite their lexical similarity. The overall concept is that a package is passive and provides the means for visibility control and structuring, whereas a task is active and provides the means for parallelism and synchronization.

In order to emphasize that a package is the main structuring tool, a task cannot be generic, cannot be a library unit, and cannot appear in a use clause.

A general subsystem might thus be a (possibly generic) package containing tasks. This general structure has the advantage of giving good control over the facilities provided. Thus protocols on the use of entries may be enforced by encapsulating their calls in a procedure.

14. Exception Handling

14.1 INTRODUCTION

The ability to handle error situations is essential for the reliability of real-time systems. In many cases, they must be designed as systems which should never halt. This definitely requires an ability to handle situations that, although rare, are quite likely to happen given enough time.

This subject of exception handling has received considerable attention over the years, and several formulations of exception handling features for programming languages have been proposed. For a presentation of these facilities the reader is referred to the extensive accounts given in [Go 75] and [Le 77]. The solutions proposed differ mainly in the level of generality at which they treat the concept of exception.

One family of solutions tends to consider exception handling as a normal programming technique for events that are infrequent, but are not necessarily errors. This viewpoint has been followed in [LMS 74], [Go 75], [PW 76], [Le 77] and [GS 77]. It means that when an exception occurs it is first treated by an *exception handler*, and then control may return to the point where the exception occurred. It also means that exception handling may be used to perform some repair actions and thereafter to continue normal execution.

A second family of proposals tends to restrict exceptions to events that can be considered (in some sense) as errors or, at least, as terminating conditions. This means that when an exception is raised in a given sequence of statements, their execution will be abandoned. Control will be passed to an exception handler but will never return to the point where the exception was raised. The handler may decide to restart the same sequence of actions under better conditions, but it will do so by a different invocation of these actions, not by a simple resumption. This second family of solutions includes *recovery blocks* [HLMR 74, Ra 75] and a proposal by Bron, Fokkinga, and De Haas [BFH 76].

Naturally, what is considered as an error is rather subjective, and moreover the ability of a handler to reinvoke a subprogram that raised an exception will permit the use of exception handling both for making repairs and for the treatment of rare events. The problem domains that can be addressed by the two families of solutions are hence comparable; but they require different underlying mechanisms and they lead to different programming styles.

The exception handling facility provided in Ada belongs to this second family. It provides a facility for local termination upon detection of errors. It has been inspired by the Bron proposal and has some similarities with the Bliss *signal enable* construct.

The discussion of exception handling starts with an overall presentation, followed by examples that illustrate the main classes of use. The interactions between exceptions and parallel processing are then presented, and we conclude with a discussion of several technical issues.

14.2 PRESENTATION OF EXCEPTION HANDLING IN ADA

There exist situations that prevent the completion of an action; for example, where a constraint is violated. An exception is a name that is attached to such a situation; for example, the name CONSTRAINT_ERROR is attached to the violation of a constraint. *Raising* an exception means telling the invoker of an action that the corresponding error situation has occurred; and *handling* an exception means executing some actions in response to this occurrence.

The definition of the exception handling facility will provide answers to the following questions:

- How are exceptions declared?

- What are exception handlers and in which part of a program can they appear?

- How are exceptions raised?

- Which handler gets executed when an exception is raised?

- How can the same exception be raised again?

We first examine these different questions in the case of sequential programs; then the case of parallel tasks is discussed in section 14.4.

14.2.1 Declaration of Exceptions

An exception declaration associates a name with a particular error situation. The form of an exception declaration is shown by the following example:

```
SINGULAR : exception;
```

Conceptually, we may view an exception declaration as declaring a constant of some type called "exception", whose values may only be mentioned in exception handlers and in raise statements. Thus the above declaration has the meaning that SINGULAR is one of the possible exceptions. Like any other declaration, an exception declaration has a scope, which is the region of text in which the corresponding name can be written in order to refer to the exception. However, as this analogy suggests, the error situation associated with an exception will exist beyond this region.

Declarations of the predefined exceptions, namely CONSTRAINT_ERROR, NUMERIC_ERROR, PROGRAM_ERROR, STORAGE_ERROR, and TASKING_ERROR, are provided in the package STANDARD that defines the predefined environment.

14.2.2 Exception Handlers

Exception handlers are the sections of the program to which control is passed when exceptions occur. Each exception handler has the form of a sequence of statements prefixed by the reserved word **when** followed by the names of the exceptions that are serviced by the handler considered (or the reserved word **others**, as described below).

Exception handlers may only appear at the end of a block statement or at the end of the body of a subprogram, package, or task unit; after the reserved word **exception**. In each of these cases, the construct includes the following part, called a *frame*:

```
begin
    sequence_of_statements
exception
    exception_handler
    {exception_handler}
end
```

The exception handlers given after the reserved word **exception** in a frame apply to the sequence of statements given after the reserved word **begin** in the same frame. As an example the following block contains a single handler that services the exception SINGULAR:

```
begin
  -- sequence of statements
exception
  when SINGULAR =>
    PUT("Matrix is singular");
end;
```

A handler that starts with **when others** services all exceptions that have no explicit handler in the same frame. Note finally, that where we want to localize the effect of handlers to some specific statements, we may always do so by enclosing these statements and handlers within a block statement.

14.2.3 The Raise Statement

There are two possible reasons for an exception to be raised in a given program unit. It may either be explicitly raised by a raise statement or, as we will explain later, it may be *propagated* by subprograms (including operators), package bodies and blocks executed by the program unit considered. (Violation of a constraint is treated as propagation.)

The normal form of raise statement includes the reserved word **raise** and the name of the exception that is raised:

```
raise SINGULAR;
raise IO_EXCEPTIONS.DEVICE_ERROR;
```

The name of the exception must of course be visible at the point of the raise statement. It may have the form of a selected component, as in the above case of the exception DEVICE_ERROR declared in the package IO_EXCEPTIONS.

14.2.4 Association of Handlers with Exceptions

We next examine the question of determining which handler gets executed when a given exception is raised. The case of an exception raised within a sequence of statements is treated here; the case of an exception raised during the elaboration of declarations will be considered later (see 14.5.1).

Note that if a frame contains a raise statement for a given exception, it does not necessarily contain a handler for that exception. For example, in the procedure P given below, both the procedures P and R provide a handler for SINGULAR and have no explicit raise statement for that exception. On the other hand, the procedure Q contains an explicit raise statement for SINGULAR but provides no handler for that exception.

```
procedure P is
   ...
   SINGULAR : exception;
   ...
   procedure Q is
   begin
      ...
      if DETERMINANT = 0 then
         raise SINGULAR;
      end if;
      ...
   end Q;

   procedure R is
   begin
      ...
      Q;
      ...
   exception
      when SINGULAR => ...
               -- inner handler for SINGULAR
   end R;

begin     -- P
   ...
   R;
   ...
   Q;
exception
   when SINGULAR => ...
            -- outer handler for SINGULAR
end P;
```

When an exception is raised within the sequence of statements of a frame, the execution of this sequence of statements is always abandoned. What happens next depends on the presence or absence of appropriate exception handlers:

(a) The frame includes a handler for the exception:

In this case the execution of the sequence of statements of this handler completes the execution of the frame.

(b) The frame does not have a handler for the exception:

In this case the subsequent actions depend on the nature of the frame. For a subprogram body, the same exception is raised – implicitly – at the point of call of the subprogram; for a block statement, the same exception is raised within the frame containing the block statement itself, after this statement. In either case, we say that the exception is *propagated*.

In the above example, if the exception SINGULAR is raised during the execution of Q that is called from R:

- The execution of Q will be abandoned, since no handler is provided for SINGULAR within Q.

- This exception is then *propagated* to the caller: it is raised within R at the point of call of Q.

- Further execution of the statements of R is then abandoned – the statements following the call of Q are not executed.

- But in this case, there is a handler for SINGULAR, and it is executed. This terminates the execution of R and the exception is not further propagated. For P, this call of R therefore appears as a normal call.

Note that the outer handler for SINGULAR, that of P, would be executed if the exception were raised by the execution of Q that is called directly from within P.

With this definition of exception handling, the effect of a subprogram, which is normally completed by the sequence of statements of its body, may alternatively, when an exception occurs, be completed by a corresponding handler, if present.

The sequence of statements of a package body acts as a procedure that is implicitly called by the package for its initialization. This also applies for exceptions. A handler in a package body acts like a handler in a procedure. In the absence of a handler, an exception is propagated to the program unit that contains the package declaration. The case of task bodies is discussed in section 14.4.

After the explanation of the concept of exception propagation, it should now be clear that there is no conceptual difference between the predefined exceptions and exceptions that are declared by the user. Predefined exceptions are exceptions that can be propagated by the basic operations of the language such as indexing, accessing a value, and the arithmetic operations. As an example NUMERIC_ERROR is an exception that may be propagated by the (hardware supplied) operation of division.

14.2.5 Raising the Same Exception Again

Within a handler, the exception that caused transfer to the handler may be raised again by a normal raise statement (mentioning its name) or by an abbreviated raise statement of the form

raise;

In either case, the effect of raising the same (or another) exception within a handler is to abandon the execution of the frame and to propagate the corresponding exception (except for tasks as explained in section 14.4).

The abbreviated form for raising the same exception again is especially useful in the case of a handler for **others**. Thus, such a handler can be used to perform some general cleanup actions, such as undoing possible side-effects, before raising the same exception again. This is made possible by the fact that the exception is left anonymous both in the handler prefix and in the reraise statement.

14.2.6 Suppressing Checks

It is possible to inform the compiler that certain run-time checks need not be provided within a given frame. This is achieved by a pragma. For example, the pragma

pragma SUPPRESS(RANGE_CHECK, ON => INDEX);

allows the compiler to omit range checks for assignments to variables of subtype INDEX. Note that this pragma is not imperative, and its inclusion does not guarantee that the exception CONSTRAINT_ERROR will not be raised: it may be raised explicitly, or be propagated from a subprogram in which checks are not suppressed. Finally, the exception may be raised simply because the compiler did not inhibit the check: this is likely to be the case if hardware checks are available.

14.2.7 Order of Exceptions

A compiler may choose to evaluate the constituent terms of an expression in any order that is consistent with the precedence properties of the operators, and with the parentheses. As a consequence, the order in which exceptions might be raised in the course of the evaluation of an expression is not guaranteed by the language. The semantics of the language only defines the value of expressions whose evaluation does not raise any exception.

14.3 EXAMPLES

Several examples that show typical uses of exception handling are discussed in this section.

14.3.1 Matrix Inversion

The first example is adapted from [BFH 76]. Each iteration of a loop is supposed to read a matrix, invert it, and print the result. If the matrix is singular, a message is to be printed and the program is to proceed with the next matrix.

```
procedure MAIN is
  procedure TREAT_MATRICES(N : INTEGER) is
    SINGULAR : exception;
    --declaration of procedures READ and PRINT used below
    ...
    procedure INVERT(M : in out MATRIX) is
    begin
      -- compute inverse of determinant
      -- note : this may implicitly raise NUMERIC_ERROR
      -- complete inversion of the matrix.
    exception
      when NUMERIC_ERROR => raise SINGULAR;
    end INVERT;

    procedure TREAT_ONE is
      M : MATRIX;
    begin
      READ(M);
      INVERT(M);
      PRINT(M);
    exception
      when SINGULAR => PRINT("Matrix is singular");
    end TREAT_ONE;
```

```
begin -- TREAT_MATRICES
   for COUNT in 1 .. N loop
      PRINT("ITERATION"); PRINT(COUNT);
      TREAT_ONE;
   end loop;
end TREAT_MATRICES;

begin
   TREAT_MATRICES(20);
end MAIN;
```

As this example illustrates, the possible occurrence of NUMERIC_ERROR within INVERT is envisaged and consequently an appropriate handler has been provided. On the other hand, an occurrence of this exception within READ or PRINT would cause termination of MAIN, since no handler has been provided within MAIN.

In order to illustrate the dynamic behavior of this program, let us consider the stack situation (stacking downward) during a call to INVERT:

(1) MAIN   *calling TREAT_MATRICES*

   TREAT_MATRICES   *calling TREAT_ONE*

   TREAT_ONE   *calling INVERT*

   INVERT   *executing normal statements of INVERT*

If NUMERIC_ERROR occurs during the inversions, the corresponding handler will be executed:

(2) MAIN   *calling TREAT_MATRICES*

   TREAT_MATRICES   *calling TREAT_ONE*

   TREAT_ONE   *calling INVERT*

   INVERT   *executing the handler for NUMERIC_ERROR*

Note that during its execution, the handler has access to the local variables and parameters of INVERT. Here the only effect of this handler is to raise the exception SINGULAR. As a consequence, the activation of INVERT is deleted (any incompleted result in M is abandoned) and the exception SINGULAR is propagated within TREAT_ONE at the point of call of INVERT. The handler of TREAT_ONE for SINGULAR is then executed:

(3) MAIN   *calling TREAT_MATRICES*

     TREAT_MATRICES   *calling TREAT_ONE*

     TREAT_ONE   *executing the handler for SINGULAR*

In this case the execution of the handler terminates the execution of TREAT_ONE without propagating an exception in TREAT_MATRICES. This leads to the following stack configuration where another iteration of the loop statement can now be performed:

(4) MAIN   *calling TREAT_MATRICES*

     TREAT_MATRICES   *executing the loop statement*

The above example is characteristic of a family of problems in which a sequence of items are subjected to a given treatment. Should this treatment fail for one item of the sequence, it would be unreasonable to abort the entire sequence. Rather, the exception handling facility provides the ability to do a partial termination – that of the current item.

14.3.2 Division

Consider the following definition of the function DIVISION:

```
function DIVISION(A, B : REAL) return REAL is
--the type REAL is
--properly declared real type
begin
   return A/B;
exception
   when NUMERIC_ERROR => return REAL'LAST;
end;
```

Should NUMERIC_ERROR occur during the computation of A/B, the execution of the handler will complete the execution of the function DIVISION. Any statement that is valid within the sequence of statements of DIVISION is also valid in the handler. In particular the handler may provide the return statement

```
return REAL'LAST;
```

on behalf of the function.

This example illustrates the nature of handlers. They must be viewed as substitutes, ready to take charge of the operations in case of error.

14.3.3 A File Example

This example shows a case where exception handling is used to treat an event that is certain to happen: reaching the end of a file. Naturally this example could be formulated with an explicit check for each iteration. Assuming the file to be quite large, however, the body of the procedure TRANSFER may be efficiently represented as an (apparently) infinite loop, and the final actions of the procedure performed by the exception handler for END_ERROR.

```
with TEXT_IO;
use TEXT_IO;
procedure TRANSFER is
   INPUT  : FILE_TYPE;
   OUTPUT : FILE_TYPE;
   C      : CHARACTER;

begin
   OPEN(INPUT,  MODE => IN_FILE,  NAME => "SOURCE");
   OPEN(OUTPUT, MODE => OUT_FILE, NAME => "DESTINATION");
   loop
      GET(INPUT, C);
      PUT(OUTPUT, C);
   end loop;
exception
   when END_ERROR =>
      CLOSE(INPUT);
      CLOSE(OUTPUT);
end;
```

The procedure TRANSFER transfers the characters from the file SOURCE into the file DESTINATION. At each iteration GET is called, and eventually an END_ERROR exception will occur. Then the corresponding handler will be activated and its execution will complete the execution of TRANSFER.

This example shows that although many exceptions will represent error conditions, some of them may just be normal conditions for termination.

14.3.4 A Package Example

The example below reproduces a skeleton of the TABLE_MANAGER package that is described in the Reference Manual section 7.5.

```
package TABLE_MANAGER is
  type ITEM is ...
  ...
  procedure INSERT    (NEW_ITEM : in ITEM);
  procedure RETRIEVE(FIRST_ITEM : out ITEM);
  TABLE_FULL : exception;    -- raised by INSERT when table full
end;

package body TABLE_MANAGER is
  ...
  procedure INSERT(NEW_ITEM : in ITEM) is
  begin
    if FREE_LIST_EMPTY then
      raise TABLE_FULL;
    end if;
    -- remaining code for INSERT
  end;
  ...
end TABLE_MANAGER;
```

The interface of the table manager defines the operations INSERT and RETRIEVE, and the exception TABLE_FULL. Any procedure that uses the package may provide a local handler for this exception; for example:

```
    with TABLE_MANAGER;
    procedure APPLICATION is
      use TABLE_MANAGER;
      ...
      procedure SAFE_INSERT(ELEMENT : in ITEM) is
        NEXT : ITEM;
      begin
        INSERT(ELEMENT);
      exception
        when TABLE_FULL =>
          RETRIEVE(NEXT);
          -- perform usual treatment of NEXT
          INSERT(ELEMENT);
      end SAFE_INSERT;
    begin
        -- includes calls of SAFE_INSERT instead of INSERT
    end APPLICATION;
```

Within procedure APPLICATION, a procedure SAFE_INSERT with a local handler for TABLE_FULL is provided. Should this exception be raised by the body of INSERT, the local handler for TABLE_FULL gains control and calls RETRIEVE before reiterating the call of INSERT. Should an exception occur again in this second call, the execution of SAFE_INSERT will be abandoned and the exception will be propagated to the caller of SAFE_INSERT.

It is worth mentioning that the body of INSERT is assumed to be programmed in a *robust* manner: it does not modify any global variable if it cannot accomplish the insertion normally. It is this property that permits SAFE_INSERT to reiterate the call of INSERT when the first call fails.

14.3.5 Example of Last Wishes

The occurrence of an exception causes termination of the procedures in the dynamic chain of calls up to (and not including) the first procedure that handles the exception. Assume, for example, that A handles a given exception, that B, C and D do not, and that:

A calls B, B calls C, C calls D

Then if the exception is raised while executing D, the execution of D is abandoned; then that of C and of B, in that order. (The propagation occurs in the reverse of the order of calls.)

One may want to let these procedures express their *last wishes* before being abandoned – for instance, to perform some cleanup actions. This can be achieved by providing a handler for others in each of these procedures. Each such handler will then issue the statement

raise;

which raises the same exception to the attention of the calling procedure. (We are thus able to achieve an effect similar to that of the *unwind* clause of Mesa without the need for a special language construct.) We illustrate last wishes with the example of a procedure that performs operations on a file:

```
procedure OPERATE(NAME : STRING) is
   FILE : FILE_TYPE;
begin
   -- initial actions
   OPEN(FILE, INOUT_FILE, NAME);
   -- perform work on the file
   CLOSE(FILE);
   -- final actions
end;
```

Should an exception occur during operations on the file, the file would be left in an open state when the body of OPERATE is left. This is avoided by expressing the appropriate corrective action in a handler:

```
procedure SAFE_OPERATE(NAME : STRING) is
   FILE : FILE_TYPE;
begin
   -- initial actions
   OPEN(FILE, INOUT_FILE, NAME);
   begin
   -- perform work on the file
   exception
     when others =>
        CLOSE(FILE);
        raise;
   end;
   CLOSE(FILE);
   -- final actions
end;
```

Now if any exception occurs, either during the initial or the final actions, it will be propagated to the caller of SAFE_OPERATE, and the file will at that time be closed. If however the exception occurs within the block, while performing work on the file, the inner handler will first close the file before propagating the exception.

Similar techniques can be used in parallel processing examples: a given task should not be left waiting forever to receive the stop signal from a task whose execution was abandoned after it sent a start signal.

14.4 TASKS AND EXCEPTIONS

The exception handling facility has so far been presented in terms of sequential programs, and the concepts presented are therefore applicable within a task body. For exception propagation there is a difference with tasks: in contrast to what is done for subprograms, if an exception is not serviced by a handler within a task body, the exception is not further propagated – the task execution is merely completed.

Note that if the exception were propagated to the parent task, it would mean that child tasks could interfere asynchronously with their parent, and it would also mean that these interferences could occur simultaneously, with disastrous results.

We will now consider two other interactions between tasking and exception handling:

- Exceptions raised during the activation of a task

- Exceptions raised during communication between tasks

14.4.1 Exceptions During Task Activation

Consider a procedure that declares three local tasks, A, B, and C. The actions performed by the procedure are partially subcontracted to these local tasks.

```
procedure PERFORM is
   task A;
   task B;
   task C;
   ...
begin
   -- activation of A, B, C, in parallel
   -- (1)
   ...
exception
   when TASKING_ERROR =>
   ...      -- (2)
end;
```

The semantics of Ada specifies that the three local tasks are activated, in parallel, after begin but before the first statement of the procedure. This means that at (1) we can rely on the fact that all three tasks are activated.

Consider now what happens if the activation of one (or more) of these tasks is not started as a consequence of the raising of an exception. It would not make much sense to execute the statements of the procedure, once it is known that one of the basic preconditions for its proper operation is not satisfied. For this reason, the execution of statements of the procedure is not started, and the predefined exception TASKING_ERROR is propagated at (1) to be handled by the exception handler at (2).

(By analogy, if A, B, and C were array declarations, the statements of the procedure would not be executed if the elaboration of any of these declarations raised an exception. The analogy stops there however, since in the case of task activation the exception is raised in the statements, and can be handled locally, whereas in the case of arrays the exception is raised in the declarative part and propagated to the caller to be dealt with. Activation of a task behaves like an implicit initialization statement – placed after **begin**.)

Note that the exception that is propagated at (1) does not depend on what caused the abandonment of task activation. What matters for the procedure is to know whether or not activations have succeeded. Should one or more of them have failed, it does not matter much whether this is by constraint violation, or by a numeric error: in any case some other treatment is needed. This therefore is the justification for the propagation of the less specific exception TASKING_ERROR. By the same reasoning, it does not matter much whether one, or more than one, task failed to be activated. Hence a single exception is raised in either case.

14.4.2 Exceptions Raised During Communication Between Tasks

When two tasks are attempting to communicate with each other, or are engaged in communication, an abnormal situation arising in one of them may have an effect on the other.

As a basis for discussing the various cases that may arise, consider a task SERVER that provides the entry UPDATE:

```
task SERVER is
   entry UPDATE(THIS : in out ITEM);
end;
```

```
    task body SERVER is
      ...
    begin
      ...
      accept UPDATE(THIS : in out ITEM) do
        -- statements for servicing the request
      end UPDATE;
      ...
    end SERVER;
```

and another task called USER, having no entry at all:

```
    task USER;
    task body USER is
      THING : ITEM;
    begin
      ...
      SERVER.UPDATE(THIS => THING);
      ...
    end USER;
```

The first interaction to consider is what happens if the USER calls an entry of the SERVER

```
    SERVER.UPDATE(THIS => THING);
```

at a time when this called task has already completed its execution. Clearly the called task will never accept the entry call, and hence there is no point in letting USER (the caller) wait forever. Consequently the exception TASKING_ERROR is propagated to the caller at the point of call: the caller is thereby informed that the call cannot be accepted. For similar reasons, this exception is also raised if the called task (SERVER) has not already completed its execution, but proceeds to do so without encountering an accept statement for the entry call.

14.4.3 Abnormal Situations in an Accept Statement

The other interactions to consider correspond to error situations that may arise while two tasks are engaged in a rendezvous. We distinguish three possible error situations:

(1) An exception is raised by the execution of the accept statement

(2) The called task (SERVER) is disrupted while executing the accept statement

(3) The caller (USER) is disrupted while the accept statement is being executed

The first situation corresponds to the usual error situations. The second and third cases are only possible if another task has issued an abort statement. For example:

```
abort SERVER;    -- in the second case
abort USER;      -- in the third case
```

Such a statement, to be used only in extreme circumstances, will eventually cause completion of the aborted task; this will in any case occur no later than when the aborted task reaches a synchronization point: a point where it causes the activation of another task; an entry call; the start or the end of an accept statement; a select statement; a delay statement; an exception handler; or an abort statement.

We next analyze the consequences of each of these possible abnormal situations, both with respect to the task issuing the entry call (USER) and with respect to the task containing the accept statement (SERVER).

An exception is raised within an accept statement

Consider a situation in which an exception, say *error*, is raised within the accept statement of SERVER:

```
task body USER is            task body SERVER is
...
SERVER.UPDATE(                   ...
      THIS => THING);
...
                             accept UPDATE(THIS : in out ITEM) do
...
                                   error
...
                             end;
end USER;                        ...
                             end SERVER;
```

From the point of view of the caller, the accept statement is analogous to a procedure body that is executed when the corresponding entry is called. Hence if an exception is raised (and not handled within the accept statement itself) it should be propagated at the point of call of SERVER.UPDATE.

However, from the point of view of the task that contains the accept statement, this statement is a normal statement of its body. Hence if an exception is raised within SERVER, it should be handled by a handler provided within that same task (outside the accept statement).

To summarize, an exception raised within an accept statement (and not handled there) is propagated both in the calling and in the called tasks. Both tasks may provide handlers for the exception.

The called task is disrupted

A different treatment must be employed if the called task (SERVER) is aborted by a third task. In this case the caller (USER) must be informed that the entry call will never be completed: For this reason, the exception TASKING_ERROR is propagated at the point of the entry call.

The calling task is disrupted

In this case, the called task (SERVER) completes the rendezvous normally: the called task is unaffected.

There are good reasons for this dissymmetry of treatment. First, we can expect servers to be programmed in a more robust manner than user tasks. Moreover it is important to ensure continuity of service, and this would not be the case if it were possible for a single unsound user to affect the service to all user tasks. In terms of the implementation, this means that the storage of an aborted task cannot be reclaimed before the end of the rendezvous: this is important if the entry has **in out** or **out** parameters that are implemented by copy, or parameters of any mode that are implemented by reference.

14.4.4 Example of Exceptions in a Rendezvous

The following program fragment shows a task USER that starts a file transfer that is performed asynchronously by a task SPOOLER. The procedure OPEN is used by SPOOLER to open the two files. If either of the files is invalid, an exception is raised, possibly after closing the other file.

```
task SPOOLER is
   entry START_TRANSFER(SOURCE, DESTINATION : in STRING);
end;

task body SPOOLER is
   INPUT  : FILE_TYPE;
   OUTPUT : FILE_TYPE;
   C      : CHARACTER;
```

```
    procedure OPEN(SOURCE, DESTINATION : in STRING) is
    begin
      OPEN(INPUT, MODE => IN_FILE, NAME => SOURCE);
      begin
        OPEN(OUTPUT, MODE => OUT_FILE, NAME => DESTINATION);
      exception
        when NAME_ERROR =>        -- also propagated to calling task
        CLOSE(INPUT); raise;
    . end;
    exception
    when NAME_ERROR => raise;
    end;

begin
  loop
    begin
      accept START_TRANSFER(SOURCE, DESTINATION : in STRING) do
        OPEN(SOURCE, DESTINATION);
      end;

      loop
        GET (INPUT, C);
        PUT (OUTPUT, C);
      end loop;
    exception
      when END_ERROR =>        -- handled locally and not propagated
        CLOSE(INPUT);
        CLOSE(OUTPUT);
      when NAME_ERROR => null;   -- restart main loop
      end;                -- the calling task has also received this
  end loop;
end SPOOLER;
```

Two forms of input-output exceptions may be raised within the body of the task
SPOOLER. The exception END_ERROR is handled locally and not propagated. The exception NAME_ERROR may be raised within the accept statement for the entry
START_TRANSFER. The handler provided within SPOOLER simply prepares it for another
iteration. In addition, the occurrence of this second exception also has an effect on the
calling task USER. The exception is propagated in that task where it can be serviced by
a local handler:

```
task body USER is
  OLD_FILE : constant STRING := ">UDD>PROJECT>JAN";
  NEW_FILE : constant STRING := ">UDD>PROJECT>FEB";
begin
  ...
  begin
    SPOOLER.START_TRANSFER(SOURCE      => OLD_FILE,
                           DESTINATION => NEW_FILE);
  exception
    when NAME_ERROR =>
      -- do something on OLD_FILE and NEW_FILE
  end;
  ...
end;
```

14.5 TECHNICAL ISSUES

The discussion of exception handling in [Go 75] classifies exceptions into three categories:

(a) *Escape* exceptions which require termination of the operation that raised the exception

(b) *Notify* exceptions, which forbid termination of the operation that raised the exception and require its resumption after completion of the actions of the handler

(c) *Signal* exceptions, which leave the choice between termination and resumption to the handler

Exceptions in Ada are of the *escape* category. They serve only for error situations and as terminating conditions, which simplifies the language: *notify* and *signal* exceptions are not provided, since these forms of exception violate program modularity and make optimization difficult, if not impossible.

The technical problems of the interactions between exceptions and parallelism have been mentioned in the previous section. The key idea was to provide a simple rule for cases where simultaneous exceptions occur in a given task. For the TASKING_ERROR exception, multiplicity can only occur in the case of nested accept statements, and then the outer exception prevails.

The remainder of this discussion will concentrate on the following issues:

• Exceptions raised during the elaboration of declarations

• Propagation of exceptions beyond their scope

• Suppression of exceptions

- Implementation of exception handling

- The case against asynchronous exceptions

- Proving programs with exceptions

14.5.1 Exceptions Raised During the Elaboration of Declarations

The elaboration of declarations may involve the evaluation of some expressions, and in consequence, exceptions may be raised during this elaboration. Consider for example the procedure

```
procedure A(N : INTEGER) is
  C : constant INTEGER := N * N;
  D : INTEGER := C;
  T : array (1 .. C) of INTEGER;
begin
  -- statements of A
exception
  -- handlers of A
end;
```

If an exception occurs during the elaboration of the constant C, the procedure will be in a state where D is not initialized, and the space for the array T is not yet allocated. Consequently, a handler may not be able to do much; any reference to D or T will be erroneous and may cause a further exception. For these reasons an exception raised by the elaboration of a declaration is never handled locally; it is propagated to the place where the elaboration of the declarations was initiated: for example, this place may be just after the call of a subprogram in whose body the declarations are written, or it may be just after a block in whose declarative part the declarations appear.

14.5.2 Propagation of an Exception Beyond its Scope

Since an exception can be propagated, it can be propagated beyond its scope. It is even possible for an exception to be propagated outside its scope and then back again within its scope. Thus, in the following example, if B calls OUTSIDE and OUTSIDE calls A, the exception ERROR raised within A will be propagated to OUTSIDE and again to B:

```
-- Assume that all that follows in the same
-- declarative region of some enclosing procedure
package D is
  procedure A;
  procedure B;
end;

procedure OUTSIDE is
begin
  ...
  D.A;
  ...
end;

package body D is
  ERROR : exception;
  procedure A is
  begin
    ... raise ERROR; ...
  end;

  procedure B is
  begin
    ...
    OUTSIDE;
    ...
  exception
    when ERROR =>
      -- ERROR may be propagated by OUTSIDE calling A
  end;
end D;
```

An exception propagated beyond its scope can only be handled there by a handler for others. It can be further propagated or raised again by the abbreviated form of the raise statement (**raise;**).

This rule provides a simple and consistent interpretation of the above example and it avoids the complexity and run-time costs that would be incurred if exceptions propagated beyond their scope were converted into a unique undefined exception. This design also considered, and rejected, the possibility of associating the names of the possibly propagated exceptions with each procedure declaration. The main reason for rejecting this possibility is the fact that this would require extra run-time code for filtering the propagation of exceptions. For example, if a procedure were declared as

```
procedure P(X : INTEGER) PROPAGATES A, B, C; -- not in Ada
```

its body would have to be compiled as the equivalent of the following procedure:

```
procedure P(X : INTEGER) is
  ...
begin
  ...
exception
  when A|B|C => raise;
  when others => raise anonymous_exception;
end P;
```

We considered the resulting code expansion to be prohibitive, especially in the case of small functions and procedures.

With the solution adopted in Ada, the user can always put similar information in comment form. The choice **others** covers all possible anonymous exceptions, not just one.

The philosophy behind the Ada model is that an exception is *not* an error situation; it is only a name that is declared for an error situation. Like any other declaration, an exception declaration has a scope. The error situation, on the other hand has no such limits, and can always be referred to as part of the **others** exception choice.

The internal codes associated with exceptions must all be distinct – as are the codes of the different literals of an enumeration type. In general, this assignment of codes to exceptions must be performed at linkage editing time.

14.5.3 Suppression of Checks

A given program unit, and in particular a procedure, may be *robust*, in that it will perform some computation, and produce some result, for any value of its input parameters. On the other hand, its validity may only be guaranteed for certain values of these parameters. The exception mechanism is a useful tool to achieve robustness, but this may be gained at some cost in efficiency, since detection of some error situations may be expensive unless aided by special hardware.

In some cases where robustness can be attained by means other than run-time checks, the programmer may not wish to incur the cost of checking for certain error situations. The pragma

```
pragma SUPPRESS(check_name);
```

indicates that the check named in the pragma need not be performed. (Should a violation of the corresponding condition occur, behavior of the program would be unpredictable.)

In the presence of such pragmas, the compiler may suppress the named checks, and will do so if this results in an optimization.

However, in the case of exceptions whose detection is aided by special hardware, inhibiting the corresponding hardware mechanisms may be costlier than actually performing the checks. Hence the pragma is not imperative – it does not mean that the checks are not done.

An alternative view of the SUPPRESS pragma would regard it as a directive indicating imperatively that no check is to be performed to detect the exception. This approach would amount to a decision to continue execution of the program *in spite of* any error situation. It would give an appearance of robustness which might be exploited in cases where the programmer knows that the error situation will have some effects that can be detected at a later time, but it is contrary to the general philosophy of the language.

In addition, the need to provide a semantics that reconciles software-and hardware-detected exceptions would have a negative effect on the efficiency of programs. If the pragma were imperative, then on a machine with hardware-detected exceptions it would be necessary to inhibit the hardware checks for a scope in which a corresponding pragma SUPPRESS is given. Thereafter, it would be necessary to enable the hardware detection again, prior to each call to a unit outside that scope, and again to inhibit the detection following a subsequent return from the call.

14.5.4 Implementation of Exception Handling

One important design consideration for the exception handling facility is that exceptions should add to execution time only if they are raised.

Several techniques may be used to reach that goal, and they may differ from one implementation to another. The essential idea is that the run-time processing costs should be concentrated on the treatment of the raise statement. Consequently, processing of a raise statement may be relatively slow. In contrast, the costs associated with exception declarations and exception handlers are only in terms of space and in terms of compilation time – they have no influence on the execution time.

As a feasibility proof, we outline a possible implementation technique in which no run-time costs whatsoever are incurred for exceptions unless they are raised. This technique has been used for some debugging systems and it bears some resemblance to the technique used in Mesa [GMS 77]. The basic principles are as follows:

(a) When an exception occurs, the specific run-time system that treats exceptions must be able to locate the addresses of the currently active procedure calls. This condition is satisfied if (as is usually the case) return addresses are stored in procedure activations.

(b) Knowing the code address of a procedure, it must be possible to locate the code address of the first handler. Similarly, given a handler, it must be possible to find the next handler. This condition can be satisfied by chaining the handlers and by storing the address of the first handler just before the code of the procedure.

(c) Each handler must start with the indication of the exception code (or codes) that it services. Some convention must be used for the handler for others, which must appear last.

(d) When effecting the association of an exception with a handler, the run-time system locates the procedure address and from there the chain of handlers. It may then inspect the exception codes to find the appropriate handler, if any.

We reiterate that this solution should only be considered as an existence proof that exceptions may be implemented at no cost unless raised. Other techniques may be more suitable, depending on the machine architecture.

14.5.5 The Case Against Asynchronous Exceptions

The normal means of communicating with a task is via entry calls. Hence most situations in which the termination of a task must be decided by another task should be programmed by calling a special entry, say STOP, of the task to be terminated (or by using a terminate alternative). The clear advantage of such a solution is the possibility thus offered of including accept statements for the STOP entry at those places where the termination can be done in an orderly fashion.

The ability for one task to raise an exception in another task must however be viewed as a possibility that has – potentially – extremely severe consequences. In no way should such externally raised exceptions be considered as being normal terminating conditions. Interfering asynchronously with the execution of a task may catch it in a state where it is not prepared to respond to such intervention. There is then always a risk of leaving the task in a state of confusion, and also of contaminating other tasks that were communicating with it.

14.5.6 Proving Programs with Exceptions

The problems of exception handling facilities such as the PL/I *on conditions*, which permit resumption after the exception, are well-known. For instance, assuming integer working, consider the consecutive statements:

```
X := P + Q;
Y := X - Q;
ASSERT (Y = P);
```

Unless overflow occurs in the evaluation of P + Q, the final assertion should be satisfied. This however would not be true if a handler for overflow were able to provide a different value for X and return to the same statement list.

This simple example shows the near impossibility of proving programs with unrestricted *signal* and *notify* exceptions. For the same reasons, such programs are extremely difficult to optimize.

In contrast, for the proposal chosen in Ada, simple proof rules may be given, as has been shown by Bron [BFH 76] and Fokkinga [Fo 77]. Additional examples may be found in the reference [DH 76]. The main idea is a consequence of the definition of the role of a handler.

As mentioned above, when an exception occurs in a procedure, the execution of the handler completes the execution of the procedure considered. Consequently the effect of a procedure is achieved either:

(a) by its body if no exception occurs

or, if the exception E occurs:

(b) by the part of its body up to the point where the exception E occurs, and then by the handler for E.

Two simple cases have been shown in the programming examples:

(1) In the SAFE_INSERT example of section 14.3.4 we have shown a case where these two rules reduce to a simpler form. The effect of SAFE_INSERT is achieved either:

   (a)   by its body if no exception occurs, or

   (b)   by the handler for TABLE_FULL if TABLE_FULL occurs.

(2) In the file example of section 14.3.3, where the exception END_ERROR is used as a terminating condition, the effect of the procedure TRANSFER is achieved by the succession of the effects of

   (a)   its body

   (b)   the body of the handler for END_ERROR.

This shows that, with adequate programming conventions, the effect of a procedure that contains an exception handler can be characterized in a simple way. This simplifies correctness proofs.

15. Representation Clauses and Machine Dependences

There is an inherent dilemma in the design of a high-order language with a systems programming capability. On the one hand we are trying to achieve reliability by raising the level of the language. For example, we provide data types and encourage the taking of an abstract view of objects, in which they are known only by the set of operations applicable to them: controlling the applicable operations enables incorrect use to be detected.

On the other hand, systems applications require the ability to stay rather close to the machine, and not only for reasons of efficiency. For example, defining a hardware descriptor must be done in terms of the physical properties, the bit positions, and so on. A mapping different from that prescribed by the hardware would not merely be inefficient – it would be incorrect and would not work at all. To produce a correct program in such cases we are forced to abandon the abstract view and to work in terms of the physical representation. This contradiction cannot be avoided. The language must deal with objects at two different levels, the logical and the representation level [Wo 72].

Clearly, dealing with physical representation is inherently dangerous. However, some control can still be achieved if the language enforces a clear separation of the logical properties from their physical representation.

This *separation principle* is discussed below, along with the problem of changing representation and an analysis of the issues raised by the different forms of representation clause available in the language. This chapter also covers the ways to specify the parameters of a given configuration, and conversely how to ascertain them by environment enquiries. Finally we present the means available for interfacing with other languages.

15.1 THE SEPARATION PRINCIPLE

The treatment of representation in Ada is done according to the separation principle discussed below.

Data type definitions are performed in two steps:

(1) The logical properties of the data are defined. They describe all the properties that programmers need to know. All algorithms are formulated in terms of these logical properties and are not based on knowledge of the representation.

(2) The representation (implementation) properties of data are either explicitly specified by the programmer or, in the usual case, chosen by default by the compiler.

There are many advantages in this separation. The most fundamental is the conceptual simplicity of formulating an algorithm in terms of abstract properties. The ability to abstract from a particular representation leads to clearer and better structured programs.

Furthermore, to establish the correctness of a program that uses a given formulation of data and a given representation, we have two disjoint proofs. First we show that the program is correct given the formulation of the data types and algorithms. Then we show that the chosen representation is a correct implementation of the data. The separation also ensures that users do not make implicit assumptions about the representation of data.

If at a later stage a different representation is selected, for example to reduce storage space, the formulation of the algorithms need not be modified. Conversely, if the algorithms of a program are modified, the representation need not be affected.

Another advantage is textual simplicity. In some cases, the representation of a data type is dictated by external considerations such as the form of a hardware interface: the description of the representation may then be correspondingly complex. However, by keeping the logical description textually distinct from that of the representation we can retain the simplicity of the logical description.

The above separation principle is reflected in Ada by a clear textual separation between the declaration of the logical properties of data and the specification of the properties of their representation. Properties of the representation are specified by representation clauses. These clauses are optional, and distinct from the declaration of the logical properties. The parts of a program that are hardware-specific are thus easy to identify.

15.2 TYPES AND DATA REPRESENTATION

In a typed language, it is important to associate representation clauses with types rather than with individual objects. The basic reasons are simplicity and uniformity. To associate representation clauses with individual objects could mean that these clauses have to be duplicated in many separate declarations and it might therefore be difficult to maintain consistency, especially after repeated modification.

Alternatively, it could mean that a name is associated with each possible representation; and that each object declaration mentions both a type name and a representation name. However such a solution would result in less readable programs. For these reasons, a simpler solution is used in Ada: a representation is associated with a type. Associating representation with type localizes this specification in one place.

The specification is thereby associated with all objects of the given type (constants, variables, formal parameters, and so on).

A further advantage of this approach is that, while every type has some representation, the user need not always be concerned with it. Explicit (user-defined) representation clauses are optional: in most cases we are quite willing to let the compiler select an efficient representation for types. This is what we normally expect from compilers although no particular default is guaranteed, so that a small change of a declaration may sometimes be reflected by a more significant change of representation. In certain cases, however, we want to regain control: not because we do not trust the compiler but because we know some information that is essential for the selection of a representation. For example we might know that a given logical type is associated with an external hardware interface, in which case we would write a representation clause to adopt the representation that is dictated by the hardware and thus override any default choice made by the compiler.

Representation clauses may be more or less restrictive; in some cases they fully specify the mapping, while in other cases they merely specify some aspects of a representation.

15.3 MULTIPLE REPRESENTATIONS AND CHANGE OF REPRESENTATION

When a program has to deal with objects that exist on an external medium, one is faced with the problem of multiple representations. For example, records may be stored in a packed form on a file; but a program may need faster access to the record components when the information is processed, and hence may require an unpacked form. This is a classic situation in which different representations for the same objects are wanted.

Although the details of the alternate representations are not part of the logical properties, we will show with the following example that the knowledge of the existence of alternate representations is, itself, a logical property.

15.3.1 A Canonical Example of Changes of Representation

Consider the problem of converting data from some external medium into a form ready to be output onto another external medium. Both data objects belong to the same enumeration type, but they have different representations, each of which is prescribed by the outside world. The following program fragment gives a hypothetical formulation (not following the Ada syntax) for the required procedure:

```
procedure CONVERT is
  -- declarations of the logical properties:

  type DAY is (MON, TUE, WED, THU, FRI, SAT, SUN);
  X, Y : DAY;

  -- representation clauses (not in the Ada syntax):

  representation FORM_A of DAY is
    (MON => 0, TUE => 1, WED => 2,
     THU => 3, FRI => 4, SAT => 5, SUN => 6);
  representation FORM_B of DAY is
    (MON => 1, TUE => 2, WED => 3,
     THU => 4, FRI => 5, SAT => 6, SUN => 7);
  for X use representation FORM_A;
  for Y use representation FORM_B;

  -- end of representation clauses (in hypothetical syntax)
begin
  ...
  Y := X;
  ...
end CONVERT;
```

In trying to establish the correctness of the above procedure, one finds that the information contained in the logical declarations of X and Y does not suffice. It can only be concluded that X and Y are of type DAY. To complete the correctness proof (that conversion is properly effected) it is necessary to consider representation clauses, and hence to violate the separation principle mentioned earlier. We are thus led to the conclusion that any attempt to hide the existence of multiple representations at the logical level ultimately leads to a violation of the separation principle.

15.3.2 One Type – One Representation Principle

It is natural and desirable to use type as a carrier for representation. The approach adopted in Ada is to have a unique representation of each type and to select the representation explicitly by representation clauses. This results in a significant simplification, since the user does not have to think in terms of multiple representations for a single type.

If we need two different representations, two different types are therefore required, although these two types should have identical logical properties: the solution to this problem is to use derived types. For example, a type B can be derived from a type A by declaring

type B **is new** A;

Since B derives its characteristics from A, both types have the same characteristics, for example the same components. However, they are distinct types and it is hence possible to specify different representations for A and for B. Change of representation can be achieved by explicit conversion between objects of types A and B since such conversions are defined for derived types. Derivation has the effect of creating a type with the same characteristics as another type, without rewriting its entire description (that would define a distinct type for which no conversions are possible).

Note:

The one type – one representation principle must be understood in terms of the knowledge that the user has from the existence (as opposed to the details) of a representation. It means that if a representation is explicitly specified for a type, then only one representation can be specified for this type. However, in cases where the representation is implicitly selected by the compiler, this does not preclude the use of different internal representations in different contexts – out of sight of the user.

15.3.3 Explicit Type Conversion and Change of Representation

The problem of change of representation is now straightforward: it can be expressed as an explicit type conversion between two derived types. As explained in Chapter 7, the type conversion appears syntactically as the call of a function with the name of the target type, for example:

```
Y := EXTERNAL_DAY(X);
```

in the conversion problem presented earlier. The full solution may be properly expressed in Ada as follows:

```
procedure CONVERT is
    -- declaration of the logical properties:

    type DAY is (MON, TUE, WED, THU, FRI, SAT, SUN);
    type EXTERNAL_DAY is new DAY; -- a derived type

    X : DAY := DAY'FIRST;
    Y : EXTERNAL_DAY;

    -- representation clauses for the two types:
```

```
    for DAY use
        (MON => 0, TUE => 1, WED => 2,
         THU => 3, FRI => 4, SAT => 5, SUN => 6);
    for EXTERNAL_DAY use
        (MON => 1, TUE => 2, WED => 3,
         THU => 4, FRI => 5, SAT => 6, SUN => 7);


    -- end of representation clauses
begin
    ...
    Y := EXTERNAL_DAY(X);
    ...
end CONVERT;
```

The correctness of this procedure can now be established without violation of the separation principle. First, we have to show that the program is correct given the definition of X and Y: Initially X contains a value of type DAY; the conversion EXTERNAL_DAY(X) is legal since the type EXTERNAL_DAY, is derived from the type DAY – it converts the value of X into a value of type EXTERNAL_DAY, which is finally assigned to Y. Secondly, it must be shown that the representations given for DAY and EXTERNAL_DAY are correct.

The same simple strategy would be used in the previously mentioned case of conversion of a record structure between a packed representation and an unpacked representation:

```
type OBJECT is
    record
        -- declaration of the components of objects
    end record;

type EXTERNAL_OBJECT is new OBJECT;
                            -- a distinct type derived from OBJECT

for EXTERNAL_OBJECT use
    record
        ...
        -- definition of the layout of record components
    end record;
X : OBJECT;
Y : EXTERNAL_OBJECT;
...
X := OBJECT(Y);            -- unpack
...
Y := EXTERNAL_OBJECT(X);   -- pack
```

15.3.4 Implementation of Representation Changes

Although they are limited to types that are conformable – having been declared to be logically equivalent – type conversions may be very costly in some cases. As an example consider a record type with variants:

```
type V(D : BOOLEAN := TRUE) is
   record
      case D is
         when TRUE  => I : INTEGER;
         when FALSE => R : REAL;
      end case;
   end record;

type W is new V;

for V use ...
for W use ...

X : V;
Y : W;
...
X := V(Y);
```

The implementation of the above assignment cannot be achieved as simply as for a normal record assignment. It must be done on a field by field basis, which is equivalent to the following program (apart from the restriction on assignment to the discriminant):

```
X.D := Y.D;          -- not legal Ada
case Y.D is
     when TRUE  => X.I := Y.I;
     when FALSE => X.R := Y.R;
end case;
```

Producing such code is well within the capability of present compilation techniques. Nevertheless it is complex and can be somewhat costly on some computers (note that there might be variants within variants). Expressing changes of representation as explicit conversions warns the user of the potentially high cost of these operations.

15.4 PRESENTATION OF THE DATA REPRESENTATION FACILITY

The language provides two possible degrees of control of representation. The first degree is provided by representation pragmas such as PACK. The compiler is merely provided with criteria for the selection of a representation: the pragma expresses the intent only, and the program remains portable. The second degree is provided by representation clauses, in which case the compiler is left no choice and *must* adopt the specified representation (if at all feasible).

15.4.1 Representation Pragmas

The pragma PACK is used to request a packed representation for objects of the type specified by its argument. The use of this pragma is for situations in which we try to minimize the storage space of a given composite type, even at the cost of complicating the access to components; but in which the exact mapping used by the compiler remains unimportant.

Consider the case of an array of a given component type. For each component the compiler must allocate a storage field with a certain number of bits. There may also be some gaps (that is, unused bit fields) between two consecutive components. The effect of the pragma PACK is to instruct the compiler to minimize such gaps. For example, to request a packed representation for boolean matrices, one would write:

```
type BIT_MAP is array (1 .. 100, 1 .. 100) of BOOLEAN;
...
pragma PACK(BIT_MAP);
```

On the other hand, if the component type is itself a composite type, it may also contain internal gaps: these gaps are unaffected by the packing specification given for the array type. Minimization of such gaps could be achieved by a prior packing specification given for the component type itself.

The language also provides the representation pragma OPTIMIZE, with the argument values SPACE and TIME, to inform the compiler about which of these two criteria is more important in a given part of the program.

15.4.2 Length Clauses

The simplest kind of representation clause is a length clause. Its form is as follows:

for *representation_attribute* **use** *expression*;

where the expression specifies a value for the given representation attribute. For example, it is possible to use a length clause to specify the size to be used for objects of a given type: for cases where a user wants to optimize access time to frequently used record components of this type, without having to specify the entire record layout.

```
type NIBBLE is range 0 .. 15;
for NIBBLE'SIZE use 4;
```

For a fixed point type, a length clause can be used to specify exactly the representation of the smallest representable value. For example:

```
type WEIGHT is delta 0.01 range 0 .. 250;
for WEIGHT'SMALL use WEIGHT'DELTA;
```

Without the length clause, the compiler would use a value of WEIGHT'SMALL that was a power of 2 – in fact 1/128 – and this has the advantage of simplifying multiplications by other fixed point types, since rescaling reduces to shift operations. Should weights actually be obtained from a sensor for which a value of 2#0000 0000 0000 0001# corresponds to exactly a centigram, then the above length clause instructs the compiler to use this representation – even if it causes multiplications to be less efficient.

For task types a length clause can be used to provide an upper bound for the storage needed by the execution of a corresponding task object; for example, if the task contains recursive procedure calls, dynamic arrays, or local access types. Note that such a clause does not dictate the actual allocation strategy used for tasks: it could be at the time of task activation or at the time of elaboration of the task declaration. The length clause only supplies information for this allocation.

```
for LINE_TO_CHAR'STORAGE_SIZE use 200;
```

For access types, a length clause provides the size of the storage space to be reserved for all dynamically allocated objects of the designated type (and of any types derived from it). The collection associated with an access type that has such a length specification is allocated all at once (upon elaboration of the representation clause) and is reclaimed all at once, as for an array declaration given at the place of the access type declaration. Hence it permits the use of access types with their notational and efficiency advantages (component selection is cheaper than array indexing for arrays of records) without necessarily incurring the potential costs of a more dynamic allocation strategy. (See Chapter 6 for further explanation.)

To define sufficient storage space it is necessary to know the storage size required for one element. For a type T, the attribute T'SIZE can be used for this purpose. For example the size of a collection large enough to contain *approximately* 400 dynamically allocated PLACEs can be expressed as follows:

```
type PLACE;
type LIST is access PLACE;

type PLACE is
  record
    SUCC, PRED : LIST;
    VALUE      : INTEGER;
  end record;

for LIST'STORAGE_SIZE use
  (400 * PLACE'SIZE) / SYSTEM.STORAGE_UNIT;
```

The number of dynamically allocated records is only known as an approximation, since the storage allocator may need some extra space, and also because records with variant parts may not all be of the same size.

A length clause can also be used to achieve a biased representation for an integer type. For example, if we have a type ranging from 10_000 to 10_127, any value of this type can be represented in only 8 bits (including the sign bit). Specifying a length of 8 bits for this type will result in the compiler using a biased representation. For example:

```
type SKEWED is new INTEGER range 10_000 .. 10_127;
for SKEWED'SIZE use 8;
```

15.4.3 Record Representation Clauses

A record representations clause allows one to specify the layout of the components of a record type. This is done by giving the order of the record components, their positions, and their sizes in machine-dependent terms. All the expressions included in such a representation clause must be static expressions: their values must be known at compilation time. A global alignment clause can also be specified.

Storage Units:

The storage unit is a configuration-dependent quantity that represents the machine's quantum of storage. Its value is given by the named number SYSTEM.STORAGE_UNIT; it is the unit of addressing implicitly used to denote the position of a component.

Bit Ranges:

A bit range is used to specify the position of a component inside a storage unit. The two expressions in the range represent the positions of the first and last bits respectively. This implies that the bit ordering inside a storage unit must be known to the user; such an ordering is implementation-defined. The first bit of a storage unit is always numbered 0. For example, the component clause:

```
SYSTEM_MASK at 0 range 0 .. 7;
```

specifies that the component SYSTEM_MASK needs 8 bits of storage, starting from the beginning of the storage unit. The storage size specified for a component must of course be large enough for the component. The compiler must check that the specified size is compatible with the minimum needed for the representation of values of the component type.

Bit numbering may extend through consecutive storage units; thus the component clause:

```
PROTECTION_KEY at 0 range 8 .. 11;
```

may be legal, even if the storage unit has eight bits on the machine considered.

At Clauses:

The at clause specifies the position of a component by giving the position of the storage unit relative to which the bit range is counted. This position is itself relative to the first storage unit of the record, which is numbered 0. For example,

```
TRACK at 2 range 0 .. 15
```

means that the component TRACK occupies 16 bits starting with bit 0 of the storage unit numbered 2. If the value of SYSTEM.STORAGE_UNIT were 8, the last bit of TRACK could actually be bit 7 in the adjacent storage unit numbered 3, depending on the implementation. Overlapping components are allowed only when they belong to distinct variants, and the compiler must actually check the absence of overlap within each variant. For example, the overlap of LINE_COUNT and CYLINDER in the following clause is legal because they belong to different variants:

```
type DEVICE is (PRINTER, DISK, DRUM);
type PERIPHERAL(UNIT : DEVICE := DISK) is
  record
    case UNIT is
      when PRINTER =>
        LINE_COUNT : INTEGER range 1 .. 50;
      when others =>
        CYLINDER : CYLINDER_INDEX;
        TRACK    : TRACK_NUMBER;
    end case;
  end record;

-- assuming SYSTEM.STORAGE_UNIT = 8 bits
```

```
for PERIPHERAL use
   record at mod 4;
      UNIT       at 0 range 0 .. 7;
      LINE_COUNT at 1 range 0 .. 7;
      CYLINDER   at 1 range 0 .. 7;
      TRACK      at 2 range 0 .. 15;
   end record;
```

When the record representation clause is incomplete – that is, if it does not specify the layout for all components – the compiler is free to map the unspecified components in any way that is consistent with the logic of the record type declaration. Compilers should be able to produce listings of record mappings upon request.

Alignment Clauses:

When it is important that the objects of a given record type be allocated on a given storage boundary, this can be specified by means of an alignment clause. The alignment is expressed as a number of storage units, and all addresses at which the objects are allocated must be exact multiples of the specified number of storage units (the address modulo the alignment expression must be zero).

```
for PAGE_BUFFER use at mod 512;
```

15.4.4 Address Clauses

An address clause can be used to force the storage space of a given variable to be allocated at a given address, which is specified in storage units:

```
for TTY_STATUS_REGISTER use at 16#40#;
```

This form of clause can also be used for specifying the address of the code of a subprogram, or to link an interrupt with a given entry. The address given after the reserved word at has the system-dependent type SYSTEM.ADDRESS (assumed to be an integer type in the above example).

15.4.5 Enumeration Representation Clauses

An enumeration representation clause is used to specify the mapping of the values of an enumeration type onto the specific internal codes used to represent the elements.

The mapping is specified using an aggregate in which the values of the type are enumerated one by one. The type of such an aggregate is a one-dimensional array whose component type is *universal_integer* and whose index subtype is the enumeration type itself. For example, consider a program that generates object code for a given machine and in which the operation codes for the machine are defined by an enumeration type. It is necessary to map the enumeration values into actual operation codes and this can be achieved as follows:

```
type MIX_CODE is (ADD, SUB, MUL, LDA, STA, STZ);

for MIX_CODE use
    (ADD => 1, SUB => 2, MUL => 3, LDA => 8, STA => 24, STZ => 33);
```

In this example the array aggregate is of type

array (MIX_CODE) **of** *universal_integer*

All enumeration values must be provided with distinct universal integer codes and these codes must be known at compilation time. Moreover, in order to get an efficient implementation of order relations, the internal codes must follow the same ordering as the enumeration values. The order relations are then known through the internal codes, and there is no need for the compiler to generate tables that contain the order relation.

As illustrated above, the specified internal codes need not be successive integers. We discuss the implications of this issue in the next section.

15.5 ENUMERATION TYPES WITH NONCONTIGUOUS REPRESENTATIONS

The specified internal codes of an enumeration type need not have contiguous values. This degree of generality is required if character types are to be represented by enumeration types, since many character sets have noncontiguous internal values.

We next discuss the implications of noncontiguous representations on assignment and comparison, indexing and case selection, and finally on iteration.

15.5.1 Assignment and Comparison with Noncontiguous Enumeration Types

An assignment only results in moving a value from one location to another, and thus is not influenced by the noncontiguity of a representation. Similarly, noncontiguity has no impact on comparison.

15.5.2 Indexing and Case Statements with Noncontiguous Enumeration Types

The simplest way to treat an array indexed by an enumeration type that has a non-contiguous representation is to implement it as a normal array, but leaving *holes* (that is, unused positions) in the storage used. No conversion is then needed between the internal code and the actual index to storage, since they have the same value. In a similar way, the internal jump table used for a case statement could have holes.

Note that no problem arises when such arrays are passed as parameters to subprograms since the index type is part of the array type and the same mapping will be used inside and outside the subprogram.

The user should be aware of the hidden storage costs involved: these costs are certainly preferable to prohibiting the use of types with noncontiguous representations for indexing and in case statements. If we consider character sets, for instance, the proportion of holes remains at an acceptable level.

15.5.3 Iteration Over Noncontiguous Enumeration Types

We are faced with a more severe problem when a loop parameter ranges over the values of a noncontiguous enumeration type: simply incrementing the value of the loop parameter by a constant at each iteration will not work! To keep the same underlying mechanism, the compiler may use a *characteristic vector*, that provides information on holes. For every such loop, the compiler will include code to interrogate the characteristic vector.

This mechanism is illustrated by the following example. Consider the type MIX_CODE, for which a noncontiguous representation has been specified.

```
type MIX_CODE is (ADD, SUB, MUL, LDA, STA, STZ);
for MIX_CODE use
   (ADD => 1, SUB => 2, MUL = > 3, LDA => 8, STA => 24, STZ => 33);
```

A loop statement that iterates over the values of the MIX_CODE type can be written as follows:

```
for N in MIX_CODE loop
   DISPLAY(N);
end loop;
```

The compiler could produce object code equivalent to the following text (apart from typing rules):

```
PRESENT : constant array (1 .. 33) of BOOLEAN :=
              (1|2|3|8|24|33 => TRUE, others => FALSE);

for J in PRESENT'RANGE loop
  if PRESENT(J) then
    DISPLAY(J);
  end if;
end loop;
```

As illustrated above, the compilation involves a characteristic vector (PRESENT) which is used to generate the integer values corresponding to the enumeration type MIX_CODE. Thus we see that iterating over such types is possible, but involves extra cost.

Another technique is to use a *representation vector* that maps the ordinals into the enumeration values:

```
REPRESENTATION : constant array (0 .. 5) of INTEGER :=
                     (1,2,3,8,24,33);
for J in REPRESENTATION'RANGE loop
  DISPLAY(REPRESENTATION(J));
end loop;
```

Similar techniques are used to implement 'SUCC, 'PRED, 'POS and 'VAL.

15.5.4 Character Types

Character types are a typical example of enumeration types with not necessarily contiguous representations. The predefined character type CHARACTER that denotes the full ASCII character set of 128 characters is contiguous, but the same is not true for other widely used character sets such as EBCDIC. Such character sets will generally be defined in library modules, which will include both the character type declaration and the associated representation specification. It may be convenient to provide such a definition in two steps. For example:

type CHAR **is** (*enumeration of all EBCDIC characters*);

type EBCDIC **is new** CHAR; -- same characters as CHAR

for EBCDIC **use** (*codes corresponding to EBCDIC characters*);

A user to whom the internal code is relevant (perhaps because he is performing input-output) will declare objects of type EBCDIC. For other uses, especially if such characters are to be used as indices, in case statements and in iterations, the user might prefer to use the type CHAR. Since no representation specification is given for this type, the translator will adopt a default representation that is convenient for indexing and iteration. Explicit conversion between the two types can be performed.

Note however that CHAR and EBCDIC will have their values in the same order, so the user cannot be relieved of all the problems associated with this data type.

15.6 CONFIGURATION SPECIFICATION AND ENVIRONMENT ENQUIRIES

To generate object code, some machine – and configuration-dependent properties such as the machine model, memory size, and special hardware options must be available to the compiler. Hence the specification of configuration-dependent features must be possible. Typical uses of such information are for the detection of exhaustion of various resources, and the generation of special-purpose instructions for the target machine.

Conversely, programs may need to access information that is known to the compiler. There are many uses for such information. A user-level input-output subprogram may need to invoke different algorithms depending on the object machine configuration (with the discrimination being made at compilation time); similarly, it may need to know the size of the storage unit for the object machine, and the size of the objects transferred.

The approach used in Ada is to group such system-dependent information in a package called SYSTEM and to provide certain specific pragmas to establish certain characteristics that may vary between different configurations of the system considered.

15.6.1 The Package System

The package SYSTEM includes the definition of system-dependent information. At the minimum it will include what is shown in the skeleton given below:

```
package SYSTEM is
   type ADDRESS is implementation_defined;
   type NAME    is implementation_defined_enumeration_type;

   SYSTEM_NAME   : constant NAME := implementation_defined;

   STORAGE_UNIT  : constant := implementation_defined;
   MEMORY_SIZE   : constant := implementation_defined;

   -- System-Dependent Named Numbers:
```

```
MIN_INT      : constant := implementation_defined;
MAX_INT      : constant := implementation_defined;
MAX_DIGITS   : constant := implementation_defined;
MAX_MANTISSA : constant := implementation_defined;
FINE_DELTA   : constant := implementation_defined;
TICK         : constant := implementation_defined;

-- Other System-Dependent Declarations

subtype PRIORITY is INTEGER range implementation_defined;

...
end SYSTEM;
```

The type ADDRESS defines what addresses are, on the machine considered: on some machines it will be an integer type, on some others an arbitrary record type. The type NAME is an enumeration type that defines names of alternative machine configurations that are handled by the system. For example we could have:

```
type NAME is (MODEL_20, MODEL_40, MODEL_45, MODEL_70);
```

As this example suggests, these possible variations are meaningful when dealing with variations of a machine that all have the same type ADDRESS. Although nothing forbids it, it would not make much sense to have a type such as

```
type NAME is (VAX_11, IBM_370, APPLE_II);
```

since the other quantities defined in the package SYSTEM are unlikely to be the same for these alternative machines. For example, the following constants are defined in the package:

- SYSTEM_NAME: the name of the current configuration.

- STORAGE_UNIT: the number of bits per storage unit:

- MEMORY_SIZE: the number of storage units in the configuration.

It is a consequence of the visibility rules that a declaration given in the (library) package SYSTEM can be made visible within a program unit that has a with clause that mentions SYSTEM. For example:

```
with SYSTEM;
procedure SPECIAL_APPLICATION is
   ...
   SIZE : constant := SYSTEM.MEMORY_SIZE;
   ...
end;
```

The fact that SYSTEM needs to be mentioned in the above manner provides an easy way of finding out which program units make direct use of system-dependent properties.

15.6.2 Pragmas for Configuration Specification

A particular configuration of the package SYSTEM, with a certain configuration name, storage unit size, and memory size can be specified by means of corresponding pragmas. For example:

```
pragma SYSTEM_NAME(MODEL_45);
pragma STORAGE_UNIT(8);       -- 8 bits
pragma MEMORY_SIZE(2#1#E18); -- 256 kbytes
```

This has the effect of establishing the corresponding constants:

```
SYSTEM.SYSTEM_NAME  = MODEL_45
SYSTEM.STORAGE_UNIT = 8
SYSTEM.MEMORY_SIZE  = 262_144
```

15.6.3 Representation Attributes

Representation attributes provide an environment enquiry mechanism that can be used to obtain information that is known by the compiler; for example to obtain the address of an object, subprogram, or entry, the position of record components, or the size of objects of a given type.

As mentioned in the section on lexical issues, an attribute designator is always preceded by an apostrophe. The corresponding identifiers are consequently not reserved. Some typical examples are given below.

```
OLD_PSW'ADDRESS   -- the address in storage units of OLD_PSW
X.MASK'POSITION   -- the starting position of the component MASK in X
X.MASK'FIRST_BIT  -- the position of the first bit of MASK
X.MASK'LAST_BIT   -- the position of the last bit of MASK
INTEGER'SIZE      -- the implemented size of INTEGER in bits
```

15.6.4 Configuration Specification and Conditional Compilation

Sometimes it is desirable to write and compile a program in which portions vary according to the object machine configuration. Such *conditional* compilation can be achieved by conditional statements that select from alternative program fragments. For example, a program that provides different algorithms for different systems may appear as follows:

```
pragma SYSTEM_NAME(MODEL_45);
...
case SYSTEM.SYSTEM_NAME is
  when MODEL_45 |MODEL_70 =>
     ...
     -- part specific to models with full floating-point support

  when MODEL_40 =>
     ...
     -- part specific to models with some floating-point support

  when MODEL_20 =>
     ...
     -- part specific to models without floating-point support
end case;
```

The system name established by the pragma is known at compilation time, and the compiler is therefore able to optimize the case statement and generate only the code that corresponds to the current system name. Thus the program can be tailored to a given machine.

This conditional compilation facility is somewhat primitive. More powerful mechanisms for conditional compilation are likely to be provided by the support environments built around the Ada language.

15.7 INTERFACE WITH OTHER LANGUAGES

A limited and implementation-dependent facility for machine code insertions has been included in Ada. This facility has the advantage of clearly isolating the use of machine language. Furthermore, its use is heavier than direct use of an assembler: the facility offered should be sufficient for cases where there is an actual need, but its style will inhibit overuse.

Each machine instruction appears as a code statement, which is a record aggregate of a record type that defines the corresponding instruction. Such record definitions will generally be available in a system-dependent library package called MACHINE_CODE. This package must also contain the representation of the record that describes the machine instruction format. Code statements may be used only in procedures whose bodies consist entirely of code statements.

The following example illustrates the use of a set system mask instruction on an IBM 370. The package MACHINE_CODE could be as follows

```
package MACHINE_CODE is
   type REGISTER     is range 0 .. 16#F#;
   type DISPLACEMENT is range 0 .. 16#FFF#;
   type OPCODE       is ( ... , SSM, ... );

   type RR is ...
   type RX is ...
   type SI is
     record
       CODE : OPCODE;
       B    : REGISTER;
       D    : DISPLACEMENT;
     end record;
   ...
   for OPCODE use ( ... , SSM => 16#80#, ... );
   ...
   for SI use
     record
       CODE at 0 range 0 .. 7;
       B    at 0 range 16 .. 19; -- bits 8 .. 15 unused
       D    at 0 range 20 .. 31;
     end record;
   ...
end MACHINE_CODE;
```

We will assume in what follows that the set system mask operation is defined as part of a package, along with similar operations:

```
package SPECIAL_COMMANDS is
   ...
   procedure SET_SYSTEM_MASK(X : MASK);
   pragma INLINE(SET_SYSTEM_MASK);
   ...
end;
```

```
with MACHINE_CODE;
package body SPECIAL_COMMANDS is
   ...
   procedure SET_SYSTEM_MASK(X : MASK) is
      use MACHINE_CODE;
   begin
      SI'(CODE => SSM, B => X'BASE_REG, D => X'DISP);
   end;
   ...
end SPECIAL_COMMANDS;
```

For the body of this package, a with clause mentioning MACHINE_CODE is required: this rule will enable programming support environments to enforce certain management rules concerning the use of machine code insertions. This example also shows the need to use implementation-specific predefined attributes in code statements, such as X'BASE_REG (the base register used for X) and X'DISP (the displacement of X). Additional implementation-specific pragmas may be needed to specify the register and linkage conventions.

Obviously such pragmas cannot be machine-independent; the only order that may be brought by a high level language to such a matter is to standardize the conventions to be used for such specifications, and this is what we achieve in Ada by recourse to pragmas. Finally, pragmas can also be used to specify that a subprogram called from an Ada program is written in another language. Consider for example the reuse of functions defined in the Fortran library, from an Ada program. To achieve this, we declare a package

```
package FORTRAN_LIB is
   function SQRT (X : FLOAT) return FLOAT;
   function EXP (X : FLOAT) return FLOAT;
   ...
private
   pragma INTERFACE(FORTRAN, SQRT);
   pragma INTERFACE(FORTRAN, EXP);
   ...
end FORTRAN_LIB;
```

For each function needed we have declared an Ada function in the usual manner, and this function can then be called using the normal Ada syntax. However, the bodies of these functions are not written in Ada and we indicate this by INTERFACE pragmas. These inform the compiler about the corresponding linkage conventions, and also to expect the object code to be provided later (at linkage editing time). Of course compilers may impose restrictions on the form of parameters that are allowed (for example, passing two-dimensional arrays may be complex, given the internal representation used by Fortran). Not all compilers need provide this machine code insertion capability.

15.8 UNCHECKED CONVERSIONS

The conversions allowed between numeric types and between types that are derived from each other are safe conversions that do not violate the rules of type checking.

Unchecked type conversions can be achieved in any language that permits code insertions or address clauses. Such conversions may, for example, be needed if a user wants to define his own allocation strategy for access types. In this case, conversions from integer to access values are necessary to define an ALLOCATE procedure and a converse FREE procedure.

From the point of view of programming management (and also of maintainability) it is desirable to provide a standard way to achieve such unchecked conversions. In this way the parts of a program that use such dangerous features are made easier to identify. The following generic library function is predefined to that effect.

```
generic
   type SOURCE is limited private;
   type TARGET is limited private;

function UNCHECKED_CONVERSION(S : SOURCE) return TARGET;
```

A program unit that uses unchecked type conversions must mention this generic function in its with clauses. A possible scenario is indicated with the package LIST_HANDLING given below:

```
package LIST_HANDLING is
   type PLACE;
   type LIST is access PLACE;

   type PLACE is
     record
       SUCC, PRED : LIST;
       VALUE      : INTEGER;
     end record;
   ...
   procedure ALLOCATE (X : out LIST);
   procedure FREE     (X : in out LIST);
   ...
   pragma CONTROLLED(LIST);    -- no garbage collection
   for LIST'STORAGE_SIZE use 0; -- new will not be usable
end;
```

```
with UNCHECKED_CONVERSION;
package body LIST_HANDLING is
  function INT_TO_LIST is
    new UNCHECKED_CONVERSION(SOURCE => INTEGER,
                   TARGET => LIST);
  ...
  procedure ALLOCATE(X : out LIST) is
    ADDRESS : INTEGER;
  begin
    ...
    -- Compute address, Then:
    X := INT_TO_LIST(ADDRESS);
  end;
  ...
end LIST_HANDLING;
```

The function INT_TO_LIST is obtained within the body of LIST_HANDLING by instantiation of UNCHECKED_CONVERSION, and is used to convert an integer address into a LIST.

The programming environment may be able to control and restrict the programs that are allowed to get access to the function UNCHECKED_CONVERSION.

16. Input-Output

16.1 INTRODUCTION

Input-output is one of the most difficult areas to define in any programming language. The requirements of individual problem domains vary widely, and it is probably impossible to satisfy one domain completely without seriously compromising the needs of another. For example, the requirements for input-output for a commercial stock control problem are quite different from those of an embedded machine controlling a steel works, or a bare board controlling a missile. There is major conflict between flexibility, variety of facilities, and raw efficiency and compactness, which have different priorities in the different domains.

Another problem is that, whereas the general facilities required of a procedural language are reasonably well understood and likely to remain stable, the requirements for input-output are likely to change dramatically during the lifetime of Ada, as the means of communication between man and machine evolve during the next few decades.

It is clear therefore that any attempt to define a permanent and fully comprehensive set of facilities, intrinsically bound into Ada, would have been very likely to fail: either the language would rapidly have become obsolete, or it would have been threatened with frequent change, in attempting to cope with changing demands. Indeed, Fortran is an obvious example of an old language that has suffered from these problems – its built-in input-output has restricted its utility in a number of domains of growing importance.

A further difficulty with built-in input-output is that special syntactic forms are almost inevitably used: examples are the format lists in Fortran and the variable numbers of parameters of the special *write* procedures in Pascal. These special forms make it impossible to change the intrinsic input-output whilst retaining the normal interface to the user; it is, for example, very difficult to insert local *filtering* into the input-output calls for monitoring and debugging purposes (that is, to replace these calls by calls to normal procedures which in turn call *write*).

Having rejected the possibility of successfully defining an intrinsic, complete, comprehensive, and stable set of facilities for all input-output for all time, one could contemplate the opposite extreme view of ignoring the whole problem in the hope that appropriate sets of facilities would emerge, defined on top of the base language.

This was the view taken by Algol 60, and undoubtedly was a prime reason for the premature obsolescence of that language and its dominance by Fortran. Individual developers of early Algol 60 compilers provided their customers with quite different sets of procedures for input-output, thereby destroying the portability of Algol 60 programs, and this resulted in the fragmentation of the user base. The later provision of a recommended standard came too late to be widely used, and the language died.

Another risk with the approach of leaving all input-output to be built on top of the base language is that the absence of appropriate syntactic support can lead to an unfriendly, clumsy, and possibly inefficient set of facilities. This was certainly also a problem with Algol 60, which required a plethora of differently named procedures to cope with the demand for flexibilty in areas such as formatting.

The approach taken in Ada lies between the two extremes of all or nothing. Input-output is not built into the syntax of the language; instead, a number of standard input-output packages are defined, using the normal extension mechanisms that the language provides. As we shall see, Ada is sufficiently rich in these mechanisms to overcome the clumsiness that plagued Algol 60. This solves the problems outlined above and, in particular, ensures the portability of the mainstream of programs without compromising the needs of special applications. Furthermore, it allows easier evolution if this is needed in the future.

The main purpose of this chapter is thus to show how the Ada extension facilities described in the previous chapters have been used in the definition of the standard input-output packages. This also serves the purpose of showing, in principle, how Ada can be used to develop other sets of packages, tailored for major classes of specialized applications; this is important, since we take the view that the standard packages are indeed just one possibility, and are not designed to deal with every foreseeable circumstance in the future.

16.2 BASIC REQUIREMENTS

Having decided to treat input-output as an application area, we next need to look at the various requirements that are imposed.

Conventional file-based input-output addresses a number of basic issues. These are:

- The identification of files from within the program as abstract entities

- The connection of these abstract files to real external files

- The control of access rights to the files, so that permission to read or to write can be granted separately

- The type and format of the items to be transmitted

- The means of initiating actual data transfer

A major distinction regarding format concerns whether the files are considered solely as repositories of information for later reading by machine, or as the representation of information for later direct interpretation by the human eye. In the first case, the information can conveniently be held (externally) in a format very similar to the internal bitwise representation, whereas the second case requires considerable transformation into some conventional textual format. The two styles are so obviously different that quite different packages seem appropriate for their implementation. Thus we have a package TEXT_IO specifically for the textual format, and in fact two rather similar packages, SEQUENTIAL_IO and DIRECT_IO, for the more general binary input-output – for sequential and for directly indexed files respectively.

Since Ada is a typed language, we need ways of allowing the transmission of data items of different types without infringing the basic rules of the type model. In the case of binary input-output, the approach taken is to insist that each file contains items of just one type. This is conveniently done using the generic mechanism, and so SEQUENTIAL_IO and DIRECT_IO are generic packages with just one formal parameter, namely the type concerned. In the case of TEXT_IO the external form is in all cases a simple stream of characters, and so there is no problem concerning the externally held type. Instead, we need ways of reading and writing values of various internal types *from* and *to* this one external character type; this is done by providing a number of overloaded procedures, with parameters of different types, although once again the generic mechanism is required to cope with the variety of numeric and enumeration types, as we shall see later.

In embedded systems there is also a requirement for a much lower level of input-output, whereby data is transferred directly to or from various external devices. Because of the enormous potential generality of devices, it is not possible realistically to provide a great deal in the way of standard facilities. The solution chosen, therefore, is just to provide a simple package LOW_LEVEL_IO which, in essence, suggests a common framework for this area.

The remainder of this chapter considers the more important aspects of these requirements in more detail, with especial emphasis on how they are met through the use of various normal features of Ada.

16.3 DESIGNATION OF FILES

Input-output operations effect data exchanges between a processor, running on behalf of the user program, and some peripheral device. Traditionally, the notion of a file, seen as a repository of information, is often distinguished from that of a device. However, the logical behavior of a program as a processor of information must not depend on the source or destination of data, as long as the data represents the desired information. For example, it is perfectly reasonable to interface the same program with a disk file at one time, and with a terminal at another time.

Consequently, the conventions used to designate the target of an input-output operation should not necessarily distinguish between file names, device names, volume names, and so on. In addition, these conventions should not conflict with those of any operating system under which the language is implemented. Thus we need to reconcile the ability to communicate with files in arbitrary operating systems with the retention of as much portability as possible in the greater part of the program. This is done by distinguishing an *external* physical file, whose general properties – in particular the lifetime – are quite outside the realm of the Ada program, from an *internal* abstract Ada object, upon which the program can operate with a well-defined set of abstract operations.

The external file is conveniently designated by a string, whose interpretation is completely implementation-dependent. A string is used for this purpose because of its generality and accommodating nature. This string is thus a parameter (called NAME) of those procedures that need to identify an external file. There are in fact two of these: CREATE which establishes a new external file, and OPEN which refers to an existing external file. In addition, it has proved convenient to provide a second string parameter (called FORM), through which arbitrary auxiliary information can be supplied. The default value for each of these parameters is the null string; in the case of the name, this is conveniently taken to indicate a temporary and anonymous file, whereas in the case of the form it merely indicates the absence of explicit auxiliary information.

Within the Ada program, the file is referred to via an Ada object of a limited private type. The type is *limited* (rather than just private) so that the user cannot make arbitrary copies of file objects, and thereby prevent the file package from having complete control over file access and over the deallocation of internal buffer storage; for a more extensive discussion of this technique see section 9.2.3.

The connection between the internal file object and the external file is made by passing the object as a further parameter to CREATE or OPEN. All access to the external file is then made by referring to the internal object. This includes calls of CLOSE and DELETE, which sever the connection between the external file and the internal file object and, in the case of DELETE, actually delete the external file itself.

16.3.1 Access Control

There is a need to provide a degree of access control, in order to reduce the risk of inadvertently misusing files. Typically, a file would have a MODE, which would allow read-only, write-only, or read-and-write access. This could be done in a variety of ways, such as:

- By providing three quite distinct file types, such as IN_FILE, OUT_FILE and INOUT_FILE, corresponding to the access modes. (This was the approach taken in the Green language.)

- By introducing an enumeration type FILE_MODE, with possible literal values IN_FILE, OUT_FILE and INOUT_FILE, and then using a single file type with a discriminant thus:

  type FILE_TYPE(MODE : FILE_MODE) **is limited private**;

- By having a single file type, without any discriminant, but associating each file object with a dynamic property that is a value of the enumeration type FILE_MODE. This is the approach actually taken by Ada.

At first sight, the first approach looks attractive. It means that the correct use of mode can be ensured at compilation time, with apparent subsequent cost savings at run time. In practice, however, there are a number of serious problems:

- It is not possible to change the mode of a file without closing it, and then reopening it using a different file object; this makes the provision of temporary files rather awkward. Of course, such files could be declared as INOUT, but this removes the security of access we were looking for in the first place, and is counter to the concept of sequential files.

- The individual file types make it impossible to write single general procedures that apply to all files.

- The individual types cause an excessive number of overloaded subprograms.

Furthermore, the apparent run-time saving is usually illusory, since the underlying operating system inevitably carries out its own access checks anyway. (This would not necessarily apply in the case of a system specifically written to support just Ada.)

We therefore reject the first approach, and consider approaches using a single type. The use of a discriminant to govern the access mode appears neat; it solves the problems of multiple types, and keeps the access information within the type concept but yet visible to the user. However, since the type is limited, the user is unable to change the discriminant anyway, and so this approach is unfruitful.

We thus come to the third of the possibilities outlined at the beginning of this section. This offers a practical solution, which has been adopted.

There is a single type, FILE_TYPE, which applies to all files and, in addition, a quite separate property of each file, which governs its access mode. This property is set when a file is opened or created, through a parameter to OPEN or CREATE, and can also be changed by calling the procedure RESET. The specifications of these procedures are thus

```
procedure CREATE (FILE : in out FILE_TYPE;
                  MODE : in     FILE_MODE := OUT_FILE;
                  NAME : in     STRING := "";
                  FORM : in     STRING := "");

procedure OPEN   (FILE : in out FILE_TYPE;
                  MODE : in     FILE_MODE;
                  NAME : in     STRING;
                  FORM : in     STRING := "");

procedure RESET  (FILE : in out FILE_TYPE;
                  MODE : in     FILE_MODE);
```

Note that the MODE has a default value of OUT_FILE in the case of CREATE. This is sensible, since it is appropriate that the first action on a newly created file is to write to it. (In the case of direct files, the default is INOUT_FILE; this mode does not apply to sequential and text files.)

The procedure RESET repositions a file at the beginning, and can also be used to change the mode so that, having written a file, we can now read it. There is also a further overloading of RESET which omits the second parameter and just repositions the file without changing its mode.

We conclude this section by observing that, although the system does not give the compilation time security that one would have liked, nevertheless a special secure system of the first category could be built on top of the more flexible current one using derived types. However, the reverse is not possible, and so the present solution has the additional merit of leaving more options open for special circumstances.

16.3.2 Default Files

It is often the case that a number of operations are performed in sequence on the same file. This applies particularly in the case of TEXT_IO, where a line of text typically comprises a mixture of numbers and strings that are output by a series of different calls, such as

```
PUT(RESULTS, "value is "); PUT(RESULTS, VALUE); NEW_LINE(RESULTS);
```

in which the repetition of the file name RESULTS is rather verbose.

In order to overcome this, the various procedures have two overloaded forms, one with the file parameter and one without – for example, in the case of the type character:

```
procedure PUT(FILE : in FILE_TYPE; ITEM : in CHARACTER);
procedure PUT(ITEM : in CHARACTER);
```

If the file parameter is omitted, an appropriate default file is used – there is one for input and one for output. These default files are initially set to two standard files, but can be changed by the user. Thus we can more conveniently write

    SET_OUTPUT(RESULTS);

followed by

    PUT("value is "); PUT(VALUE); NEW_LINE;

The subprograms provided for the manipulation of the default files are

    procedure SET_OUTPUT(FILE : in FILE_TYPE);
    function   STANDARD_OUTPUT return FILE_TYPE;
    function   CURRENT_OUTPUT return FILE_TYPE;

with corresponding subprograms for input. As the names suggest, SET_OUTPUT sets the default to the specified file, STANDARD_OUTPUT returns the initial standard file, and CURRENT_OUTPUT returns the file that is the present default file.

It is thus possible to set the default file to that required locally, and then to reset it to the standard, by:

    SET_OUTPUT(local_file);
    -- do the I/O
    SET_OUTPUT(STANDARD_OUTPUT);

A more general requirement (in a widely used standard subprogram, perhaps) might be to surround the local use of a default file by statements which preserve and then restore the existing default file. The function CURRENT_OUTPUT is provided so that this can be done.

16.4 INDEXED AND SEQUENTIAL FILES

Files are conceived essentially as one-dimensional arrays. Each element in the file has an index value associated with it, the first element having the index value 1. In the case of SEQUENTIAL_IO this index value is hidden from the user, whereas in the case of DIRECT_IO the index value can be directly manipulated.

Considering SEQUENTIAL_IO in more detail, its specification commences:

```
with IO_EXCEPTIONS;
generic
   type ELEMENT_TYPE is private;
package SEQUENTIAL_IO is
   type FILE_TYPE is limited private;
   type FILE_MODE is (IN_FILE, OUT_FILE);
   ...
end SEQUENTIAL_IO;
```

(The package IO_EXCEPTIONS is explained in section 16.6 below.)

The one generic parameter gives the type of elements in the file. Note that this is private but not limited. This reflects the fact that input-output cannot be performed on limited types, since to do so would indirectly permit assignment; it also forbids attempts to output task values.

The declarations of FILE_TYPE and FILE_MODE then follow. Note that FILE_MODE has only two values – read-write access is not defined for sequential files.

The specification then contains the various file management procedures, CREATE, OPEN, CLOSE, DELETE, and RESET, which were discussed above.

Next come a group of functions which give access to the properties of a file; they are

```
function MODE    (FILE : in FILE_TYPE) return FILE_MODE;
function NAME    (FILE : in FILE_TYPE) return STRING;
function FORM    (FILE : in FILE_TYPE) return STRING;
function IS_OPEN (FILE : in FILE_TYPE) return BOOLEAN;
```

These functions will be found useful when writing general-purpose procedures that manipulate files passed as parameters. They enable the general state of a file to be checked before it is used, and thereby avoid raising exceptions.

Actual input and output is performed by procedures READ and WRITE, which have the specifications:

```
procedure READ  (FILE : in FILE_TYPE; ITEM : out ELEMENT_TYPE);
procedure WRITE (FILE : in FILE_TYPE; ITEM : in  ELEMENT_TYPE);
```

Calls of READ and WRITE access the file element at the current position and then move on, ready to access the next element. In other words they increment the hidden index value.

The function

function END_OF_FILE(FILE : **in** FILE_TYPE) **return** BOOLEAN;

which only applies to files of mode IN_FILE, returns TRUE if there are no more elements to be read.

The package specification concludes with the renaming declarations of various exceptions, as explained in section 16.6 below.

The package DIRECT_IO is very similar. The differences are that the mode now has three values

type FILE_MODE **is** (IN_FILE, INOUT_FILE, OUT_FILE);

and there are additional subprograms for direct manipulation of the index. These are

```
procedure SET_INDEX (FILE : in FILE_TYPE;
                     TO : in POSITIVE_COUNT);
function INDEX (FILE : in FILE_TYPE) return POSITIVE_COUNT;
function SIZE  (FILE : in FILE_TYPE) return COUNT;
```

where

type COUNT **is range** 0 .. *implementation_defined*;
subtype POSITIVE_COUNT **is** COUNT **range** 1 .. COUNT'LAST;

are declared within DIRECT_IO and specify the type of the index values.

The procedure SET_INDEX sets the current index of the given index value, which may exceed the current size of the file. If the given index value exceeds the current size of the file, item-sized "gaps" will occur which are undefined items.

The function INDEX returns the current index value. The function SIZE gives the number of items in the file, which includes both defined and undefined items.

Finally there are overloadings of READ and WRITE with a further parameter giving the index value:

```
procedure READ (FILE : in  FILE_TYPE;
                ITEM : out ELEMENT_TYPE;
                FROM : in  POSITIVE_COUNT);

procedure WRITE (FILE : in FILE_TYPE;
                 ITEM : in ELEMENT_TYPE;
                 TO   : in POSITIVE_COUNT);
```

Thus a call of READ or WRITE can specify a specific index value or, on the other hand, it can be omitted, in which case the normal sequential behavior will occur. This is an illustration of the use of overloading to achieve an effect similar to that of default parameters.

16.5 TEXT FILES

As stated earlier, in the case of TEXT_IO the external file essentially comprises a sequence of characters. We require, therefore, a number of subprograms that can map the various different Ada types onto the type character. In addition, there is a need to be able to specify the format of the externally held item – in the case of an integer it could be in decimal or some other base, it might be padded with leading blanks to fit a fixed field, and so on. Furthermore, there are many circumstances in which it is convenient to be able to use default formats, in order to avoid having to supply the detailed format on each individual call.

16.5.1 Overloading PUT and GET

The use of PUT and GET for all types (and all formats) is an excellent example of the usefulness of overloading. Without overloading (as is the situation with Algol 60), we would need to declare differently named procedures for each type and formatting style:

```
PUT_CHARACTER
PUT_STRING
PUT_INTEGER
PUT_FLOAT
...
PUT_INTEGER_FORMATTED
...
```

Thus in Algol 60 we had to write something like

```
integer I;
real X;
...
PUTSTRING("results are: "); PUTINT(I); PUTREAL(X);
```

whereas in Ada we can much more neatly write

```
I : INTEGER;
X : REAL;
...
PUT("results are: "); PUT(I); PUT(X);
```

Moreover, without overloading it would be almost impossible to provide facilities for arbitrary user-defined numeric and enumeration types. With overloading we are able to use PUT for the output of all types and all formats; identification of the proper procedure is resolved by the normal rules, and no particular problems arise.

However, even with overloading, there are two limitations of the strict procedural approach. First the language does not have any concept equivalent to the straightening of Algol 68. If *straightening* were provided, a procedure such as PUT (which is defined for the type INTEGER) would be automatically extended (by iteration) to arrays of integers. Similarly if PUT were defined for the types of the components of a record, it would also be defined for the record type itself. The second limitation concerns parameter lists. It is traditional to perform several output operations with a single statement but this is not permitted by a strictly procedural form. Conceivably one could use another separator (say //) to permit multiple argument lists for a procedure:

```
PUT("results are: " // I // X); -- not in Ada
```

For simplicity neither straightening nor multiple parameter lists have been introduced. The choice of short identifiers such as PUT much reduces the inconvenience of the procedural form.

16.5.2 Generic Treatment of Numeric and Enumeration Types

It would be possible to provide procedures PUT and GET for the predefined numeric types: INTEGER, LONG_INTEGER, FLOAT, LONG_FLOAT, and so on. However, this would not be in the style of Ada, which, for the sake of abstraction and portability, encourages the user to declare application-specific numeric types such as:

```
type REAL is digits 10;
R : REAL;
```

It is desirable to be able to write

```
PUT(R);
```

where the particular PUT has formatting and other properties relevant to the type R, rather than, say,

```
PUT(FLOAT(R));
```

which introduces portability problems because the default format will depend upon the properties of the predefined type FLOAT, and this will of course vary with the implementation.

A convenient solution is provided by generic packages that are declared within TEXT_IO and are visible outside of this package. There are four of these, covering integer types, floating types, fixed types, and enumeration types. Each of these packages has one generic parameter that determines the particular type. Thus in the case of floating types the package has the form:

```
generic
   type NUM is digits <>;
package FLOAT_IO is
   ...
   procedure PUT(ITEM : in NUM; ... );
   ...
end FLOAT_IO;
```

The user can then instantiate this generic package in the usual way, and thereby obtain the desired effect:

```
declare
   use TEXT_IO;
   package REAL_IO is new FLOAT_IO(NUM => REAL);
   use REAL_IO;
begin
   PUT(R);                -- calls REAL_IO.PUT
   ...
end;
```

16.5.3 Use of Default Parameters for Formatting

It is important for the user to have good control over the format of output items. This applies particularly to the numeric types, and to a lesser extent to enumeration types. On the other hand, it is often convenient to use some default format in order to avoid the tedious repetition of standard parameters. The ability to provide default expressions for in parameters enables such facilities to be provided in a convenient manner. We will illustrate the techniques with the packages for integer and enumeration types; the same principles apply to the real types.

The specification of INTEGER_IO is

```
generic
   type NUM is range <>;
package INTEGER_IO is

   DEFAULT_WIDTH : FIELD := NUM'WIDTH;
   DEFAULT_BASE  : NUMBER_BASE := 10;
   ...
   procedure PUT (ITEM  : in NUM;
                  WIDTH : in FIELD := DEFAULT_WIDTH;
                  BASE  : in NUMBER_BASE := DEFAULT_BASE);
   ...
end INTEGER_IO;
```

For simplicity we have just shown the procedure PUT that takes the default output file; there is another procedure PUT with an additional and leading parameter that gives the file explicitly, as discussed in 16.3.2.

The parameters of PUT are as follows:

ITEM   The numeric value to be output

WIDTH   The width of the field in which the value is to be placed. The type mark FIELD is just a suitable subtype of INTEGER. The value is right justified in the field, with padding leading spaces and a minus sign if appropriate. If the field is not wide enough, then it is expanded as necessary.

BASE   The number base to be used. If this is 10 then normal decimal notation is used, otherwise the syntax of based literal is used (with any letters in upper case). Again, the type mark NUMBER_BASE, is a suitable subtype of INTEGER.

The default expressions for the format parameters should be noted. They are the values of the variables DEFAULT_WIDTH and DEFAULT_BASE which are also declared in the visible part of the generic package INTEGER_IO. The initial value of DEFAULT_WIDTH is the attribute NUM'WIDTH – this gives a field just large enough to hold all values of the type, including a prefixed minus sign or space. The initial value of DEFAULT_BASE is 10.

We now have the desired behavior. The format can be specified on each call, or, alternatively, one or both parameters can be omitted, in which case the relevant defaults will be obtained.

The fact that default expressions for parameters are evaluated on each use is very important. It means that the current values of the variables DEFAULT_WIDTH and DEFAULT_BASE are always used, and not just their initial values. As a consequence, the default values can be changed dynamically. Moreover, since the variables DEFAULT_WIDTH and DEFAULT_BASE are declared in the visible part of the package INTEGER_IO, the user can change them by direct assignment. The user can now write

```
declare
   type INDEX is range 0 .. 511;
   package INDEX_IO is new INTEGER_IO(NUM => INDEX);
   use INDEX_IO;
   ...
   I : INDEX;
begin
   I := 471;

   PUT(I);                          -- b471
   PUT(I, 6);                       -- bbb471
   PUT(I, BASE => 8);               -- 8#727#

   INDEX_IO.DEFAULT_WIDTH := 7;
   INDEX_IO.DEFAULT_BASE  := 8;

   PUT(I);                          -- b8#727#
   ...
end;
```

(The letter b in the above comments stands for one blank space.)

Note that INDEX'WIDTH (the initial DEFAULT_WIDTH) is 4; this allows for three digits plus a leading space. It is important to realize that the WIDTH attribute is a property of the subtype and not of the base type – this is very appropriate, because the base type will be derived from one of the predefined types, and could indeed be the type INTEGER; it would not be appropriate to use the WIDTH pertaining to this, since it would vary with the implementation.

Observe also that the package name has been used when assigning to the defaults. This will be necessary if a number of instances of these generic packages have been declared.

In the case of ENUMERATION_IO we have:

```
generic
   type ENUM is (<>);
package ENUMERATION_IO is
```

```
    DEFAULT_WIDTH    : FIELD := 0;
    DEFAULT_SETTING : TYPE_SET := UPPER_CASE;
      ...
    procedure PUT (ITEM  : in ENUM;
                   WIDTH : in FIELD := DEFAULT_WIDTH;
                   SET   : in TYPE_SET := DEFAULT_SETTING);
      ...
  end ENUMERATION_IO;
```

Here the format parameters control the field width and the case of characters (lower case or upper case, with upper being the norm). TYPE_SET is itself an enumeration type declared in TEXT_IO as follows:

```
type TYPE_SET is (LOWER_CASE, UPPER_CASE);
```

The behavior is as expected. Values are by default output in a minimal field – since the default width is zero – and in upper case. Furthermore, the user can provide an explicit format, and also change the default. Padding is by trailing blanks.

16.6 EXCEPTIONS AND RENAMING

Input-output can very easily be misused, and consequently there is a need for reporting errors. As might be expected, this is done through the raising of certain exceptions, which for convenience are declared together in the package IO_EXCEPTIONS, thus:

```
package IO_EXCEPTIONS is
    STATUS_ERROR      : exception;
    MODE_ERROR        : exception;
    NAME_ERROR        : exception;
    USE_ERROR         : exception;
    DEVICE_ERROR      : exception;
    END_ERROR         : exception;
    DATA_ERROR        : exception;
    LAYOUT_ERROR      : exception;
  end IO_EXCEPTIONS;
```

Note that it would be very inconvenient for these exceptions to be declared in each of the packages SEQUENTIAL_IO, DIRECT_IO, and TEXT_IO. Each instantiation of SEQUENTIAL_IO, for example, would then give rise to a different exception, and it would consequently be tedious to write a general purpose handler, since it would need to refer explicitly to all the instances.

For this reason the three packages all contain renaming declarations such as

STATUS_ERROR : exception renames IO_EXCEPTIONS.STATUS_ERROR;

This has the advantage that the user (and indeed the writer of the IO package bodies) need not refer explicitly to IO_EXCEPTIONS.

16.7 LOW LEVEL INPUT-OUTPUT

Low level input-output facilities are especially needed in embedded computer systems, since signal processing and interaction with non-standard peripheral devices are common. Clearly, major system dependences cannot be avoided in this area. At best the language can provide a set of standard calling conventions for dealing directly with peripherals. The specific device and data descriptions cannot however be given.

Interaction with peripheral devices involves three kinds of action: starting an operation on a device, interrogating the status of the device, and waiting for completion of an operation. The third case can be dealt with by the entry mechanism, coupled with the specification of an address clause that links the entry to an interrupt. The first two cases, however, constitute requests from the program. For these, two procedure names are introduced: SEND_CONTROL to start an operation, and RECEIVE_CONTROL to interrogate the status. Each takes two arguments: DEVICE identifies a particular peripheral device, and DATA corresponds to the information that should be exchanged with the device (hence DATA is an **in out** parameter).

For the definition of such procedures we are faced with two problems: efficiency and generality. Efficiency dictates that an operation that normally requires a small number of machine instructions should not be surrounded by lengthy checks. This could be achieved by making the low level primitives built-in to a given compiler. However, generality requires the ability to write the appropriate SEND_CONTROL and RECEIVE_CONTROL operations whenever a new device is added to the system, without forcing a recompilation of the compiler. Hence these operations cannot be built-in.

In order to satisfy these apparently conflicting goals, subprogram overloading and code statements can be used. As many *device types* should be introduced as are required by the interfacing conventions of the system. Similarly, for each device type, appropriate *data types* should be introduced. For each meaningful combination of device type and data type, overloaded definitions of SEND_CONTROL and RECEIVE_CONTROL can be given, and the corresponding subprogram bodies may use appropriate code statements.

The general form of the package LOW_LEVEL_IO is as follows

```
package LOW_LEVEL_IO is
   -- declarations of different device types
   -- declarations of different data types

   ...
   -- declarations of overloaded procedures for these types:
   procedure SEND_CONTROL    (DEVICE  :  device_type;
                              DATA    :  in out data_type);
   procedure RECEIVE_CONTROL(DEVICE  :  device_type;
                              DATA    :  in out data_type);

   ...
end LOW_LEVEL_IO;
```

Thus if a user needs to introduce a new device, then the appropriate types and procedures can be added independently of existing ones; this only requires recompilation of the package LOW_LEVEL_IO.

16.8 CONCLUSION

We have seen how the general features of Ada can be used in order to provide flexible and convenient input-output facilities, without adding to the syntactic framework of the language itself in any way. The following features have been particularly useful in doing this:

- overloading of subprograms

- default parameters, including their dynamic evaluation

- limited types

- exceptions

- generic units, and especially the different formal types

- attributes of derived types

This chapter has provided an excellent demonstration of the capability of Ada as an application language. It illustrates that once a language has an adequate richness of mechanisms it passes some kind of threshold, and then effectively becomes self-extending and able to lend itself to varied domains of application, including such demanding areas as input-output. Ada is the first real language to have achieved this.

Bibliography

"[Ba 70]" Balzer, R.M., Ports, A method for dynamic interprogram communication and job control, Rand Corporation (R605 ARPA) (1970).

"[BFH 76]" Bron, C., Fokkinga, M.M. and De Haas, A.C.M., A proposal for dealing with abnormal termination of programs, Twente University of Technology, Mem. Nr. 150, The Netherlands (Nov. 1976).

"[BJ 78]" Bert, D., Jacquet, P., Some Validation Problems with Parameterized Types and Generic Functions, Proc. 3rd International Symposium on Programming, Paris, Dunod (1978), pp. 279-292.

"[BH 70]" Brinch Hansen, P., The Nucleus of a Multiprogramming System, Comm. ACM 13,4 (April 1970), pp. 238-241.

"[BH 73]" Brinch Hansen, P., Operating System Principles, Prentice Hall, N.J., 1973.

"[BH 75]" Brinch Hansen, P., The Programming Language Concurrent Pascal, IEEE Trans. Software Eng. 1,2 (June 1975), pp. 199- 207.

"[BH 77]"   Brinch Hansen, P., Distributed processes, a concurrent programming concept, Computer Science Department, University of Southern California - Los Angeles (1977).

"[BH 78]"   Brinch Hansen, P., Distributed processes: A Concurrent Programming Concept, Comm. ACM 21, 11 (Nov. 1978), pp. 934- 941.

"[Br 78]"   Brown, W.S., A Realistic Model of Floating Point Computation, Numerical Software, Vol. 3 (ed., Rice), Academic Press, 1978.

"[CH 74]"   Campbell, R.H., Habermann, A.N., The Specification of process synchronization by path expressions, Lecture notes in computer science, Vol. 16, Springer (1974), pp. 89-102.

"[Co 63]"   Conway, M.E., Design of a Separable Transition-Diagram Compiler, Comm. ACM 6,7 (July 1963), pp. 396-408.

"[DDH 72]"   Dahl, O-J, Dijkstra, E.W., Hoare, C.A.R., Structured Programming, Academic Press, London 1972.

"[DH 76]"   De Haas, A.C.M., Escape Clauses in Programming Languages, Twente University of Technology, The Netherlands (Sept. 1976).

"[Di 68]"   Dijkstra, E.W., Cooperating Sequential Processes, in Programming languages, (ed. F. Genuys), Academic Press, London, 1968, pp. 43-112.

"[Di 72]"   Dijkstra, E.W., Notes on Structured Programming, in Structured Programming, Academic Press, London, 1972.

"[DoD 77]"   Department of Defense, Revised Ironman requirements for high order computer programming languages, July 1977.

"[DoD 78]"   Department of Defense, Steelman requirements for high order computer programming languages, June 1978.

"[DoD 80]"   Requirements for Ada Programming Support Environments: STONEMAN; February 1980. United States Department of Defense, Office of the Under Secretary of Defense for Research and Engineering. NTIS-AD- A100 404/3.

"[Fo 77]"   Fokkinga, M.M., Axiomatization of declarations and the formal treatment of an escape construct, Twente University of Technology, Mem. Nr. 176, The Netherlands (Sept. 1977).

"[Fr 77]"   Francez, N., Another advantage of Keyword Notation for Parameter Communication with Subprograms, Comm. ACM 20,8 (Aug. 1977), pp. 604-605.

"[GH 75]"   Gannon, J.D., Horning, J.J., Language design for programming reliability, IEEE Trans. Software Eng. SE-1,2 (June 1975), pp. 179-191.

"[GK 77]"   Goos, G., Karstens, P., A Comparison of Modularization Facilities in Four Languages, IFIP Working Conference on the Production of Reliable Software, Novosibirsk 1977, North Holland.

"[GM 75]"   Geschke, C.G., Mitchell, J.G., On the problem of uniform references to data structures, IEEE Trans. Software Eng. SE- 1,2 (June 1975), pp. 207-219.

"[Go 75]"   Goodenough, J.B., Exception Handling: Issues and a Proposed Notation, Comm. ACM 18,12 (Dec. 1975), pp. 683-696.

"[Gu 77]"   Guttag, J., Abstract Data Types and the Development of Data Structures, Comm. ACM 20,6 (June 1977), pp. 396-404.

384 *Bibliography*

"[GS 77]"   Geschke, C.M., Satterthwaite, E.H., Exception Handling in Mesa, XE-
              ROX PARC report, Palo Alto (1977).

"[Ha 77]"   Hartmann, A.C., A Concurrent Pascal Compiler for a mini computer,
              Lecture Notes in Comp. Science, vol. 50, Springer Verlag (1977).

"[Hab 73]"   Habermann, A.N., Critical comments on the programming language Pas-
              cal, Acta Informatica, 3 (1973), pp. 47-57.

"[Har 76]"   Hardgrave, W.T., Positional versus keyword parameter communication in
              programming language, ACM, SIGPLAN Notices 11,5 (May 1976), pp.
              52-58.

"[HF 76]"   Hague, S.J., and Ford, B., Portability, Prediction and Correction, Soft-
              ware - Practice and Experience, Vol. 6 (1976), pp. 61-69.

"[Hi 63]"   Higman,B. What everybody should know about Algol. Computer Journal
              6,1 (1963), pp. 50-56.

"[HLMR 74]"   Horning, J.J., Lauer, H.C., Melliar-Smith, P.M., Randell, B., A program
              structure for error definition and recovery, in Operating Systems, Gelenbe
              and Kaiser (Eds.), Springer Verlag, N.Y. (1974), pp. 171-187.

"[Ho 74]"   Hoare, C.A.R., Monitors: An Operating System Structuring Concept,
              Comm. ACM 17, 10 (Oct. 1974), pp. 549-557.

"[Ho 78]"   Hoare, C.A.R., Communicating sequential processes, Comm. ACM 21, 8
              (Aug. 1978), pp. 666-677.

"[HW 73]"   Hoare, C.A.R., and Wirth, N., An Axiomatic Definition of the Program-
             ming Language Pascal, Acta Informatica, Vol.2 (1973), pp. 335-355.

"[I 79]"   Ichbiah, J.D, et al., Rationale of the Design of the Ada Programming
             Language, ACM, SIGPLAN Notices 14, 6 (June 1979), Part B.

"[IF 77]"   Ichbiah, J.D., Ferran, G., Separate Definition and Compilation in LIS
             and its Implementation, Cornell Symposium on the Design of High Order
             Languages, in Lecture Notes in Computer Science, Springer Verlag, N.Y.
             (1977).

"[Ka 74]"   Kahn, G., The semantics of a simple language for parallel programming,
             Proc. IFIP Congress 74, North Holland (1974).

"[KBL 80]"   Krieg-Brueckner, B., Luckham, D.C., ANNA: Towards a Language for
             Annotating Ada Programs, ACM, SIGPLAN Notices 15, 11 (Nov. 1980),
             pp.128-138.

"[Le 77]"   Levin, R., Program Structures for Exceptional Condition Handling (PhD
             Thesis), Dept. of Computer Science, Carnegie Mellon University (June
             1977).

"[LMS 74]"   Lampson, B.W., Mitchell, J.G., Satterthwaite, E.H., On the transfer of
             control between contexts, Lecture notes in Computer Science, Vol. 19,
             Robinet (Ed.) Springer Verlag, N.Y. (1974), pp. 181-203.

"[LSAS 77]" Liskov, B., Snyder, A., Atkinson, R., Schaffert, C., Abstraction mecha-
             nisms in CLU, Comm. ACM 20,8 (Aug. 1977), pp. 564-576.

"[Or 50]"   Orwell, G., "1984", Harcourt, Brace and Co., N.Y. (July 1950).

"[Pa 71]"   Parnas, D.L., Information distribution aspects of design methodology, Information Processing 71, North Holland Pub. Co., Amsterdam (1971), pp. 339-344.

"[PW 74]"   Presser, L., White, J., Making Global Variables Beneficial, Proceedings IFIP Congress 1974 (Aug. 1974).

"[PW 76]"   Parnas, D.L., Wurges, H., Response to Undesired Events in Software Systems, Proc. 2nd Int'l. Conf. on Software Engineering (October 1976).

"[Ra 75]"   Randell, B., System Structure for Fault Tolerance, Proc. Int'l. Conf. on Reliable Software, Los Angeles (1975), and SIGPLAN Notices, Vol. 10,6 (Jun. 1975).

"[Ro 70]"   Ross, D.T., Uniform referents: An essential property for a software engineering language, in Software Engineering (J.TOU, Ed.), Vol. 1, Academic Press (1970), pp. 91-101.

"[SW 74]"   Scowen, R.S., Wichmann, B.A., The definition of comments in Programming Languages, Software - Practice and Experience, Vol. 4,2 (April 1974), pp. 181-188.

"[SWKW]"   Symm, G.T., Wichmann, B.A., Kok, J., Winter, D.T., Guidelines for the design of large modular scientific libraries in Ada. National Physical Laboratory Report DITC 37/84 (March 1984).

"[VH 75]"   Von Henke, F.W., On Generating Programs from Data Types: An Approach to Automatic Programming. Proc. Int'l. Symposium on Proving and Improving Programming (Arc-et-Senans) IRIA (1975), pp. 57-70.

"[Wa 72]"   Walden, D.C., A System for Interprocess Communication in a Resource Sharing Computer Network, Comm. ACM 15,4 (April 1972), pp. 221-230.

"[We 78]"   Welsh, J., Economic Range Checks in Pascal, Software - Practice and Experience, Vol. 8, 1 (Jan. 1978), pp. 85-98.

"[Wi 71]"   Wirth, N., Program development by stepwise refinement, Comm. ACM 14,4 (April 1971), pp. 221-227.

"[Wo 72]"   Woodger, M., Levels of Language, in High Level Languages, INFOTECH, State of the Art Report, No. 7 (1972), pp. 201-215.

"[WSH 77]"   Welsh, J., Sneeringer, M.J., Hoare, C.A.R., Ambiguities and Insecurities in Pascal, Software - Practice and Experience, Vol. 7,6 (Nov. 1977), pp. 685-696.

"[Za 74]"   Zahn, C.T., A control Statement for natural top-down structured programming, in Lecture Notes in Computer Science, No. 19, Robinet(Ed.), Springer Verlag, N.Y. (1974), pp. 170- 180.

LANGUAGES

"Ada"   Reference Manual for the Ada programming language (ANSI/MIL- STD 1815 A). US government, Ada Joint Program Office (Jan. 1983).

"Algol 60"   Naur, P. (ed.), Revised Report on the algorithmic language Algol 60, Comm. ACM, Vol.6,1 (Jan, 1963), pp. 1-17.

"Algol 68"   Van Wijngaarden, A., et al., Revised Report on the algorithmic language Algol 68, Acta Informatica, Vol. 5, Fasc.1-3 (1975), pp. 1-236.

"Alphard"   Wulf, W.A., London, R.L., and Shaw, M., Abstraction and verification in Alphard: Introduction to language and methodology, USC Inform. Sci. Institute Technical Report, University of Southern California, Los Angeles (1976).

"Bliss-II"   Digital Equipment Corporation, BLISS-II Programmer's Manual, Maynard, Mass. (1974).

"Clu"   Liskov, B., A Note on CLU, Computation Structures Group Memo 112, MIT Project MAC, Cambridge, Mass. (Nov. 1974).

"Coral 66"   Woodward, P.M., Wetherall, P.R., and Gorman, B., Official Definition of CORAL 66, Her Majesty's Stationery Office (1970).

"CS-4"   Brosgol, Ben M., et al., CS-4 Language Reference Manual and Operating System Interface, Report IR-130-2, Intermetrics, Inc., Cambridge, Mass. (Oct. 1975).

"EL1"   Wegbreit, B., The Treatment of Data Types in EL1, Comm. ACM, Vol. 17,5 (May, 1974), pp. 251- 264.

"Euclid"   Lampson, B.W., Horning, J.J, London, R.L., Mitchell, J.G, and Popek, G.J., Report on the Programming Language Euclid, SIGPLAN Notices, Vol. 12,2 (Feb. 1977).

"Fortran"   ANSI (formerly USASI) - X3.9 - 1978 (USA Standard Fortran).

"Jovial"   Perstein, M.H., The JOVIAL (J3) Grammar and Lexicon, SDC technical report TM-555 (1966).

"Lis"   Ichbiah, J.D., Rissen, J.P., Heliard, J.C., Cousot, P., The System Imple-
               mentation Language LIS, Reference Manual, CII-HB Technical Report
               4549 E/EN, CII-HB, Louveciennes, France (Dec. 1974).

"Mary"   Rain, M., Mary Programmer's Reference Manual, R Unit, Trondheim
               (1974).

"Mesa"   Mitchell, J.G., Maybury, W., Sweet, R., Mesa Language Manual, Version
               5.0, Xeros PARC Report CSL-79-3(Apr. 1979).

"Modula"   Wirth, N., Nodula: A Programming Language for Modular Multipro-
               cessing, Software - Practice and Experience, Vol. 7,1 (June 1977), pp.
               3-35.

"Modula-2"   Wirth, N., Programming in Modula-2, Springer Verlag (1983)

"Pascal"   Wirth, N., The programming language Pascal, Acta Informatica, Vol. 1,
               No. 1 (1971), pp. 35- 63, Springer Verlag.

"RTL/2"   Barnes, J.G.P., RTL/2 Design and Philosophy, Heyden, London (1976).

"Simula 67"   Dahl, O.J., Nygaard, K., Myhrhaug, B., The Simula 67 common base
               language, Pub S-22, Norwegian Computing Center, Oslo (1969).

"Sue"   Clark, B.L., Horning, J.J., The System Language for Project Sue, SIG-
               PLAN Notices, Vol. 6,9 (Oct. 1971), pp. 79-88.

"Tartan"   Shaw, M., Hilfinger, P., Wulf, W.A., TARTAN - Language design for the
               Ironman Requirements: Reference Manual, SIGPLAN Notices, Vol. 13,9
               (September 1978), pp. 36-58.

Index

DATE DUE

	261-2500		Printed in USA